# 400 CALORIE FIX™

## SLIM IS SIMPLE:
### 400 Ways to Eat 400 Calorie Meals

By Liz Vaccariello
Editor-in-Chief of **Prevention**®
WITH MINDY HERMANN, RD

RODALE®

This book is intended as a reference volume only, not as a medical manual. The information given here is designed to help you make informed decisions about your health. It is not intended as a substitute for any treatment that may have been prescribed by your doctor. If you suspect that you have a medical problem, we urge you to seek competent medical help.

Mention of specific companies, organizations, or authorities in this book does not imply endorsement by the author or publisher, nor does mention of specific companies, organizations, or authorities imply that they endorse this book, its author, or the publisher. The brand-name products mentioned in this book are trademarks or registered trademarks of their respective companies. Internet addresses and telephone numbers given in this book were accurate at the time it went to press.

Prevention is a registered trademark of Rodale Inc.
400 Calorie Fix is a trademark of Rodale Inc.

Printed in the United States of America
Rodale Inc. makes every effort to use acid-free ∞, recycled paper ♺.

Photographs by Ted Morrison with additional photos by Mitch Mandel
Book design by Jill Armus
Photo Editor: Rebecca Simpson Steele

**Library of Congress Cataloging-in-Publication Data**

Vaccariello, Liz.
    400 calorie fix : Slim Is Simple: 400 Ways to Eat 400 Calorie Meals /
Liz Vaccariello, with Mindy Hermann.
        p.    cm.
    Includes index.
    ISBN-13 978-1-60529-515-2 hardcover
    ISBN-10 1-60529-515-9 hardcover
    1. Reducing diets—Recipes.   I. Hermann, Mindy G.    II. Title.
III. Title: Four hundred calorie fix.
    RM222.2.V25   2010
    641.5'635—dc22                    2009044206

2   4   6   8   10   9   7   5   3   1   hardcover

RODALE
LIVE YOUR WHOLE LIFE™

We inspire and enable people to improve their lives and the world around them

For more of our products visit **rodalestore.com** or call 800-848-4735

# DEDICATION

*For Steve, Sophia, and Olivia*
—LIZ

*For Eric, David, and Jon*
*and to my late father, Fred Hermann,*
*who would have been so proud*
—MINDY

# CONTENTS

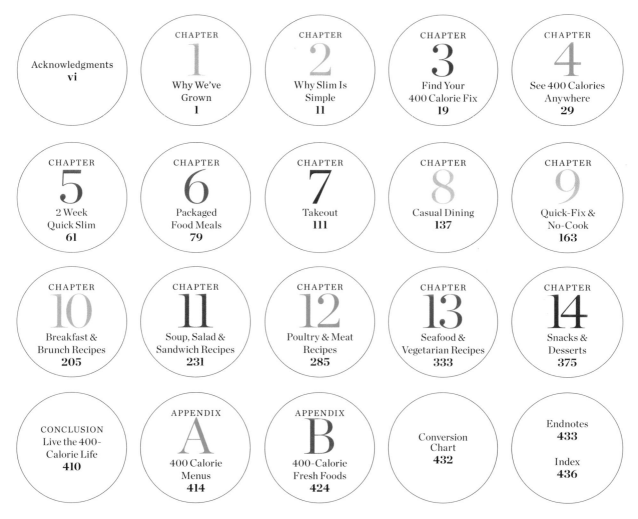

# ACKNOWLE

MY GRATITUDE TO THE RODALE FAMILY. For generations, through their magazines, books, and online properties, they have remained committed to a special mission, that of giving people the tools and inspiration to live their whole lives. My most heartfelt thanks to CEO Maria Rodale for her leadership, vision, and support throughout this project and from my earliest moments at Rodale.

Very special thanks to Karen Rinaldi and Gregg Michaelson for their enthusiasm, wisdom, and guidance always. And to Janine

# DGMENTS

Slaughter, who made a good idea even better. To Sindy Berner and Lori Magilton, who took my vision and communicated it to the masses. To Mary Murcko, whose passion for the *Prevention* brand knows no bounds. Thank you to Bethridge Toovell and Lauren Paul for their early and tenacious enthusiasm (book it! book it! book it!). To Jenny Sucov, who showed me the lens. And to the lovely woman on my left and Steve Madden on my right, for their in-flight cover wisdom.

But now I must go back to the beginning—and acknowledge the inspiration of *Prevention*'s brilliant creative director, Jill Armus, who loved *Flat Belly Diet!* and suggested a whole book of 400-calorie meals. Her vision for this project is reflected in every page of this gorgeous and infinitely useful book.

Endless gratitude to Andrea Au Levitt, who has kept *400 Calorie Fix* so close to her heart and been a careful, caring steward of this project every step of the way. This book would not have been possible without her or her team, including Marielle Messing, Hope Clarke, Chris Krogermeier, Sara Cox, JoAnn Brader, Brooke Myers, Liz Krenos, and Jennifer Giandomenico.

A zillion thanks to this project's unsung heroes: A huge shout out to Rebecca Simpson Steele, who made more than 700 pictures happen in 2 months; Katie Kackenmeister, who never met a calorie she couldn't count; Carol Angstadt, who ran photo shoots with one hand while marshalling production troops in two cities with the other; Kerrie Keegan and John Mok, who mastered the art of managing the art (among many other things!); David Bonom, who helped to develop the most delicious 400-calorie recipes ever; and Marlea Clark, who masterminded the 400 Calorie Fix extravaganzas. Thanks also to Leah McLaughlin for bringing us Mindy! And of course to Mindy Hermann, the fastest, smartest, most organized, and most good-natured coauthor a gal could ever have—thanks for giving up your nights and weekends to the 400-calorie cause!

We'd also like to extend our gratitude to our 400 Calorie Fix test panel, which was conducted in the summer of 2009. Thank you, Sandi (Fagan) Hill, Patti Robbins, Janet Sartorius, Donna Agajanian, Virginia Simpson, Judi Herrmann, Denise Bernstein, Gladys DiSisto, Melody Rubie, Bill Berkowsky, Jordan and Ronni Metzger, Francesca Minerva, Kristin Lewandowski, Helen Cannavale, and Lisa Frankel for providing us with the essential insights that helped us develop this book into a diet plan any type of eater could love. Thanks also to Alyssa Shaffer, Teresa Dumain, Diana Kelly, Marisa Bardach, Amanda Junker, Lisa Schnettler, and Deborah Wilburn, who've all touched and shaped this brand in many vital ways. And to Elizabeth Goodman, Alyson Cameron, Jenelle Wagner, Sunny Stafford, Paul Kramer, and Will Pelkey for their timely assistance.

As always, thanks to Courtenay Smith, Polly Chevalier, Jonathan Bigham, Fotoulla Euripidou, and Bill Stump for their counsel and wisdom around all things *Prevention*. And to the smartest photo and art team in the business, including *Prevention*'s Helen Cannavale, Leah Vinluan, Maureen O'Brien, Jessica Sokol, Donna Agajanian, Mallory Craig, and Tiffany Lee. And finally a huge hug for the lovely Susan Graves for keeping me . . . heck, all of us . . . sane (and running on time).

Finally, to the photographers and their teams, for bringing the 400 Calorie Lens to life: Ted Morrison, Cyd McDowell, Cindy DiPrima, Philip Shubin, Mitch Mandel, and Christine Langfield.

# 1.
# Why We've GROWN

IT SEEMED TO DEFY LOGIC. I was in my late thirties and exercising a dozen hours a week, eating healthfully, and coming off a 7-year stint as a senior-level editor at a popular fitness magazine. I was intimately familiar with the major tenets of exercise, nutrition, and weight loss. After all, we informed and inspired millions of women every month, and I proudly lived the advice I doled out. I was strong, fit, full of energy. And yet.

And yet I was also 10 pounds heavier than I wanted to be. The more I exercised, the hungrier I was. And, because I exercised so much, I usually ate whatever food I wanted, in whatever amount satisfied me. I mostly ate healthy foods—fresh fruits and vegetables, whole grains, lean proteins, lots of fat-free milk—so I didn't think to watch my portions too carefully. The trouble was, my laissez-faire attitude about the food—the calories—I was putting into my mouth meant I was gradually, stealthily gaining a pound or two a year. It wasn't anything to worry about, but the rising numbers on the scale were enough to make me look up one day and realize what an impact a little inattention to calories can have. It was my *job* to understand how to achieve a healthy weight, and yet the pounds crept up even on me! I could easily imagine the frustration of people whose lives didn't revolve around health.

Then I came upon this statistic: In 2007 the average American consumed close to 2,800 calories per day. In 1970 it was 2,200 calories per day.[1] That 600-calorie difference might not seem like a lot, but eating an extra 500 calories a day can translate into 1 pound of extra fat per week!

Most of us don't gain a pound a week (52 pounds in a year is pretty extreme), but putting on an extra 2 or 5 or 10 is pretty common. And it's why so many of us look up one day and think, "Where did this weight come from?"

### THE STORY OF CALORIE CREEP

Why, exactly, are we eating more calories than our bodies need? The good news is: It's not our fault. For starters, portions have grown . . . and grown and grown. They are bigger everywhere, as pointed out by Brian Wansink, PhD, Cornell University professor and researcher, whose revealing work shows that when packages, plates, and portions are larger, we eat more. It's bad news, then, that our plates and bowls have gotten about 36 percent bigger since 1960,[2] and many beer and wine glasses have swelled to accommodate more than a single serving. (A "portion," by the way, is the amount of food that you serve yourself, while a "serving" is the measured amount recommended on the label or by the government and contains a specific number of calories. Confused? You're not alone. Only about half of us know the difference between the two.[3])

Whereas the tall, skinny highball and champagne glasses of the past held a more reasonable 6- to 8-ounce serving (and deceived our eyes into thinking we were getting more than we were), today's oversize glasses hold 10 to 16 ounces or more! Even nutrition experts, who should know better, serve themselves bigger portions—and eat more—when they have bigger bowls, bigger serving spoons, and bigger packages, according to a recent study.[4]

Making your own meals is usually healthier than eating takeout, but even your cookbook may not be as slimming as you think. Classic cookbooks like *The Joy of Cooking* have upsized: A recent study found a 42 percent increase in recipe portion size and a 170-calorie increase per serving since 1931.[5]

Wait. There's more. Like so many Americans, I was raised by clean-your-plate parents who applauded the finished dinner and scorned the untouched serving. And like many of us, I've been finishing everything that was in front of me ever since, thanks to this sense of duty, my own frugal-minded distaste of waste, and sometimes even boredom or mindless eating. What I didn't realize was that all that extra food shouldn't have been there in the first place. It shouldn't have been there at my first apartment, where I piled pasta onto my oversize Pottery Barn plates, whose massive circumference tricked my eye into serving way more than I needed. Nor should it have been there at my favorite restaurants. Restaurant portions are nearly double (or triple) what

they used to be, with some meals clocking in at upwards of 1,500 calories, close to what most people need for an entire day.

Finally—and here's the real rub—it doesn't help that so few of us know how many calories we need, let alone how many we are putting into our mouths. A survey found that almost 90 percent of adults have no clue how many calories they should eat on any given day.[6] And in New York City, where chain restaurants have recently been required to post calorie counts on their menus, one

## MY FAVORITE 400-CALORIE MEAL

### ROBIN'S STUFFED CHICKEN BREAST

I love this dish because it's loaded with flavor and healthy ingredients, and it's ready in a flash. First, mix together 1 chopped McIntosh apple, ½ cup each toasted slivered almonds and crumbled blue cheese, and 1 tablespoon chopped fresh parsley. Then, using a small knife, create pockets in four chicken breasts by slicing into the side about three-quarters of the way through. Transfer the chicken to a shallow roasting pan that's been coated with cooking spray and stuff the apple mixture into the pockets. Coat the chicken with cooking spray and season with salt and black pepper. Bake at 400°F for 25 minutes or until the chicken is cooked through, and pair it with roasted asparagus or another vegetable, and you've got a heart-smart, gourmet meal in just minutes!

—*Robin Miller, nutritionist, host of the Food Network's* Quick Fix Meals, *and author of* Robin Rescues Dinner

study conducted in 2007 showed that only 4 percent even noticed the information. People buying fast food purchased meals that averaged more than 800 calories, with about one-third of those being more than 1,000 calories.[7]

Like millions of us, I was being swept along by a stealth calorie creep.

### THE HAPPY, HEALTHY SOLUTION

Food may have been the problem, but as someone with a deep appreciation for the power food has to heal, fuel, and energize, I know that food can also be the solution. And, as the editor-in-chief of *Prevention* magazine and a coauthor of the blockbuster *Flat Belly Diet!*, I see a clear, simple, back-to-basics trend emerging: Managing weight comes down to calories.

I talk to nutritionists and researchers about the many diet trends that have come and gone over the past 20 years. We started with the low-fat diets of the 1980s and '90s, which were inspired by research showing that people whose diets are filled with low-fat foods have less body fat. Turns out, those diets work only as long as they mainly include foods like fruits, vegetables, and lean meats; they don't work well at all when people load up on fat-free cookies and snacks. Why? Because they contain too many calories.

The pendulum then swung in the opposite direction. Low carb (in some cases, high fat) took its place as the diet du jour and remains popular today. The basic premise is that you eliminate foods such as bread and pasta from your diet in exchange for large, and sometimes unlimited, portions of meat, eggs, and high-fat indulgences like bacon and whipped cream. Although pounds melt away at first, weight loss eventually slows. Worst of all, once you start eating simple carbs again, weight finds its way back quickly. Why? Because your calorie count shoots up.

Then there's what I call the no-brainer diet: prepackaged low-calorie meals and shakes, and even meals that are delivered to your doorstep every morning to take the guess-work out of dieting—no cooking, no shopping, no planning. But they're not long-term solutions. Why? Because they don't teach you what you need to know about calories!

## WHAT'S A HEALTHY WEIGHT?

You know you need to control calories to reach and maintain a healthy weight, but how do you know how much you should weigh? The body mass index (BMI) is a number calculated using height and weight. Generally, BMIs range from the mid- to high teens for a thin adult to over 30 for obese adults, with a healthy weight corresponding to a BMI of 24.9. Go to www.prevention.com and search for "BMI" to figure out your BMI and find out the range of healthy weights for your height.

In recent years, however, a welcome spate of more balanced Mediterranean-type diet plans, including the South Beach Diet and the Flat Belly Diet, have emerged that actually encourage eating healthy fats and whole grains, both of which benefit your heart and other vital organs and lower your risk for many diseases. These types of diets may even diminish extra stores of visceral (belly) fat, which experts now know can increase your risk of heart disease, diabetes, even certain kinds of cancers. These diets (the Flat Belly Diet in particular) also put a cap on calorie consumption—and they start to teach you how to do it for life.

In fact, the latest scientific studies are backing up calorie control as the smartest means to achieving a healthy weight and a long life. Yes, it's just that simple: The only way to lose weight and keep it off long-term is to learn how to spot and control calories. Here's some of the recent research that got me excited:

❖ More than 800 overweight adults who were assigned to one of four lower-calorie diets—low fat, high carb; low fat, moderate carb; high fat, low carb; and high fat, very low carb—lost about the same amount of weight over two years, *regardless of which diet they were on.*[8] Diets were about 750 calories less than what researchers calculated that participants needed to maintain weight. Results of this National Institutes of Health–funded study appeared in 2009 in the *New England Journal of Medicine.*

❖ Blood pressure, fasting blood glucose, and insulin levels and resistance to insulin all decreased in a group of adults who were on a 1-year, calorie-controlled weight-loss diet, according to a 2009 study conducted in Adelaide, Australia, and published in the *American Journal of Clinical Nutrition.*[9]

❖ Several studies on calorie control were linked to better sensitivity to insulin and potentially to longer life in humans.[10] This comes from a research review—just one of a growing number of reviews on the health benefits of eating less—that appeared in the journal *Molecular and Cellular Endocrinology.*

Of course, counting calories is nothing new. In fact, as far back as 1918, Lulu Hunt Peters introduced the concept in her book, *Diet and Health, with Key to the Calories,* and doctors have been telling people they should cut calories in order to trim pounds ever since. If the answer is so simple and we've known the secret for so many years, why are so many of us still overweight?

I'm here to tell you, it goes way beyond willpower. Most of us don't know how many calories we really should be eating. (In fact, the 2008 International Food Information Council Foundation (IFIC) Food and Health Survey found that only 15 percent of adults know how many calories a person of their age, height, and activity level should eat to maintain a healthy weight—the rest either estimated incorrectly or were totally unaware.[11]) Most of us

*(continued on page 9)*

# QUIZ: HOW MANY CALORIES ARE IN . . .

**1.** 2 CUPS OATMEAL CRISP CRUNCHY ALMOND CEREAL + 1 CUP FAT-FREE MILK

**2.**

DUNKIN' DONUTS EGG WHITE TURKEY SAUSAGE FLATBREAD SANDWICH + 8 OUNCES ORANGE JUICE

**3.**

ARBY'S PECAN CHICKEN SALAD SANDWICH

**4.**

LEAN CUISINE BBQ RECIPE CHICKEN PIZZA + WHOLE FRUIT STRAWBERRY FRUIT BAR

**5.**
AU BON PAIN
MEDITERRANEAN WRAP

**8.**
1 OUNCE CHEDDAR CHEESE + 1 OUNCE
BRIE CHEESE + 4 REDUCED-FAT TRISCUITS
+ 5 OUNCES WHITE WINE

**11.**
RED LOBSTER MAUI
LUAU SHRIMP AND SALMON

**6.**
3 OUNCES TOSTITOS MULTIGRAIN
TORTILLA CHIPS + ½ CUP DESERT
PEPPER TRADING COMPANY CORN,
BLACK BEAN, ROASTED PEPPER SALSA

**9.**
STIR-FRIED BEEF AND BROCCOLI
WITH BROWN RICE

**12.**
3 OUNCE BROWNIE SHOT
+ ¼ CUP WHIPPED CREAM

**7.**
20-OUNCE BOTTLE ARIZONA GREEN
TEA WITH GINSENG AND HONEY
+ 2.25-OUNCE PACKAGE OF EMERALD
TROPICAL BLEND TRAIL MIX

**10.**
RUBY TUESDAY AVOCADO
TURKEY BURGER

**13.**
MCDONALD'S SMALL
STRAWBERRY TRIPLE THICK SHAKE

TURN
THE PAGE
FOR THE
ANSWERS
> > > > > >

# AND THE CALORIES ARE . . .

1. **2 CUPS OATMEAL CRISP CRUNCHY ALMOND CEREAL (480 calories) + 1 CUP FAT-FREE MILK (80 calories) = 560 calories**
*The serving sizes (and corresponding calories) on cereal boxes range from ½ cup to 1 cup. Most people eat double that or more.*

2. **DUNKIN' DONUTS EGG WHITE TURKEY SAUSAGE FLATBREAD SANDWICH (280 calories) + 8 OUNCES ORANGE JUICE (110 calories) = 390 calories**
*Thanks to the egg whites, sausage, and spinach, this grab-and-go sandwich stands out as a smart, filling fast-food choice.*

3. **ARBY'S PECAN CHICKEN SALAD SANDWICH = 769 calories**
*Although this sandwich is built on whole grain bread and contains fruit and chicken, it's loaded with calories thanks to the generous amount of fat-laden mayonnaise.*

4. **LEAN CUISINE BBQ RECIPE CHICKEN PIZZA (340 calories) + WHOLE FRUIT STRAWBERRY FRUIT BAR (70 calories) = 410 calories**
*Single-serving pizzas can provide instant portion control, but check the label—some supply more than 750 calories apiece!*

5. **AU BON PAIN MEDITERRANEAN WRAP = 610 calories**
*Vegetarian doesn't automatically mean low-cal. And wraps aren't necessarily a better option than bread: They're big, allowing for more spreads and fillings.*

6. **3 OUNCES TOSTITOS MULTIGRAIN TORTILLA CHIPS (450 CALORIES) + ½ CUP DESERT PEPPER TRADING COMPANY CORN, BLACK BEAN, ROASTED RED PEPPER SALSA (80 CALORIES) = 530 calories**
*Choose baked chips instead for the same amount of fiber and 30 fewer calories per ounce. Salsa is healthy, but a jar without beans or corn will be the lowest in calories.*

7. **20-OUNCE BOTTLE ARIZONA GREEN TEA WITH GINSENG AND HONEY (175 CALORIES) + 2.25-OUNCE PACKAGE OF EMERALD TROPICAL BLEND TRAIL MIX (296 CALORIES) = 471 calories**
*Although nuts and dried fruits contain nutrients and fiber, they're calorie-dense. Watch out for oversize, oversweetened drinks (even ones that may sound healthy), which make an innocent-looking snack a fairly big-calorie meal.*

8. **1 OUNCE CHEDDAR CHEESE + 1 OUNCE BRIE CHEESE + 4 REDUCED-FAT TRISCUITS + 5 OUNCES WHITE WINE) = 400 calories**
*Choose sensible portions of creamy cheese, crispy crackers, and refreshing wine to treat yourself well without overdoing on calories.*

9. **STIR-FRIED BEEF AND BROCCOLI WITH BROWN RICE = 410 calories**
*When you prepare this dish at home using our 400-calorie recipe (page 321), you won't have to guess how much sugar and salt—or how many calories—you're eating. A lunch bowl of beef and broccoli (with white rice) at P.F. Chang's contains nearly double the calories (790).*

10. **RUBY TUESDAY AVOCADO TURKEY BURGER = 1,130 calories**
*When you're eating out, don't assume that a turkey burger is lower in calories than a beef burger. It all depends on the fat content of the meat (ground turkey sometimes has turkey skin mixed in for moisture) and the weight of the patty. With the high-cal toppings, including avocado, bacon, and cheese, this burger contains almost three meals' worth of calories—and that's without fries!*

11. **RED LOBSTER MAUI LUAU SHRIMP AND SALMON = 790 calories**
*Seafood can be a big calorie bargain, but not this meal. You probably know to avoid battered and fried dishes, but also look out for sweet or rich sauces, dips, and butters.*

12. **3 OUNCE BROWNIE SHOT + 1/4 CUP WHIPPED CREAM = 430 calories**
*Although it's a lower-calorie choice than other dessert options, especially in restaurants, this "three-bite" dessert counts as a meal when it comes to calories.*

13. **MCDONALD'S SMALL STRAWBERRY TRIPLE THICK SHAKE = 420 calories**
*The "small" size (12 fluid ounces) of this shake doesn't change the fact that it packs a lot of calories. Order a Strawberry Sundae and you'll save 140 calories.*

*(continued from page 5)*

don't know how many calories are in the foods we eat. And most of us don't really want to have to count calories.

Bottom line: We're intimidated by and underinformed about calories.

✤ In one study, 120 men and women selected premeasured foods from a buffet line, then told the research team how much food they thought they ate. Fewer than one-third were able to estimate portions correctly.[12] (The good news is that practice makes perfect. People who train using portion-size shortcuts, such as likening a deck of cards to a 3-ounce serving of meat, improve accuracy.[13])

✤ Close to 200 survey respondents who were asked to estimate the calories and fat in nine restaurant entrées generally were off by 100 percent—they thought that a meal with more than 1,300 calories had only 642 calories![14] Respondents had the most difficulty estimating calories in the most unhealthy items. For example, a serving of cheese fries with ranch dressing weighed in at 3,000-plus calories; they guessed 1,000.

That's my inspiration for this book: We all need delicious calorie-controlled meals *and* the tools to view and choose food through a healthy calorie lens. Along the way, you'll discover that weight loss doesn't have to mean forbidden food groups and deprivation. It *is* possible to reach your

goals by following a moderate, flexible, easy-to-follow eating plan that controls calories but also allows for splurges and favorite foods.

To help me put together meals that were not only calorie-controlled but also nutritionally balanced *and* tasty, I enlisted the help of Mindy Hermann, RD, whose expertise in food and nutrition spans 30 years. Mindy is a registered dietitian, busy mom, and great cook, and she's a professional who understands the challenge of marrying healthy eating with the realities of a hectic life. As we pulled together the research on hidden calories, I learned to modify my favorite meals with a healthier balance of nutrients and more reasonable portions. My go-to meal for years has been a lemon salad dinner. Simple, scrumptious, and now I know it's just 400 calories a serving—toss together 3 cups romaine lettuce, ¼ cup Romano cheese, the juice of a lemon, and 2 teaspoons olive oil, and enjoy with a 16-ounce glass of fat-free milk.

That's one example of my reality. Now let's try to understand yours.

# 2.
# WHY SLIM IS SIMPLE

ONE OF THE THINGS THAT READERS TOLD ME THEY LOVE MOST about *Prevention*'s Flat Belly Diet is the ever-so-simple "rule" that you must eat four 400-calorie meals a day. The *400 Calorie Fix* was inspired by that basic idea.

## 400: THE MAGIC NUMBER

If you're a woman of average size and average activity level, you need about 1,600 calories per day to maintain a healthy weight (that's four 400-calorie meals a day). But when it comes to weight and calories, one size does not fit all. According to government estimates, most men need about 2,000 calories a day; hence, the use of a 2,000-calorie standard on food package labels. Athletes and other people who are very active may need more. Now, if you're trying to lose weight, you probably need fewer calories. Instead, most of us tend to eat more: According to the USDA, the average American eats about 2,800 calories a day.[1]

Regardless of our total calorie needs, though, we all need food to fuel us throughout the day. If you skip breakfast, have a light lunch, and then eat a really big dinner (which many of us do), you won't meet your body's daily need for calories and nutrients. Eating 1,600 daily calories that way—that is, almost all in one meal—is a recipe for moodiness and exhaustion. You'll be hungry and suffer from low blood sugar during the day, *plus* your body won't metabolize fat as efficiently, especially at night.[2]

Instead, study after study illustrates the benefits of spacing out your meals at regular intervals and keeping them all about the same size. Eating meals at regular intervals has been linked to greater calorie burning after eating, better response to insulin, and lower fasting blood cholesterol levels.[3-5] When you eat throughout the day, you're less likely to become ravenous and overeat when you do sit down. You also keep your blood sugar (and energy) levels balanced, your metabolism revved, and your mood stable.

Historically, some calorie-controlled diets were hard to follow because they didn't account for hunger—or acknowledge the best types of foods to keep energy levels up and cravings at bay. Mindy and I chose 400 calories as our per-meal "fix" because it's the right amount to keep you active and satiated until your next meal. Plus, it allows for variety: Go any lower and it would be difficult to get a good mix of tastes and textures on your plate, as well as enough body-building, disease-fighting nutrients.

## WHAT MAKES 400 CALORIE FIX A POWERFUL WEIGHT-LOSS SOLUTION?

If you're reading this book, chances are you've tried to lose weight before and are looking for a different approach that fits your lifestyle and calls on the foods you like to eat. You've had enough of diets that rely on low-calorie foods (grapefruit and celery sticks come to mind) without interesting flavors. The 400 Calorie Fix tackles weight management head-on with a commitment to taste.

Successful weight loss *does* require lifestyle changes—but the beauty of the 400 Calorie Fix is that you don't have to drastically alter your routine or avoid the foods, activities, or social occasions you love. You can mix and match 400-calorie meals from this book, or create your own. If you're looking for more structure, you can follow one of the specific plans described in Chapter 3. Whether you like to watch movies and eat popcorn with your family, order takeout for yourself after work, or hit the town for dinner and drinks with friends, the 400 Calorie Fix lets you live your life exactly how you want to live it.

But don't take my word for it. Mindy and I recruited 16 regular folks, men and women ranging in age from 35 to 57, all with busy work and social lives, and asked them to try out the 400 Calorie Fix. You'll learn more about their life- and body-changing experiences in Chapter 5. As they found, the secret to the 400 Calorie Fix is adapting your food choices to fit the life you have, not the other way around!

You will not find lists of foods that you can or cannot eat in this book. You will not be instructed to read labels for specific ingredients. You will not have to cook every day (unless you want to) or invest in tasteless meal replacements or untested supplements. Instead, we give you a guide for right-sizing out-of-control portions and keeping calories in check at every meal in every situation. We did the work for you so you can eat what you want, when and where you want, just by looking at your meals—and food in general— through the 400 Calorie Lens.

I wanted to create a solution that is truly adaptable to any lifestyle, taste preference, and weight-loss goal. This flexibility is what makes the 400 Calorie Fix such a powerful weight-loss solution; after all, a diet only works as long as you follow it. The 400 Calorie Fix is filled with strategies to customize the way you eat, as you'll learn in Chapter 3.

### HOW MANY 400-CALORIE MEALS CAN I EAT?

Here's how it works: Each of the 400-plus meals in this book delivers between 380 and 420 calories. You should eat three, four, or five meals a day, depending on your gender

## MY FAVORITE 400-CALORIE MEAL

### DAWN'S CURRIED QUINOA SALAD

For a fast, flavorful 400-calorie meal, I cook up this salad, which is a quick way to get the health benefits of whole grains and the disease-fighting antioxidant power of curry. Bring ½ cup water to a boil and add ¼ cup dry quinoa and ½ teaspoon curry powder. Simmer, covered, for 10 minutes. Add ½ cup shredded carrots, 2 tablespoons dried cranberries, and 1 chopped scallion to the cooked quinoa and season with salt and pepper to taste. Serve with 1 cup steamed broccoli and 3 ounces of your favorite grilled protein, such as lean steak, salmon, chicken breast, or—my favorite—a grilled tofu cutlet. **—Dawn Jackson Blatner, RD,** *spokesperson for the American Dietetic Association and author of* The Flexitarian Diet

and activity level (and how much weight you want to lose). So if you choose three meals daily, you'll get about 1,200 calories, four daily meals provide about 1,600 calories, and five daily meals serve up 2,000 calories.

As we learned in Chapter 1, few people know what a healthy weight is for them, and only about 15 percent know how many calories they need to eat each day to reach and stay at that healthy weight. And no wonder! Determining the number of calories you should eat each day can be complicated. Numerous calorie counters can be found online that will take into account your age, gender, current weight, metabolism, activity level, even how much weight you want to lose by when, and then plug all of these into a series of complex equations and eventually tell you an exact number of calories you should eat in order to meet your goal weight. But you could drive yourself crazy if you tried to hit that exact number every day.

The good news is that you don't need to. We've simplified your task and added up the numbers for you. We consulted the American Dietetic Association's Evidence Analysis Library (EAL) for guidance. Studies summarized by the EAL show that having four or five meals or snacks each day is linked to lower or no obesity risk. In contrast, people who eat three or fewer, or more than six, daily meals or snacks may have a higher risk of obesity. A French study also found that participants who cut down from four to three daily meals—but ate the same number of calories—actually gained body fat.[6]

Consult the chart to the left to determine the number of meals you should eat per day (and, hence, your daily calorie count). When you're ready, turn to Chapters 6 to 14 and choose whichever meals suit you! (To find out more about your daily calorie needs, visit www.prevention.com/healthtracker.)

## HOW MUCH FOOD DO I GET FOR 400 CALORIES?

Worried that eating just 400 calories a meal will leave you hungry? I promise you'll be pleasantly surprised at how satisfied you are with the 400-calorie meals in this book. Sandi Hill, one of our 2 Week Quick Slim

---

## "How Many Meals Should I Eat?"

### Women

| WEIGHT GOAL/ ACTIVITY LEVEL | SEDENTARY | SOMEWHAT ACTIVE/ACTIVE | VERY ACTIVE |
|---|---|---|---|
| Lose | 3 meals | 3-4 meals | 4 meals |
| Maintain | 3-4 meals | 4 meals | 4-5 meals |

### Men

| WEIGHT GOAL/ ACTIVITY LEVEL | SEDENTARY | SOMEWHAT ACTIVE/ACTIVE | VERY ACTIVE |
|---|---|---|---|
| Lose | 3-4 meals | 4 meals | 4-5 meals |
| Maintain | 4 meals | 4-5 meals | 5+ meals |

**SEDENTARY:** You sit most of the day and drive everywhere, and you log plenty of hours of screen time each day. **SOMEWHAT ACTIVE:** You get about 30 minutes of physical activity daily. Nothing too strenuous, generally the equivalent of walking about 1½ to 3 miles daily, or 3,000 to 6,000 steps on a pedometer.

**ACTIVE:** You like to move around and clock 30 to 60 minutes of daily physical activity by hitting the gym, climbing stairs at the office, and parking farther away at the market along with moderate exercise, the equivalent of walking more than 3 miles per day, or more than 6,000 steps on a pedometer. **VERY ACTIVE:** You're more than a weekend warrior; you thrive on high-intensity sports and rigorous activities that total more than 60 minutes per day.

panelists, noted, "At first, 400 calories per meal seemed really drastic and I expected to be hungry. In fact, I felt satisfied after eating each meal."

If you make smart choices, 400 calories are enough to supply good nutrition and give you plenty of energy. With 400 calories, you can even enjoy rich and flavorful foods like cheese and chocolate that typical diets tell you to avoid. How? By eating right-size portions that fit into the 400-calorie framework. Check out our Domino's Hawaiian Feast Brooklyn Crust Pizza (page 115) and Microwave S'mores (page 195). They're perfect examples of ways to indulge a little.

As you'll see in the following pages, you *can* get a lot of food for 400 calories. There are no puny salads or lonely bits of lettuce here! Our Mexican Flag Salad with Crispy Tortilla Topping (page 263), for example, is piled high with lettuce, tomato, avocado, *queso blanco,* and crispy tortilla strips. Here's the trick: Experts at the University of Pennsylvania say that when your eyes see a portion of food that looks small, your brain sends a message that the amount of food is inadequate, even if the food is something like chocolate that is high in fat and calories.[7] Our 400-calorie meals look substantial and contain lots of colorful low-calorie fruits and vegetables to make them look even more appetizing.

## WHAT CAN I EAT FOR 400 CALORIES?

To help you feel full and satisfied, most of your meals should feature at least one filling food: Vegetables and fruits, protein-rich

foods, nuts and other foods with good fats, and foods high in fiber have all been proven by researchers to increase satiety, or feelings of fullness. Almost all of our 400-calorie meals adhere to this strategy, and we'll show you how to construct your own meals this way, too. As you'll learn in Chapter 3, these are the foundations of our 4 Star Nutrition System and each gets a different colored star.

★ *Protein.* Foods rich in protein are even better hunger beaters than foods rich in carbohydrates or fat, and they actually stimulate hormones and neurotransmitters that signal fullness. So naturally we've filled the 400 Calorie Fix with plenty of meals that feature protein. Richard Mattes, MPH, PhD, RD, and his colleagues at Purdue University have conducted extensive research on satiety. In one study, they compared a high-protein breakfast to a standard breakfast in men on a calorie-restricted diet. The high-protein

FIX IT
FAST

Eat your fruit or
vegetables toward
the beginning of
the meal. Because
they're high in
water, they'll help
fill you up and
make your meal
more satisfying.

breakfast led to greater and longer-lasting feelings of fullness.[8] Barbara Rolls, PhD, Penn State, also looked at the relationship between protein and feeling full. She found that chicken breast (high protein) is more satiating than celery with cream cheese (high fat), lemon candy (high carbohydrate), or chocolate (high fat and high carbohydrate).[9] Protein might also stimulate the body to burn more calories and help maintain muscle mass, which uses up more calories than fat does.[10] We've marked our higher-protein meals—the BBQ Spice-Rubbed Pork Loin Roast (page 326) is just one of dozens of meals—with a blue star.

★ **Fiber.** Foods that are highest in fiber, typically fruits and vegetables, legumes such as chickpeas and kidney beans, and whole grains, are in short supply in many low-carb weight-loss plans. Another big mistake. The Nurse's Health Study of more than 70,000 female nurses found that eating

a lot of fruits, vegetables, and other high-fiber foods lowered the chances of becoming overweight.[11, 12] In a study of 500 Finnish men and women, those who ate the most fiber lost the most weight.[13] So we made sure to include these foods in many of our meals. In *400 Calorie Fix,* meals that are highest in fiber, like the Vegetarian Paella (page 364), are marked with an orange star.

★ **Good Fats.** Not all that long ago, nuts topped the list of forbidden foods for people trying to lose weight. Big mistake! Thanks to studies done by Mattes and others, peanuts, almonds, and other nuts, all high in monounsaturated fats (MUFAs), are now considered an important part of weight-management plans. Researchers became interested in the link between nuts and body weight when they discovered that people who eat nuts frequently have a lower body mass index (BMI) than people who eat them less often. How can eating a high-calorie food not lead to weight gain? Research at Purdue revealed that nuts are so satiating that people eat fewer calories throughout the day.[14] Also, the body doesn't absorb all of the fat (and therefore calories) in nuts because the fat is tucked away behind heavy cell walls that are virtually impossible for the human body to break down.

What if you don't like or are allergic to nuts? Olives, avocados, fatty fish like tuna and salmon, most vegetable oils, and even dark chocolate also are rich in healthy fats. In fact, you get a double benefit from many of these foods, which not only contain belly-

flattening MUFAs but also heart-healthy omega-3 fatty acids. MUFAs in a meal can help you feel fuller longer;[15] add taste and satisfaction to a healthy eating plan, making it easier to follow;[16] and possibly boost weight loss.[17] In one study, a group of men and women eating a moderate-fat diet that contained MUFAs lost more weight over 14 months than did a group following a low-fat diet. Including foods with MUFAs during weight loss and maintenance is also good for heart health.[18] Omega-3 fatty acids, found in fatty fish, flaxseed, and other foods, can help lower blood pressure.[19] You'll notice that meals with nuts and other healthy fats, namely MUFAs and omega-3s, are marked with a red star. Be sure to try the Quick-Fix Grilled Salmon Sandwich (page 181).

★ *Fruits/Veggies.* We were inspired to include plenty of produce in this plan because of the work of Rolls and her team. They have conducted numerous studies showing that fruits and vegetables enhance feelings of fullness because they are natu-rally high in water and fiber. Better yet, they help you stay satisfied on fewer calories. In one of her earlier studies, Rolls instructed participants to serve themselves as much as they wanted from one of three entrées; participants who ate the entrée with the most vegetables ate fewer calories overall.[20]

Mindy is especially fond of vegetables for weight management because most are low in calories and rich in vitamins and minerals. In fact, a lot of veggies, mostly those that are green, made her list of "free" vegetables on page 38. These can be eaten in almost unlimited amounts and enjoyed as desired with meals and snacks. You can also pick out meals that are particularly high in vegetables or fruits—try our Quick-Fix Pumped-Up Fruit Salad (page 171) or our recipe for 7-Layer Mexican Dinner Dip (page 362)—by looking for the green fruits and vegetables star.

# 3.
## FIND YOUR
## 400 CALORIE
## FIX

NOW THAT YOU UNDERSTAND THE SCIENCE BEHIND MANAGING your weight through calorie control and you've learned how many calories you need to eat, it's time to start putting these principles into practice. Where do you start? You need tools. And we've got 'em!

### THE 400 CALORIE FIX: YOUR LIFE, YOUR WAY

I wrote *400 Calorie Fix* to fit all sorts of food personalities and dieting styles. If you want structure, we offer set meal plans. If you prefer more flexibility, you can mix and match any of the 400-plus choices in the book. If you like to cook, try our delicious recipes; if you don't, go for the packaged or restaurant meals. If you don't have time for even that, you'll find tips and tricks to choose smart 400-calorie meals wherever you go, from the salad bar to the office party to the vending machine.

And now for the really good part: Fun. Food should be fun, and the absolute last thing I want to do is tell you what you can't have, whether it's an ice-cold beer, a glass of red wine, or a decadent dessert. Heck, I've been known to have a bowl of ice cream and call it dinner—more than once. You should be able to do these things too, and still maintain a healthy weight. The secret is moderation, but as portions have doubled, tripled, and quadrupled, this word has lost its meaning. My goal with the 400 Calorie Fix is to bring back into focus what moderation looks like.

### WHAT'S YOUR 400-CALORIE PERSONALITY?

We created five main tools with varying levels of structure to customize the 400 Calorie Fix to your life, your tastes, and your goals. Pick the ones that appeal to you most.

❖ *400 Calorie Meals.* If you just want to learn how to eat 400-calorie meals, try any and all of the four hundred 400 Calorie Meals in Chapters 6 to 14. Look in the chapter with the type of meal that you want—prepared foods, takeout, casual dining, quick fix, or recipe.

❖ *400 Calorie Lens.* If you're a visual person and you frequently find yourself in situations where food choices are limited, our 400 Calorie Lens in Chapter 4 gives you simple visual tricks and shortcuts to help you gauge how much food really adds up to 400 calories.

❖ *2 Week Quick Slim.* If you want to jump-start healthy eating and lose weight on a structured program, turn to Chapter 5 for the 2 Week Quick Slim, 14 days of planned meals to help you drop pounds quickly and get you motivated and excited about the 400-calorie frame of mind.

❖ *400 Calorie Menus.* If you're a planner or have specific health needs or eating challenges—for instance, you're at risk for diabetes, you travel a lot, or you're cooking for a whole family—check out our 400 Calorie Menus in Appendix A. These ready-made meal plans are designed to match your tastes and lifestyle and provide an instant shortcut for mapping out your day's food.

✤ *4 Star Nutrition System.* If you're primarily concerned about good nutrition, the 4 Star Nutrition System described later in this chapter helps you mix and match meals to get a healthy balance of protein, fiber, good fats, and fruits and vegetables throughout the day.

Now, let's look at each of these tools in a bit more detail.

## FOUR HUNDRED 400 CALORIE MEALS

Confession: I have eaten the same turkey sandwich on whole wheat with a side of baby carrots for lunch nearly every workday for 20 years. Talk about a food rut! But, in fact, most of us eat the same 10 or so meals week after week. By learning to eat the 400-calorie way, you're already expanding your diet horizons!

Most of the 400 meals in this book weigh in at 380 to 420 calories and were designed to fit into a hectic lifestyle, whether you slog away at a desk, hit the road for business or pleasure, or spend most of your time coordinating the schedules of loved ones. We crafted meals using foods from many different places—the aisles of the supermarket, the vending machine, national fast-food chains, and restaurants—so that you can look for foods that work in your day. Maybe you don't have the time or the inclination to cook: Our quick-fix and no-cook meals are perfect for you! If you eat at your desk, you can choose from dozens of 400-calorie meals made from packaged foods—frozen meals, frozen items, canned soups, and plenty of other quick and convenient choices. If you eat out, you'll enjoy the broad range of takeout and casual meals, including a steak dinner, a sushi lunch, and a deli-style sandwich.

For people who do like to cook, we searched the globe and developed 150 scrumptious recipes from cuisines around the world, including Mexican, Asian, and Italian. The recipes are simple to follow and include right-size portions. We've added side dishes

## MY FAVORITE 400-CALORIE MEAL

### ELLIE'S GARLIC-BASIL SHRIMP

My recipe for Garlic-Basil Shrimp is so delicious and beautiful that I chose it for the cover of my newest book. For 4 servings, I sauté 1¼ pounds shrimp with 3 cloves minced garlic, then add a splash of white wine. Then I toss in 1½ cups chopped fresh tomatoes and ¼ cup basil leaves and serve it over 3 cups cooked whole wheat orzo. It's a fast and elegant meal for 380 calories per serving!—*Ellie Krieger, RD,* author of So Easy: Luscious, Healthy Recipes for Every Meal of the Week

# MOVE IT, MOVE IT, MOVE IT!

Exercise lifts your mood, boosts your energy level, prevents disease, and enhances confidence. That's why I am practically begging you to include exercise as part of the 400-calorie lifestyle. The more active you are, the more 400-calorie meals you can eat in a day. Here are some examples:

## *Ways to Burn 400 Calories*

| ACTIVITY | TIME NEEDED TO BURN 400 CALORIES* |
|---|---|
| Running a 10-minute mile (6 miles per hour) | 35 minutes |
| Working out on a stairclimbing machine | 39 minutes |
| Mountain biking | 42 minutes |
| Playing singles tennis | 44 minutes |
| Swimming laps at the Y (moderate) | 50 minutes |
| Sweating it out in aerobics class (moderate) | 54 minutes |
| Riding a bike at a leisurely pace | 59 minutes |
| Shoveling snow | 59 minutes |
| Rearranging furniture in your house | 59 minutes |
| Ice-skating for fun | 1 hour 4 minutes |
| Walking for exercise (4 miles per hour) | 1 hour 11 minutes |
| Kayaking | 1 hour 11 minutes |
| Weeding the garden | 1 hour 18 minutes |
| Playing outside with kids (moderate) | 1 hour 28 minutes |
| Walking for exercise (3.5 miles per hour) | 1 hour 33 minutes |
| Playing Dance Dance Revolution | 1 hour 35 minutes |
| Vacuuming pesky pet hair off the carpet | 1 hour 41 minutes |
| Strength training/lifting weights (moderate) | 1 hour 58 minutes |
| Practicing downward-facing dog, sun salutation, and child's pose (hatha yoga) | 2 hours 21 minutes |
| Watching a *Dancing with the Stars* marathon | 5 hours 53 minutes |
| Sleeping | 6 hours 32 minutes |

*Calculations based on a 150-pound person.

Source: Ainsworth BE. (2002, January) The Compendium of Physical Activities Tracking Guide. Prevention Research Center, Norman J. Arnold School of Public Health, University of South Carolina. Retrieved 5/15/2009 from the World Wide Web.

and other foods so that each meal adds up to 400 calories. Personally, I'm crazy about the recipes calling for the slow cooker, as this inexpensive piece of equipment is supereasy and cranks out crowd-pleasing meals.

Smart nutrition is important for both health and weight loss, so most of the meals (yes, even the prepackaged and fast-food ones) dish up several food groups that are essential for good health. For example, most breakfasts have fruit and a calcium-rich dairy food. The 4 Star Nutrition System helps ensure that you get the right balance of foods.

## THE 400 CALORIE LENS
It's really hard to eyeball and estimate food portions and calories, no matter how many diets you've been on. As studies have shown, even the experts have trouble!

The 400 Calorie Lens will help refocus your eye so that you instinctively know what a 400-calorie meal looks like. To estimate how many calories are in any given food, you need to know (1) what you're eating; (2) how much of it you're eating; and (3) how it's prepared. The 400 Calorie Lens, including visual cues and other tricks, will teach you how to answer these questions.

## THE 2 WEEK QUICK SLIM
If you want to jump-start weight loss and/or would like a structured plan laid out for

# IT'S HOW YOU PLAY THE GAME
Hooked on "exergames" like those available for the Nintendo Wii? Here's how long it would take you to burn 400 calories playing virtual Wii Sports, compared with the traditional activities.*

## *To Burn 400 Calories, You'd Need to . . .*

| | |
|---|---|
| **PLAY WII GOLF FOR:** | **2 hours 9 minutes** |
| Hit golf balls at a driving range for: | 1 hour 58 minutes |
| Walk the golf course while carrying clubs for: | 1 hour 18 minutes |
| **PLAY WII BOWLING FOR:** | **1 hour 43 minutes** |
| Challenge friends in a game of lawn bowling for: | 1 hour 58 minutes |
| Head to the lanes and bowl for: | 1 hour 58 minutes |
| **PLAY WII TENNIS FOR:** | **1 hour 15 minutes** |
| Grab a paddle and play table tennis for: | 1 hour 28 minutes |
| Square off in a doubles match on the court: | 59 minutes |
| Go one-on-one on the court for: | 44 minutes |

*Calculations based on a 150-pound person.

Sources: Ainsworth BE. (2002, January) The Compendium of Physical Activities Tracking Guide. Prevention Research Center, Norman J. Arnold School of Public Health, University of South Carolina. Retrieved 5/15/2009 from the World Wide Web.

Anders, Mark. "As Good as the Real Thing?" *ACE Fitness Matters.* Vol. 14, No. 4 (2008): 7-9.

## COUNT ON CALCIUM

Most Americans fall far short of the daily recommendation for calcium, which is found mainly in dairy products and some fortified foods. To check how you're doing, use the calcium info for each meal, expressed as a percentage of the Daily Value of 1,000 milligrams (1,200 for adults 51 and older).

you, try the 2 Week Quick Slim described in Chapter 5. We tested the 2 Week Quick Slim on 16 men and women with amazing results—a total loss of more than 96 pounds and an average loss of 6 pounds per person. This 2-week plan gives you three daily meals for about 1,200 calories, a level that will promote weight loss of up to 2 pounds per week in most people, although our test panel lost even more. This is a relatively low-calorie eating plan, but the foods and meals are well balanced and were chosen to deliver the important nutrients you need. You probably won't want to stay at this low a calorie level indefinitely, but it's certainly safe to return to this 2-week plan any time you feel that you need to retrain your eye to reset your portion sizes.

### THE 400 CALORIE MENUS

The 400 Calorie Menus are ready-made meal plans for different tastes and lifestyles. Check out Appendix A to find the meal plan that is best for you. Say you don't have much time to eat, let alone cook. The From the Freezer Menu includes make-ahead and freezer-friendly fare that you can put together quickly on a weekend or weekday evening. If that requires too much planning for you, the On the Run Menu includes mostly no-cook and quick-fix meals. The Dining-Out Menu offers mostly restaurant meals, which will be particularly helpful to the frequent traveler. The Family-Friendly Menu serves up classic dishes the whole family will enjoy and is designed to be quick to prepare and easy on the wallet. We also provide Vegetarian, Heart-Healthy, and Diabetes-Friendly menus. You can also refer to the menus as a general guide for creating your own daily eating plan or for putting together meals with a particular theme.

### THE 4 STAR NUTRITION SYSTEM

For optimal health, energy, and brainpower, you need nutrients as well as calories. That's where the 4 Star Nutrition System comes in. The 4 Star Nutrition System will help you eat for health *and* nutrition while following a 400-calorie lifestyle. To create the 4 Star Nutrition System, Mindy identified four important features in healthy meals: protein, fiber, good fats, and fruits and vegetables—the satisfying building blocks we mentioned in Chapter 2. We assigned each a colored star—blue for protein, orange for fiber, red for good fats, and green for fruits and veggies—and determined a threshold for each, awarding stars accordingly. Some of the meals have just one star. Others have two, three, even four stars because they qualify in more than one category. A few meals have zero stars. These are our Fun Meals, like ice cream, cake, and ballpark food, which fall short of our nutrition guidelines but still have a place in a healthy (real) life.

Mindy designed each of the 400-plus meals in this book to be as nutritionally balanced as possible. Almost all the meals—even some of our Fun Meals—include more than one of these four key elements. In other words, just because a meal doesn't have a protein star doesn't mean it doesn't have any protein in it; it just doesn't have quite enough to qualify for that star. If you chose four meals from this book at random, chances are you'd get reasonable amounts of protein, fiber, good fats, and fruits and vegetables. Which begs the question, why bother with the 4 Star Nutrition System?

Because it is virtually impossible to get enough of all four components in one meal, it's more important to look at the balance of protein, fiber, good fats, and fruits and vegetables over the course of a day. Government health agencies have established basic nutritional guidelines that recommend specific daily amounts of each nutrient and food group that research indicates are optimal for adults. You'll see these in the USDA's My Pyramid Food Guidance System and in the recommended daily intakes listed on food labels. But it's a pain to have to calculate how many grams of fiber are in each meal or to track how many cups of fruits and vegetables you're eating per day. With the 4 Star Nutrition System, you don't have to. By collecting each star at least once during the day, you'll be on the road to meeting these recommendations.

You may notice that the threshold we've set for each star does not match the government's daily recommendations. This is because government guidelines apply to the entire day's meals, not just one meal. Take protein, for example: You don't really want to have all of your day's protein in one meal. But because we've included protein in almost every meal, as long as you make sure to include at least one high-protein meal (at least 20 grams), you'll almost definitely make up the remainder of your daily quota of 50 to 70 grams (experts are debating exact requirements) through the rest of your meals. Similarly, the daily recommendation for fiber is about 20 grams in a 1,600-calorie diet. We award a fiber star to meals with at least 7 grams; together with the smaller amount of fiber in your other meals, this will get you to about 20 grams over the course of the day. The government recommends about $4\frac{1}{2}$ cups of fruits and vegetables each day, so look for the fruits and vegetables star—awarded if a meal supplies at least 1 cup—and add extra veggies from the freebie list in Chapter 4. Meals with the good fats star have at least one food item that is a key source of monounsaturated and/or omega-3 fats.

Using the 4 Star Nutrition System is as simple as collecting colors. Your goal? Collect at least one star of each of the four colors by the end of the day. And the more stars, the better. That's it. See, I told you it was easy!

Enjoy a Fun Meal—no stars—up to three times per week to stay happy and stave off feelings of deprivation, which lead to cravings. This lets you indulge without overdoing it.

## BE SMART ABOUT SODIUM

Salt (sodium chloride) is so widely used in packaged and restaurant foods that many Americans eat far more than the 2,400-milligram Daily Value (the amount of sodium in a teaspoon of table salt). After you eat a salty meal, your body may retain extra water and your weight may go up. Many of our recipes call for using lower-sodium ingredients; rinsing canned beans, tuna, and salmon; and seasoning with salt-free herb and spice blends by companies such as McCormick, Penzeys, Mrs. Dash, and Spice Hunter (see page 41).

# HEALTHY OR

## YOU ONLY THINK IT'S LOW-CALORIE!

Many foods that sound healthy really aren't, and even those that are nutritious aren't necessarily low-calorie. Here are some common examples, with the lowdown on whether or not it's worth making the switch. In the next chapter, you'll learn how to spot these sneaky calorie busters wherever they lurk—and, of couse, how to fix them.

### MULTIGRAIN BREADS AND BAGELS

Multigrain is the way to go for more nutrition—especially fiber—but the heavier whole grain flours also make for heavier and higher-calorie breads and rolls. **FIX IT FAST:** Multigrain and whole grain are worth it for nutrition and satiety, but watch portion size.

### REDUCED-FAT (2%) MILK

Reduced-fat milk contains about 120 calories per cup, compared to 150 for whole milk (3.7% fat). Low-fat and fat-free milks, at 100 and 80 calories per cup, respectively, offer more dramatic calorie savings. **FIX IT FAST:** Use low-fat or fat-free milk.

### FRUIT JUICE

A cup of juice generally has more calories than a piece of fruit. Also, liquid calories are much less filling. **FIX IT FAST:** Opt for a piece of fresh fruit. Or, instead of drinking a whole cup, add just a splash of juice to sparkling water.

### SMOOTHIES

The calories in a smoothie can add up quickly, particularly if it's made with calorie-dense ingredients like banana and fruit juice. **FIX IT FAST:** Stick to the smallest size and choose a combo of fresh fruits with milk or yogurt for extra calcium and protein.

### GRANOLA

The wholesomeness of granola, with its oat flakes, raisins, and seeds, belies its high calorie count. **FIX IT FAST:** Buy lower-fat granola or make your own (see page 206). You'll save about 70 calories per ½-cup portion.

### LOW-FAT MUFFINS

Reduced-fat and low-fat muffins often contain additional sugar for chewiness that helps compensate for the loss of texture and flavor contributed by the fat. **FIX IT FAST:** Don't bother unless you prefer the flavor.

### BAKED CHIPS AND CRACKERS

Extra potato or flour makes up the lost weight of the oil and adds back some of the calories. **FIX IT FAST:** Baked chips and crackers often don't offer much calorie savings.

### EGG-WHITE OMELET

Although you do save 56 calories per yolk by choosing egg whites, eggs aren't the biggest issue when it comes to omelets. It's what you fold into it that really makes calories add up. **FIX IT FAST:** Stuff your omelet with more veggies and less cheese.

# HEFTY?

## FROZEN YOGURT AND DOUBLE-CHURNED ICE CREAM

Super-premium and boutique brands have the most calories, sometimes even more than regular ice cream.
**FIX IT FAST:** Don't spend more than 150 calories on a half-cup serving.

## FRUIT SORBET, POPSICLES, AND ITALIAN ICES

Ice pops and Italian ices usually have no real fruit; they're made from water, sugar and other sweeteners, and flavorings.
**FIX IT FAST:** Pick sugar-free popsicles and ices if you're looking for a cold treat with almost no calories.

## DRIED FRUIT

The drying process creates bite-size bits that are concentrated in calories. Worse, many varieties, including cranberries, mango, kiwifruit, and papaya, contain added sugar.
**FIX IT FAST:** Eat in small amounts as a garnish for cereals and salads.

## WRAP SANDWICHES

The wrapper may be skinny but the calories aren't. In fact, it takes a big wrap to hold even a modest amount of filling. Figure on possibly twice the number of calories that you would get from a couple of slices of bread. A 10" wrapper, a typical size, has 220 calories while an 8" has 140.
**FIX IT FAST:** Eat just half your sandwich. Or put the filling from half of your wrap onto a plate and toss the rest of the wrapper.

## LIGHT SALAD DRESSING

Although lower in fat and calories than regular dressing, light dressing is hardly free of fat or calories.
**FIX IT FAST:** Switch to salad dressing spray when you can, for only 1 calorie or so per spray. Or use only 1 to 2 tablespoons of light dressing. If you have a few flavorful ingredients like olives or beets, you might not need dressing at all. Just be careful: Many of these ingredients are also high in calories.

## CHICKEN BREAST FILLET

Skinless chicken breasts have almost no fat—but most restaurants cook them with fat.
**FIX IT FAST:** Stay away from chicken breasts that are oily or breaded. When making your own, marinate first to boost flavor and moisture, and cook until just done to avoid dryness.

## FISH SANDWICH OR TACOS

Most fish is naturally much leaner and lower in calories than beef or chicken. In restaurant and fast-food fare, however, it often is breaded and/or fried.
**FIX IT FAST:** Switch to charbroiled and save about 10 percent of the calories at one national chain.

## VEGGIE SIDE DISHES

Sometimes they're freshly cooked with just a little extra fat, and sometimes they're soggy and caloric from sitting in a puddle of oil or sauce.
**FIX IT FAST:** Ask how cooked veggies are prepared; or, go raw.

## ALL-VEGGIE CHINESE ENTRÉES

Restaurant veggie dishes are stir-fried in a lot of oil, adding gobs of fat. Steamed veggies are lower in calories but can leave you hungry.
**FIX IT FAST:** Add tofu and ½ cup of brown rice to steamed veggies.

## ORGANIC FOODS

The organic designation has nothing to do with calories.
**FIX IT FAST:** If you choose to buy organic, do so for its safety and nutritional profile.

# 4.
# SEE
## 400 CALORIES
## ANYWHERE

RECENTLY, AN EDITOR (WE'LL CALL HER BETH) who works with me at *Prevention* had what I call a 400-calorie moment. With a 40th birthday approaching, Beth is anxious to lose the 20 extra pounds she's carrying on an already curvy frame (her words). She's been exercising almost daily, walking part of the way to work, and trying to be smarter about her diet. A few days ago she bought what she thought was the perfect "diet" lunch: a plain, grilled chicken breast paired with a to-go container of fruit- and nut-studded quinoa, a healthy whole grain. She ate the whole thing and felt unpleasantly full after, so she did a little online research and realized that, although her meal was healthy, the serving sizes were huge: The chicken breast was about three times the recommended 3- to 4-ounce serving and the quinoa, about five times the recommended $\frac{1}{2}$ cup. Her rough estimate of her diet lunch? Nine hundred calories—more than half of what she should be eating each day in order to lose weight.

I use this story to illustrate how vital it is to start looking at your meals through the 400 Calorie Lens. In the previous chapters, I've told you that to successfully follow this program you need to make this important shift in perspective. In this chapter, I'm going to *show* you how to start retraining your mind to see food the 400-calorie way, especially when you find yourself in places with limited choices. Don't be intimidated by the lessons and information we present here. It's still possible (and simple!) to eat the 400-calorie way just by picking and choosing from our 400-plus meals and combos throughout the book. But heed the tips and tricks that follow and it will change your outlook (and diet).

## THE MYSTERY OF PORTION CONTROL

If you've been on diets before, you might feel pretty confident about your ability to put together a meal with close to the right number of calories. In fact, several of our test panel participants didn't want to measure their foods because they said that they knew portion sizes from other diets. Guess what? When we asked them to pull out the scale and measuring cups, they were shocked that their portion estimates were so off.

Research backs this up. We have trouble estimating portions and we tend to eat foods in amounts that are pretty out of whack with government and expert recommendations for serving sizes. In one study, for example, 177 college students were asked to serve themselves typical portions of breakfast, lunch, and dinner foods from a buffet table.[1] Their portions were secretly measured by food service staff, who weighed the buffet platters before and after each student took food. Fewer than half of the breakfast food portions and only about a third of the lunch and dinner food portions were close to recommended serving sizes.

Why are portions, and the calories in them, so hard for us to gauge? Because the appropriate portion of food varies depending on the type of food and the way it's prepared. Pound for pound, nuts pack more calories than an apple, an apple more than lettuce, lettuce dipped in creamy salad dressing more than plain lettuce, and so on.

### 400 CALORIE LENS

To estimate how many calories are in any given meal, you need to know (1) what food you're eating; (2) how much of it you're eating; and (3) how it's prepared.

Since there are multiple factors that affect your portions, we are going to give you multiple tools. Use as many as you find helpful.

### Weigh and Measure

I know that weighing and measuring meals is not a lot of fun, not to mention being inconvenient, boring, and tough to keep up for more than a couple of days. But there's no getting around the fact that it's the most accurate way to tell how much food you're eating.

We've given you a hand by calling for common, standard measurements, like 1 cup of cereal, ½ cup of fruit, 1 tablespoon of salad dressing, 1 teaspoon of soy sauce. Items from each food group follow general portion standards, although in some cases we adjust portions to keep calories within our range of 380 to 420 calories per meal. But believe me:

Investing in and using a food scale and a set of measuring cups and measuring spoons will change your diet, your body, and your life. Of course, weighing and measuring are easiest to do when you're preparing your own meals in your own kitchen.

Keep in mind that measuring will be more accurate if you use tools that are specifically designed for liquids or solids. Here's what you need (and may already have):

• Nested measuring cups for dry foods and ingredients
• 2-cup liquid measuring cup
• Set of measuring spoons
• Inexpensive digital kitchen scale for weighing food
• ½-cup, 1-cup, 2-cup, and 4-cup sealable plastic containers for storage and quick measuring

## MY FAVORITE 400-CALORIE MEAL

### ASHLEY'S BERRY PARFAIT

Parfait means "perfect" in French—and that's what this equally delicious and nutritious 400-calorie treat is! In a tall champagne flute, layer 10 ounces Oikos plain Greek yogurt (150 calories), ½ cup Nature's Path Vanilla Almond Flax Plus Granola (168 calories), and 1 cup organic blueberries or mixed berries (80 calories). Enjoy it for breakfast or lunch. —*Ashley Koff, RD, Los Angeles–based nutritionist*

# *It's a ball, it's a hand, it's a portion*

| | BALL | HAND | PORTIONS | EXAMPLES |
|---|---|---|---|---|
| | small marble | tip of the thumb | 1 teaspoon | oil, butter, margarine, sugar |
| | large marble | thumb to the first knuckle | 1 table-spoon | chopped nuts, honey, ketchup |
| | two large marbles | whole thumb | 2 table-spoons/ 1 ounce liquid | salad dressing, grated cheese, raisins |
| | golf ball | cupped handful | ¼ cup | beans, chopped vegetables, salsa, hummus |
| | hockey puck | palm of the hand | ½ cup/ 4 oz (¼ lb) raw meat, poultry, fish | burger patty, beef, pork, chicken, turkey, fish |
| | tennis ball | open handful | ½ cup | pasta, fruit salad, melon balls, small roll, scrambled eggs |
| | Wiffle ball | very loose cupped handful | 1 cup/ 1 to 2 ounces chips | potato chips, tortilla chips, popcorn, pretzels |
| | baseball | whole fist | 1 cup | cereal, lettuce, vegetables, strawberries, soup |

In addition, you'll want to have small plates on which to serve your 400-calorie meals:

- 8" salad plates
- 8–12 oz soup/salad bowls
- Tall, skinny drinking glasses
- Small serving bowls and spoons
- 8–10 oz mugs for latte, hot cocoa

### See the Visual Cues

When you're eating away from home and don't have access to measuring cups and spoons, use visual cues to eyeball, say, a steak or a bowl of pasta to get a reasonably good idea of how big or small it is. The 400 Calorie Fix gives you a choice of two different sets of visual shortcuts, one using your hand as a reference, the other using a series of different-size balls.

You'll notice that most of these are volume measurements (teaspoons, tablespoons, and cups), which is the easiest way to visualize most foods, from oil to yogurt to rice. But some foods, like chips and pretzels and meat, poultry, and fish, are awkward shapes and don't fit neatly into either a real or an imaginary spoon or cup.

You'll usually see foods like these measured by weight; hence, we've given you the corresponding weight measurements here. (A note about pretzels: Like chips, you'll want to measure them in a loose cupped handful, but keep in mind that pretzels are heavier than most chips. In fact, a loose cupped handful can weigh up to 2 ounces, depending on the shape and size of the pretzels.)

Also, you'll see that we've listed 4 ounces here as a serving size for meat, poultry, and fish, even though the most frequently recommended serving size for meat is 3 ounces. It's not a mistake: 4 ounces refers to the raw weight, 3 ounces to the cooked weight. For more details on how weight measurements match up to volume measurements, see the Conversion Chart on page 432.

## Know Your Common Foods

Of course, you can't memorize all the foods in the world and their calorie counts, but over time you'll probably get to know the right portions for your favorite foods. Throughout this book, we've given you lists of common foods that you'll find in various places. Charts and photos show you how similar foods compare in portion size and calories.

For example, in the 400 Calorie Salad Bar sidebar on page 44, you can see just how many calories you save by choosing a light dressing rather than regular one (potentially as much as 130!).

In the 400 Calorie Mexican sidebar on page 156, you can compare calories between different sizes and types of tortillas (a 12-inch tortilla has twice as many calories as a 7½-inch tortilla) and see exactly how much you can eat for 400 calories (either one 12-ounce margarita, one fajita, or one-quarter of a tostada salad).

Want to cook up your own 400-calorie meal? Check out Appendix B for a guide to calorie counts for fresh foods that you can use as building blocks. You'll learn, for instance, that for the same number of calories (200) you could eat twice as much tuna (6 ounces) as ground beef (3¼ ounces). Check out your favorites to see how they stack up.

## Learn the 1-2-3-400-Calorie Trick

After you have some idea of the appropriate portions for individual foods, it's time to put them together into balanced meals. Here's a handy trick for filling your plate at mealtime. It's a quick 1-2-3-400-Calorie system to give you the right balance of nutrients while staying in the 400-calorie ballpark. Here's how to do it.

# PLATE SIZE MATTERS

Use smaller plates to make your meal appear larger and to help you control how much you eat. Brian Wansink, PhD, of Cornell University found that even nutrition experts served themselves bigger portions—and ate more—when they had bigger bowls and serving spoons.[2] A portion that looks too small to your eyes triggers you to eat more. Compare the three plates above, which all provide exactly the same amount of food.

Mentally divide your plate into six sections:

- Fill **one** section with one serving of a protein. For meat, chicken, or fish, that's 3 ounces cooked (4 ounces raw), about the size of a hockey puck. One cup of milk or yogurt also provides one serving of protein.

- Fill **two** sections with two servings of a grain food like rice, pasta, or bread. For rice and pasta, that is ⅔ cup, or slightly less than a baseball-size scoop. For bread, it's two slices (no butter, though!).

- Fill **three** sections with three servings of vegetables. Each serving is 1 cup, so pile on three baseball-size heaps of greens and other veggies.

You might want to dish up these sample portions at home so you can start training your eyes to see meals through this lens.

You may notice that not all of our 400-plus 400-calorie meals follow this 1-2-3-400-Calorie trick. It's important to get a good balance of nutrients, but meals could get boring if they all have to have exactly the same proportion of meat to grain to fruits and vegetables. Unfortunately, the system isn't always precise because of the way that foods are prepared. Specifically,

# FIND THE FAT

What is the difference between these two fast-food meals?

THEY MAY LOOK SIMILAR, but their calories are wildly different, about 400 for the burger and salad on the top and 765 for the meal on the bottom! The difference is fat. The meal on the bottom has mayonnaise and a small slice of cheese on the burger and a full packet of regular dressing on the salad. The burger on top has ketchup and pickles but no mayo or cheese and the salad has a light Italian dressing.

## SIGNS IT'S SOAKED

It's hard to tell if prepared foods are made with a lot of fat. When in doubt, look for these telltale signs:

- Oil slicks on the side or bottom of the plate
- A high gloss shine, even under dim lighting
- White paste on top of and lodged between pieces of chicken, tuna, pasta, or potatoes in a salad
- White coating on foods that are not naturally white
- Beads of a liquid on the surface of vegetables
- A creeping dark stain on a popcorn or other paper bag
- An oil ring on a napkin or paper plate

## WORDS TO WATCH FOR

These words are like a neon sign flashing FAT HERE!

- Creamy
- Crispy
- Fried
- Crunchy
- Breaded (and fried)
- Flaky
- Trans fat free (still has fat, just not this type of fat)

## FATTY FOODS CHEAT SHEET

In many food categories, you can choose among several fat levels: regular, which usually is full fat; reduced fat, with 25 percent less fat; light, with 50 percent less fat or one-third fewer calories; low-fat, with no more than 3 grams of fat per serving; and fat-free. Cutting fat saves calories, but sometimes not as much as you might think.

**8 OZ GLASS OF MILK**
FAT-FREE
80 calories
LOW-FAT 1%
100 calories
REDUCED-FAT 2%
120 calories
WHOLE MILK
150 calories

**1 OZ CHEDDAR CHEESE**
FAT-FREE
50 calories
LIGHT
70 calories
LIGHT, 50% REDUCED-FAT
90 calories
REGULAR
110 calories

**1 CUP NEW ENGLAND CLAM CHOWDER**
98% FAT-FREE
110 calories
REGULAR
120 calories

**2 TABLESPOONS ITALIAN DRESSING**
FAT-FREE
15 calories
REDUCED-FAT/LIGHT
20 calories
REGULAR
90 calories

**1 TEASPOON BUTTER**
I CAN'T BELIEVE IT'S NOT BUTTER
15 calories
WHIPPED BUTTER
20 calories
BUTTER
35 calories

**1 OUNCE COFFEE CREAMER**
SKIM MILK
10 calories
FAT-FREE HALF-AND-HALF
20 calories
WHOLE MILK
20 calories
HALF-AND-HALF
40 calories

**1 OUNCE POTATO CHIPS**
BAKED
130 calories
REGULAR
160 calories

**½ CUP VANILLA ICE CREAM**
FAT FREE
90 calories
LOW-FAT
110 calories
REGULAR
140 calories
SUPER-PREMIUM
290 calories

# SPOT THE SUGAR

What's the difference between these two coffee drinks?

THESE TWO STAR-BUCKS Frappuccinos look exactly the same, but the light version has about half the calories and a little more than half the sugar. Removing 6½ teaspoons of sugar saves more than 100 calories in sugar alone. Lower-fat creamy ingredients in the light Frappuccino account for the rest of the calorie savings.

## WORDS TO WATCH FOR

If the grams of sugars on the Nutrition Facts panel make up at least half of the total carbohydrates, you can be sure pretty sure that at least one of these caloric sweeteners is on the ingredient list.

| | |
|---|---|
| ■ Glucose | 8 calories per teaspoon |
| ■ Invert sugar | 12 calories per teaspoon |
| ■ Fructose | 15 calories per teaspoon |
| ■ Dextrose | 16 calories per teaspoon |
| ■ Evaporated cane juice | 16 calories per teaspoon |
| ■ Sucrose/sugar | 16 calories per teaspoon |
| ■ Brown sugar | 17 calories per teaspoon |
| ■ Syrups | 17 calories per teaspoon |
| ■ High fructose corn syrup | 18 calories per teaspoon |
| ■ Molasses | 19 calories per teaspoon |
| ■ Honey | 21 calories per teaspoon |

## CALORIE-FREE SWEETENERS

Food products often contain a combination of calorie-free sweeteners to optimize taste, and some blend caloric with noncaloric.

- ■ Saccharin (Sweet'N Low)
- ■ Aspartame (Equal, NutraSweet, SugarTwin)
- ■ Acesulfame K (Sweet One, Sunett, ace-K)
- ■ Sucralose (Splenda)
- ■ Stevia (Truvia, PureVia, SweetLeaf)

## SUGARY SNACKS CHEAT SHEET

Going sugar-free saves big calories in beverages, cereals, ice pops, and fat-free nondairy creamer, but not as many in desserts and chocolate candies that have high-calorie ingredients like fats and flour.

**12–OUNCE CAN COLA**
DIET
zero calories,
zero grams sugars
REGULAR
140 calories,
39 grams sugars

**8-OUNCE BOTTLE CRANBERRY JUICE**
DIET
5 calories,
2 grams sugars
LIGHT
40 calories,
10 grams sugars
REGULAR
(100% juice)
140 calories,
36 grams sugars

**8-OUNCE BOTTLE SNAPPLE LEMON TEA**
DIET
zero calories,
zero grams sugars
REGULAR
100 calories,
23 grams sugars

**6-OUNCE CARTON BLUEBERRY YOGURT**
LIGHT
80 calories,
11 grams sugars
REGULAR
140 calories,
25 grams sugars

**½ CUP BRAN CEREAL**
FIBER ONE ORIGINAL
60 calories,
zero grams sugars
ALL-BRAN ORIGINAL
80 calories,
6 grams sugars

**CRACKERS**
15 TRISCUITS THIN CRISPS
(about 1 ounce)
130 calories,
zero grams sugars
16 WHEAT THINS
(about 1 ounce)
140 calories, 4 grams sugars

**BREAD**
1 SLICE 100% WHOLE WHEAT BREAD
80 calories,
2 grams sugars
1 SLICE CINNAMON BREAD
80 calories, 4 grams sugars

**½ CUP SCOOP VANILLA ICE CREAM**
SUGAR-FREE
70 calories, 6 grams sugars
REGULAR
140 calories, 12 grams sugars

**CHOCOLATE PUDDING SNACK CUP**
NO SUGAR ADDED
60 calories, 1 gram sugars
REGULAR
120 calories, 16 grams sugars

**2 TABLESPOONS COOL WHIP**
SUGAR-FREE
20 calories, zero grams sugars
REGULAR
25 calories, 1 gram sugars

**POPSICLE**
SUGAR-FREE
15 calories,
zero grams sugars
REGULAR
45 calories, 8 grams sugars

many dishes have hidden calories from fats and sugars. And often, foods within the same food group can have very different calories. Like all the fixes we're giving you, the 1-2-3-400-Calorie trick won't apply to every meal, but it can be a handy guide for balanced nutrition when you're constructing your own meals.

### Spy Hidden Calories

As the nutrient with the most calories per gram, fat creates particular challenges when you're trying to eat 400-calorie meals. The first challenge is obvious: If you stack your meal with high-fat foods, you don't get to eat very much. The second is more subtle—hidden fats you might not spot unless you know just what to look for. See the sidebar on page 34 for more details on how to "find the fat."

It's easy to blame fat for calorie creep, but sugar can be just as sneaky. We're eating more calories from added sugars than ever before. If a food is sweet, figure that it contains added sugars. Count on all soft drinks, fruit drinks, desserts, and candy to contain sugars unless the label says otherwise. You'll also find sugars in foods that you might not think of as overly sweet, such as ketchup, barbecue sauce, and breakfast cereals. Read labels carefully to spot hidden sugar, or choose sugar-free alternatives. The sidebar at left can help you "spot the sugar" in the foods you like to eat.

### YOUR 400-CALORIE WORLD

In order to make 400-calorie meals, you

need a 400-calorie kitchen filled with a variety of foods. To help you, we've given you a guide for stocking your pantry and freezer with staples. We've picked out a few sample brands and highlighted what we like about them, along with tips on how to combine them with fresh foods to make delicious and filling 400-calorie meals. You'll also find a list of beverages to consider when planning your meals.

But don't worry, you don't need to be confined to the kitchen to make the 400 Calorie Fix work for you! Most weight loss books will tell you that the only way you can be sure of how many calories you're eating is to prepare food yourself, weighing and measuring every ingredient as you go. We know that's not realistic . . . and of course the real challenge comes when you're eating away from home and the best choices are not absolutely clear.

You want and need shortcuts for choosing the least caloric and most satisfying and nutritious options—everywhere. So we visited some of the places you go—the office vending machine, the bar, a party, a hot buffet, a salad bar, a ballpark, a cookout, and the movies—and handpicked the best 400-calorie choices. Good news: There's lots to choose from! In these pages, we tell you how many calories are in typical portions of various foods, so that you can see what foods are really worth the calories. Then we give you some examples of how you can combine more reasonable servings of these foods into 400-calorie combos that let you indulge your tastebuds without expanding your waistline.

And if that still isn't enough for you, we've given you a list of "freebies"—these are foods that are so low in calories, you almost don't need to count them. These fall into three categories: vegetables that add fiber and water to your meals to help you feel full; condiments that add flavor without adding calories to help you feel satisfied; and beverages with no calories to help you round out your meal.

# FREEBIES

Although freebies are not entirely calorie-free, they are low enough that most people would find it difficult to overdo. The free veggies and condiments are particularly well suited to sandwiches, burgers, and salads.

| RAW VEGGIES | CONDIMENTS |
|---|---|
| Alfalfa sprouts | Capers |
| Bean sprouts | Hot pepper sauce |
| Bell peppers | Ketchup* |
| Broccoli | Lemon juice |
| Cabbage | Mustard |
| Celery | Prepared horseradish |
| Cucumber | Tomato-pepper salsas |
| Dill pickles | Soy sauce* |
| Jalapeño chile peppers | Vinegars |
| Lettuce | Worcestershire sauce |
| Mushrooms | *Reduced- or low-sodium* |
| Onions | |
| Sauerkraut | **BEVERAGES** |
| Spinach | Black coffee or tea with no or |
| Tomato | noncaloric sweeteners |
| | Diet colas or sports drinks |
| | Sparkling water |

# 400 CALORIE BEVERAGE

LIQUID CALORIES CAN ADD UP QUICKLY. Worst of all, calories in beverages are not as filling as calories in foods, so it's possible to sip down a lot of liquids and still be hungry.

## FRUIT AND VEGETABLE JUICES

**1 CUP TOMATO JUICE**
40 calories
**1 CUP LOW-CALORIE CRANBERRY JUICE COCKTAIL**
40 calories
**1 CUP V8 JUICE**
50 calories
**1 CUP ORANGE JUICE**
110 calories
**1 CUP APPLE JUICE**
110 calories
**1 CUP CRANBERRY JUICE COCKTAIL**
140 calories

## MILKS

**1 CUP ALMOND MILK**
60 calories
**1 CUP LIGHT SOY MILK**
60 calories
**1 CUP FAT-FREE MILK**
80 calories
**1 CUP LOW-FAT MILK**
100 calories
**1 CUP REGULAR SOY MILK**
110 calories
**1 CUP REDUCED-FAT CHOCOLATE MILK**
120 calories
**1 CUP REDUCED-FAT MILK**
120 calories
**1 CUP RICE MILK**
120 calories
**1 CUP WHOLE MILK**
150 calories

## SODAS AND FLAVORED DRINKS

**1 CUP SELTZER WATER**
zero calories
**1 CUP DIET COLA**
zero calories
**1 CUP DIET SNAPPLE ICED TEA**
5 calories
**1 CUP SUGAR-FREE LEMONADE**
5 calories
**1 CUP VITAMINWATER**
50 calories
**1 CUP GATORADE**
60 calories
**1 CUP COLA**
100 calories
**1 CUP REGULAR LEMONADE**
100 calories
**1 CUP SNAPPLE ICED TEA**
100 calories

## HOT BEVERAGES

**1 CUP BLACK COFFEE, BLACK TEA, OR GREEN TEA**
zero calories
**1 CUP DIET HOT COCOA**
50 calories
**1 CUP REGULAR HOT COCOA**
120 calories

## ADD

**1 TSP SUGAR**
16 calories
**1 TBSP SKIM MILK**
5 calories
**1 TBSP WHOLE MILK**
10 calories
**1 TBSP HALF-AND-HALF**
20 calories
**1 TBSP AMARETTO NONDAIRY CREAMER**
25 calories

# 400 CALORIE PANTRY

IF YOU'RE HUNGRY AND THERE'S NOTHING HEALTHY in sight, you're more likely to eat, and maybe overeat, whatever is available. So stock your pantry with smart choices. Here are some of our healthy (and tasty) picks.

## GRAINS Eat with a protein and vegetables.

**UNCLE BEN'S WHOLE GRAIN BROWN READY RICE** (110 calories per ½ cup) **OR MINUTE BROWN RICE** (150 calories per ⅔ cup) ◆ Quick to fix and a simple side for several different meals.

**GIA RUSSA, HEARTLAND, DE CECCO, BARILLA, DREAMFIELDS, TRADER JOE'S, OR OTHER WHOLE WHEAT PASTA** (about 200 calories, 5 g fiber per ⅔ cup) ◆ Whole wheat pasta is a delicious and higher-fiber alternative to regular pasta.

**WHOLE WHEAT COUSCOUS** (about 150 calories, 5 g fiber per ⅔ cup) ◆ A form of pasta, couscous cooks up quickly and is a perfect base for Mediterranean vegetable and meat dishes.

## SOUPS Add a salad or sandwich.

**CAMPBELL'S SELECT HARVEST 98% FAT FREE NEW ENGLAND CLAM CHOWDER** (110 calories, 480 mg sodium per cup) ◆ Campbell's has been quietly lowering sodium in its soups; this is significantly lower in calories than the cream-based version.

**HEALTH VALLEY ORGANIC SPLIT PEA SOUP** (120 calories, 480 mg sodium per cup) ◆ Bean soups are both filling and a reliable source of fiber.

**PROGRESSO 50% LESS SODIUM CHICKEN GUMBO** (110 calories, 450 mg sodium per cup) ◆ It's easy to turn this soup into a meal by adding vegetables and rice or pasta.

## LEGUMES

Use in meal salads, hearty soups, or stews.

**CANNED OR DRIED BLACK BEANS** ◆ Best in soups, salsas, and bean dips.

**CANNED OR DRIED CHICKPEAS** ◆ The foundation for hummus and a delicious ingredient in couscous salads.

**CANNED OR DRIED WHITE BEANS** ◆ A creamy base for soups and dips.

**CANNED OR DRIED SPLIT PEAS** ◆ The longer you cook them, the creamier and smoother they become.

## PASTA SAUCES Pair with pasta and add protein and vegetables.

**CLASSICO TRADITIONAL SWEET BASIL PASTA SAUCE** (70 calories, 520 mg sodium per ½ cup) ◆ A versatile sauce that pairs well with all types of pasta dishes.

**MUIR GLEN CHUNKY TOMATO & HERB PASTA SAUCE** (60 calories, 350 mg sodium per ½ cup) ◆ A well-established organic brand with a broad line of sauces to choose from.

## NO-CALORIE, LOW-SODIUM SEASONING BLENDS

The American diet is too high in sodium, and experts are calling on us to cut back. Rather than stock up on individual herbs that become stale before you've made a dent in your supply, try these versatile combos that happen to be salt-free.

| SEASONING BLEND | MAIN FLAVORS | BEST FOR |
|---|---|---|
| Bell's Lemon Pepper | lemon, pepper, onion | seafood |
| Bell's Onion and Herb | onion, thyme, basil | chicken |
| Bell's Tomato Basil | garlic, basil, tomato | beef |
| Chef Paul Prudhomme's Magic Salt Free Seasoning | paprika, herbs, spices | potatoes, poultry, meats |
| McCormick Perfect Pinch Garlic & Herb | garlic, oregano, rosemary | poultry, pasta, salad dressing |
| McCormick Perfect Pinch Italian | marjoram, thyme, rosemary | pasta sauce, garlic bread, pizza |
| McCormick Super Spice All-Purpose Salt-Free | chile pepper, garlic, onion | meat, beans |
| Mrs. Dash Chicken Grilling Blend | garlic, onion, chili powder | poultry, pork, shrimp |
| Mrs. Dash Fiesta Lime Seasoning Blend | chile pepper, cumin, garlic | salsa, ground beef, chicken |
| Mrs. Dash Table Blend | onion, black pepper, chile pepper | salads, vegetables, potatoes |
| Penzeys Green Goddess | basil, dill, scallion | salad dressing, dip, fish |
| Penzeys Singapore Seasoning | curry | chicken, fish |
| Penzeys Sunny Paris Seasoning | shallots, chives | poultry, vegetables, rice |
| The Spice Hunter Fajita Seasoning Blend | onion, garlic, ginger, paprika | grilled meats, marinades, dips |
| The Spice Hunter Herbes de Provence Blend | thyme, marjoram, rosemary | eggs, vegetables, fish |
| The Spice Hunter Thai Seasoning Blend | sesame seeds, chile pepper, coriander | soups, seafood, poultry |

# FIXES

**1** Create a master list of staples that you always want to have on hand. Refer to it when you make your weekly shopping list.

**2** Avoid buying items that you don't really want just because they're on sale.

**3** To make healthy choices easier, limit the variety of similar items that you have at any one time. For example, stock just a couple of different pasta sauces and replace them as you use them.

**4** Limit the number of different cookies, crackers, snack foods, breakfast cereals, and other foods that might be tempting. Taste buds love variety and yours may lead you back to the snack cupboard for a new flavor.

**5** Always have a variety of canned beans. They're like the perfect black dress—they can go anywhere. Puree beans for a quick dip, combine with low-sodium broth for soup, add to a salad, or mash into a sandwich filling.

**6** Compare brands to find items with fewer calories, lower fat, and lower sodium.

## STOCK UP

It's easy to have lots of fruits, vegetables, lean meats, and breads on hand in your freezer. Here's how to shop and store properly:

### FROZEN VEGETABLES

✦ Go for vegetable combos
✦ Buy brands without sauce
✦ Avoid bags and boxes with large clumps, which usually mean the veggies have thawed and refrozen
✦ Keep frozen for up to 8 months

### FROZEN FRUITS

✦ Buy large bags sold in warehouse stores
✦ Avoid varieties frozen in sugar or syrup
✦ Keep frozen for up to 1 year

### BREAD

✦ Keeps longer in the freezer than in the fridge or at room temperature
✦ Look for brands with a whole grain as the first ingredient
✦ Wrap well to help ward off freezer burn
✦ Keep frozen for 3 months

### MEATS AND POULTRY

✦ Take advantage of sales to stock up on favorite cuts
✦ Freeze in convenient-size portions
✦ Avoid refreezing items that were frozen and defrosted
✦ Keep frozen for 4–12 months if well wrapped

### NUTS

✦ Buy larger quantities sold in warehouse stores
✦ Keep frozen for up to 1 year

# 400 CALORIE FREEZER

THE FREEZER GETS AN UNDESERVED BAD RAP as a repository for frozen meals and desserts. It's anything but, and it offers such a simple way to stock up on healthy foods that won't spoil. For each item, we've provided nutritional information for one serving.

# BREAKFAST
Add dairy and fruit.

## WAFFLES

**VAN'S ALL NATURAL MULTIGRAIN WAFFLES** (180 calories, 7 g fat, 3 g fiber in 2 waffles) ◆ Terrific lineup of whole grains like barley, rye, and oats, plus whole wheat flour as the first ingredient.

**KASHI HEART TO HEART WAFFLES** (160 calories, 3 g fat, 3 g fiber in 2 waffles) ◆ The Kashi brand has become the poster child for whole grain, healthy breakfast foods.

**AUNT JEMIMA LOW FAT WAFFLES** (160 calories, 3 g fat, 1 g fiber in 2 waffles) ◆ They're not whole grain but they're pretty darn good.

**KELLOGG'S EGGO NUTRI-GRAIN BLUEBERRY WAFFLES** (180 calories, 5 g fat, 3 g fiber in 2 waffles) ◆ The entire Nutri-Grain line is higher in fiber than other brands.

## BURRITOS, QUESADILLAS, AND POCKETS

**AMY'S BREAKFAST BURRITO** (250 calories, 7 g fat, 5 g fiber) With protein from the beans and tofu and fiber from the beans and veggies, this is a really filling breakfast option.

**WEIGHT WATCHERS SMART ONES BREAKFAST QUESADILLA** (220 calories, 6 g fat, 6 g fiber) ◆ This classic has been lightened up with egg whites and turkey bacon, and the cheese gives its calcium content a nice bump.

**LEAN POCKETS HAM, EGG & CHEESE** (130 calories, 4 g fat, 1 g fiber) ◆ They're relatively low in calories, so you could even eat two and still have calories left for fruit and yogurt.

# LUNCHES AND DINNERS
Round out the meal with more vegetables.

**WEIGHT WATCHERS SMART ONES HONEY MANGO BARBECUE CHICKEN** (240 calories, 3.5 g fat, 0 g fiber) ◆ Among the few frozen entrées that include fruit, and mango is rich in vitamins A and C.

**HEALTHY CHOICE HEARTY BEEF STROGANOFF** (300 calories, 6 g fat, 5 g fiber) ◆ Designed to be a complete meal, this dish includes both vegetables and fruit.

**CEDARLANE GARDEN VEGETABLE ENCHILADAS** (140 calories, 3 g fat, 3 g fiber) ◆ A tasty meatless option with protein from cheese and black beans.

**AMY'S ORGANIC ASIAN NOODLE STIR-FRY** (290 calories, 7 g fat, 4 g fiber) ◆ Amy's meatless entrées offer a world's menu of different options.

# PIZZA
Enjoy with a salad.

**AMY'S CHEESE PIZZA** (290 calories, 12 g fat, 2 g fiber) ◆ A good basic pizza that is easy to customize with your favorite vegetable or even fruit toppings.

**DIGIORNO RISING CRUST SPINACH, MUSHROOM & GARLIC PIZZA** (300 calories, 9 g fat, 3 g fiber) ◆ Lower in fat than many varieties of frozen pizza. You may want to add extra mushrooms and spinach.

**KASHI ROASTED VEGETABLE THIN CRUST PIZZA** (250 calories, 9 g fat, 4 g fiber) ◆ With its whole grain crust, the Kashi brand pizza is a bit higher in fiber than most brands.

# FIXES

1 Get into the habit of putting new freezer foods toward the back of the shelf so that older items get used up before developing freezer burn.

2 Wrap leftovers well and label and date before freezing. Once a month, take stock and use up the oldest ones.

3 Defrost frozen items in the refrigerator rather than on the counter. Leave the wrapping on to prevent moisture from forming on the food as it thaws.

4 Take advantage of sales on frozen dinners to stock up so that you always have a couple of choices available.

5 Limit the number of tempting freezer foods like breakfast items and desserts.

6 Store bread in the freezer. Nuts, too. They last longer frozen than in the refrigerator or on the counter.

7 Cut meats and poultry into single servings and wrap each individually. Put them in the fridge to thaw the day before you need them, or defrost in the microwave immediately before cooking.

## FREEBIES

While these aren't zero or negative calories, they're so low that you can pretty much go to town and not worry. Each of these is 20 calories for ¼ cup.

RAW BROCCOLI
SHREDDED CABBAGE
SLICED CUCUMBER
SLICED RAW PEPPERS
CHOPPED CELERY
RAW SPINACH
BEAN SPROUTS
SHREDDED CARROTS
SLICED RED ONION
ICEBERG, ROMAINE,
RED LEAF, GREEN LEAF,
BOSTON, OR BABY
LETTUCE

## FEAR THESE

A couple of tablespoons here and there can add up quickly. Except where indicated, each item equals ¼ cup, or the amount in a rounded salad-bar scoop

CRUMBLED BLUE
CHEESE (2 TBSP)
60 calories
CRISPY CHINESE
NOODLES (2 TBSP)
70 calories
PASTA AND
VEGETABLE SALAD
80 calories
POTATO SALAD
80 calories
CAESAR PASTA SALAD
90 calories
COLESLAW
90 calories
CARROT-RAISIN SALAD
100 calories
CHOPPED WALNUTS
100 calories
MACARONI SALAD
110 calories
EGG SALAD
120 calories
TUNA SALAD
130 calories

### MIXED BABY LETTUCE GREENS
1 CUP
10 calories

All lettuces and greens are fair game. Darker greens are richest in nutrients. Go to town with the freebies on the left.

### AVOCADO
1 ROUNDED SCOOP
(¼ CUP)
60 calories

Although it's relatively high in calories for a fruit, avocado is rich in good fats, which can help you feel full.

### CANNED KIDNEY OR GARBANZO BEANS
1 ROUNDED SCOOP
(¼ CUP)
70–90 calories

Mixed beans in a dressing have extra fat from the oil, so drain the liquid.

### TOMATOES
2 ROUNDED SALAD-BAR SCOOPS (½ CUP SLICED OR 8 GRAPE TOMATOES)
20–25 calories

Make sure they're not shiny, a sure sign they've been tossed with oil.

# 400 CALORIE SALAD BAR

HOORAY FOR SALAD BARS! A well-built salad can be a satisfying and slimming meal. Prepared dishes and toppings can send calories soaring, though, so choose carefully.

### ARTICHOKE HEARTS
3 CUT PIECES,
ABOUT ¼ HEART EACH
25 calories

These are plain, canned hearts. If they're shiny and flecked with herbs, they're probably marinated, with extra calories from oil.

### SLICED OLIVES
1 FLAT SCOOP (2 TBSP)
20 calories

Calories from whole olives—5 to 10 calories apiece depending on size—add up faster than chopped or sliced because it takes more to spread throughout your salad.

### DICED BEETS
1 ROUNDED SCOOP (¼ CUP)
15 calories

A root vegetable, beets are a storehouse of vitamin C, folate, iron, and other vitamins and minerals. Pickled beets can be slightly higher in calories because they're often prepared with sugar.

### SALAD DRESSINGS
2 TBSP

Vinaigrettes and oil-based dressings usually have fewer calories than creamy dressings. "Fat-free" dressings are lighter than "light" dressings. Vinegars are virtually calorie-free.

FAT-FREE
20–50 calories
LIGHT
50–80 calories
REGULAR
100–150 calories

### TOPPINGS
1 FLAT SCOOP (2 TBSP)

Toppings add color and crunch, but also calories. Limit to one or two and keep portions small.

RAISINS AND DRIED CRANBERRIES
50 calories
CROUTONS (8 LARGE)
50 calories
BACON BITS
70 calories
NUTS AND SEEDS
100 calories

### CHEESES
Assume most are full-fat.
COTTAGE CHEESE (1 ROUNDED SCOOP OR ¼ CUP)
50 calories
GRATED CHEDDAR CHEESE
(1 FLAT SCOOP OR 2 TBSP)
60 calories

### CHOPPED EGG
1 FLAT SCOOP (2 TBSP)
30 calories

A flat scoop is about equal to half an egg. Pick out just the egg white and you'll spend only 15 calories.

### SLIVERED DELI TURKEY OR HAM
1 FLAT SCOOP (2 TBSP)
30 calories

Turkey breast is almost all protein with very little fat, and deli ham can be pretty close. Ham that's cut into chunks is usually not as lean.

## 400-CAL COMBOS

2 cups mixed greens
+ 1 cup sliced cucumbers
+ 1 cup tomatoes
+ ½ cup chickpeas
+ 2 Tbsp regular dressing
= **400 CALORIES**

4 Tbsp egg
+ 2 Tbsp slivered deli turkey
+ 1 cup chopped celery
+ ½ cup avocado
+ 2 Tbsp fat-free ranch dressing
+ 4 Tbsp grated cheese
= **400 CALORIES**

⅓ cup carrot-raisin salad
+ ¼ cup potato salad
+ ¼ cup tuna salad
+ 2 large croutons
= **375 CALORIES**

## 400-CAL COMBOS

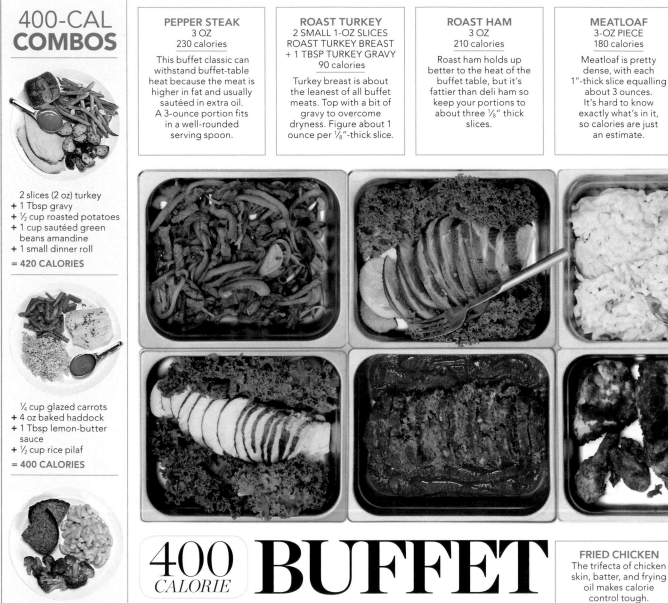

2 slices (2 oz) turkey
+ 1 Tbsp gravy
+ ½ cup roasted potatoes
+ 1 cup sautéed green beans amandine
+ 1 small dinner roll
= **420 CALORIES**

¼ cup glazed carrots
+ 4 oz baked haddock
+ 1 Tbsp lemon-butter sauce
+ ½ cup rice pilaf
= **400 CALORIES**

3 oz meatloaf
+ ½ cup mac and cheese
+ ¼ cup steamed broccoli
= **400 CALORIES**

### PEPPER STEAK
3 OZ
230 calories

This buffet classic can withstand buffet-table heat because the meat is higher in fat and usually sautéed in extra oil. A 3-ounce portion fits in a well-rounded serving spoon.

### ROAST TURKEY
2 SMALL 1-OZ SLICES ROAST TURKEY BREAST + 1 TBSP TURKEY GRAVY
90 calories

Turkey breast is about the leanest of all buffet meats. Top with a bit of gravy to overcome dryness. Figure about 1 ounce per ⅛"-thick slice.

### ROAST HAM
3 OZ
210 calories

Roast ham holds up better to the heat of the buffet table, but it's fattier than deli ham so keep your portions to about three ⅛" thick slices.

### MEATLOAF
3-OZ PIECE
180 calories

Meatloaf is pretty dense, with each 1"-thick slice equalling about 3 ounces. It's hard to know exactly what's in it, so calories are just an estimate.

# 400 CALORIE BUFFET

BUFFETS ARE A 400-CALORIE CHALLENGE. But if you load up on veggies, stick to lean meats, and choose calorie-free drinks, you may even be able to go back for seconds.

### FRIED CHICKEN
The trifecta of chicken skin, batter, and frying oil makes calorie control tough.
1 BREAST
360 calories

1 DRUMSTICK
190 calories

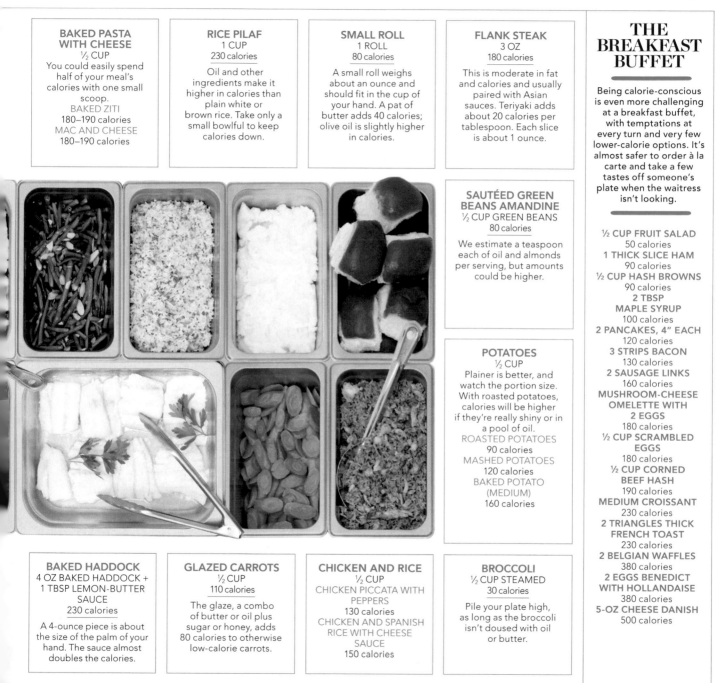

### BAKED PASTA WITH CHEESE
½ CUP
You could easily spend half of your meal's calories with one small scoop.
BAKED ZITI
180–190 calories
MAC AND CHEESE
180–190 calories

### RICE PILAF
1 CUP
230 calories

Oil and other ingredients make it higher in calories than plain white or brown rice. Take only a small bowlful to keep calories down.

### SMALL ROLL
1 ROLL
80 calories

A small roll weighs about an ounce and should fit in the cup of your hand. A pat of butter adds 40 calories; olive oil is slightly higher in calories.

### FLANK STEAK
3 OZ
180 calories

This is moderate in fat and calories and usually paired with Asian sauces. Teriyaki adds about 20 calories per tablespoon. Each slice is about 1 ounce.

### THE BREAKFAST BUFFET

Being calorie-conscious is even more challenging at a breakfast buffet, with temptations at every turn and very few lower-calorie options. It's almost safer to order à la carte and take a few tastes off someone's plate when the waitress isn't looking.

½ CUP FRUIT SALAD
50 calories
1 THICK SLICE HAM
90 calories
½ CUP HASH BROWNS
90 calories
2 TBSP MAPLE SYRUP
100 calories
2 PANCAKES, 4" EACH
120 calories
3 STRIPS BACON
130 calories
2 SAUSAGE LINKS
160 calories
MUSHROOM-CHEESE OMELETTE WITH 2 EGGS
180 calories
½ CUP SCRAMBLED EGGS
180 calories
½ CUP CORNED BEEF HASH
190 calories
MEDIUM CROISSANT
230 calories
2 TRIANGLES THICK FRENCH TOAST
230 calories
2 BELGIAN WAFFLES
380 calories
2 EGGS BENEDICT WITH HOLLANDAISE
380 calories
5-OZ CHEESE DANISH
500 calories

### SAUTÉED GREEN BEANS AMANDINE
½ CUP GREEN BEANS
80 calories

We estimate a teaspoon each of oil and almonds per serving, but amounts could be higher.

### POTATOES
½ CUP
Plainer is better, and watch the portion size. With roasted potatoes, calories will be higher if they're really shiny or in a pool of oil.
ROASTED POTATOES
90 calories
MASHED POTATOES
120 calories
BAKED POTATO (MEDIUM)
160 calories

### BAKED HADDOCK
4 OZ BAKED HADDOCK + 1 TBSP LEMON-BUTTER SAUCE
230 calories

A 4-ounce piece is about the size of the palm of your hand. The sauce almost doubles the calories.

### GLAZED CARROTS
½ CUP
110 calories

The glaze, a combo of butter or oil plus sugar or honey, adds 80 calories to otherwise low-calorie carrots.

### CHICKEN AND RICE
½ CUP
CHICKEN PICCATA WITH PEPPERS
130 calories
CHICKEN AND SPANISH RICE WITH CHEESE SAUCE
150 calories

### BROCCOLI
½ CUP STEAMED
30 calories

Pile your plate high, as long as the broccoli isn't doused with oil or butter.

## WINE

Wine is among the lower-calorie alcoholic beverages, and there's not much calorie difference between white, red, and rosé. While you could drink two-thirds of a bottle for 400 calories, you might want to swap some wine for food.

**5-OZ GLASS OF CHAMPAGNE**
110 calories
**5-OZ GLASS OF WINE**
120 calories

## PASSED HORS D'OEUVRES

You can make an entire meal out of passed hors d'oeuvres.

**2 LARGE SHRIMP WITH 2 TSP COCKTAIL SAUCE**
20 calories
**2 MINI CHICKEN SATAY SKEWERS (ABOUT 1¼ OZ TOTAL)**
60 calories
**2 SLICED PUMPER-NICKEL SNACK BREAD TOPPED WITH SMOKED SALMON, CHOPPED EGG, CAPERS, ONION**
70 calories
**2 MINI MUSHROOM TURNOVERS**
80 calories
**2 SMALL SPINACH AND CHEESE TARTS**
100 calories
**2 BOCCONCINI AND CHERRY TOMATO SKEWERS**
100 calories
**2 SCALLOPS WRAPPED IN BACON**
100 calories

## PÂTÉ
2 TBSP
120 calories

Fat contributes more than 80 percent of the calories in pâté, so calories are high for a relatively small portion.

## BUFFALO WINGS
4 WINGS + 2 TBSP BLUE CHEESE DRESSING
340 calories

This modest portion adds up to almost an entire meal's calories.

## PIGS IN A BLANKET
1 PIG
60 calories

They're so cute and little, and about 60 calories of almost pure fat apiece.

## CHEX MIX
1 CUP
190 calories

Cereal is healthy enough by itself, but Chex Mix's added fat and sugar push up the calories.

# 400 *CALORIE* PARTY

IT'S THE SCARIEST SETTING FOR A DIETER. Count on party food to be indulgent and the atmosphere to encourage eating and drinking. But if you arrive armed with a plan and choose wisely, you can enjoy your favorite treats and still stay within your 400 calories. One strategy: To help manage temptation, circulate and socialize to avoid standing next to the food tables.

## CHEESES
1 OUNCE

Cheeses average about 100 calories per ounce (the size of your thumb or two large marbles).
SOFT GOAT CHEESE
80 calories
BRIE CHEESE
90 calories
GOUDA CHEESE
100 calories
CHEDDAR CHEESE
110 calories

### DIP, CHIPS, AND CRUDITÉS
Mix a packet of onion soup mix with plain yogurt for a light dip.
1 CUP CRUDITÉS
50 calories
¼ CUP ONION DIP +
1 OZ POTATO CHIPS
260 calories

### VANILLA ICE CREAM
½ CUP SCOOP
A ½-cup serving is about the size of a tennis ball.
REGULAR VANILLA
140 calories
SUPER-PREMIUM VANILLA
310 calories

### PIE
1 SLICE (9" PIE)
Keep slices to about half the size of your hand.
PUMPKIN PIE  320 calories
CHERRY PIE  330 calories
BANANA CREAM PIE  370 calories
APPLE PIE  410 calories

## 400-CAL COMBOS

5 oz champagne
+ 1 cup crudités
+ 2 mini mushroom turnovers
+ 1 cup Caesar salad
= 390 CALORIES

5 oz wine
+ ½ cup seafood salad
+ ½ slice pumpkin pie
= 420 CALORIES

1 cup Chex Mix
+ 1 oz Cheddar cheese
+ 2 ⅓-oz chocolate chip cookies
= 420 CALORIES

### OFFICE PARTY SALADS
½ CUP
Deli and catered salads usually have a lot of hidden fat in the form of dressing, mayonnaise, and olive oil, so keep portions small.
CAESAR SALAD
75 calories
SEAFOOD SALAD
140 calories
TORTELLINI SALAD
190 calories

### COOKIES
TWO ⅓-OZ COOKIES
A ⅓-oz cookie has about the same diameter as a golf ball.
SUGAR
100 calories
OATMEAL
110 calories
CHOCOLATE CHIP
120 calories
PEANUT BUTTER
120 calories

### CAKE
2¼-OZ PIECE
A thin slice, the width of two fingers, likely has fewer calories than a supersize cupcake.
CHOCOLATE CAKE WITH CHOCOLATE FROSTING
230 calories
YELLOW CAKE WITH CHOCOLATE FROSTING
240 calories
YELLOW CUPCAKE (3 OZ) WITH FROSTING
530 calories

## MIND YOUR MEAT

Decide on one main item, usually a hamburger or hot dog, and build your meal from there. And don't overdo it with sauces and condiments, like barbecue sauce, ketchup, and relish, which often contain added sugar. Unless you go meatless, doubling up on burgers or dogs will put you over 400 calories.

### BURGER
3 OZ

Higher fat means more calories but a juicier burger. All of these include a standard-size hamburger bun.

**LEAN GROUND BEEF PATTY (10% FAT)**
305 calories

**GROUND TURKEY PATTY**
310 calories

**GROUND BEEF PATTY (20% FAT)**
350 calories

### HOT DOGS
1¾ OZ

Hot dogs vary in calories, with regular dogs topping the list and veggie dogs near the bottom of the calorie lineup. All of these include a standard-size hot dog bun.

**SMART DOG (1½ OZ)**
165 calories

**TURKEY DOG (1⅝ OZ)**
220 calories

**REDUCED-FAT BEEF FRANK**
240 calories

**BEEF FRANK**
270 calories

### WATERMELON
1" WEDGE
90 calories

About 1/16 of a medium-size melon, a wedge will set you back less than 100 calories.

### BROWNIE
2" BROWNIE
240 calories

Make them with dark or bittersweet chocolate for extra good fats.

### S'MORES
2 S'MORES
400 calories

For fewer calories, stick with plain toasted marshmallows at a mere 25 calories apiece.

### BARBECUE CHICKEN
2 BARBECUE CHICKEN THIGHS + 2 TBSP BARBECUE SAUCE
270 calories

Brush sauce on skinless chicken for maximum flavor and minimum calories.

## 400 CALORIE COOKOUT

EVERYTHING LOOKS AND SMELLS good at a cookout, regardless of whether it's the first of the season or one in a long line of outdoor meals. Choose wisely and you can enjoy a full cookout meal guilt-free—and a beer, too!

### GRILLED VEGETABLES
1 SLICE EGGPLANT + ½ RED PEPPER + ½ PORTOBELLO CAP
90 calories

Use just a light coating of oil or a spritz of cooking spray to prevent sticking.

### VEGGIES AND DIP
6 BABY CARROTS, 2 HALF CELERY STALKS, 4 CHERRY TOMATOES, 4 BROCCOLI FLORETS + ¼ CUP FRENCH ONION DIP
150 calories

Most calories are from dip.

### LEMONADE
8-OZ GLASS
100 calories

Make your own low-calorie version with fresh-squeezed lemon juice and a noncaloric sweetener to save almost 200 calories.

### BRISKET
3 OZ COOKED BRISKET
170 calories

Slow-cooking on the grill turns gristly brisket into a tender and moist cookout favorite. About two ¼"-thick slices equal 3 ounces.

# 400-CAL COMBOS

1 slice eggplant
+ ½ red pepper
+ ½ portobello cap, grilled
+ 1 medium ear corn on the cob
+ 2 tsp butter
+ 3 oz brisket
= **410 CALORIES**

3 oz ground turkey burger
+ lettuce
+ tomato
+ bun
+ 1" thick watermelon wedge
= **400 CALORIES**

3 oz baby back ribs
+ 8 oz lemonade
= **410 CALORIES**

### CORN ON THE COB
MEDIUM EAR CORN + 2 TSP BUTTER
150 calories

Corn is so sweet and juicy it's delicious without the calories and fat of butter. Add a dash of salt to bring out the flavor.

### GARLIC BREAD
1¾-OZ PIECE
190 calories

Pick a piece about the size of your palm, and try to find one that's not too greasy.

### BABY BACK RIBS
3 OZ ROASTED
310 calories

They're pretty high in fat, so take just two 4" ribs. And remember, barbecue sauce tends to have added sugar.

### SALAD SIDES
¼ CUP
Keep a lid on oil and mayo.
POTATO SALAD
80 calories
COLESLAW
90 calories
MACARONI SALAD
110 calories

## 400-CAL COMBOS

Small hot dog on a bun
+ mustard
+ onions
+ 12 oz regular beer
= **400 CALORIES**

½ soft pretzel
+ 2 chicken tenders
+ 1 Tbsp barbecue sauce
+ 12 oz diet cola
= **395 CALORIES**

3 deep-fried Oreos
+ 1 oz cotton candy
+ 20 oz bottled water
= **420 CALORIES**

### CRACKER JACK
2.875-OZ BAG
350 calories

It will be hard to find single-serving boxes of this snack at the ballpark, so be mindful of how many times you reach into the bag.

### CHICKEN TENDERS
4 TENDERS + 2 TBSP BARBECUE SAUCE
400 calories

Because these chicken bites come in many shapes and sizes, portion sizes vary even within the same stadium.

### GRILLED SAUSAGE ON BUN WITH PEPPERS AND ONIONS
450 calories

Choose a sausage about the size of a regular hot dog.

### COTTON CANDY ON A STICK
1 OZ
120 calories

Embrace your inner child if you're looking for something sweet. Cotton candy sold in bags is double or triple the size.

### SNOW CONE
3 OZ
250 calories

Ask the vendor if he has sugar-free syrups. Since snow cones are just ice and syrup, that would substantially cut calories.

# 400 CALORIE BALLPARK

PLAY BALL TO BURN CALORIES. But watching the game is a different story. To help you navigate the sea of vendors, we've provided ballpark figures (pun intended!) for the most common concessions at the stadium, carnival, or amusement park.

### DEEP-FRIED OREOS
6 OREOS
600 calories

We estimate these crunchy-on-the-outside, gooey-on-the-inside gut-busters at a minimum of 100 calories a pop.

### NACHOS WITH CHEESE
18 CHIPS
880 calories

For 400 calories, get a small portion of just the basics—6 to 8 nachos with cheese and a few jalapeño chile peppers.

### SOFT PRETZEL
4 OZ
390 calories

A 4-ounce pretzel—about 6"—satisfies your 400-calorie goal; jumbo varieties (5 to 7 ounces) have 500 or more calories each.

### BANANA SPLIT DIPPIN' DOTS
1 CUP
340 calories

A different way to eat ice cream with a similar calorie content.

### LARGE CORN DOG
6"
380 calories

It's a complete meal on a stick, with room for a few tablespoons of ketchup for dipping.

## BEVERAGES

Ballpark drinks are oversize in volume and calories.

### "MALTERNATIVE"
12-OZ GLASS
230 calories

Malt beverages, like Mike's Hard Lemonade and Bacardi Mojito, are higher in calories than beer. If it comes in a 16-ounce plastic bottle, calories are about 300.

### SOUVENIR CUP OF REGULAR BEER
24 OZ
300 calories

Alcoholic beverages are pricey, so larger sizes can be a better value. But remember to count your beers by ounces and not servings. This "cup" holds two standard-size beers.

### THICK SHAKE
20 OZ
590 calories

The more upscale shakes are made with super-premium ice cream. It's highest in calories and fat.

## *FIX IT FAST*

Drink water. Walking around the park or sitting in the bleachers on a sunny day while eating high-sodium foods can leave you dehydrated.

### FRENCH FRIES
6 OZ
520 calories

Stick with the smallest portion and the traditional shape. Add on another 100 or so calories if you top them with cheese sauce.

### ZEPPOLES WITH POWDERED SUGAR
3 ZEPPOLES
300 calories

It's a good thing these nutritionally empty fried treats are relegated to carnivals and fairs.

### MEDIUM HOT DOG WITH BUN
350 calories

A medium hot dog is about 6" long and the diameter of a quarter. If you want a beer, have a small dog (250 calories, about the diameter of a nickel).

### SHELL-ON PEANUTS
8-OZ BAG
900 calories

Nuts are calorie-dense, so buying them in the shell will stop you from downing them in a handful. Just don't eat the whole bag.

## FOOD

**17 TINY TWIST PRETZELS (1 OZ)**
110 calories

**ROUNDED CUPPED HANDFUL (⅓ CUP) WASABI PEAS**
120 calories

**20 FRIES (3½ OZ) PLUS 2 TBSP KETCHUP**
160 calories

**CUPPED HANDFUL (¼ CUP) MIXED NUTS**
200 calories

**CUPPED HANDFUL (¼ CUP) DRY-ROASTED PEANUTS**
210 calories

**3 CHEDDAR BACON POTATO SKINS**
210 calories

**10 MEDIUM ONION RINGS**
240 calories

**4 BUFFALO CHICKEN WINGS + 2 TBSP BLUE CHEESE DRESSING**
340 calories

**FOUR 1" CHEDDAR CUBES + 8 RITZ CRACKERS**
400 calories

**18 TORTILLA CHIPS + ¼ CUP QUESO DIP**
460 calories

| BLOODY MARY | GIN AND TONIC | RUM AND COKE | SCREWDRIVER |
|---|---|---|---|
| 8 OZ | 8 OZ | 8 OZ | 8 OZ |
| 120 calories | 150 calories | 160 calories | 170 calories |

| MARTINI | RED, WHITE, OR ROSÉ WINE | BLENDED PIÑA COLADA | COSMO |
|---|---|---|---|
| 3 OZ | 5 OZ | 6 OZ (half ice, half liquor) | 5 OZ |
| 170 calories | 120 calories | 250 calories | 250 calories |

# 400 CALORIE BAR

WE HAVE A SOCIAL LIFE TOO.
Learn to divide your 400 calories between drink and food.

**SHOT VODKA, RUM, WHISKEY, OTHER HARD LIQUORS**
1½ OZ
100 calories

**BOTTLE STOUT**
12 OZ
200 calories

**BOTTLE PALE ALE**
12 OZ
190 calories

**BOTTLE LIGHT BEER**
12 OZ
100 calories

**BLENDED MARGARITA**
6 OZ (half ice, half liquor)
190 calories

**BOTTLE PORTER**
12 OZ
220 calories

**BOTTLE REGULAR BEER**
12 OZ
150 calories

## 400-CAL COMBOS

2 light beers
+ ¼ cup mixed nuts
= **400 CALORIES**

1 bottle stout
+ 2 Buffalo wings
+ 1 Tbsp blue cheese dressing
= **370 CALORIES**

two 5-oz glasses wine
+ 25 tiny pretzels
= **400 CALORIES**

**SUGAR-FREE RED BULL**
1 CAN
15 calories

**RED BULL**
1 CAN
110 calories

**REGULAR SOFT DRINK**
12 OZ
160 calories

**SCOTCH ON THE ROCKS**
2 OZ
140 calories

## 400-CAL COMBOS

16 oz slush
+ 3 blocks Hershey's Special Dark Chocolate
= 390 CALORIES

¼ order pretzel bites with cheese
+ 16 Crunch Dibs
= 410 CALORIES

3½ cups popcorn (½ small order), no topping
+ 16 oz regular soda
= 410 CALORIES

| GOOD & PLENTY | JUNIOR MINTS | SOUR PATCH KIDS | DOTS | MILK CHOCOLATE M&M'S | PEANUT M&M'S |
|---|---|---|---|---|---|
| 100 PIECES | 38 PIECES | 43 PIECES | 34 PIECES | 90 PIECES | 32 PIECES |
| 400 calories | 405 calories | 405 calories | 400 calories | 405 calories | 415 calories |
| About ⅔ of a 6-oz box | About ¾ of a 4-oz box | About 1¹⁄₁₀ of a 3½-oz box | About ½ of a 7.5-oz box | About ½ of a 5.3-oz bag | About ½ of a 5.3-oz bag |

# 400 CALORIE MOVIES

KIT KAT KING SIZE
1 FULL BAR
400 calories
One 3-oz bar

SNACKS AT THE THEATER will hit you hard in the wallet and on the waistline. Here's what we could find for 400-calorie portions in New York City movie theaters.

**MILK DUDS**
31 PIECES
405 calories

About ⅔
of a 5-oz box

**REESE'S PIECES**
105 PIECES
400 calories

About ⅔ of
a 4-oz box

**MIKE AND IKE**
66 PIECES
400 calories

About ⅜ of
a 9 ½ -oz box

**BUTTER-FINGER MINIS**
9 BARS
405 calories

About ⁹⁄₁₀ of
a 3 ½ -oz box

**RAISINETS**
105 PIECES
380 calories

One 3½-oz box

**HERSHEY'S SPECIAL DARK CHOCOLATE**
7 BLOCKS
395 calories

About ½ of
a 6.8-oz bar

**POPCORN**
7 CUPS
(1 SMALL ORDER)
NO TOPPING
420 calories

**SODA**
32-OZ
COCA-COLA
CLASSIC
400 calories

**NACHOS**
½ ORDER OF
NACHOS
390 calories

**PRETZEL BITES**
½ ORDER OF
PRETZEL BITES WITH
CHEESE
420 calories

**SLUSH**
32-OZ ICEE
440 calories

**SKITTLES**
100 PIECES
405 calories

About ½ of a
7.2 oz bag

**WHOPPERS**
40 PIECES
400 calories

About 1¼ of
a 2¾-oz box

**TWIZZLERS BLACK LICORICE**
11 PIECES
415 calories

About ½ of a
7-oz package

**TWIZZLERS RED LICORICE**
12 PIECES
390 calories

About ⅔
of a 7-oz
package

**ICE CREAMS**
32 CRUNCH DIBS
400 calories

1⅓ HÄAGEN-DAZS VANILLA & ALMONDS ICE CREAM BARS
413 calories

1⅓ NESTLÉ FROZEN LEMONADE CUP
400 calories

# 400 CALORIE VENDING MA

NOTHING BECKONS LIKE A WELL-STOCKED VENDING MACHINE when you're stuck at the airport, or your midafternoon slump hits. Sadly, it's almost impossible to put together a nutritious vending-machine meal. But if you must, here's the calorie lowdown.

## BEST CHOICES

Snacks that combine moderate calories with the ability to satisfy your hunger.

TRISCUIT CRACKERS
GRANOLA BAR
CEREAL MIX
NUTS
TRAIL MIX

## WORST CHOICES

Foods that use up calories but aren't filling.

REGULAR CHIPS
COOKIES
CHOCOLATE BARS
CANDY
BREAKFAST PASTRIES

### TRISCUIT ORIGINAL
1.94 OZ
240 calories

With 6 grams of fiber, among the highest fiber snacks.

### LAY'S POTATO CHIPS
1⅛ OZ
280 calories

50 percent more volume and calories than the standard 1 ounce serving.

### BAKED LAY'S
1⅜ OZ
160 calories

The bag weighs a bit less and they're about 25 percent lower in calories than regular.

### SNYDER'S OF HANOVER SOUR-DOUGH SPECIALS PRETZELS
1.65 OZ
160 calories

Most pretzels are not made with fat, so they're lower in calories than other snacks.

### WELCH'S FRUIT SNACKS
2¼ OZ
210 calories

Although fruit juice concentrate is the first ingredient, they still have plenty of other sweeteners.

### ANDY CAPP'S HOT FRIES
1 OZ
150 calories

Nutritionally similar to corn and potato chips.

### CHEEZ-IT REDUCED FAT
1½ OZ
190 calories

You save about a teaspoon of fat by picking these instead of regular Cheez-Its.

### MINI CHIPS AHOY!
2 OZ
270 calories

Chocolate chip cookies will never top a nutrition list, but they sure taste good.

### DORITOS NACHO CHEESE
1 OZ
150 calories

Made from whole grain corn and a bit higher in fiber.

### ENTENMANN'S JUMBO ICED HONEY BUN
½ BUN
330 calories

Even the package describes a serving as half a bun.

### TRADITIONAL CHEX MIX
1¾ OZ
220 calories

Made from breakfast cereal, which makes it seem healthy, but it's nutritionally similar to other salty snacks.

### SUNCHIPS
1 OZ
140 calories

Whole grains give it a nutritional halo, but the calorie count is not much different from potato chips.

# CHINE

### PEANUT BUTTER RITZ BITS
3 OZ
420 calories

To control calories, limit yourself to just half of the 3-ounce bag.

### FRITOS CORN CHIPS
3⅜ OZ
560 calories

Close in calories to potato and flavored tortilla chips.

### CHEDDAR GOLDFISH
1½ OZ
200 calories

The perfect choice for keeping your kids happy.

### SUGARLESS GUM
5 STICKS OR PIECES
25 calories

Chewing gum helps manage weight.

### TIC TAC FRESHMINTS
5 PIECES
10 calories

So low in calories that they almost don't count.

### KELLOGG'S RICE KRISPIES TREATS
0.78 OZ
90 calories

A classic treat, with extra B vitamins coming from the Rice Krispies.

### SNICKERS BAR
2.07 OZ
280 calories

No better or worse than most candy bars.

### PLANTERS SALTED PEANUTS
2 OZ
330 calories

They're filling and packed with healthy monounsaturated fats.

### NATURE VALLEY GRANOLA BAR
1 BAR
90 calories

One of the original granola bars, and relatively low in calories.

### REESE'S PEANUT BUTTER CUPS
1½ OZ
220 calories

If the machine has only the bigger 2¼-ounce size, try to eat half today and save the rest for tomorrow.

### BREATH SAVERS
12 MINTS
60 calories

At 5 calories per mint, these have about one-third the calories of a Life Saver.

### DOUBLEMINT GUM
5 STICKS
50 calories

The same weight loss benefits as sugarless gum but not as good for your teeth.

### LIFE SAVERS
1 ROLL (14 LIFE SAVERS)
210 calories

It's easier to stop at a roll instead of a bag.

### CERTS BREATH MINTS
5 MINTS
25 calories

One of the original breath products, and about the same calories as the rest.

### HO HOS
3 OZ
70 calories

The problem with snack cakes and other desserts is that you can eat a lot of calories and not feel very full.

### BUBBLE YUM ORIGINAL GUM
5 PIECES
125 calories

A pillow-shape piece weighs more than a stick of gum.

### KELLOGG'S LOW FAT GRANOLA CRUNCHY BLENDS
1½ OZ
160 calories

A pretty smart pick, especially if paired with a carton of yogurt.

### FUNYUNS
1¼ OZ
175 calories

Onion rings in snack-food form.

### WHEAT THINS TOASTED CHIPS
1¾ OZ
220 calories

One of the higher-sodium snacks, but with close to 2 grams of fiber from whole grain.

### SKITTLES ORIGINAL FRUIT
61 GRAMS
250 calories

More than 2 ounces of pure sugar and not much else.

### PLANTERS TRAIL MIX NUT & CHOCOLATE
2 OZ
320 calories

Nuts have a lot of calories, but they also help keep hunger at bay.

### FAMOUS AMOS CHOCOLATE CHIP COOKIES
3 OZ
450 calories

The portion size is the problem, so share with a couple of friends.

# 5.
## 2 Week
# QUICK
## SLIM

DO YOU WANT TO LOSE WEIGHT? Are you looking for an easy entry into the 400-calorie lifestyle that virtually guarantees the pounds will come off? Then I encourage you to try the 2 Week Quick Slim. Here we've taken a no-brainer approach to dropping pounds (eat 400-calorie meals) and made it even easier. We've done all the work for you, pulling together a simple 2-week plan that will jump-start your weight loss by giving you a set 14-day meal plan with three 400-calorie meals (about 1,200 calories a day). Our 2 Week Quick Slim test panelists loved the results: They lost an average of 6 pounds and 8 inches, with some dropping as many as 11 pounds and more than 15 inches, including 3 inches off the waistline!

For most of you, 1,200 calories will sound low. But try it! Mindy designed the Quick Slim to be satisfying by including filling and fun foods like pancakes, cheese pizza, rotisserie chicken, and steak. You'll find sweet treats (like Chocolate Chip Scones, a favorite of the test panelists) and enjoy reasonable portions of a wide variety of foods. Our 2 Week Quick Slim test participants told us that the meal plan was filling and easy to stick to, despite being relatively low in calories. "I was really surprised by how satisfied I felt on the plan—I love to graze, but I didn't feel the need to snack once during the whole two weeks!" notes Ronni Metzger, age 50, who dropped an inch off her waist during the Quick Slim. Judi Herrmann, 44, who lost 6 pounds and 6¼ inches, loved the fact that "I could eat real food without having to eliminate or give up any type. It was easy to just order some sushi and easily get my 400 calories. My favorite food was the Chocolate Chip Scones—they were wonderful!"

What I love about the 2 Week Quick Slim is that it's easy to follow and can be followed almost anywhere. We've included frozen entrées, packaged foods, and restaurant meals—even fast food—knowing that it's tough for many people to find the time to cook every day.

If you're a stay-at-home mom or dad, you might prefer meals that you can cook or prepare quickly and easily. If you're a road warrior, our selection of restaurant meals gives you variety and lets you eat meals you're likely to find wherever your travels take you. You'll see that the menus follow the 4 Star Nutrition System to give you a balance of protein, fiber, good fats, and fruits and vegetables through the day. "I loved that I didn't have to worry about what I would eat or where I would shop," says Virginia Simpson, 57, who lost 10 pounds in 2 weeks. "I could eat some of the same things that I always do, I just became more mindful of my portions," adds Donna Agajanian, 64, who lost more than 10 pounds on the 2-week plan.

# HOW TO DO THE QUICK SLIM

**1. To determine if you need to lose weight,** find your BMI by visiting www.prevention.com and searching for "BMI Calculator."

**2. Set an initial goal** to lose up to 10 percent of your current weight. Weigh yourself and take key measurements—waist, hips, thighs, upper arms—before you start.

**3. Eat three daily meals:** breakfast, lunch, and dinner.

**4. You are permitted to swap meals—** breakfasts can be switched with other breakfasts, lunches and dinners for different lunches or dinners—so that you can choose among home-cooked, quick-fix, restaurant, and packaged meals.

**5. Follow each meal exactly as written;** however, you can add herbs, spices, and other calorie-free seasonings as desired. Many of the recipes make four or more servings; eat just one serving at a meal. If you are allergic to any foods on the list, you can find comparable foods and meals in other sections of the book.

**6. We suggest including a supplement** that contains 100 percent of the Daily Value (DV) for vitamins and minerals each day, to ensure that you're getting adequate amounts of important nutrients.

**7. Continue or step up** your current exercise regimen to get at least 30 minutes of moderate-intensity physical activity **three times a week, preferably more often.**

**8. Keep a food log** to help you follow what you're eating and stay on track.

**9. Weigh yourself on a regular basis,** at least once a week, and take your measurements to monitor your progress. Aim for a steady loss of up to 2 pounds per week. If you're losing 4 pounds or more per week, increase calories by adding a fourth meal to your day. Choose any of the Quick Slim meals as your additional meal and adjust meal times so that you're eating every 4 to 5 hours.

## MY FAVORITE 400-CALORIE MEAL

### JEREMY AND NATALIA'S CITRUS-MARINATED FISH

Use a simple citrus marinade for fatty fish that are high in omega-3 fatty acids such as trout, salmon, tuna, and mackerel. The vitamin C in the citrus fruit will help protect the fragile omega-3 fatty acids in the fish, so that it can absorb better. Combine the juice of 1 lime, lemon, or orange with 2 tablespoons canola or olive oil, 2 cloves minced garlic, a pinch of sugar, and a dash each of sea salt and black pepper. Marinate for 15 minutes and bake, sear, or grill over a low flame until desired doneness.—*Jeremy Bearman, executive chef, and Natalia Rusin, RD, culinary nutritionist, of Rouge Tomate in New York City*

# FREQUENTLY ASKED QUESTIONS ABOUT THE QUICK SLIM

### What can I drink on the Quick Slim?

All noncaloric beverages are fine, including water (with a lemon slice, if desired), sparkling water, diet soft drinks, coffee, and tea. You may use noncaloric sweeteners. Wine and beer are not allowed for this 2-week period.

### Can I break up a meal into two smaller meals, half for now and half for later?

No, each meal should be eaten in a single sitting. We've designed the meal to provide enough calories and food to be satisfying and to help keep hunger at bay. Smaller meals would not have the same effect.

### Should I eat at set mealtimes?

Set mealtimes are not necessary, but try to allow no more than 4 to 5 hours between meals. Noncaloric beverages can be consumed with and between meals.

### Can I add extra salt or seasoning?

You can add salt or seasonings with fewer than 5 calories per serving. The recipes are designed to be sodium-smart; that is, most call for less salt and fewer high-sodium ingredients. Over time, your taste buds will get used to eating foods that are not as salty.

### Can I make substitutions?

The Quick Slim allows you to interchange meals—for example, Day 10 breakfast instead of Day 5 breakfast. Breakfast is not interchangeable with lunch and dinner because it is the only meal that usually includes fruit and a calcium-rich item since these are typical breakfast foods. Lunch is designed to be the most suitable for taking to work. You may substitute soy products for dairy products, as long as they provide a similar number of calories and are fortified with calcium.

### Can I eat a favorite meal on more than one day?

From a calorie standpoint, you can eat the same meal every day. A balanced diet needs variety, however, so we encourage you to include as many different meals as possible.

### Do I have to buy the brands listed in the meal plans and recipes?

We've selected particular brands because of their taste, quality, availability, and nutritional value, including calorie count. If you can't or prefer not to use that brand, however, replace it with a comparable food with as close to the same calorie, fat, fiber, and sodium levels as possible.

### Do I have to exercise?

You should try to exercise at least three times per week, but it is not required. Weight loss is most successful when you combine moderate calorie restriction with regular physical activity. Exercise burns calories, but also builds muscle tissue, which means you'll burn more calories even at rest.

### I have to eat out for business frequently; can I still be on this plan?

The 2 Week Quick Slim includes options for the business traveler, including restaurant meals and meals that would be easy for a restaurant to prepare for you. Day 6 dinner, for example, includes a grilled salmon fillet with brown rice and spinach. Also look through the meals to identify those that would be easy to find on the road, such as the McDonald's breakfast, the deli sandwich, and the Japanese sushi dinner.

**As a tall man, I've been told that I need at least 1,800 to 2,000 calories per day to be healthy. Is 1,200 calories really okay for me?**

Because the Quick Slim is only 2 weeks, 1,200 calories should be fine. It takes a deficit of about 500 calories per day to lose a pound per week, putting you in the right calorie range to accomplish that. If you lose weight rapidly—

more than 4 pounds during the first week—or are not feeling well while on the plan, consider adding a meal to slow down your loss. Too-rapid weight loss can sap your energy and cause your metabolism to slow down so much that in the long term you'll find it harder to maintain a healthy weight.

**Why do I need to take a multivitamin?**

At this calorie level, it's very difficult to get the dietary recommendations for all vitamins and minerals—even in a nutritionally balanced plan such as ours—so we recommend a multivitamin to help cover all the bases. This is also one of the reasons why we don't suggest staying at this calorie level indefinitely.

### STAR SYSTEM

★ PROTEIN
★ FIBER
★ GOOD FATS
★ FRUITS/VEGGIES

# Day 1

### KASHI GOLEAN CEREAL (page 81)

★ ★ ★

| | calories |
|---|---|
| Kashi GOLEAN cereal, 1 cup | 140 |
| Low-fat or fat-free milk, 1 cup | 100 |
| Blueberries, 1 cup | 80 |
| Hard-boiled egg, 1 | 80 |
| **Total = 400** | |

### DELI SANDWICH (page 183)

★ ★

| | calories |
|---|---|
| Whole wheat bread, 2 slices | 140 |
| Lean roast beef, two 1-oz slices | 120 |
| Deli turkey breast, two 1-oz slices | 60 |
| Lettuce, 2 leaves | 10 |
| Tomato, 2 slices | 10 |
| Deli mustard, 1 tsp | 5 |
| Fresh fruit salad, ½ cup | 50 |
| **Total = 395** | |

### THAI-INSPIRED CHICKEN LETTUCE WRAPS (page 306)

★ ★ ★

| | calories |
|---|---|
| Thai-Inspired Chicken Lettuce Wraps, 2 wraps | 280 |
| Brown rice, ½ cup cooked | 110 |
| **Total = 390** | |

# Day 2

## FIBER ONE HONEY CLUSTERS
(page 164)

| ★ ★ | calories |
|---|---|
| Fiber One Honey Clusters, 1 cup | 160 |
| Sliced banana, ½ medium | 50 |
| Chopped walnuts, 2 Tbsp | 100 |
| Low-fat or fat-free milk, 1 cup | 100 |
| **Total = 410** | |

## LEAN CUISINE STEAK TIPS DIJON (page 99)

| ★ | calories |
|---|---|
| Lean Cuisine Steak Tips Dijon, 1 | 280 |
| Red wine, 5 oz | 120 |
| **Total = 400** | |

## GRILLED MAHI-MAHI (page 146)

| ★ ★ | calories |
|---|---|
| Grilled mahi-mahi, 4 oz | 120 |
| Broccoli, 1 cup sautéed in 1 tsp olive oil | 70 |
| Whole wheat roll, medium, with 1 tsp butter | 130 |
| Cappuccino, 16 oz, made with 8 oz fat-free milk | 80 |
| **Total = 400** | |

# Day 3

## ENGLISH MUFFIN WITH NUT BUTTER (page 168)

| ★ ★ ★ | calories |
|---|---|
| Toasted whole wheat English muffin, 1 | 130 |
| Peanut or almond butter, 4 tsp | 130 |
| Sliced banana, ½ medium | 50 |
| Low-fat or fat-free milk, 1 cup | 100 |
| **Total = 410** | |

## VEGETABLE MEDLEY SALAD (page 173)

| ★ ★ | calories |
|---|---|
| Romaine or other lettuce mix, 2 cups | 20 |
| Canned chickpeas, rinsed and drained, ½ cup | 140 |
| Alpine Lace Swiss cheese, cut into thin strips, one ½-oz slice | 45 |
| Tomato, cut into wedges, 1 medium | 20 |
| Sliced cucumber, ¼ cup | 5 |
| Plain croutons, ½ cup | 60 |
| Mrs. Dash Tomato Basil Garlic Seasoning Blend, few shakes | 0 |
| Olive oil, 2 tsp, mixed with 1 Tbsp balsamic vinegar | 90 |
| **Total = 380** | |

## SUSHI (page 146)

| ★ | calories |
|---|---|
| Miso soup, 1 cup | 40 |
| California roll (real or mock crabmeat) or salmon roll, 4 pieces | 150 |
| Spicy tuna roll, 4 pieces | 140 |
| Orange wedges, 8 | 70 |
| **Total = 400** | |

# SUCCESS STORY

## Sandi Hill

AGE: 37    HEIGHT: 5 feet 9 inches

START WEIGHT: 256 pounds

AFTER 2 WEEKS: 245 pounds

RESULTS: Lost 11 pounds, 9½ inches (including 2 inches from waist and 2 inches from hips)

SANDI IS NO STRANGER TO DIETS. Over the years she's tried everything from point plans to liquid fasts, with the same result: She'd lose the weight, then quickly gain it back. And always, she says, she felt constrained by the program and the choices she had to make.

But her experience with the 2 Week Quick Slim opened her eyes to a new way of eating. "I never really felt like I was on a diet. I always felt satisfied, and it didn't feel like I was making too many sacrifices," Sandi says. "I was really surprised that I could lose weight while eating real food." While normally her stomach would be growling by the time lunch came around, adding foods like nuts to her oatmeal kept her feeling full for hours. "I wasn't really tempted to snack or cheat."

An early childhood arts teacher, Sandi would plan out her meals the night before, then pack breakfast and lunch to take to school with her. "I'd sit there with my Chocolate Chip Scone and Starbucks coffee and think, 'Am I really on a diet?'"

After 2 weeks, Sandi dropped 11 pounds and several inches from her waist, hips, and thighs. And she had significantly more energy, for both her charges at work and her own 3-year-old daughter, who has inspired her to continue with her weight loss. "I want to be healthier so I can keep up with her!" she laughs. "I think I'm on my way toward reaching goals that I once couldn't touch and getting to a healthy weight for life."

**BEFORE:** 256 pountds

**SANDI LOST 11 LBS!**

**AFTER:** 245 pounds

# Day 4

### CHOCOLATE CHIP SCONES
(page 210)

| ★ ★ | calories |
|---|---|
| Chocolate Chip Scone, 1 | 160 |
| Part-skim ricotta, ¼ cup | 70 |
| Sliced almonds, 1 Tbsp | 30 |
| Strawberries, 1 cup | 50 |
| Latte made with ¾ cup low-fat milk | 80 |
| **Total = 390** | |

### GRILLED CHICKEN SANDWICH
(page 143)

| ★ ★ ★ ★ | calories |
|---|---|
| Whole wheat roll, medium | 100 |
| Grilled chicken breast, 3 oz | 140 |
| Roasted peppers, ¼ cup | 20 |
| Lettuce, 2 leaves | 10 |
| Tomato, 2 slices | 10 |
| Salsa, 1 Tbsp | 0 |
| Guacamole, 1 Tbsp | 30 |
| Coleslaw, ¼ cup | 50 |
| Strawberries, 1 cup | 50 |
| **Total = 410** | |

### DILL SALMON BURGERS (page 337)

| ★ ★ ★ ★ | calories |
|---|---|
| Dill Salmon Burger, 1 | 320 |
| Carrot sticks, ½ cup | 25 |
| Baked potato chips, ½ oz | 60 |
| **Total = 405** | |

# Day 5

### CREAMY ONE-DISH BREAKFAST OATS (page 214)

| ★ | calories |
|---|---|
| Creamy One-Dish Breakfast Oats, 1¼ cups | 380 |
| **Total = 380** | |

### PROGRESSO HEARTY BLACK BEAN WITH BACON SOUP
(page 89)

| ★ ★ | calories |
|---|---|
| Progresso Hearty Black Bean with Bacon Soup, 1 cup | 160 |
| Pepperidge Farm 100-Calorie Pack Cheddar Goldfish, 1 | 100 |
| Broccoli florets, 1 cup, with 1 Tbsp fat-free ranch dressing | 40 |
| Watermelon chunks, 1 cup | 50 |
| Nabisco Ginger Snaps, 2 cookies | 60 |
| **Total = 410** | |

### MCDONALD'S PREMIUM SOUTHWEST SALAD WITH GRILLED CHICKEN (page 116)

| ★ ★ | calories |
|---|---|
| McDonald's Premium Southwest Salad with Grilled Chicken, 1 | 320 |
| McDonald's Newman's Own Low Fat Family Recipe Italian Dressing, 1 packet | 60 |
| **Total = 380** | |

2 WEEK QUICK SLIM **69**

# Day 6

### ENGLISH MUFFIN WITH BUTTER
(page 169)

| ★ ★ ★ | calories |
|---|---|
| Toasted whole wheat English muffin, 1 | 130 |
| Whipped butter, 2 tsp | 50 |
| Plain low-fat or fat-free yogurt, 1 cup | 150 |
| Sliced strawberries, 1 cup | 50 |
| Honey, 1 tsp | 20 |
| **Total = 400** | |

### AMY'S CHEESE PIZZA (page 94)

| ★ | calories |
|---|---|
| Amy's Cheese Pizza, ⅓ pizza | 290 |
| Cubed cantaloupe, 1 cup | 50 |
| Graham cracker squares, 2 | 60 |
| **Total = 400** | |

### GRILLED SALMON (page 186)

| ★ ★ ★ | calories |
|---|---|
| Salmon fillet, 4 oz raw, brushed with 1 tsp Mrs. Dash Spicy Teriyaki 10-Minute Marinade | 250 |
| Brown rice, ½ cup cooked | 110 |
| Spinach, 2 cups, sautéed with 1 minced clove garlic in 1 tsp peanut oil | 60 |
| **Total = 420** | |

# Day 7

### RAISIN BRAN MUFFIN (page 170)

| ★ ★ | calories |
|---|---|
| Raisin bran muffin, 2 oz | 150 |
| All-fruit strawberry jam, 2 tsp | 20 |
| Plain low-fat or fat-free yogurt, ¾ cup | 120 |
| Wheat germ, 1 Tbsp | 30 |
| Mixed berries, 1 cup | 100 |
| **Total = 420** | |

### MEDITERRANEAN CHOPPED SALAD (page 259)

| ★ ★ ★ | calories |
|---|---|
| Mediterranean Chopped Salad, 3 cups | 90 |
| Hummus, ½ cup | 210 |
| Whole wheat pita, ½ | 90 |
| **Total = 390** | |

### CHIPOTLE SALAD (page 119)

| ★ ★ ★ | calories |
|---|---|
| Romaine lettuce, 2.5 oz | 10 |
| Black beans, 4 oz | 120 |
| Fajita vegetables, 2.5 oz | 20 |
| Cilantro-lime rice, 3 oz | 130 |
| Tomato salsa, 3.5 oz | 20 |
| Cheese, 1 oz | 100 |
| **Total = 400** | |

# SUCCESS STORIES

## Patti Robbins

AGE: 53    HEIGHT: 5 feet 5½ inches

START WEIGHT: 172½ pounds

AFTER 2 WEEKS: 162 pounds

RESULTS: Lost 10½ pounds, 7¾ inches (including ½ inch from waist and 1½ inches from hips)
**After 8 weeks: Weight: 155 (lost 17½ pounds from the start)

## Gladys DiSisto

AGE: 54    HEIGHT: 5 feet 4 inches

START WEIGHT: 161½ pounds

AFTER 2 WEEKS: 156 pounds

RESULTS: Lost 5½ pounds, 6¼ inches (including 1½ inches from waist and 1½ inches from hips)
**After 8 weeks: Weight: 151 (lost 10½ pounds from the start)

TENNIS PARTNERS PATTI AND GLADYS ARE very used to supporting each other on the court. So when it came time to finally lose those last 10 to 15 pounds they'd each been complaining about, the two once again joined forces.

"Having the support of a friend made a big difference in keeping to the plan," notes Patti, who began packing on some excess weight after hitting menopause. "We'd talk a lot about the different recipes and bounced ideas off each other."

"We'd see each other on the tennis court or check in on the phone almost every day to see how it was going," adds Gladys, who says she got interested in the diet after her doctor pointed out that she'd gained about 15 pounds in 5 years.

Their teamwork paid off: After 2 weeks, Patti had lost more than 10 pounds; Gladys dropped 5½ ("She's very competitive!" Gladys laughs). Both continued to lose weight on the plan even after the 2 Week Quick Slim: Patti was down more than 17 pounds at 8 weeks and Gladys, more than 10.

"I had to buy a bunch of new clothes—including a new bathing suit—because nothing fits anymore!" says Patti, who adds that the plan gave her a better appreciation for portion sizes and calorie counts. Gladys has also noticed a difference in her appearance. "I'm wearing clothes now that I didn't dare try on before because I felt so chunky," she reports. "My body just feels more 'sucked in.'" She also notes that she's lost some of her bad eating habits. "I used to snack like crazy, especially if I felt stressed out, but now I'm a lot more in control and not as tempted to binge."

The pair expect to celebrate their joint successes with more than just new wardrobes. The two had made a pledge that when they each lost 10 pounds, they'd take a trip to a nearby spa as a well-deserved reward. "Now we're just waiting on another friend to try the plan so we can go together," Patti says.

**PATTI LOST 10½ LBS!**

**BEFORE:** 172½ pounds  **AFTER:** 162 pounds

**GLADYS LOST 5½ LBS!**

**BEFORE:** 161½ pounds  **AFTER:** 156 pounds

# Day 8

## MCDONALD'S EGG McMUFFIN
(page 114)

| ★ | calories |
|---|---|
| McDonald's Egg McMuffin, 1 | 300 |
| McDonald's Nonfat Cappuccino, large, 20 oz | 90 |
| **Total = 390** | |

## SALADE NIÇOISE (page 255)

| ★ ★ ★ | calories |
|---|---|
| Salade Niçoise, 2 cups | 290 |
| Whole wheat roll, medium | 100 |
| **Total = 390** | |

## WEIGHT WATCHERS SMART ONES CHICKEN SANTA FE
(page 99)

| ★ ★ | calories |
|---|---|
| Weight Watchers Smart Ones Chicken Santa Fe, 1 | 140 |
| Healthy Choice Old Fashioned Chicken Noodle Soup, 1 cup | 100 |
| Whole wheat tortilla, one 6" | 120 |
| Cubed cantaloupe, ½ cup | 25 |
| **Total = 385** | |

# Day 9

## AUNT JEMIMA FROZEN WHOLE GRAIN PANCAKES (page 87)

| ★ | calories |
|---|---|
| Aunt Jemima Frozen Whole Grain Pancakes, 2 | 160 |
| Maple syrup, 1 Tbsp | 50 |
| Sliced banana, 1 medium | 110 |
| Fat-free flavored yogurt, 6 oz | 80 |
| **Total = 400** | |

## GRILLED SALMON SANDWICH
(page 181)

| ★ ★ ★ | calories |
|---|---|
| 100% whole wheat bread, 2 slices | 140 |
| Grilled salmon, 3 oz | 180 |
| Plain yogurt, 2 Tbsp, mixed with 1 tsp fresh dill | 20 |
| Deli mustard, 1 tsp | 5 |
| Lettuce, 2 leaves | 10 |
| Tomato, 2 slices | 10 |
| Deli three-bean salad, ⅓ cup | 60 |
| **Total = 425** | |

## BOSTON MARKET ¼ WHITE ROTISSERIE CHICKEN (page 123)

| ★ ★ | calories |
|---|---|
| Boston Market ¼ White Rotisserie Chicken, no skin | 240 |
| Boston Market Garlic Dill New Potatoes, ½ cup | 100 |
| Boston Market Caesar Side Salad (without dressing), 1 | 40 |
| Boston Market Lite Ranch Dressing, 1 Tbsp | 20 |
| **Total = 400** | |

# Day 10

## OATMEAL (page 167)

| ★ | calories |
|---|---|
| Instant oatmeal, 1 cup cooked | 160 |
| Chopped walnuts, 2 Tbsp | 100 |
| Raisins, 2 Tbsp | 50 |
| Latte made with ¾ cup low-fat milk | 80 |
| **Total = 390** | |

## SUBWAY VEGGIE DELITE (page 125)

| ★ ★ | calories |
|---|---|
| Subway Jared Veggie Delite with 9-grain bread and provolone cheese, 6" sandwich | 280 |
| Subway Fire-Roasted Tomato Orzo Soup, 1 | 130 |
| **Total = 410** | |

## NORTH AFRICAN TURKEY MEATBALLS WITH CARAMELIZED ONIONS (page 305)

| ★ ★ ★ | calories |
|---|---|
| North African Turkey Meatballs with Caramelized Onions, 6 meatballs | 310 |
| Brown rice, ½ cup cooked | 110 |
| **Total = 420** | |

# Day 11

## ALL-IN-ONE SMOOTHIE (page 171)

| ★ ★ ★ | calories |
|---|---|
| Low-fat or fat-free milk, 1 cup | 100 |
| Banana (peel, slice, and freeze the night before), small | 90 |
| Frozen berries, ½ cup | 30 |
| Old-fashioned oats, ¼ cup | 80 |
| Peanut butter, 1 Tbsp | 90 |
| **Total = 390** | |

## CHICKEN FAJITA (page 143)

| ★ ★ | calories |
|---|---|
| Flour tortilla, one 7½" | 140 |
| Grilled chicken breast, 3 oz | 110 |
| Grilled bell peppers and onions, ½ cup | 90 |
| Salsa, 2 Tbsp | 10 |
| Guacamole, 2 Tbsp | 40 |
| **Total = 390** | |

## HEALTHY CHOICE BEEF TIPS PORTOBELLO (page 96)

| ★ ★ ★ ★ | calories |
|---|---|
| Healthy Choice Beef Tips Portobello, 1 package | 260 |
| Large salad with 2 cups lettuce, 1 tomato, 1 Tbsp chopped walnuts, and 10 sprays of salad dressing | 110 |
| Fat-free Greek yogurt, ⅓ cup | 50 |
| **Total = 410** | |

# SUCCESS STORY

## Janet Sartorius

AGE: 50   HEIGHT: 5 feet 6 inches

START WEIGHT: 218¼ pounds

AFTER 2 WEEKS: 208 pounds

RESULTS: Lost 10¼ pounds, 9 inches (including 2 inches from waist and 2 inches from hips)

JANET KNOWS WHAT IT'S LIKE TO WORK HARD AT WEIGHT LOSS, only to see the pounds slowly pile back on. A few years ago, she lost an amazing 90 pounds while on a popular weight-loss plan. She even took a new career direction—walking dogs—to help her stay more active. But after a couple of years, she regained about two-thirds of the weight and was starting to worry that she was doomed to obesity. "I felt totally hopeless, like my metabolism had shifted and there was nothing I could do to lose the weight again," she recalls.

But after starting the 2 Week Quick Slim, Janet was surprised to see that the needle on the scale was once again moving down.

"Suddenly I had hope again!" she says. "I realized I could be at a healthy weight and stay there." Having an established plan made it easier for her to say no to certain foods, and she felt satisfied for hours after eating, so she wasn't as tempted to snack or binge. "I couldn't believe I could eat things like a whole wheat roll! I was so trained to think all carbs were bad, but I learned having foods with fiber kept me more satisfied."

Her favorite foods? The North African Turkey Meatballs with Caramelized Onions and Vegetable Medley Salad. The best part? Her family loved them too! "This wasn't just something I was doing for myself, it was something my family could follow along with me because the foods were all very satisfying."

Eventually, Janet hopes to be able to slip into a size 8 pair of pants. "I know I'm moving in the right direction: I'm so much more motivated now to get healthier, for both myself and my family."

BEFORE: 218¼ pounds

AFTER: 208 pounds

JANET LOST 10¼ LBS!

# Day 12

### WESTERN FRITTATA (page 221)

| ★ ★ ★ | calories |
|---|---|
| Western Frittata, 4 wedges | 280 |
| Whole wheat toast, 1 slice | 70 |
| Grapefruit, ½ | 50 |
| **Total = 400** | |

### CHEF'S SALAD (page 174)

| ★ ★ ★ | calories |
|---|---|
| Mixed greens, 2 cups | 20 |
| Turkey, ham, and roast beef, cut into thin strips, 1 oz each | 120 |
| Sliced olives, 5 | 50 |
| Diced tomato, 1 medium | 20 |
| Diced bell pepper, ½ medium | 10 |
| Sliced almonds, 1 Tbsp | 30 |
| Olive oil, 1 tsp, mixed with 1 Tbsp balsamic vinegar | 50 |
| 100-calorie pack cookies of your choice | 100 |
| **Total = 400** | |

### LONGHORN STEAKHOUSE RENEGADE TOP SIRLOIN
(page 142)

| ★ ★ | calories |
|---|---|
| Longhorn Steakhouse Renegade Top Sirloin, 4 oz (½ of 8-oz steak) | 240 |
| Longhorn Steakhouse Grilled Onions, 1 order | 90 |
| Longhorn Steakhouse Fresh Steamed Asparagus, 1 order | 80 |
| **Total = 410** | |

# Day 13

### BAGEL WITH CREAM CHEESE
(page 168)

| ★ | calories |
|---|---|
| Lender's Wheat Bagel, 1 | 210 |
| Light cream cheese, 2 Tbsp | 70 |
| Fat-free flavored yogurt, 6 oz | 80 |
| Banana, ½ medium | 50 |
| **Total = 410** | |

### AMY'S MEXICAN CASSEROLE
(page 95)

| ★ ★ | calories |
|---|---|
| Amy's Mexican Casserole (Light in Sodium), 1 serving | 370 |
| Low sodium V8 juice, 1 cup | 50 |
| **Total = 420** | |

### FISH EN PAPILLOTE (page 340)

| ★ ★ ★ | calories |
|---|---|
| Fish en Papillote | 250 |
| Breyer's Smooth & Dreamy Vanilla Bean Ice Cream, ½ cup | 110 |
| Cascadian Farm Harvest Berries, ½ cup | 30 |
| **Total = 390** | |

# Day 14

## BREAKFAST (page 83)

| ★ ★ | calories |
|---|---|
| Jimmy Dean D-Lights Breakfast Bowl, 1 | 230 |
| Whole wheat toast, 1 slice | 70 |
| Orange juice, 6 oz | 80 |
| **Total = 380** | |

## ITALIAN SALAD (page 262)

| ★ ★ ★ | calories |
|---|---|
| Italian Salad, 3 cups | 400 |
| **Total = 400** | |

## RED LOBSTER SHRIMP SCAMPI (page 142)

| ★ | calories |
|---|---|
| Red Lobster Shrimp Scampi, 1 order | 130 |
| Red Lobster Wild Rice Pilaf, 1 order | 180 |
| Red Lobster Garden Salad with 1 Tbsp Red Lobster Fat-Free Ranch Dressing | 110 |
| **Total = 420** | |

# Congratulations!
## YOU'VE FINISHED THE 2 WEEK QUICK SLIM!

Now, assess your progress.

✤ **If you want to lose more weight,** continue to eat three meals daily. You can keep following the 2 Week Quick Slim menus, or try putting together your own menu with the four hundred 400-calorie meals in Chapters 6 through 14. Just make sure that you follow the 4 Star Nutrition System and collect all four stars each day (this means that at least one meal will need to have more than one star).

Maintain your journal and track your weight so that you can monitor your progress. Don't worry if your rate of weight loss slows down. Just stick with your eating plan and add some exercise, and you'll overcome this natural slowdown. By the end of your second round, for a total of 4 weeks on the Quick Slim, your weight loss is likely to have stabilized at a couple of pounds per week.

If you're continuing to lose weight rapidly, you probably are not getting enough calories and should consider adding a fourth meal each day.

✤ **If you lost weight and want to maintain your new weight,** add a fourth meal to your day. For maximum satisfaction, this meal should be eaten in one sitting. Even at four meals a day, you may continue to lose some weight, but at a slower pace.

As Gladys points out, this plan "isn't about eliminating foods; it's about making smart choices with real foods and just focusing on portion sizes. Even [after] being on it for just 2 weeks I can see how this type of eating can be incorporated into my diet for the long run."

Keep it up and you just might find that there are even more benefits besides a slimmer waist and healthier body. "Eating in moderation rather than just eating everything all the time gave me a feeling that I could take control of other aspects of my life, like saving more money out of my paycheck each week. Everyone is commenting on how great I look, and I really feel it!" Melody raves.

# SUCCESS STORY

## Melody Rubie

AGE: 48    HEIGHT: 5 feet 1 inch

START WEIGHT: 153 pounds

AFTER 2 WEEKS: 148 pounds

RESULTS: Lost 5 pounds, 9 inches (including 3 inches from waist and 2 inches from hips)
**After 8 weeks: Weight: 138½ (lost 14½ pounds from the start)

LIKE MANY MOMS, Melody found it difficult to lose the weight she'd gained with the birth of her son, Benjamin, now 6½. She attributed this partly to her age and partly to the stresses of being a new mom. Eventually she resigned herself to living as a size 12.

But when Melody heard about the 400-Calorie Fix, she says, something in her clicked. "I wanted my son to see what I really looked like, and this sounded like a reasonable approach." She immediately took to the menu plans and meal ideas. "It was so easy to see what I wanted to eat; it was all laid out for me," says Melody.

Melody's also no ordinary working mom: She's a regular cast member in Broadway's famed *Phantom of the Opera*, where she says her excess weight often slowed her down. "On the days where we do both a matinee and an evening performance, I really would be dragging at the end. We work hard on stage and off." But after just 2 weeks on the program, she says her energy levels are at an all-time high. "I feel like I can keep going as long as I need to."

Even after the 2 Week Quick Slim was over, Melody continued to lose weight, dropping nearly 10 more pounds and getting close to her final goal weight of 135 pounds. She continues to keep tabs on her hunger levels, writing down when and what she eats to help keep her appetite in check. She also power walks across town to fit in more exercise after dropping off her son at school.

"I feel so empowered," she says. "I have a much greater sense of control and it's spilling into other areas of my life—work, home. I feel like I can do almost anything now!"

BEFORE: 153 pounds

AFTER: 148 pounds

MELODY LOST 5 LBS!

# 6.
# PACKAGED FOOD MEALS

KELLOGG'S
SPECIAL K
BLUEBERRY
CEREAL
420

# BREAKFASTS

## KELLOGG'S SPECIAL K BLUEBERRY CEREAL
★ ★

We suggest topping the cereal with milk and one of the peaches, then eating the other peach and the almonds as "dessert."

| | calories |
|---|---|
| Kellogg's Special K Blueberry Cereal, ¾ cup | 100 |
| Reduced-fat milk "box," 8 oz | 120 |
| Peaches, 2 medium | 120 |
| Almonds, 10 whole | 80 |

**420 calories,** 12 g fat, 3.5 g saturated fat, 294 mg sodium, 67 g carbohydrate, 6 g fiber, 16 g protein, 60% calcium

## KASHI GOLEAN CEREAL
★ ★ ★

GOLEAN provides plenty of protein and fiber to help keep you full. We added even more protein with the hard-boiled egg.

| | calories |
|---|---|
| Kashi GOLEAN cereal, 1 cup | 140 |
| Blueberries, 1 cup | 80 |
| Low-fat or fat-free milk, 1 cup | 100 |
| Hard-boiled egg, 1 | 80 |

**400 calories,** 9 g fat, 3 g saturated fat, 255 mg sodium, 64 g carbohydrate, 13 g fiber, 29 g protein, 35% calcium

## QUAKER OATMEAL SQUARES
★ ★ ★

Oatmeal squares are hearty enough to have for a snack. For a change of pace, we top the cereal with canned peaches rather than fresh fruit.

| | calories |
|---|---|
| Quaker Oatmeal Squares, ⅔ cup | 150 |
| Low-fat or fat-free milk, ¾ cup | 80 |
| Peaches canned in juice, drained, 1 cup chopped | 110 |
| Chopped pecans, 1 Tbsp | 50 |

**390 calories,** 9 g fat, 2 g saturated fat, 269 mg sodium, 70 g carbohydrate, 7 g fiber, 13 g protein, 42% calcium

## CASCADIAN FARM FRUIT & NUT GRANOLA
★ ★ ★

We love granola, but it's usually very high in calories and fat. Not so with this brand. If you prefer, substitute a flavored fat-free 80-calorie yogurt for the plain yogurt.

| | calories |
|---|---|
| Cascadian Farm Fruit & Nut Granola, ½ cup | 140 |
| Stonyfield Farm Fat Free Plain Yogurt, 6 oz | 80 |
| Blueberries, 1 cup | 80 |
| Walnut halves, 2 Tbsp | 80 |

**380 calories,** 12.5 g fat, 1.5 g saturated fat, 191 mg sodium, 58 g carbohydrate, 7 g fiber, 14 g protein, 33% calcium

*easy fix*

CASCADIAN FARM FRUIT & NUT GRANOLA

+

+

+

EQUALS

**380**
CALORIES

## STAR SYSTEM

★ PROTEIN
★ FIBER
★ GOOD FATS
★ FRUITS/VEGGIES

## easy fix

QUAKER
INSTANT
OATMEAL

+

+

## EQUALS

# 400
## CALORIES

---

## KOZY SHACK MAPLE BROWN SUGAR READY GRAINS

★

Kozy Shack is best known for its puddings, so you might find this ready-to-heat cereal in the dairy case rather than the cereal aisle. Either stir in the dried fruit or eat as is, along with a small glass of milk.

| | calories |
|---|---|
| Kozy Shack Maple Brown Sugar Ready Grains, 7 oz | 190 |
| Dried fruit, ¼ cup | 120 |
| Low-fat or fat-free milk, ¾ cup | 80 |

**390 calories,** 4 g fat, 2 g saturated fat, 265 mg sodium, 70 g carbohydrate, 9 g fiber, 14 g protein, 37% calcium

## QUAKER INSTANT OATMEAL

★

Doubling up with two packets of oatmeal makes this a higher-fiber and more satisfying meal.

| | calories |
|---|---|
| Quaker Instant Oatmeal, Original, 2 packets | 200 |
| Dried fruit, ¼ cup | 120 |
| Steamed low-fat or fat-free milk, ¾ cup, with 2 Tbsp sugar-free syrup | 80 |

**400 calories,** 6 g fat, 1 g saturated fat, 245 mg sodium, 75 g carbohydrate, 8 g fiber, 15 g protein, 40% calcium

---

## KELLOGG'S RAISIN BRAN

★ ★

This breakfast is a classic. Try different brands of raisin bran to find the one that you like best.

| | calories |
|---|---|
| Kellogg's Raisin Bran, 1 cup | 190 |
| Low-fat or fat-free milk, ¾ cup | 80 |
| Banana, 1 medium | 110 |

**380 calories,** 3.5 g fat, 1 g saturated fat, 435 mg sodium, 81 g carbohydrate, 10 g fiber, 12 g protein, 22% calcium

## CHEERIOS

★ ★

Another cereal classic; we suggest adding nuts for good fats and added satiety.

| | calories |
|---|---|
| Cheerios, 1½ cups | 150 |
| Sliced almonds, 4 Tbsp | 130 |
| Low-fat or fat-free milk, 1 cup | 100 |

**380 calories,** 17 g fat, 2.5 g saturated fat, 392 mg sodium, 47 g carbohydrate, 8 g fiber, 18 g protein, 50% calcium

## FIBER ONE BLUEBERRY MUFFIN
★ ★

This blueberry muffin, made from a mix, has more fiber than conventional blueberry muffins. Try scrambling the egg with the tomato or putting the tomato on top once the egg is cooked.

| | calories |
|---|---|
| Fiber One Blueberry Muffin Mix, 1 muffin | 160 |
| Scrambled egg, 1 | 70 |
| Diced tomato, ¼ cup | 10 |
| Yoplait Light (any flavor), 6 oz | 100 |
| Cubed cantaloupe, 1 cup | 50 |

**390 calories,** 11 g fat, 3.5 g saturated fat, 430 mg sodium, 62 g carbohydrate, 8 g fiber, 15 g protein, 25% calcium

## JIMMY DEAN D-LIGHTS BREAKFAST BOWL
★ ★

This breakfast bowl combines turkey sausage, egg whites, cheese, and potatoes into a hearty and protein-packed breakfast option.

| | calories |
|---|---|
| Jimmy Dean D-Lights Breakfast Bowl, 1 | 230 |
| Whole wheat toast, 1 slice | 70 |
| Orange juice, 6 oz | 80 |

**380 calories,** 8 g fat, 3 g saturated fat, 862 mg sodium, 50 g carbohydrate, 4 g fiber, 28 g protein, 19% calcium

FIBER ONE WILD BLUEBERRY MUFFIN
390

JIMMY DEAN D-LIGHTS BREAKFAST BOWL
380

## AMY'S BREAKFAST BURRITO
★ ★

To make the latte, heat milk in the microwave, with a coffee machine steamer wand, or on the stove and combine with very strong hot coffee. No calories in the coffee!

| | calories |
|---|---|
| Amy's Breakfast Burrito, 1 | 250 |
| Tomato, 4 slices | 15 |
| Honeydew, 1 cup | 60 |
| Latte made with ¾ cup low-fat milk | 80 |

**405 calories,** 9 g fat, 1.5 g saturated fat, 655 mg sodium, 65 g carbohydrate, 7 g fiber, 17 g protein, 28% calcium

THE WEIGHT Watchers Smart Ones Breakfast Quesadilla is an excellent source of fiber, a nutrient known to help boost fullness and stave off hunger.

## WEIGHT WATCHERS SMART ONES BREAKFAST QUESADILLA
★ ★ ★

Use the yogurt like sour cream on top of your quesadilla. If you prefer thicker Greek-style yogurt, be sure to compare labels, since some brands have more calories than others.

| | calories |
|---|---|
| Smart Ones Breakfast Quesadilla, 1 | 220 |
| Plain low-fat or fat-free yogurt, ¾ cup | 120 |
| Orange, 1 medium | 70 |

**410 calories,** 9 g fat, 5 g saturated fat, 839 mg sodium, 59 g carbohydrate, 9 g fiber, 24 g protein, 55% calcium

AMY'S BREAKFAST
405

WEIGHT WATCHERS SMART ONES BREAKFAST QUESADILLA
410

## AMY'S ORGANIC TOFU SCRAMBLE
★ ★

A vegan take on scrambled eggs, this dish comes with vegetables and potatoes. If you prefer Amy's Mexican version (400 calories), skip the juice.

| | calories |
|---|---|
| Amy's Organic Tofu Scramble, 1 serving | 320 |
| Grapefruit juice, 1 cup | 90 |

**410 calories,** 19 g fat, 3 g saturated fat, 582 mg sodium, 41 g carbohydrate, 4 g fiber, 20 g protein, 17% calcium

## STOUFFER'S HARVEST APPLES

Enjoy these apples a few different ways, either on top of the cream cheese and bagel, stirred into the yogurt, or by themselves.

| | calories |
|---|---|
| Stouffer's Harvest Apples, ½ cup | 130 |
| Pepperidge Farm Mini Brown Sugar Cinnamon Bagel, 1 | 120 |
| Light Philadelphia Cream Cheese, 2 Tbsp | 70 |
| Dannon Light & Fit Yogurt, 6 oz | 80 |

**400 calories,** 7.5 g fat, 3 g saturated fat, 373 mg sodium, 69 g carbohydrate, 3 g fiber, 11 g protein, 23% calcium

### ADD...

**ADDING YOGURT** or milk to a breakfast instantly improves its nutrition profile by boosting protein and calcium.

STOUFFER'S HARVEST APPLES
400

AMY'S ORGANIC TOFU SCRAMBLE
410

VAN'S ALL NATURAL MULTIGRAIN WAFFLES 390

CASCADIAN FARM HARVEST BERRIES 400

## VAN'S ALL NATURAL MULTIGRAIN WAFFLES
★ ★ ★

If you're short on time in the morning, spread these waffles with almond butter while they're still warm—it's easier to spread then—and top with sliced banana.

| | calories |
|---|---|
| Van's All Natural Multigrain Waffles, 2 | 180 |
| Almond butter, 1 Tbsp | 100 |
| Banana, 1 medium | 110 |

**390 calories,** 16 g fat, 1.5 g saturated fat, 390 mg sodium, 55 g carbohydrate, 7 g fiber, 7 g protein, 14% calcium

## CASCADIAN FARM HARVEST BERRIES
★ ★ ★

Frozen berries provide a touch of summer year-round and are among the fruits highest in fiber and healthy phytochemicals. Combine the berries, cottage cheese, and sliced banana for a refreshing meal.

| | calories |
|---|---|
| Cascadian Farm Harvest Berries, 1 cup | 60 |
| Breakstone 2% Fat Small Curd Cottage Cheese, 4 oz | 90 |
| Banana, 1 medium | 110 |
| Pepperidge Farm 100% Whole Wheat English Muffin, 1 | 140 |

**400 calories,** 5 g fat, 2 g saturated fat, 610 mg sodium, 76 g carbohydrate, 10 g fiber, 20 g protein, 2% calcium

## AUNT JEMIMA FROZEN WHOLE GRAIN PANCAKES
★

Whole grain pancakes have a nuttier flavor and a bit more fiber, even though this breakfast falls a bit short of the fiber star. If you prefer yogurt to milk, try combining an 80-calorie yogurt with the syrup and banana to put on top of the pancakes.

| | calories |
|---|---|
| Aunt Jemima Frozen Whole Grain Pancakes, 2 | 160 |
| Maple syrup, 1 Tbsp | 50 |
| Sliced banana, 1 medium | 110 |
| Fat-free flavored yogurt, 6 oz | 80 |

**400 calories,** 4 g fat, 0 g saturated fat, 386 mg sodium, 84 g carbohydrate, 5 g fiber, 9 g protein, 20% calcium

## KELLOGG'S EGGO NUTRI-GRAIN BLUEBERRY WAFFLES
★ ★

The Fiber One line of yogurts offers another alternative for boosting fiber. Check other brands if you'd prefer a larger portion of yogurt for the 80 calories.

| | calories |
|---|---|
| Kellogg's Eggo Nutri-Grain Blueberry Waffles, 2 | 180 |
| Frozen blueberries, 1 cup | 80 |
| Honey, 1 Tbsp | 60 |
| Yoplait Fiber One Yogurt, 4 oz | 80 |

**400 calories,** 5 g fat, 1.5 g saturated fat, 445 mg sodium, 88 g carbohydrate, 11 g fiber, 9 g protein, 20% calcium

## NATURE'S PATH ORGANIC STRAWBERRY TOASTER PASTRY
★

Compare labels when you're buying organic since many foods, including this toaster pastry, have about the same calories as their nonorganic counterparts.

| | calories |
|---|---|
| Nature's Path Organic Strawberry Toaster Pastry, 1 | 210 |
| Stonyfield Farm Organic Strawberry Smoothie, 6 oz | 150 |
| Fresh strawberries, 1 cup | 50 |

**410 calories,** 6.5 g fat, 3 g saturated fat, 240 mg sodium, 75 g carbohydrate, 5 g fiber, 11 g protein, 29% calcium

# LUNCH/DINNER

## EASY MAC MICROWAVEABLE SNACK PACKET

Not the most nutritious lunch and pretty high in sodium, but feels like a childhood meal.

| | calories |
|---|---|
| Easy Mac Microwaveable Snack Packet, 1 | 230 |
| Green Giant Just for One Broccoli & Cheese Sauce, 1 box | 50 |
| Kozy Shack Original Rice Pudding, 1 4-oz cup | 130 |

**410 calories,** 8.5 g fat, 5 g saturated fat, 1,115 mg sodium, 71 g carbohydrate, 4 g fiber, 13 g protein, 34% calcium

*easy fix*

EASY MAC MICROWAVEABLE SNACK PACKET

+

+

EQUALS

**410**
CALORIES

HORMEL
VEGETARIAN
CHILI WITH
BEANS
400

## HORMEL VEGETARIAN CHILI WITH BEANS
★ ★ ★

We like to crumble the tortilla into the chili and slice the cheese into the salad. Any salad dressing spray is fine since all have about 1 calorie per spray.

| | calories |
|---|---|
| Hormel Vegetarian Chili with Beans, 1 cup | 190 |
| Large salad with 2 cups lettuce, 1 tomato, salad dressing spray | 60 |
| Corn tortilla, one 6" | 60 |
| Alpine Lace Swiss cheese, two ½-oz slices | 90 |

**400 calories,** 11 g fat, 4 g saturated fat, 818 mg sodium, 57 g carbohydrate, 14 g fiber, 22 g protein, 40% calcium

## CAMPBELL'S SELECT HARVEST 98% FAT FREE NEW ENGLAND CLAM CHOWDER
★ ★ ★

Now that lower-fat versions are available, New England clam chowder can return to your favorites list. Swap for a different fruit if strawberries are out of season.

| | calories |
|---|---|
| Campbell's Select Harvest 98% Fat Free New England Clam Chowder, 1 cup | 110 |
| Kashi Roasted Vegetable Thin Crust Pizza, ⅓ pizza | 250 |
| Fresh strawberries, 1 cup | 50 |

**410 calories,** 12.5 g fat, 5 g saturated fat, 1,112 mg sodium, 58 g carbohydrate, 8 g fiber, 21 g protein, 25% calcium

## HEALTH VALLEY ORGANIC SPLIT PEA & CARROT SOUP
★ ★ ★

Split peas, like other legumes, are highly filling and filled with fiber, protein, and other key nutrients. Penn State researchers say starting your meal with soup may help you eat fewer calories.

| | calories |
|---|---|
| Health Valley Organic Split Pea & Carrot Soup, 1 cup | 120 |
| South Beach Southwestern Chicken Wrap, 1 | 240 |
| Raspberries, ½ cup | 30 |

**390 calories,** 11 g fat, 5 g saturated fat, 1,290 mg sodium, 59 g carbohydrate, 26 g fiber, 33 g protein, 31% calcium

## PROGRESSO HEARTY BLACK BEAN WITH BACON SOUP
★ ★

This meal is easy to make if you have access to a fridge and a microwave. A different 100-calorie pack can be swapped for the Goldfish. If you prefer your broccoli au naturel, skip the dressing to lose a few calories and some of the sodium.

| | calories |
|---|---|
| Progresso Hearty Black Bean with Bacon Soup, 1 cup | 160 |
| Pepperidge Farm 100-Calorie Pack Cheddar Goldfish, 1 | 100 |
| Broccoli florets, 1 cup, with 1 Tbsp fat-free ranch dressing | 40 |
| Watermelon chunks, 1 cup | 50 |
| Nabisco Ginger Snaps, 2 cookies | 60 |

**410 calories,** 6 g fat, 1.5 g saturated fat, 1,240 mg sodium, 75 g carbohydrate, 13 g fiber, 14 g protein, 14% calcium

*easy fix*

PROGRESSO
HEARTY BLACK
BEAN WITH
BACON SOUP

+

+

+

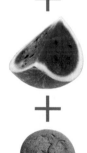

+

+

EQUALS

**410**
CALORIES

## easy fix

CHICKEN OF
THE SEA
PINK SALMON
POUCH

+

+

+

EQUALS

## 385
CALORIES

## CAMPBELL'S SOUP AT HAND 25% LESS SODIUM CLASSIC TOMATO
★

Traditional soups tend to be high in salt, so look for brands and varieties with less sodium. The cheese in the calzone gives this meal a calcium boost.

| | calories |
|---|---|
| Campbell's Soup at Hand 25% Less Sodium Classic Tomato, 1 | 120 |
| Weight Watchers Smart Ones Calzone Italiano, 1 | 290 |

**410 calories,** 6 g fat, 2 g saturated fat, 1,280 mg sodium, 74 g carbohydrate, 8 g fiber, 17 g protein, 22% calcium

## CHICKEN OF THE SEA PINK SALMON POUCH
★ ★ ★ ★

Salmon in a pouch doesn't require refrigeration, so it's easy to take with you. Any greens are fine for this salad, as is any Vita Top, since each flavor has 100 calories.

| | calories |
|---|---|
| Chicken of the Sea Pink Salmon Pouch, 1 | 90 |
| Earthbound Mixed Baby Greens, 2 cups | 15 |
| Ken's Lite Caesar, 2 Tbsp | 70 |
| Mango, 1 cup | 110 |
| Golden Corn VitaTops, 1 | 100 |

**385 calories,** 10.5 g fat, 2 g saturated fat, 1,243 mg sodium, 59 g carbohydrate, 10 g fiber, 22 g protein, 10% calcium

## BUSH'S BEST VEGETARIAN BAKED BEANS
★ ★ ★

This high-fiber, protein-filled meal will satisfy vegans and nonvegetarians alike.

| | calories |
|---|---|
| Bush's Best Vegetarian Baked Beans, ½ cup | 130 |
| Yves Zesty Italian Veggie Brat, 1 | 150 |
| Whole wheat hot dog bun, 1 | 110 |
| Watermelon chunks, ½ cup | 20 |

**410 calories,** 7 g fat, 1 g saturated fat, 1,436 mg sodium, 66 g carbohydrate, 10 g fiber, 29 g protein, 13% calcium

## THE SPICE HUNTER SPLIT PEA SOUP
★ ★ ★

The open-face ham sandwich is a perfect match for split pea soup. Check out the freezer case for other frozen treats with similar calories.

| | calories |
|---|---|
| The Spice Hunter Split Pea Soup, 1 cup | 170 |
| Rye bread, 1 slice | 80 |
| Healthy Choice Smoked Ham, two 1-oz slices | 60 |
| Deli mustard, 1 tsp | 5 |
| Lettuce, 2 leaves | 10 |
| Tomato, 2 slices | 10 |
| Low Fat Creamsicle, 1.65-oz bar | 70 |

**405 calories,** 5 g fat, 1 g saturated fat, 1,373 mg sodium, 69 g carbohydrate, 14 g fiber, 20 g protein, 6% calcium

## HEALTHY CHOICE MINESTRONE SOUP
★ ★

Try melting the cheese on the roll, a cross between an English muffin and a bun, or cut up the cheese and stir it into the soup.

| | calories |
|---|---:|
| Healthy Choice Minestrone Soup, 1 cup | 200 |
| Arnold Select Multi-Grain Sandwich Thins, 1 | 100 |
| The Laughing Cow Mini Babybel Light, 1 round | 50 |
| Seedless grapes, ½ cup | 60 |

**410 calories,** 6 g fat, 1.5 g saturated fat, 860 mg sodium, 77 g carbohydrate, 10 g fiber, 17 g protein, 32% calcium

## BOCA BURGER
★ ★ ★

Top the burger with the chili for a satisfying meatless meal.

| | calories |
|---|---:|
| Whole wheat bun, 1 | 110 |
| Boca Burger, Original, 1 patty | 100 |
| Bush's Best Red Beans in Chili Sauce, ¼ cup | 50 |
| Lettuce, 2 leaves | 10 |
| Tomato, 2 slices | 10 |
| Baby carrots, 10 | 40 |
| So Delicious Minis Chocolate Sandwich, 1 | 90 |

**410 calories,** 5.5 g fat, 1 g saturated fat, 952 mg sodium, 69 g carbohydrate, 18 g fiber, 29 g protein, 21% calcium

HEALTHY
CHOICE
MINESTRONE
SOUP
410

BOCA
BURGER
410

## *easy fix*

MORNINGSTAR
FARMS GRILLERS
PRIME VEGGIE
BURGERS

+

+

+

+

EQUALS
## 395
CALORIES

## TURKEY BURGER
★ ★

Cut up the cooked turkey burger and place it in the pita, along with tomato, cheese, and a squirt of ketchup.

| | calories |
|---|---|
| Perdue, Foster Farms, or other turkey burger, one 4-oz patty | 170 |
| Whole wheat pita, one 6" pita | 170 |
| Diced tomato, ¼ cup | 10 |
| Low-sodium ketchup, 1 Tbsp | 20 |
| Kraft 2% Milk Mexican Four Cheese Shreds, 1 Tbsp | 20 |

**390 calories,** 13 g fat, 4 g saturated fat, 510 mg sodium, 40 g carbohydrate, 7 g fiber, 28 g protein, 12% calcium

## MORNINGSTAR FARMS VEGGIE BURGER
★ ★ ★

Guacamole, or just plain mashed avocado, is a delicious good-fats alternative to standard burger spreads like mayonnaise.

| | calories |
|---|---|
| Wonder Stoneground 100% Whole Wheat Bread, 2 slices | 180 |
| Morningstar Farms Grillers Prime Veggie Burger, 1 patty | 170 |
| Lettuce, 2 leaves | 10 |
| Tomato, 2 slices | 10 |
| Guacamole, 1 Tbsp | 25 |

**395 calories,** 13.5 g fat, 1.5 g saturated fat, 836 mg sodium, 41 g carbohydrate, 9 g fiber, 24 g protein, 15% calcium

## CHICKEN OF THE SEA LIGHT TUNA POUCH
★

We like putting the tuna on the salad and broiling the English muffin with cheese on top.

| | calories |
|---|---|
| Chicken of the Sea Light Tuna Pouch, 3 oz | 90 |
| Pepperidge Farm 100% Whole Wheat English Muffin, 1 | 140 |
| Cabot 75% Reduced Fat Cheddar Cheese, 1 oz, shredded | 60 |
| Small salad, 1 cup, with 1 tsp walnuts and salad spray | 40 |
| Fudgsicle, 1.65-oz bar | 60 |

**390 calories,** 9.5 g fat, 3 g saturated fat, 965 mg sodium, 44 g carbohydrate, 4 g fiber, 37 g protein, 34% calcium

## DIGIORNO CLASSIC THIN CRUST FOUR CHEESE PIZZA

The freezer case is filled with different pizzas, so choose your favorite crust and topping. Pay attention to portion size, since it varies from brand to brand.

| | calories |
|---|---|
| DiGiorno Classic Thin Crust Four Cheese Pizza, ¼ of 19-oz pizza | 340 |
| Lemonade mixed with seltzer, ½ cup each | 60 |

**400 calories,** 15 g fat, 5 g saturated fat, 722 mg sodium, 53 g carbohydrate, 4 g fiber, 14 g protein, 20% calcium

DIGIORNO
CLASSIC THIN
CRUST
CHEESE PIZZA
400

### CALIFORNIA PIZZA KITCHEN FIVE CHEESE & TOMATO
★ ★

Feel free to swap to a different type of frozen, or even fresh, vegetable mix to put on top of your pizza.

| | calories |
|---|---|
| California Pizza Kitchen Five Cheese & Tomato, ⅓ of 12.6-oz pizza | 320 |
| Cascadian Farm Gardener's Blend, 1 cup | 80 |

**400 calories,** 15 g fat, 9 g saturated fat, 767 mg sodium, 45 g carbohydrate, 4 g fiber, 21 g protein, 35% calcium

### AMY'S CHEESE PIZZA
★

Amy's offers an organic option for pizza lovers.

| | calories |
|---|---|
| Amy's Cheese Pizza, ⅓ pizza | 290 |
| Cubed cantaloupe, 1 cup | 50 |
| Graham cracker squares, 2 | 60 |

**400 calories,** 13.5 g fat, 5 g saturated fat, 700 mg sodium, 57 g carbohydrate, 3 g fiber, 14 g protein, 22% calcium

### KASHI ROASTED VEGETABLE THIN CRUST PIZZA
★

We like to cook the extra vegetables and put them on top of the pizza. Any flavor of fat-free pudding is fine as long as the calories are the same.

| | calories |
|---|---|
| Kashi Roasted Vegetable Thin Crust Pizza, ⅓ pizza | 250 |
| Green Giant Garden Vegetable Medley, ½ cup cooked (1 cup frozen) | 70 |
| Hunt's Fat-Free Snack Pack Chocolate Pudding, 1 | 90 |

**410 calories,** 9.5 g fat, 4 g saturated fat, 990 mg sodium, 62 g carbohydrate, 6 g fiber, 18 g protein, 26% calcium

### SOUTH BEACH LIVING GRILLED CHICKEN & VEGETABLE PIZZA
★ ★

South Beach Living pizza is high in both protein and fiber to help make it more satiating. If you prefer a different frozen fruit bar, select brands with just fruit and without added cream or coconut.

| | calories |
|---|---|
| South Beach Living Grilled Chicken & Vegetable Pizza, 1 | 330 |
| Edy's Whole Fruit Strawberry Fruit Bar, 1 | 80 |

**410 calories,** 10 g fat, 4 g saturated fat, 620 mg sodium, 58 g carbohydrate, 11 g fiber, 30 g protein, 35% calcium

*easy fix*

AMY'S CHEESE PIZZA

+

+

EQUALS

**400 CALORIES**

## LEAN CUISINE CHICKEN TUSCAN PANINI
★ ★ ★

This panini sandwich has plenty of protein and is one of the lower-sodium packaged grilled sandwiches.

|  | calories |
|---|---|
| Lean Cuisine Chicken Tuscan Panini, 1 | 320 |
| Fruit salad, 1 cup | 100 |

**420 calories,** 7 g fat, 2 g saturated fat, 590 mg sodium, 67 g carbohydrate, 7 g fiber, 22 g protein, 0% calcium

## AMY'S MEXICAN CASSEROLE
★ ★

To brighten up the flavor of the juice, add a squeeze of lemon or lime juice plus a dash of Tabasco sauce.

|  | calories |
|---|---|
| Amy's Mexican Casserole (Light in Sodium), 1 serving | 370 |
| Low sodium V8 juice, 1 cup | 50 |

**420 calories,** 16 g fat, 5 g saturated fat, 531 mg sodium, 58 g carbohydrate, 9 g fiber, 14 g protein, 27% calcium

LEAN
CUISINE
CHICKEN
TUSCAN
PANINI
**420**

## AMY'S INDIAN MATTAR TOFU
★

To make Indian raita without adding extra calories, add chopped fresh mint and grated cucumber to the yogurt.

|  | calories |
|---|---|
| Amy's Indian Mattar Tofu, 1 package | 260 |
| Chobani Low Fat Plain Greek Yogurt, 6 oz | 130 |

**390 calories,** 11.5 g fat, 3 g saturated fat, 750 mg sodium, 44 g carbohydrate, 5 g fiber, 29 g protein, 20% calcium

## HEALTHY CHOICE BEEF TIPS PORTOBELLO
★ ★ ★ ★

Several companies offer beef entrées with about the same number of calories; any dish with 220 to 260 calories will keep you in the 400-calorie range for this meal.

| | calories |
| --- | ---: |
| Healthy Choice Beef Tips Portobello, 1 package | 260 |
| Large salad with 2 cups lettuce, 1 tomato, 1 Tbsp chopped walnuts, salad dressing spray | 110 |
| Fat-free Greek yogurt, ⅓ cup | 50 |

**420 calories,** 14 g fat, 2.5 g saturated fat, 628 mg sodium, 48 g carbohydrate, 8 g fiber, 26 g protein, 16% calcium

## WEIGHT WATCHERS SMART ONES STUFFED TURKEY BREAST
★ ★

Turkey makes us think of Thanksgiving, so we paired this entrée with a baked sweet potato and a quick baked apple made in the microwave.

| | calories |
| --- | ---: |
| Weight Watchers Smart Ones Stuffed Turkey Breast, 1 package | 290 |
| Baked sweet potato, 1 small | 50 |
| Apple, baked in the microwave, 1 small | 80 |

**420 calories,** 6 g fat, 2 g saturated fat, 893 mg sodium, 75 g carbohydrate, 10 g fiber, 19 g protein, 9% calcium

HEALTHY CHOICE BEEF TIPS PORTOBELLO
420

WEIGHT WATCHERS SMART ONES STUFFED TURKEY BREAST
420

## KASHI RANCHERO BEANS
★ ★

Beans are a sure bet for fiber and they're naturally low in fat. This vegetarian entrée comes with a whole grain pilaf; we've added a salad to round out the meal.

|  | calories |
|---|---|
| Kashi Ranchero Beans, 1 entrée | 340 |
| Small salad with 1 tsp walnuts, salad dressing spray | 40 |

**380 calories,** 10 g fat, 1 g saturated fat, 695 mg sodium, 61 g carbohydrate, 12 g fiber, 13 g protein, 8% calcium

## WEIGHT WATCHERS SMART ONES HONEY MANGO BARBECUE CHICKEN
★

Mango is among the more nutritious fruits, with vitamins A and C.

|  | calories |
|---|---|
| Weight Watchers Smart Ones Honey Mango Barbecue Chicken, 1 package | 240 |
| Progresso 50% Less Sodium Chicken Gumbo, 1 cup | 110 |
| Pineapple canned in juice, ½ cup | 50 |

**400 calories,** 5 g fat, 1.5 g saturated fat, 941 mg sodium, 67 g carbohydrate, 3 g fiber, 16 g protein, 8% calcium

# WE LOVE...

WE LOVE SWEET POTATOES. THEY FILL US UP EVEN THOUGH THEY'RE NOT VERY HIGH IN CALORIES, AND THEY'RE PACKED WITH NUTRIENTS LIKE VITAMINS A AND C. ROAST THEM IN THE REGULAR OVEN AND THEY'LL TURN CARAMEL SWEET.

KASHI RANCHERO BEANS
380

WEIGHT WATCHERS SMART ONES HONEY MANGO BARBECUE CHICKEN
400

### easy fix

MICHELINA'S
LEAN GOURMET
BEEF PEPPER
STEAK & RICE

+

+

### EQUALS

## 410

CALORIES

---

### HEALTHY CHOICE FRESH MIXERS ZITI & MEAT SAUCE
★ ★

We left the flavor of salad dressing up to you.

|  | calories |
|---|---|
| Healthy Choice Fresh Mixers Ziti & Meat Sauce, 1 | 340 |
| Large salad with 2 cups lettuce, 1 tomato, salad dressing spray | 60 |

**400 calories**, 9 g fat, 2 g saturated fat, 600 mg sodium, 66 g carbohydrate, 11 g fiber, 17 g protein, 8% calcium

### MICHELINA'S LEAN GOURMET BEEF PEPPER STEAK & RICE
★ ★

Any vegetables with up to 80 calories per serving are fine for this meal, or stick with the broccoli and carrots and add a green salad.

|  | calories |
|---|---|
| Michelina's Lean Gourmet Beef Pepper Steak & Rice, 1 package | 270 |
| Green Giant Broccoli & Carrots, ½ cup cooked (1¼ cup frozen) | 40 |
| Edy's Chocolate Vanilla Swirl Yogurt Blends, ½ cup | 100 |

**410 calories**, 7.5 g fat, 2.5 g saturated fat, 935 mg sodium, 78 g carbohydrate, 3 g fiber, 16 g protein, 6% calcium

---

### BIRDS EYE STEAMFRESH GRILLED CHICKEN IN ROASTED GARLIC SAUCE
★ ★

Birds Eye is best known for its vegetables, which are abundant in this quick dinner.

|  | calories |
|---|---|
| Birds Eye Steamfresh Grilled Chicken in Roasted Garlic Sauce, ½ bag | 340 |
| Fruit salad, ½ cup | 50 |

**390 calories,** 13 g fat, 5 g saturated fat, 880 mg sodium, 63 g carbohydrate, 8 g fiber, 18 g protein, 6% calcium

### LEAN POCKETS WHOLE GRAIN GRILLED CHICKEN, MUSHROOM & SPINACH
★ ★

We picked the lentil soup to add fiber to this meal, but any other soup with 130 to 170 calories is fine.

|  | calories |
|---|---|
| Lean Pockets Whole Grain Grilled Chicken, Mushroom & Spinach, 1 pocket | 250 |
| Amy's Organic Lentil Vegetable Soup, 1 cup | 150 |

**400 calories**, 10 g fat, 3.5 g saturated fat, 1,170 mg sodium, 60 g carbohydrate, 10 g fiber, 18 g protein, 26% calcium

## BIRDS EYE VOILA! BEEF AND BROCCOLI STIR FRY

★

Feel free to substitute another 100-calorie dessert of your choice.

| | calories |
|---|---|
| Birds Eye Voila! Beef and Broccoli Stir Fry, 1½ cups cooked | 310 |
| Nestlé Frozen Lemonade Cup, ⅓ container | 100 |

**410 calories,** 9 g fat, 2 g saturated fat, 1,060 mg sodium, 65 g carbohydrate, 3 g fiber, 15 g protein, 6% calcium

## LEAN CUISINE STEAK TIPS DIJON

★

Red wine is a perfect accompaniment to this French-inspired entrée.

| | calories |
|---|---|
| Lean Cuisine Steak Tips Dijon, 1 | 280 |
| Red wine, 5 oz | 120 |

**400 calories,** 7 g fat, 2.5 g saturated fat, 656 mg sodium, 37 g carbohydrate, 5 g fiber, 21 g protein, 1% calcium

## SOUTH BEACH LIVING CHICKEN CAESAR WRAP

★ ★ ★ ★

In this meal, the wrap sandwich dishes up a lot of fiber and protein, while the salad kit delivers veggies, plus almonds for good fats.

| | calories |
|---|---|
| South Beach Living Chicken Caesar Wrap, 1 | 230 |
| Dole Asian Island Crunch Salad Kit, 1½ cups | 130 |
| Breyer's Pure Fruit Fruit Bar, 1 | 40 |

**400 calories,** 18 g fat, 5 g saturated fat, 820 mg sodium, 46 g carbohydrate, 16 g fiber, 27 g protein, 25% calcium

## WEIGHT WATCHERS SMART ONES CHICKEN SANTA FE

★ ★

If you prefer, switch to Campbell's Healthy Request chicken soup with egg noodles for similar calories and nutrition. Tortilla sizes and weights vary a lot, so compare labels.

| | calories |
|---|---|
| Weight Watchers Smart Ones Chicken Santa Fe, 1 | 140 |
| Healthy Choice Old Fashioned Chicken Noodle Soup, 1 cup | 110 |
| Whole wheat tortilla, one 6" tortilla | 120 |
| Cubed cantaloupe, ½ cup | 25 |

**385 calories,** 4.5 g fat, 0 g saturated fat, 1,572 mg sodium, 63 g carbohydrate, 9 g fiber, 34 g protein, 9% calcium

*easy fix*

WEIGHT WATCHERS SMART ONES CHICKEN SANTA FE

+

+

+

EQUALS

**385** CALORIES

### *easy fix*

BETTY CROCKER
SUDDENLY
SALAD CLASSIC
PASTA SALAD MIX

+

+

+

**EQUALS**

## 380
CALORIES

---

## HEALTHY CHOICE ROASTED SESAME CHICKEN
★ ★ ★

For almost the same number of calories, you can have this entrée, Stouffer's Grilled Chicken Teriyaki, or, if you prefer meatless, Amy's Organic Asian Noodle Stir-Fry.

| | calories |
|---|---|
| Healthy Choice Roasted Sesame Chicken, 1 package | 340 |
| Mixed greens, 1 cup, with salad dressing spray | 30 |
| Blueberries, ½ cup | 40 |

**410 calories,** 10 g fat, 1.5 g saturated fat, 711 mg sodium, 69 g carbohydrate, 9 g fiber, 20 g protein, 8% calcium

---

## BETTY CROCKER SUDDENLY SALAD CLASSIC PASTA SALAD MIX
★

Pasta salad mixes save time because almost everything you need is in the box. We like to add vegetables to make the dish more filling.

| | calories |
|---|---|
| Betty Crocker Suddenly Salad Classic Pasta Salad Mix, ¾ cup prepared | 230 |
| Broccoli, 1 cup | 20 |
| Canned chickpeas, drained and rinsed, ⅓ cup | 90 |
| Shredded part-skim mozzarella cheese, 2 Tbsp | 40 |

**380 calories,** 11 g fat, 3 g saturated fat, 989 mg sodium, 59 g carbohydrate, 6 g fiber, 15 g protein, 15% calcium

---

## MRS. T'S POTATO & ONION PIEROGIES
★

Greek yogurt is a much lower-fat and lower-calorie alternative to regular sour cream, and it has more protein and calcium than fat-free sour cream.

| | calories |
|---|---|
| Mrs. T's Potato & Onion Pierogies, 4 | 230 |
| Fage Total 0% Yogurt, ½ cup | 60 |
| Campbell's Chunky Classic Chicken Noodle Soup, 1 cup | 110 |

**400 calories,** 5.5 g fat, 1 g saturated fat, 1,493 mg sodium, 65 g carbohydrate, 3 g fiber, 25 g protein, 17% calcium

---

## SEVIROLI SPINACH & CHEESE RAVIOLI
★ ★

Your local market may carry a regional brand of ravioli with similar calories. It's fine to switch to plain cheese, since there's too little spinach to make much nutritional difference.

| | calories |
|---|---|
| Seviroli Spinach & Cheese Ravioli, 5 | 200 |
| Classico Triple Mushroom Sauce, ½ cup | 70 |
| Broccoli, 1 cup steamed | 60 |
| Chopped garlic, 1 clove | 5 |
| Seedless grapes, ½ cup | 60 |

**395 calories,** 8 g fat, 3 g saturated fat, 469 mg sodium, 67 g carbohydrate, 10 g fiber, 17 g protein, 23% calcium

MRS. T'S
POTATO &
ONION
PIEROGIES
400

## AIDELLS CHICKEN AND TURKEY SAUSAGE WITH PORTOBELLO MUSHROOMS
★ ★

Most whole wheat pastas have similar calories, and we prefer them for their fiber and other nutrients. The pasta sauce flavor is up to you.

| | calories |
|---|---|
| Aidells Chicken and Turkey Sausage with Portobello Mushrooms, 3 oz | 130 |
| Whole wheat pasta, ⅔ cup cooked | 120 |
| Pasta sauce, ½ cup | 80 |
| Green Giant Asparagus Cuts (no sauce), ½ cup cooked (⅔ cup frozen) | 20 |
| Ocean Spray Light Cranberry Juice, 1 cup | 40 |

**390 calories,** 11.5 g fat, 2 g saturated fat, 1,233 mg sodium, 51 g carbohydrate, 5 g fiber, 23 g protein, 19% calcium

## BREADED FROZEN SHRIMP
★ ★

We couldn't recommend a specific brand of frozen shrimp because different brands are available in different stores. Keep your shrimp serving at no more than 250 calories.

| | calories |
|---|---|
| Breaded frozen shrimp, 7 | 240 |
| Uncle Ben's Ready Whole Grain Medley Vegetable Harvest, ½ cup | 110 |
| Green Giant Valley Fresh Steamers, Asian Style Medley, ½ cup cooked (1 cup frozen) | 50 |

**400 calories,** 13 g fat, 2 g saturated fat, 1,045 mg sodium, 56 g carbohydrate, 7 g fiber, 18 g protein, 6% calcium

## GORTON'S CLASSIC GRILLED SALMON
★ ★ ★

Packaged, prepared fish is a convenient freezer staple that cooks up quickly.

| | calories |
|---|---|
| Gorton's Classic Grilled Salmon, 1 fillet | 100 |
| Uncle Ben's Ready Rice Whole Grain Brown, ½ cup cooked | 110 |
| Green Giant Broccoli & Carrots (Family Size bag), 1 cup cooked (2½ cup frozen) | 80 |
| Nabisco Ginger Snaps, 4 cookies | 120 |

**410 calories,** 8 g fat, 0.5 g saturated fat, 868 mg sodium, 59 g carbohydrate, 5 g fiber, 23 g protein, 8% calcium

## BOCA MEATLESS GROUND CRUMBLES
★ ★ ★

Meat eaters will barely notice that the meat is missing. Pasta sauce varies a lot in calories, so if you're switching flavors, choose one with no more than 100 calories per half cup.

| | calories |
|---|---|
| Boca Meatless Ground Crumbles, ¼ cup | 60 |
| Whole wheat macaroni, ⅔ cup cooked | 120 |
| Muir Glen Italian Herb Pasta Sauce, ½ cup | 60 |
| Kraft Natural Shredded Low-Moisture Part-Skim Mozzarella, ¼ cup | 80 |
| Large salad with 2 cups lettuce, 1 tomato, salad dressing spray | 60 |

**380 calories,** 10 g fat, 3.5 g saturated fat, 843 mg sodium, 53 g carbohydrate, 11 g fiber, 28 g protein, 28% calcium

## WE LOVE...

WINE GOES WELL WITH FISH AND SEAFOOD, SO FEEL FREE TO SWAP ANY 120-CALORIE FOOD FOR A 5-OUNCE GLASS OF YOUR FAVORITE WHITE, ROSÉ, OR RED.

AIDELLS
CHICKEN
AND TURKEY
SAUSAGE WITH
PORTOBELLO
MUSHROOMS
390

GORTON'S
CLASSIC
GRILLED
SALMON
410

BREADED
FROZEN
SHRIMP
400

BOCA
MEATLESS
GROUND
CRUMBLES
380

# SNACKS/DESSERTS

## SOUTH BEACH LIVING CHOCOLATE PEANUT BUTTER CRISPY MEAL BAR
★ ★ ★

Buy ready-made fruit mix or make your own with your choice of fruits. Measure out the chopped dried fruit into ¼-cup portions and put them in plastic bags so that they're ready to go.

| | calories |
|---|---|
| South Beach Living Chocolate Peanut Butter Crispy Meal Bar, 1 | 210 |
| Dried fruit, ¼ cup | 120 |
| Cappuccino, 16 oz, made with 8 oz fat-free milk | 80 |

**410 calories,** 7 g fat, 3 g saturated fat, 440 mg sodium, 66 g carbohydrate, 8 g fiber, 28 g protein, 40% calcium

SOUTH BEACH LIVING CHOCOLATE PEANUT BUTTER CRISPY MEAL BAR
410

## HEALTHY CHOICE ICE CREAM SANDWICH
★ ★ ★

This snack has two parts—the ice cream sandwich and the fruit topped with granola and pistachios. For a healthy twist on a sundae, you can swap the ice cream sandwich for a scoop of ice cream or frozen yogurt with the same calories.

| | calories |
|---|---|
| Healthy Choice Ice Cream Sandwich, 1 | 130 |
| Fruit salad, 1 cup | 100 |
| Cascadian Farm Fruit and Nut Granola, ½ cup | 140 |
| Chopped pistachios, 1 Tbsp | 40 |

**410 calories,** 10 g fat, 2 g saturated fat, 181 mg sodium, 77 g carbohydrate, 8 g fiber, 9 g protein, 15% calcium

## KELLOGG'S NUTRI-GRAIN YOGURT BAR VANILLA YOGURT
★

Greek yogurts tend to be higher in calories because they are more concentrated—some of their liquid is removed to increase thickness. Any yogurt with between 140 and 180 calories will work in this meal.

| | calories |
|---|---|
| Kellogg's Nutri-Grain Yogurt Bar, Vanilla Yogurt, 1 | 140 |
| Fruit salad, 1 cup | 100 |
| Chobani Strawberry 0% Greek Yogurt, 6 oz | 140 |

**380 calories,** 4.5 g fat, 0.5 g saturated fat, 191 mg sodium, 71 g carbohydrate, 6 g fiber, 17 g protein, 42% calcium

## POWERBAR HARVEST DOUBLE CHOCOLATE CRISP

★ ★ ★

This bar is more like a meal replacement than a snack. You can swap a banana or a cup of fruit salad for the apple.

| | calories |
|---|---|
| PowerBar Harvest Double Chocolate Crisp, 1 | 250 |
| Apple, 1 medium | 100 |
| Unsalted sunflower seed kernels, 1 Tbsp | 50 |

**400 calories,** 9 g fat, 3 g saturated fat, 140 mg sodium, 69 g carbohydrate, 10 g fiber, 12 g protein, 0 calcium

## CHOCOLATE COCONUT LÄRABAR

★

LäraBars are made mostly from dried fruit and have a very chewy consistency. It's okay to substitute another light cheese for the string cheese.

| | calories |
|---|---|
| Chocolate Coconut LäraBar, 1 | 220 |
| Sargento Light String Cheese, 1 piece | 50 |
| Seedless grapes, 1 cup | 110 |

**380 calories,** 15.5 g fat, 4 g saturated fat, 180 mg sodium, 55 g carbohydrate, 6 g fiber, 11 g protein, 21% calcium

## CLIF MOJO HONEY ROASTED PEANUT BAR

★ ★

Shelf-stable servings of milk in aseptic drink boxes are easy to store and take with you. Fat-free or low-fat milk boxes can be hard to find, but feel free to make the swap if you can locate them.

| | calories |
|---|---|
| Clif Mojo Honey Roasted Peanut Bar, 1 | 200 |
| Dried apricots, 4 whole or 8 halves | 70 |
| Reduced-fat milk "box," 8 oz | 120 |

**390 calories,** 14.5 g fat, 5 g saturated fat, 320 mg sodium, 50 g carbohydrate, 4 g fiber, 19 g protein, 38% calcium

## KASHI TLC CHEWY TRAIL MIX GRANOLA BAR

★ ★ ★

This combo is easy to put together at home or buy when you're on the road. Mini-mart packs of peanuts are pretty big, so measure out your portion and save the rest for other meals.

| | calories |
|---|---|
| Kashi TLC Chewy Trail Mix Granola Bar, 1 | 140 |
| Dannon Light & Fit Yogurt, 6 oz | 80 |
| Peanuts, 1 Tbsp | 50 |
| Banana, 1 medium | 110 |

**380 calories,** 9.5 g fat, 1 g saturated fat, 185 mg sodium, 65 g carbohydrate, 8 g fiber, 13 g protein, 15% calcium

### *easy fix*

KASHI TLC CHEWY TRAIL MIX GRANOLA BAR

+

+

+

EQUALS

# 380
CALORIES

## *easy fix*

### HOMEMADE TRAIL MIX

+

+

+

EQUALS

## 400 CALORIES

## TRADITIONAL CHEX MIX

Chex Mix is a good vending machine option.

| | calories |
|---|---|
| Traditional Chex Mix, 1.75 oz | 220 |
| Snapple Iced Tea, 16 fl oz | 200 |

**420 calories,** 6.5 g fat, 1 g saturated fat, 651 mg sodium, 87 g carbohydrate, 2 g fiber, 3 g protein, 0% calcium

## HOMEMADE TRAIL MIX
★

The peanuts help make this snack more satisfying.

| | calories |
|---|---|
| 100-Calorie Pack Mini Teddy Grahams, 1 | 100 |
| Dried cherries and cranberries, 2 Tbsp each | 110 |
| Shelled peanuts, 2 Tbsp | 100 |
| Mini M&Ms, 4 tsp | 90 |

**400 calories,** 17 g fat, 4 g saturated fat, 128 mg sodium, 59 g carbohydrate, 5 g fiber, 7 g protein, 0% calcium

## LUNA CHOCOLATE PEPPERMINT STICK BAR
★ ★

Luna bars are designed for women—hence the high calcium count. Any flavor between 180 and 220 calories will fit into this snack.

| | calories |
|---|---|
| Luna Chocolate Peppermint Stick Bar, 1 | 180 |
| Latte made with 1 cup fat-free milk | 100 |
| Unsalted cashews, 2 Tbsp | 100 |

**380 calories,** 13 g fat, 4 g saturated fat, 245 mg sodium, 47 g carbohydrate, 4 g fiber, 22 g protein, 70% calcium

## NATURE VALLEY ROASTED ALMOND GRANOLA BAR
★

We like to put the trail mix on top of the yogurt and then crumble in the granola bar, but you can enjoy this meal any way you like.

| | calories |
|---|---|
| Nature Valley Roasted Almond Granola Bar, 1 | 90 |
| Trail mix, ¼ cup | 170 |
| Fage Total 2% Peach Yogurt, 5.3 oz | 130 |

**390 calories,** 17 g fat, 4 g saturated fat, 216 mg sodium, 49 g carbohydrate, 3 g fiber, 17 g protein, 13% calcium

## QUAKER CHEWY 90 CALORIE PEANUT BUTTER GRANOLA BARS

★

A mixed melon salad can take the place of the honeydew.

| | calories |
|---|---|
| Quaker Chewy 90 Calorie Peanut Butter Granola Bars, 2 | 180 |
| Hard-boiled eggs, 2 | 160 |
| Cubed honeydew, 1 cup | 60 |

**400 calories,** 15 g fat, 3 g saturated fat, 384 mg sodium, 52 g carbohydrate, 3 g fiber, 18 g protein, 27% calcium

## KELLOGG'S SPECIAL K CHOCOLATE PEANUT BUTTER PROTEIN MEAL BAR

★ ★

This meal is perfect for eating at your desk or on the go.

| | calories |
|---|---|
| Kellogg's Special K Protein Meal Bar Chocolate Peanut Butter, 1 | 180 |
| LäraBar Apple Pie Bar, 1 bar | 180 |
| Dried apricots, 4 halves | 30 |

**390 calories,** 16 g fat, 4.5 g saturated fat, 236 mg sodium, 56 g carbohydrate, 10 g fiber, 14 g protein, 26% calcium

## CHIPS AHOY CHOCOLATE CHIP PACKS 2 GO!

★

For 190 calories, you can choose any type of cookie. Portion sizes will vary.

| | calories |
|---|---|
| Chips Ahoy Chocolate Chip Packs 2 Go!, 1 pack | 190 |
| Low-fat or fat-free milk, 1 cup | 100 |
| Banana, 1 medium | 110 |

**400 calories,** 11.5 g fat, 4 g saturated fat, 247 mg sodium, 66 g carbohydrate, 4 g fiber, 11 g protein, 29% calcium

## SNYDER'S OF HANOVER HONEY WHEAT STICKS

★ ★

Honey wheat pretzels have become pretty popular—for good reason—and calories are about the same from brand to brand. As an alternative to the string cheese, have four wedges of The Laughing Cow Light cheese. They're only 35 calories each.

| | calories |
|---|---|
| Snyder's of Hanover Honey Wheat Sticks, 1 oz | 120 |
| Kraft String-Ums, String Cheese, 2 pieces | 160 |
| Baby carrots, 10 | 40 |
| Apple, 1 medium | 100 |

**420 calories,** 14 g fat, 7 g saturated fat, 670 mg sodium, 59 g carbohydrate, 9 g fiber, 18 g protein, 33% calcium

*easy fix*

SNYDER'S OF HANOVER HONEY WHEAT STICKS

+

+

+

EQUALS

**420**
CALORIES

# BREAKFAST

## STARBUCKS APPLE BRAN MUFFIN
★

Be sure to look up nutrition info before walking into Starbucks in a caffeine-deprived fog. But a few of their baked goodies do fit into a 400-calorie framework, like the apple bran muffin, which even qualifies for a fiber star. Fat-free milk and sugar-free syrup options help make Starbucks coffees a nutritionally smart option.

| | calories |
|---|---|
| Starbucks Apple Bran Muffin, 1 | 310 |
| Starbucks Skinny Caramel Latte, tall (12 oz) | 90 |

**400 calories,** 7 g fat, 2 g saturated fat, 565 mg sodium, 72 g carbohydrate, 7 g fiber, 15 g protein, 50% calcium

STARBUCKS
APPLE BRAN
MUFFIN
**400**

## STARBUCKS PERFECT OATMEAL
★

Starbucks offers this tasty and satisfying breakfast at a discounted price, making it an even better nutrition bargain. We hope that it stays on the menu forever.

| | calories |
|---|---|
| Starbucks Perfect Oatmeal, 1 bowl | 140 |
| Starbucks Nut Medley, 1 packet | 100 |
| Starbucks Brown Sugar, 1 packet | 50 |
| Starbucks Skinny Latte, tall (12 oz) | 100 |

**390 calories,** 11.5 g fat, 1.5 g saturated fat, 225 mg sodium, 55 g carbohydrate, 5 g fiber, 17 g protein, 47% calcium

## DUNKIN' DONUTS EGG WHITE TURKEY SAUSAGE FLATBREAD SANDWICH
★ ★

Not a bad combo for a donut chain, and the sandwich has plenty of protein. You can have a coffee drink instead of the juice, but you'll lose the fruits/veggies star.

| | calories |
|---|---|
| Dunkin' Donuts Egg White Turkey Sausage Flatbread Sandwich, 1 | 280 |
| Orange juice, 1 cup | 110 |

**390 calories,** 6.5 g fat, 2.5 g saturated fat, 820 mg sodium, 62 g carbohydrate, 3 g fiber, 21 g protein, 17% calcium

## DUNKIN' DONUTS GLAZED DONUT

The reality is that sometimes you just have to have a donut, and this meal shows how to make it work for 400 calories. To earn this meal a fruits/veggies star, switch to a small cappuccino and bring a cup of fruit salad from home.

|  | calories |
| --- | --- |
| Dunkin' Donuts glazed donut, 1 | 220 |
| Dunkin' Donuts Coffee Coolatta with milk, small (16 oz) | 170 |

**390 calories,** 13 g fat, 6.5 g saturated fat, 395 mg sodium, 60 g carbohydrate, 1 g fiber, 7 g protein, 15% calcium

## CHICK-FIL-A CHICKEN BREAKFAST BURRITO
★

A fast-food chicken chain may not be an automatic pick for breakfast, but this chicken burrito fits the bill.

|  | calories |
| --- | --- |
| Chick-fil-A Chicken Breakfast Burrito, 1 | 410 |

**410 calories,** 18 g fat, 7 g saturated fat, 890 mg sodium, 41 g carbohydrate, 4 g fiber, 22 g protein, 25% calcium

DUNKIN'
DONUTS
GLAZED
DONUT
390

## MCDONALD'S EGG MCMUFFIN

★

The original fast-food breakfast, an Egg McMuffin is not as high in calories as you might think. Café-style drinks make breakfast even more enjoyable.

| | calories |
|---|---|
| McDonald's Egg McMuffin, 1 | 300 |
| McDonald's Nonfat Cappuccino, large (20 oz) | 90 |

**390 calories,** 12 g fat, 5 g saturated fat, 950 mg sodium, 43 g carbohydrate, 2 g fiber, 27 g protein, 65% calcium

# LUNCH/DINNER

## MCDONALD'S HAMBURGER

If you have to have a burger, the smallest one on the menu generally is the smartest pick. And why not end the meal with an ice cream, which happens to be pretty low in fat?

| | calories |
|---|---|
| McDonald's Hamburger, 1 | 250 |
| McDonald's Vanilla Ice Cream Cone, 1 | 150 |

**400 calories,** 12.5 g fat, 5.5 g saturated fat, 580 mg sodium, 55 g carbohydrate, 2 g fiber, 16 g protein, 20% calcium

## BURGER KING DOUBLE HAMBURGER

★

It's hard to pick a winner in the burger wars, so use nutrition info to pick a burger that fits into the 400-calorie framework.

| | calories |
|---|---|
| Burger King Double Hamburger, 1 | 420 |

**420 calories,** 22 g fat, 9 g saturated fat, 590 mg sodium, 30 g carbohydrate, fiber n/a, 26 g protein, calcium n/a

## BURGER KING BK VEGGIE BURGER
★ ★

Vegetarians are out of luck at most burger places. We hope more chains will follow the lead of Burger King and put a veggie burger on the menu.

| | calories |
|---|---|
| Burger King BK Veggie Burger (no mayo), 1 | 340 |
| American cheese, 1 slice | 45 |

**385 calories,** 12 g fat, 3.5 g saturated fat, 1,250 mg sodium, 47 g carbohydrate, 7 g fiber, 25 g protein, calcium n/a

## WENDY'S CHILI
★ ★

Chili tends to be really filling and is a good alternative to a burger.

| | calories |
|---|---|
| Wendy's Chili, large, 1 | 280 |
| Wendy's Saltine Crackers, 1 package | 30 |
| Wendy's Shredded Cheddar Cheese, 2 Tbsp | 70 |

**380 calories,** 15.5 g fat, 6.5 g saturated fat, 1,425 mg sodium, 35 g carbohydrate, 7 g fiber, 26 g protein, calcium n/a

WENDY'S CHILI 380

## PIZZA HUT FIT 'N DELICIOUS GREEN PEPPER, RED ONION & DICED RED TOMATO PIZZA
★ ★

It can be surprisingly hard to craft a balanced 400-calorie meal at a pizza chain. Here, we asked for extra veggies on top and brought along an orange for dessert. The Fit 'n Delicious pizza gave us the best balance of crust, cheese, and vegetables for the calories.

| | calories |
|---|---|
| 12" Fit 'n Delicious Green Pepper, Red Onion & Diced Red Tomato Pizza, 2 slices | 300 |
| Extra pepper, onion, tomato topping, ¾ cup | 50 |
| Orange, 1 medium | 70 |

**420 calories,** 8 g fat, 3 g saturated fat, 805 mg sodium, 76 g carbohydrates, 10 g fiber, 15 g protein, 8% calcium

## DOMINO'S HAWAIIAN FEAST BROOKLYN CRUST PIZZA
★

Take a look at Domino's online or in-store nutrition info ahead of time so that you can order your favorites in the right 400-calorie combo of crust and toppings. To round out calories and boost satiety, we added a side salad.

| | calories |
|---|---|
| Domino's 14" Hawaiian Feast Brooklyn Crust Pizza, 1 slice | 310 |
| Domino's Garden Fresh Salad, 1 | 70 |
| Domino's Light Italian Dressing, 1 packet | 20 |

**400 calories,** 17 g fat, 8.5 g saturated fat, 1,710 mg sodium, 40 g carbohydrates, 4 g fiber, 19 g protein, 30% calcium

*ADD...*

**ADD AS MANY EXTRA VEGGIES** as possible. They have almost no calories, add nutrition, and make your meal bigger and more satisfying.

## ARBY'S MARKET FRESH CHOPPED FARMHOUSE GRILLED CHICKEN SALAD
★ ★

Arby's is best known for beef sandwiches, but this salad is a good alternative. You'll have to ask for the bun since it doesn't come standard with the salad.

| | calories |
|---|---|
| Arby's Market Fresh Chopped Farmhouse Grilled Chicken Salad, 1 | 260 |
| Arby's Balsamic Vinaigrette Dressing, 1 Tbsp | 40 |
| Arby's Sesame Bun, ½ regular bun | 90 |

**390 calories,** 18.5 g fat, 8.5 g saturated fat, 1,084 mg sodium, 29 g carbohydrate, 3 g fiber, 29 g protein, 25% calcium

## UNO CHICAGO GRILL SPINACH, CHICKEN & GORGONZOLA SALAD
★ ★

A dependable option in the airport terminal, Uno offers several different salads. If you can get Wi-Fi service, check out calorie counts on Uno's Web site before ordering something other than the salad below.

| | calories |
|---|---|
| Uno Chicago Grill Spinach, Chicken & Gorgonzola Salad | 370 |
| Breadstick, ¼ | 50 |
| Half-Half Lemonade + Diet Iced Tea, 20 oz | 0 |

**420 calories,** 25 g fat, 5.5 g saturated fat, 745 mg sodium, 29 g carbohydrate, 4 g fiber, 22 g protein, 15% calcium

## MCDONALD'S PREMIUM SOUTHWEST SALAD WITH GRILLED CHICKEN
★ ★

To stay at the 400-calorie threshold, ask for your chicken grilled and request just one packet of low-fat dressing. A fully loaded salad with crispy chicken and regular dressing has more than 500 calories.

| | calories |
|---|---|
| McDonald's Premium Southwest Salad with Grilled Chicken, 1 | 320 |
| McDonald's Newman's Own Low Fat Family Recipe Italian Dressing, 1 packet | 60 |

**380 calories,** 11.5 g fat, 3 g saturated fat, 1,690 mg sodium, 38 g carbohydrate, 6 g fiber, 31 g protein, 15% calcium

## JACK IN THE BOX ASIAN CHICKEN SALAD WITH GRILLED CHICKEN
★ ★ ★ ★

This meal is packed with nutrition. Just watch the amount of dressing you use to avoid going over the calorie limit.

| | calories |
|---|---|
| Jack in the Box Asian Chicken Salad with Grilled Chicken, 1 | 180 |
| Roasted slivered almonds, 1 order (3 Tbsp) | 110 |
| Asian sesame dressing, ½ serving (2 Tbsp) | 100 |

**390 calories,** 17.5 g fat, 1.5 g saturated fat, 700 mg sodium, 34 g carbohydrate, 8 g fiber, 27 g protein, calcium n/a

# WENDY'S MANDARIN CHICKEN SALAD WITH GRILLED CHICKEN BREAST

★ ★ ★

Personalize your salad by asking for grilled chicken—less than half the calories of spicy or homestyle—skipping the crispy noodles, and using half the packet of dressing.

| | calories |
|---|---|
| Wendy's Mandarin Chicken Salad with Grilled Chicken Breast, 1 | 180 |
| Wendy's Roasted Almonds, 1 packet | 130 |
| Wendy's Oriental Sesame Dressing, ½ packet | 90 |

**400 calories,** 18 g fat, 2.5 g saturated fat, 880 mg sodium, 30 g carbohydrate, 4 g fiber, 29 g protein, calcium n/a

# KFC ROASTED CHICKEN CAESAR SALAD

★ ★

Now that KFC has added roasted chicken to its menu, putting together a 400-calorie meal is much easier. Be sure to ask for the fat-free dressing. Otherwise, your salad may have more calories than the fried chicken that you're trying to resist.

| | calories |
|---|---|
| KFC Roasted Chicken Caesar Salad, 1 | 190 |
| Hidden Valley The Original Ranch Fat Free Dressing, 1 packet | 40 |
| Parmesan Garlic Croutons, 1 pouch | 70 |
| KFC Home-Style Biscuit, ⅔ | 120 |

**420 calories,** 14.5 g fat, 7 g saturated fat, 1,435 mg sodium, 36 g carbohydrate, 4 g fiber, 35 g protein, calcium n/a

WENDY'S MANDARIN CHICKEN SALAD
400

KFC ROASTED CHICKEN CAESAR SALAD
420

AU BON PAIN
THAI PEANUT
CHICKEN
SALAD
400

COSI
SIGNATURE
SALAD LIGHT
370

## AU BON PAIN THAI PEANUT CHICKEN SALAD

★ ★ ★

Each regular-size oatmeal cookie has 230 calories and it's just too hard to stop at a half, so we opted for the mini cookies instead.

|  | calories |
| --- | --- |
| Au Bon Pain Thai Peanut Chicken Salad, 1 | 240 |
| Au Bon Pain Thai Peanut Dressing, 1 Tbsp | 40 |
| Au Bon Pain Mini Oatmeal Raisin Cookies, 2 | 120 |

**400 calories,** 14 g fat, 2 g saturated fat, 565 mg sodium, 42 g carbohydrate, 6 g fiber, 25 g protein, calcium n/a

## COSI OUR LIGHTER SIDE SIGNATURE SALAD

★ ★

No guesswork involved with this meal, which includes a delicious mix of greens, fruits, nuts, and cheese. Note, however, that the Cosi bread (which is included with the meal) adds 265 calories.

|  | calories |
| --- | --- |
| Cosi Our Lighter Side Signature Salad (with light dressing, no bread), 1 | 370 |

**370 calories,** 19 g fat, saturated fat n/a, 485 mg sodium, 45 g carbohydrate, 5 g fiber, 9 g protein, calcium n/a

## STARBUCKS TARRAGON CHICKEN SALAD SANDWICH

★

On its own, this sandwich goes over the 400-calorie limit, so eat half and take the other half home. Starbucks menu options vary regionally.

|  | calories |
| --- | --- |
| Starbucks Tarragon Chicken Salad Sandwich, ½ sandwich | 240 |
| Starbucks Mocha Frappuccino Light Blended Coffee, grande (16 oz) | 140 |

**380 calories,** 6.5 g fat, 1 g saturated fat, 835 mg sodium, 60 g carbohydrate, 5 g fiber, 23 g protein, calcium n/a

## CHIPOTLE SALAD

★ ★ ★

All salads are made to order, so you can ask for exactly what you want. Take a look at the menu or Web site to find additional topping options.

|  | calories |
| --- | --- |
| Romaine lettuce, 2.5 oz | 10 |
| Black beans, 4 oz | 120 |
| Fajita vegetables, 2.5 oz | 20 |
| Cilantro-lime rice, 3 oz | 130 |
| Tomato salsa, 3.5 oz | 20 |
| Cheese, 1 oz | 100 |

**400 calories,** 13 g fat, 5.5 g saturated fat, 1,225 mg sodium, 56 g carbohydrate, 14 g fiber, 20 g protein, 32% calcium

**SOME SALADS** have more calories than a burger and fries because they're drenched in regular dressing—as much as 400 calories or more in a 2-ounce packet.

## UNO CHICAGO GRILL GRILLED CHICKEN SANDWICH
★

Look up or ask about calorie counts before you order, since Uno changes its menu often.

|  | calories |
|---|---|
| Uno Chicago Grill Grilled Chicken Sandwich, 1 | 380 |

**380 calories,** 13 g fat, 3 g saturated fat, 1,010 mg sodium, 34 g carbohydrate, 2 g fiber, 34 g protein, 8% calcium

## DQ GRILLED CHICKEN WRAP

Here's a way to enjoy fast-food fries and even have a small sandwich.

|  | calories |
|---|---|
| DQ Grilled Chicken Wrap, 1 | 200 |
| DQ Fries, child size | 190 |
| Ketchup, 1 Tbsp | 15 |

**405 calories,** 20 g fat, 4 g saturated fat, 1,017 mg sodium, 40 g carbohydrate, 3 g fiber, 14 g protein, 10% calcium

## ARBY'S SUPER ROAST BEEF SANDWICH
★

The type of sandwich Arby's is best known for.

|  | calories |
|---|---|
| Arby's Super Roast Beef Sandwich, 1 regular | 430 |

**430 calories,** 18 g fat, 6 g saturated fat, 1,070 mg sodium, 44 g carbohydrate, 3 g fiber, 20 g protein, 8% calcium

## CHICK-FIL-A CHARGRILLED CHICKEN SANDWICH
★ ★

Mayonnaise is a notorious calorie buster, so it's best to go without it or ask for light mayo. This chain is one of the few that offers a light option, as well as fruit salad.

|  | calories |
|---|---|
| Chick-fil-A Chargrilled Chicken Sandwich, 1 | 260 |
| Light mayonnaise, 1 packet | 40 |
| Chick-fil-A Fruit Cup, 1 | 100 |

**400 calories,** 7 g fat, 1 g saturated fat, 1,385 mg sodium, 60 g carbohydrate, 10 g fiber, 28 g protein, 8% calcium

## KFC TOASTED WRAP WITH TENDER ROAST FILET
★ ★

Ordering dishes without sauce or with sauce on the side is a good habit to get into, since most sauces are surprisingly high in calories.

|  | calories |
|---|---|
| KFC Toasted Wrap with Tender Roast Filet (no sauce), 1 | 250 |
| KFC Honey BBQ Dipping Sauce, 1 packet | 40 |
| KFC Corn on the Cob, 3" | 70 |
| KFC Green Beans, 1 order | 25 |

**385 calories,** 8.5 g fat, 3.5 g saturated fat, 1,340 mg sodium, 54 g carbohydrate, 5 g fiber, 25 g protein, calcium n/a

## PANERA BREAD FUJI APPLE CHICKEN SALAD

★ ★

People love Panera Bread for its generous portions and tasty food. Unfortunately, larger portions mean more calories. Share this salad with a friend or pack up half for tomorrow.

| | calories |
|---|---|
| Panera Bread Fuji Apple Chicken Salad, ½ salad | 190 |
| Reduced Sugar Asian-Sesame Vinaigrette, ¾ order | 70 |
| Panera Bread Whole Grain Loaf, two 1-oz slices | 140 |

**400 calories,** 16.5 g fat, 3 g saturated fat, 870 mg sodium, 41 g carbohydrate, 6 g fiber, 21 g protein, 10% calcium

PANERA BREAD FUJI APPLE CHICKEN SALAD
**370**

## BAJA FRESH BAJA ENSALADA WITH SAVORY PORK CARNITAS

★ ★ ★

Using pico de gallo or salsa instead of salad dressing saves lots of calories and gives your salad a spicy kick.

| | calories |
|---|---|
| Baja Fresh Baja Ensalada with Savory Pork Carnitas, 1 | 370 |
| Baja Fresh Pico de Gallo, ½ cup | 25 |

**395 calories,** 18 g fat, 6 g saturated fat, 1,855 mg sodium, 26 g carbohydrate, 9 g fiber, 36 g protein, calcium n/a

BAJA FRESH BAJA ENSALADA WITH SAVORY PORK CARNITAS
**395**

BOSTON MARKET ¼ WHITE ROTISSERIE CHICKEN
400

## BOSTON MARKET ¼ WHITE ROTISSERIE CHICKEN
★ ★

Chicken has a membrane that separates the skin from the meat, so cooking with the skin on keeps the meat moist but doesn't infuse it with fat. Remove the skin before eating, of course.

| | calories |
|---|---|
| Boston Market ¼ White Rotisserie Chicken, no skin, 1 | 240 |
| Boston Market Garlic Dill New Potatoes, ½ cup | 100 |
| Boston Market Side Caesar Salad (without dressing), 1 | 40 |
| Boston Market Lite Ranch Dressing, 1 Tbsp | 20 |

**400 calories,** 9 g fat, 3.5 g saturated fat, 1,155 mg sodium, 24 g carbohydrate, 3 g fiber, 55 g protein, calcium n/a

## QUIZNOS TUSCAN TURKEY ON ROSEMARY PARMESAN ROLL
★ ★

Sandwich chains usually are a good bet because you can customize your sandwich to get exactly what you want. Of all the sandwich fillings, turkey breast is lowest in calories.

| | calories |
|---|---|
| Quizno's Tuscan Turkey on Rosemary Parmesan Roll (no dressing), 1 | 340 |
| Orange, 1 medium | 70 |

**410 calories,** 10 g fat, 2.5 g saturated fat, 1,080 mg sodium, 62 g carbohydrate, 5 g fiber, 22 g protein, calcium n/a

## PANERA BREAD SMOKED TURKEY BREAST SANDWICH ON SOURDOUGH
★ ★

Panera always offers several different soups, with calorie info available in an in-store brochure. Bean soups are particularly high in fiber and good for keeping hunger at bay.

| | calories |
|---|---|
| Panera Bread Smoked Turkey Breast Sandwich on Sourdough (no mayonnaise), ½ sandwich | 240 |
| Panera Bread Low-Fat Vegetarian Black Bean Soup, 8 oz | 150 |

**390 calories,** 5 g fat, 0 g saturated fat, 2,320 mg sodium, 69 g carbohydrate, 13 g fiber, 27 g protein, 9% calcium

QUIZNOS TUSCAN TURKEY ON ROSEMARY PARMESAN ROLL
**410**

## BOSTON MARKET ROASTED TURKEY

★ ★ ★

Use your 400 Calorie Lens to estimate portion size, since portions can vary from server to server and may be bigger or smaller than what we recommend.

| | calories |
|---|---|
| Boston Market Roasted Turkey, 5 oz | 180 |
| Boston Market Poultry Gravy, 4 oz | 50 |
| Boston Market Fresh Steamed Vegetables, 1 order | 60 |
| Boston Market Garlic Spinach, 1 order | 130 |

**420 calories,** 16 g fat, 7.5 g saturated fat, 1,550 mg sodium, 24 g carbohydrate, 8 g fiber, 45 g protein, calcium n/a

## COSI HUMMUS AND FRESH VEGGIES SANDWICH

★

Hummus is made from chickpeas and generally is a healthy option.

| | calories |
|---|---|
| Cosi Hummus and Fresh Veggies Sandwich, 1 | 400 |

**400 calories,** 7 g fat, saturated fat n/a, 592 mg sodium, 72 g carbohydrate, 7 g fiber, 13 g protein, calcium n/a

## SUBWAY OVEN ROASTED CHICKEN SANDWICH

★

Pile on extra veggies for a more substantial sandwich.

| | calories |
|---|---|
| Subway Double Oven Roasted Chicken Sandwich on 9-grain bread with lettuce, tomato, onion, bell peppers, and mustard, 6" | 400 |

**400 calories,** 8 g fat, 2.5 g saturated fat, 1,160 mg sodium, 51 g carbohydrate, 6 g fiber, 38 g protein, 8% calcium

## AU BON PAIN SALMON SALSA VERDE SANDWICH

★ ★

As with most sandwiches, this one is too big for just one meal. A vegetable-based soup rounds out the meal nicely and makes it more filling.

| | calories |
|---|---|
| Au Bon Pain Salmon Salsa Verde Sandwich, ½ sandwich | 280 |
| Au Bon Pain Carrot Ginger Soup, medium | 140 |

**420 calories,** 12 g fat, 2.5 g saturated fat, 1,460 mg sodium, 55 g carbohydrate, 4 g fiber, 19 g protein, calcium n/a

SUBWAY VEGGIE DELITE
410

## SUBWAY VEGGIE DELITE
★ ★

Subway spokesman Jared lost a lot of weight eating 6" sandwiches from Subway. The trick is to avoid straying to a bigger size and to say no to Subway's oil-based dressing. You can substitute Chicken Tortilla Soup for the tomato soup if it's available.

|  | calories |
|---|---|
| Subway Veggie Delite on 9-grain bread with provolone cheese, 6" sandwich | 280 |
| Subway Fire-Roasted Tomato Orzo Soup, 1 | 130 |

**410 calories,** 8 g fat, 3.5 g saturated fat, 1,035 mg sodium, 68 g carbohydrate, 7 g fiber, 19 g protein, 26% calcium

## CHIPOTLE CRISP TACO
★ ★ ★

You can combine dishes any number of ways to get to 400 calories at Chipotle.

|  | calories |
|---|---|
| Taco shells, 2 | 120 |
| Steak, 4 oz | 190 |
| Romaine lettuce, 1 oz | 5 |
| Guacamole, ¼ cup | 90 |
| Green Tomatillo Salsa, 2 Tbsp | 10 |

**415 calories,** 18 g fat, 4 g saturated fat, 564 mg sodium, 27 g carbohydrate, 7 g fiber, 34 g protein, 8% calcium

TACO BELL FRESCO CHICKEN BURRITO SUPREME
410

## TACO BELL FRESCO CHICKEN BURRITO SUPREME
★ ★

Choose foods from Taco Bell's Fresco menu for items that are a bit lower in calories and higher in nutrition. Guacamole is rich in healthy MUFAs.

|  | calories |
|---|---|
| Taco Bell Fresco Chicken Burrito Supreme, 1 | 340 |
| Taco Bell Guacamole side, 1 order | 70 |

**410 calories,** 13 g fat, 3.5 g saturated fat, 1,560 mg sodium, 54 g carbohydrate, 8 g fiber, 19 g protein, calcium n/a

## QDOBA MEXICAN GUMBO
★ ★

The combination of fiber-rich beans and protein-rich chicken makes this a particularly satisfying meal. To turn up the heat, add a tablespoon of salsa.

|  | calories |
|---|---|
| Qdoba Mexican Gumbo with pinto beans, chicken, 1 bowl | 410 |

**410 calories,** 15 g fat, 4 g saturated fat, 1,580 mg sodium, 32 g carbohydrate, 10 g fiber, 35 g protein, 6% calcium

IF ALL YOUR sandwich choices are too high in calories, eat half and round out your meal with soup and/or salad.

## PANDA EXPRESS BROCCOLI BEEF
★

Just because you're hungry an hour after eating Chinese food doesn't mean that it's low in calories. For more variety, take a couple of friends and order more dishes to share.

| | calories |
|---|---|
| Panda Express Broccoli Beef, 1 order | 150 |
| Panda Express Steamed Rice, ⅔ cup | 260 |

**410 calories,** 6 g fat, 1.5 g saturated fat, 720 mg sodium, 69 g carbohydrate, 3 g fiber, 16 g protein, calcium n/a

## LONG JOHN SILVER'S GRILLED PACIFIC SALMON
★ ★

Salmon is available on so many menus that you can enjoy this MUFA-rich food almost anywhere. Use your 400 Calorie Lens to make sure that portions are close to the size we recommend.

| | calories |
|---|---|
| Long John Silver's Grilled Pacific Salmon, 2 fillets | 150 |
| Long John Silver's Vegetable Medley, 4 oz | 50 |
| Long John Silver's Rice, ¾ cup | 180 |

**380 calories,** 8 g fat, 2 g saturated fat, 1,270 mg sodium, 47 g carbohydrate, 5 g fiber, 29 g protein, 8% calcium

PANDA EXPRESS BROCCOLI BEEF 410

# SNACKS/DESSERTS

## PANDA EXPRESS CHICKEN POTSTICKERS
★

Not the most nutritious meal, but a snack to consider during a long afternoon of shopping at the mall. Soy sauce will push up the sodium but doesn't add calories.

| | calories |
|---|---|
| Panda Express Chicken Potstickers, 3 | 220 |
| Panda Express Veggie Spring Roll, 2 | 160 |
| Panda Express fortune cookie, 1 | 30 |

**410 calories,** 19 g fat, 3.5 g saturated fat, 908 mg sodium, 55 g carbohydrate, 8 g fiber, 11 g protein, calcium n/a

## JAMBA JUICE MEGA MANGO
★ ★

This smoothie is all fruit, but Jamba has plenty of others made with milk or yogurt. Calories can vary widely, depending on size and ingredients.

| | calories |
|---|---|
| Jamba Juice Mega Mango, 16 oz | 230 |
| Jamba Juice Omega-3 Chocolate Brownie Cookie, 1 | 150 |

**380 calories,** 4 g fat, 1 g saturated fat, 15 mg sodium, 87 g carbohydrate, 6 g fiber, 5 g protein, 6% calcium

## AU BON PAIN STRAWBERRY SMOOTHIE
★

The bigger the cup, the greater the calories, so stick with the medium size.

| | calories |
|---|---|
| Au Bon Pain Strawberry Smoothie, medium | 310 |
| Au Bon Pain Chocolate Covered Pretzel, 1 pretzel | 80 |

**390 calories,** 4 g fat, 2 g saturated fat, 215 mg sodium, 78 g carbohydrate, 3 g fiber, 6 g protein, calcium n/a

## DQ CHOCOLATE DIPPED CONE
Yum! Just wish it could be bigger.

| | calories |
|---|---|
| DQ Chocolate Dipped Cone, 1 small | 330 |
| DQ Rainbow Sprinkles, 1 serving | 70 |

**400 calories,** 17.5 g fat, 7 g saturated fat, 105 mg sodium, 52 g carbohydrate, 0 g fiber, 6 g protein, 20% calcium

JAMBA JUICE MEGA MANGO
380

# FIXES

**1** Pick the smallest size possible, usually a single burger, regular-size hot dog, small fries, or small shake.

**2** Have it your way and take control of your order by specifying what you do and don't want. Ask for no sauce or mayonnaise. Specify the type of bun or bread you want. Bulk up your meal by requesting calorie-safe toppings like lettuce, tomato, sliced onions, and pickles, along with ketchup and mustard. Say no to supersizing and value meals that add extra items.

**3** Look up or ask for calorie information from your favorite chain, since portion sizes and definitions can vary, especially with fries. Medium fries at McDonald's, for example, have 100 fewer calories than medium fries at Burger King.

**4** Splitting an order with a friend is a good way to keep calories under control.

### FISH SANDWICH
- FILET-O-FISH SANDWICH (McDonald's) 380 calories
- PREMIUM FISH FILLET SANDWICH, WITHOUT TARTAR SAUCE (Wendy's) 390 calories
- BK BIG FISH SANDWICH, WITHOUT TARTAR SAUCE (Burger King) 460 calories

### POTATOES AND ONION RINGS
- SOUR CREAM AND CHIVES POTATO (Wendy's) 320 calories
- SMALL FRIES (Burger King) 340 calories
- MEDIUM FRIES (McDonald's) 380 calories
- MEDIUM ONION RINGS (Burger King) 450 calories

### BURGER
- DOUBLE STACK (Wendy's) 345 calories
- ½ DOUBLE WHOPPER, WITHOUT MAYO (Burger King) 380 calories
- QUARTER POUNDER (McDonald's) 410 calories
- DOUBLE HAMBURGER (Burger King) 420 calories

# 400 CALORIE DRIVE THRU

WE ALL KNOW THAT FAST FOOD can be fattening, but close to half of us love fast food too much to give it up, according to a February 2009 Synovate survey. If you eat smart, you can eat in a 400-calorie way at the drive thru.

## GRILLED CHICKEN SANDWICH

- TENDERGRILL CHICKEN SANDWICH, WITH KETCHUP, NO MAYO (Burger King) 380 calories
- 1½ GRILLED CHICKEN GO WRAPS (Wendy's) 380 calories
- 1½ GRILLED CHICKEN HONEY MUSTARD SNACK WRAPS (McDonald's) 390 calories

## BREADED CHICKEN SANDWICH

- CRISPY CHICKEN SANDWICH (Wendy's) 360 calories
- MCCHICKEN SANDWICH (McDonalds) 360 calories
- ½ TENDERCRISP CHICKEN SANDWICH (Burger King) 400 calories

## CHICKEN NUGGETS

- 8 CHICKEN TENDERS (Burger King) 360 calories
- 8 CHICKEN NUGGETS (Wendy's) 380 calories
- 7½ CHICKEN MCNUGGETS WITH 1 PACKAGE BARBEQUE SAUCE (McDonald's) 400 calories

## HOT DOGS

- ORIGINAL CHILI CHEESE DOG (Wienerschnitzel) 340 calories
- ALL BEEF CHILI AND CHEESE DOG (DQ) 380 calories

## BREAKFAST BREADS AND PASTRIES

- APPLE FRITTER (Dunkin' Donuts) 400 calories
- ⅞ SESAME BAGEL WITH REDUCED-FAT CREAM CHEESE (Dunkin' Donuts) 410 calories
- ⅘ BLUEBERRY MUFFIN (Dunkin' Donuts) 410 calories

## BREAKFAST SANDWICH

- BACON, EGG, AND CHEESE BISCUIT (McDonald's) 420 calories
- BACON, EGG, AND CHEESE BISCUIT (Burger King) 420 calories

## BEVERAGES

- LARGE COCA-COLA (40 OZ, WITH ICE) (Wendy's) 270 calories
- STRAWBERRY TRIPLE THICK SHAKE (12 OZ) (McDonald's) 420 calories
- SMALL STRAWBERRY SHAKE (16 OZ) (Burger King) 440 calories

# FIGHT THE FAT

Hold the mayo. At about 100 calories per tablespoon, mayonnaise and sauces made with mayonnaise, like tartar sauce and ranch dressing, can add up to almost half your calories for the meal.

# SHUN THE SUGAR

Barbecue sauce and sweet-and-sour sauce are almost entirely sugar. Honey-mustard sauce also contains oil.

A small shake contains the equivalent of 10 to 15 teaspoons of sugar.

BIG BAGELS have become an every day favorite.

**PLAIN BAGEL WITH LOX**
BAGEL SHOP PLAIN BAGEL 290 calories + 1 TBSP CREAM CHEESE 50 calories + 1 OZ LOX 40 calories + 1 THICK SLICE TOMATO 5 calories

385 CALORIES

**BAGEL WITH TUNA SALAD**
HOLLOWED-OUT BAGEL STORE PLAIN BAGEL 210 calories + 1/3 CUP TUNA SALAD 170 calories

380 CALORIES

**EGG BAGEL WITH CHEESE**
BAGEL SHOP EGG BAGEL 290 calories + 1 OZ SWISS CHEESE 110 calories

400 CALORIES

**CINNAMON RAISIN BAGEL WITH BUTTER**
BAGEL SHOP CINNAMON RAISIN BAGEL 240 calories + 4 TSP UNSALTED BUTTER 140 calories

380 CALORIES

# 400 CALORIE BAGEL

WHEN IT COMES TO BAGELS, is bigger better? Usually not. If your bagel is bigger than 4 inches across, or about 3½ ounces, you won't have many calories to spare for toppings and fillings. We've used the 4 inch bagel as a standard for bagel shops, though be aware that sizes can vary quite a bit from shop to shop.

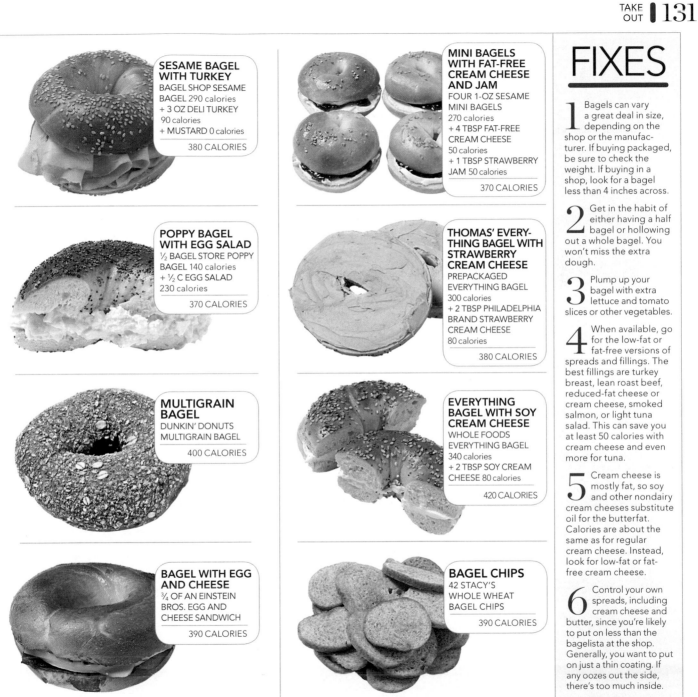

### SESAME BAGEL WITH TURKEY
BAGEL SHOP SESAME BAGEL 290 calories
+ 3 OZ DELI TURKEY 90 calories
+ MUSTARD 0 calories

**380 CALORIES**

### POPPY BAGEL WITH EGG SALAD
½ BAGEL STORE POPPY BAGEL 140 calories
+ ½ C EGG SALAD 230 calories

**370 CALORIES**

### MULTIGRAIN BAGEL
DUNKIN' DONUTS MULTIGRAIN BAGEL

**400 CALORIES**

### BAGEL WITH EGG AND CHEESE
¾ OF AN EINSTEIN BROS. EGG AND CHEESE SANDWICH

**390 CALORIES**

### MINI BAGELS WITH FAT-FREE CREAM CHEESE AND JAM
FOUR 1-OZ SESAME MINI BAGELS 270 calories
+ 4 TBSP FAT-FREE CREAM CHEESE 50 calories
+ 1 TBSP STRAWBERRY JAM 50 calories

**370 CALORIES**

### THOMAS' EVERY-THING BAGEL WITH STRAWBERRY CREAM CHEESE
PREPACKAGED EVERYTHING BAGEL 300 calories
+ 2 TBSP PHILADELPHIA BRAND STRAWBERRY CREAM CHEESE 80 calories

**380 CALORIES**

### EVERYTHING BAGEL WITH SOY CREAM CHEESE
WHOLE FOODS EVERYTHING BAGEL 340 calories
+ 2 TBSP SOY CREAM CHEESE 80 calories

**420 CALORIES**

### BAGEL CHIPS
42 STACY'S WHOLE WHEAT BAGEL CHIPS

**390 CALORIES**

# FIXES

1 Bagels can vary a great deal in size, depending on the shop or the manufacturer. If buying packaged, be sure to check the weight. If buying in a shop, look for a bagel less than 4 inches across.

2 Get in the habit of either having a half bagel or hollowing out a whole bagel. You won't miss the extra dough.

3 Plump up your bagel with extra lettuce and tomato slices or other vegetables.

4 When available, go for the low-fat or fat-free versions of spreads and fillings. The best fillings are turkey breast, lean roast beef, reduced-fat cheese or cream cheese, smoked salmon, or light tuna salad. This can save you at least 50 calories with cream cheese and even more for tuna.

5 Cream cheese is mostly fat, so soy and other nondairy cream cheeses substitute oil for the butterfat. Calories are about the same as for regular cream cheese. Instead, look for low-fat or fat-free cream cheese.

6 Control your own spreads, including cream cheese and butter, since you're likely to put on less than the bagelista at the shop. Generally, you want to put on just a thin coating. If any oozes out the side, there's too much inside.

# 400 CALORIE PIZZA

A SINGLE SLICE OF CHEESE PIZZA from a traditional 14" (large) New York-style pie weighs in at about 320 calories. But picking pizza today can be pretty complicated, with sizes, crusts, and toppings all varying quite a bit.

**FIND THE FAT**
Meat toppings are highest in fat and calories; raw veggie toppings are lowest.

MUSHROOM (¼ CUP)
**325** CALORIES

BBQ CHICKEN (¼ CUP)
**380** CALORIES

THE WORKS
**480** CALORIES

EIGHT SLICES eight toppings

SAUSAGE (1 OZ)
**420** CALORIES

HAM AND PINEAPPLE
**375** CALORIES

BROCCOLI (¼ CUP)
**335** CALORIES

PEPPERONI (½ OZ)
**390** CALORIES

CHEESE
**320** CALORIES

**FIND THE FAT**
The orange slick on the surface of your pizza is mainly fat that separated from the [illegible] napkin or fold your slice in half and allow the oil to drip off.

# TOPPINGS

Pizza toppings and amounts differ from pizzeria to pizzeria, so we've gathered info for standard portions of the most popular toppings:

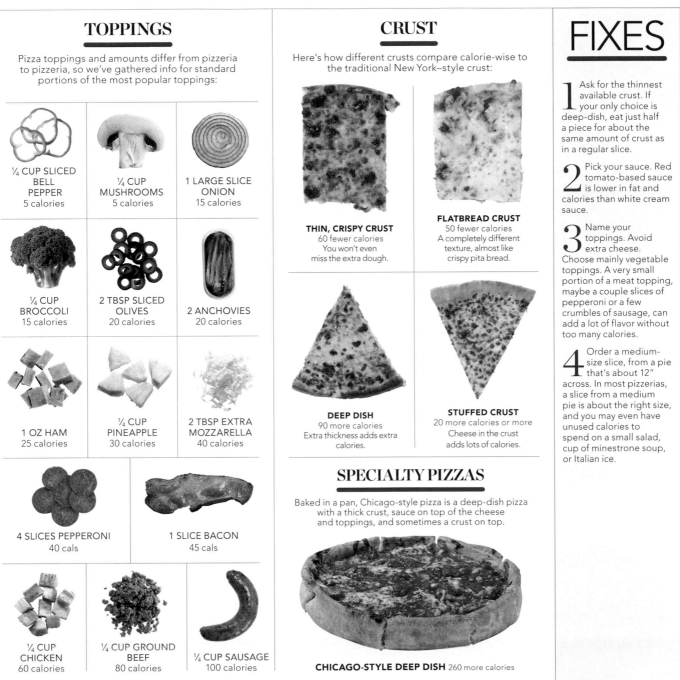

¼ CUP SLICED BELL PEPPER
5 calories

¼ CUP MUSHROOMS
5 calories

1 LARGE SLICE ONION
15 calories

¼ CUP BROCCOLI
15 calories

2 TBSP SLICED OLIVES
20 calories

2 ANCHOVIES
20 calories

1 OZ HAM
25 calories

¼ CUP PINEAPPLE
30 calories

2 TBSP EXTRA MOZZARELLA
40 calories

4 SLICES PEPPERONI
40 cals

1 SLICE BACON
45 cals

¼ CUP CHICKEN
60 calories

¼ CUP GROUND BEEF
80 calories

¼ CUP SAUSAGE
100 calories

# CRUST

Here's how different crusts compare calorie-wise to the traditional New York–style crust:

**THIN, CRISPY CRUST**
60 fewer calories
You won't even miss the extra dough.

**FLATBREAD CRUST**
50 fewer calories
A completely different texture, almost like crispy pita bread.

**DEEP DISH**
90 more calories
Extra thickness adds extra calories.

**STUFFED CRUST**
20 more calories or more
Cheese in the crust adds lots of calories.

# SPECIALTY PIZZAS

Baked in a pan, Chicago-style pizza is a deep-dish pizza with a thick crust, sauce on top of the cheese and toppings, and sometimes a crust on top.

**CHICAGO-STYLE DEEP DISH** 260 more calories

# FIXES

1 Ask for the thinnest available crust. If your only choice is deep-dish, eat just half a piece for about the same amount of crust as in a regular slice.

2 Pick your sauce. Red tomato-based sauce is lower in fat and calories than white cream sauce.

3 Name your toppings. Avoid extra cheese. Choose mainly vegetable toppings. A very small portion of a meat topping, maybe a couple slices of pepperoni or a few crumbles of sausage, can add a lot of flavor without too many calories.

4 Order a medium-size slice, from a pie that's about 12" across. In most pizzerias, a slice from a medium pie is about the right size, and you may even have unused calories to spend on a small salad, cup of minestrone soup, or Italian ice.

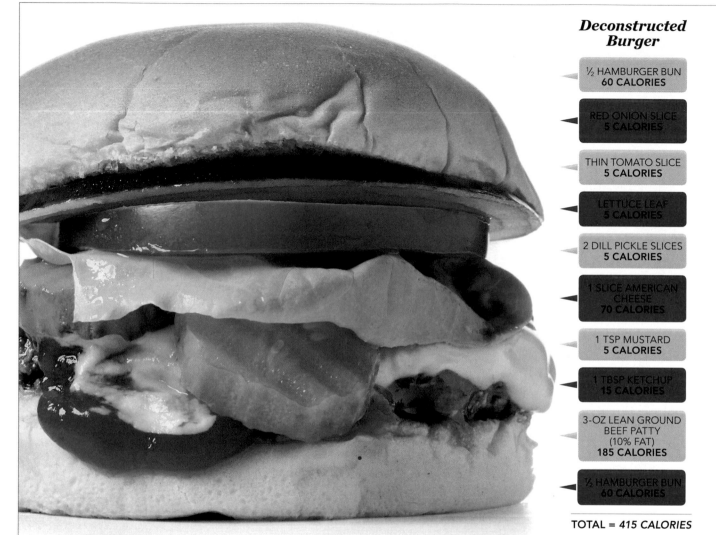

### Deconstructed Burger

½ HAMBURGER BUN
**60 CALORIES**

RED ONION SLICE
**5 CALORIES**

THIN TOMATO SLICE
**5 CALORIES**

LETTUCE LEAF
**5 CALORIES**

2 DILL PICKLE SLICES
**5 CALORIES**

1 SLICE AMERICAN CHEESE
**70 CALORIES**

1 TSP MUSTARD
**5 CALORIES**

1 TBSP KETCHUP
**15 CALORIES**

3-OZ LEAN GROUND BEEF PATTY (10% FAT)
**185 CALORIES**

½ HAMBURGER BUN
**60 CALORIES**

**TOTAL = 415 CALORIES**

**FIND THE FAT**
Sautéed or grilled onions, mushrooms, and other veggies are low in calories if you prepare them at home with just a little oil. Otherwise, they can be a hidden source of extra fat and calories.

# 400 *CALORIE* BURGER

NO MATTER HOW YOU LIKE YOUR BURGER, you can enjoy a satisfying meal from dozens of different burger, bun, and topping combos.

# TOPPINGS

### FREEBIES
### (UP TO 5 CALORIES)

LETTUCE
ALFALFA SPROUTS
BABY SPINACH
DILL PICKLES
SLICED MUSHROOMS
RAW ONIONS
SAUERKRAUT
TOMATO SLICES
HOT-PEPPER SAUCE
SALSA
JALAPEÑO CHILE
PEPPERS
MUSTARD
HORSERADISH

### 10–25 CALORIES

ROASTED RED BELL
PEPPERS, 1 OZ
KETCHUP, 1 TBSP
STEAK SAUCE, 1 TBSP
SWEET PICKLE CHIPS
3 PICKLE RELISH, 1 TBSP
BARBECUE SAUCE,
1 TBSP

### 35–60 CALORIES

TURKEY BACON,
1 SLICE (¼ OZ)
SAUTÉED MUSHROOMS,
2 TBSP (¼ CUP RAW
+ 1 TSP OIL)
BACON (¼ OZ),
1 SLICE
LIGHT MAYONNAISE,
1 TBSP
THOUSAND ISLAND
DRESSING, 1 TBSP
SAUTÉED ONIONS,
2 TBSP
(¼ CUP RAW +
1 TSP OIL)

### 75–80 CALORIES

CHILI WITH BEANS,
¼ CUP
AVOCADO SLICES,
¼ AVOCADO
PESTO, 1 TBSP

# BURGERS
### (COOKED WEIGHT)

1 PORTOBELLO
MUSHROOM CAP
+ 1 TSP OLIVE OIL
60 calories

3.5-OZ VEGGIE
BURGER
(BOCA BURGER
ORIGINAL)
100 calories

3-OZ LEAN
GROUND
TURKEY BREAST
PATTY
110 calories

3-OZ LEAN
GROUND
BEEF PATTY
(10% FAT)
185 calories

3-OZ GROUND
TURKEY PATTY
190 calories

3-OZ GROUND
BISON PATTY
200 calories

3-OZ GROUND
BEEF PATTY
(20% FAT)
230 calories

# BUNS/BREADS

REDUCED-
CALORIE
HAMBURGER BUN
85 calories

WHOLE WHEAT
HAMBURGER BUN
115 calories

HAMBURGER BUN
120 calories

POTATO ROLL
120 calories

ENGLISH MUFFIN
130 calories

SANDWICH
ROLL WITH
SESAME SEEDS
150 calories

6½" DIAMETER
PITA
165 calories

KAISER OR
CRUSTY ROLL
170 calories

# CHEESES

1 TBSP FETA
CRUMBLES
25 calories

1 TBSP BLUE
CHEESE CRUMBLES
30 calories

1 SLICE (¾ OZ)
AMERICAN
CHEESE
70 calories

1 SLICE (1 OZ)
SWISS, CHEDDAR,
OR JACK CHEESE
100 calories

# FIXES

1 Think first about the burger, since that's the source of at least half the calories. Lean ground beef has fewer calories than regular, but it is not as juicy. Veggie, soy, turkey breast, and bison are all leaner options than beef. Pay attention to the size of the patty, too! Many restaurant portions are well over the recommended serving size of 3 ounces of cooked meat (4 ounces raw, sometimes called a quarter-pounder).

2 Next, consider your bun. There isn't much calorie difference between a regular, whole wheat, or sesame hamburger bun, but you can find reduced-calorie versions—and try English muffins, pitas, or other breads for variety. A lettuce "wrap" is only 10 calories, if you'd rather spend your calories on meat and toppings than bread. Or compromise by having your burger open-faced.

3 Finally, be mindful of creamy or meaty toppings like mayo, avocado, and chili, where the calories can add up quickly.

# 8.
# CASUAL DINING

# BREAKFAST

## DENNY'S EGG BEATERS

With less than half the calories of a whole egg, liquid egg "substitutes" are a great way to have your eggs and eat them too. Share an order of bacon with a friend since calories (and sodium) add up quickly.

| | calories |
|---|---|
| Denny's Egg Beaters, 1 | 60 |
| Denny's Hash Browns, 1 | 200 |
| Denny's Bacon, 1 strip (out of 4) | 40 |
| Denny's Cinnamon Apples, 1 | 100 |

**400 calories,** 15 g fat, 4 g saturated fat, 934 mg sodium, 46 g carbohydrate, 1 g fiber, 16 g protein, calcium n/a

## STAR SYSTEM

- ★ PROTEIN
- ★ FIBER
- ★ GOOD FATS
- ★ FRUITS/VEGGIES

DENNY'S
EGG BEATERS
400

## BOB EVANS FIT FROM THE FARM BREAKFAST

★

We were pleasantly surprised to find this breakfast with a choice of a crepe, mini yogurt parfait, or oatmeal. The oatmeal gives just the right balance between calories and satisfaction. The crepe adds another 110 calories. The parfait saves 120 calories, but you may not feel full afterward.

| | calories |
|---|---|
| Bob Evans Fit from the Farm Breakfast with Oatmeal, 1 | 370 |

**370 calories,** 9 g fat, 3 g saturated fat, 813 mg sodium, 46 g carbohydrate, 3 g fiber, 26 g protein, calcium n/a

## IHOP SPINACH, MUSHROOM & TOMATO OMELETTE

★

The healthier IHOP for Me menu includes this omelette with a reasonable calorie count. A slice of whole wheat toast—no butter—brings the meal up to the 400-calorie mark.

| | calories |
|---|---|
| Spinach, Mushroom & Tomato Omelette, 1 | 330 |
| Whole wheat toast, 1 slice | 70 |

**400 calories,** 8 g fat, 3 g saturated fat, 790 mg sodium, 49 g carbohydrate, 2 g fiber, 34 g protein, 2% calcium

# LUNCH/DINNER

## RUBY TUESDAY WHITE BEAN CHICKEN CHILI

★ ★ ★

Bean chili is almost always a smart choice because of everything good about beans. They supply protein, are packed with fiber, have other key nutrients, and are really filling. Ask your server about other vegetable or fruit side dish choices.

| | calories |
|---|---|
| Ruby Tuesday White Bean Chicken Chili, 1 | 320 |
| Ruby Tuesday Fresh Steamed Broccoli, 1 | 90 |

**410 calories,** 16 g fat, saturated fat n/a, sodium n/a, 43 g carbohydrate, 13 g fiber, 29 g protein, calcium n/a

## CHILI'S CHICKEN ENCHILADA SOUP

★ ★

Even with a salad dressed with just balsamic vinegar, this meal is a bit higher in calories and fat than we would like. At 210 calories, the house salad is more than just a bowl of greens.

| | calories |
|---|---|
| Chili's Chicken Enchilada Soup, 1 cup | 220 |
| Chili's Side House Salad (no dressing; with balsamic vinegar) | 210 |

**430 calories,** 25 g fat, 11 g saturated fat, 1,000 mg sodium, 26 g carbohydrate, 4 g fiber, 25 g protein, calcium n/a

RUBY TUESDAY WHITE BEAN CHICKEN CHILI
**410**

## ROMANO'S MACARONI GRILL WARM SPINACH SALAD

★ ★

This salad is a full meal, with meat, cheese, and plenty of vitamin A-rich spinach. Skip the bread—it adds about 70 calories per slice.

| | calories |
|---|---|
| Romano's Macaroni Grill Warm Spinach Salad, ½ | 380 |

**380 calories,** 24 g fat, 8 g saturated fat, 1,010 mg sodium, 22 g carbohydrate, 7 g fiber, 19 g protein, calcium n/a

## FRENCH ONION SOUP
★

Is it possible to enjoy French onion soup while eating the 400-calorie way? Yes, as long as you stick to a modest-size bowl topped with a slice of bread and just a few ounces of Gruyère cheese.

| | calories |
|---|---|
| French onion soup, 1 bowl | 380 |

**380 calories,** 23 g fat, 14 g saturated fat, 1,166 mg sodium, 20 g carbohydrate, 2 g fiber, 24 g protein, 63% calcium

## CHEVY'S FRESH MEX SANTA FE CHOPPED SALAD
★ ★ ★

In this salad, we say no to cheese and bacon.

| | calories |
|---|---|
| Chevy's Fresh Mex Santa Fe Chopped Salad (no cheese or bacon), 1 | 320 |
| Sweet Corn Tamalito, 3 Tbsp | 90 |

**410 calories,** 14.5 g fat, 3.5 g saturated fat, 507 mg sodium, 42 g carbohydrate, 10 g fiber, 40 g protein, calcium n/a

## RED ROBIN MIGHTY CAESAR SALAD WITH GRILLED CHICKEN
★ ★ ★

Ask your server to cut you off on the garlic bread after the first slice.

| | calories |
|---|---|
| Red Robin Mighty Caesar Salad with Grilled Chicken, 1, with 2 Tbsp grated Parmesan cheese, 2 garlic croutons, and 3 Tbsp balsamic vinaigrette | 400 |

**400 calories,** 16 g fat, saturated fat n/a, 1,031 mg sodium, 25 g carbohydrate, 7 g fiber, 35 g protein, calcium n/a

## ATLANTA BREAD COMPANY BALSAMIC BLEU SALAD
★ ★

You can get your blue cheese fix from what's in the salad, and the natural sweetness of balsamic vinegar makes it a perfect and virtually calorie-free dressing alternative.

| | calories |
|---|---|
| Atlanta Bread Company Balsamic Bleu Salad (balsamic vinegar only), 1 | 330 |
| Rye loaf, one ¼-oz slice | 90 |

**420 calories,** 19 g fat, 6 g saturated fat, 580 mg sodium, 53 g carbohydrate, 7 g fiber, 14 g protein, 22% calcium

## CHILI'S GUILTLESS CEDAR PLANK TILAPIA
★

Fish that has been cooked on a cedar plank has a deliciously subtle smokiness.

| | calories |
|---|---|
| Chili's Guiltless Cedar Plank Tilapia, 1 | 200 |
| Chili's Rice, 1 cup | 190 |

**390 calories,** 5 g fat, 2 g saturated fat, 1,260 mg sodium, 50 g carbohydrate, 6 g fiber, 38 g protein, calcium n/a

CHILI'S
GUILTLESS
CEDAR PLANK
TILAPIA
390

## RUBY TUESDAY SMART EATING CREOLE CATCH
★

You have a choice—the virtuous option of green beans on the side or the almost equally virtuous mini chocolate chip cookie. We picked the cookie and ate it in small bites.

| | calories |
|---|---|
| Ruby Tuesday Smart Eating Creole Catch, 1 | 320 |
| Ruby Tuesday Mini Chocolate Chip Cookie, 1 | 80 |

**400 calories,** 20 g fat, saturated fat n/a, sodium n/a, carbohydrate n/a, 2 g fiber, protein n/a, calcium n/a

## RED LOBSTER GARLIC SHRIMP SCAMPI
★

Shrimp is so low in calories that most of the calories in shrimp dishes come from the sauce.

| | calories |
|---|---|
| Red Lobster Garlic Shrimp Scampi, 1 | 130 |
| Red Lobster Wild Rice Pilaf, 1 | 180 |
| Red Lobster Garden Salad with 1 Tbsp Red Lobster Fat-Free Ranch Dressing | 110 |

**420 calories,** 15 g fat, 2.5 g saturated fat, 1,615 mg sodium, 53 g carbohydrate, fiber n/a, protein n/a, calcium n/a

## CHICKEN SATAY ENTRÉE
★ ★ ★

The peanut sauce, filled with good-fat MUFAs, adds flavor to the chicken and the rice.

| | calories |
|---|---|
| Chicken satay, 5 pieces (about 3 oz) | 150 |
| White rice, ½ cup cooked | 100 |
| Peanut sauce, 2 Tbsp | 90 |
| Fresh pineapple chunks, ½ cup | 40 |

**380 calories,** 3.5 g fat, 1 g saturated fat, 906 mg sodium, 59 g carbohydrate, 8 g fiber, 30 g protein, 9% calcium

## LONGHORN STEAKHOUSE RENEGADE TOP SIRLOIN
★ ★

Choose lean cuts and save half for a delicious steak sandwich the next day.

| | calories |
|---|---|
| LongHorn Steakhouse Renegade Top Sirloin, 4 oz (½ of 8-oz steak) | 240 |
| LongHorn Steakhouse Grilled Onions, 1 | 90 |
| LongHorn Steakhouse Fresh Steamed Asparagus, 1 | 80 |

**410 calories,** 21.5 g fat, 5 g saturated fat, 1,145 mg sodium, 16 g carbohydrate, fiber n/a, protein n/a, calcium n/a

RED LOBSTER GARLIC SHRIMP SCAMPI
420

## GRILLED CHICKEN SANDWICH
★ ★ ★ ★

Commercial coleslaw is surprisingly high in calories, even in a small restaurant side serving.

| | calories |
|---|---|
| Whole wheat roll, medium | 100 |
| Grilled chicken breast, 3 oz | 140 |
| Roasted bell peppers, ¼ cup | 20 |
| Lettuce, 2 leaves | 10 |
| Tomato, 2 slices | 10 |
| Salsa, 1 Tbsp | 0 |
| Guacamole, 1 Tbsp | 30 |
| Coleslaw, ¼ cup | 50 |
| Strawberries, 1 cup | 50 |

**410 calories,** 11 g fat, 2 g saturated fat, 717 mg sodium, 44 g carbohydrate, 8 g fiber, 33 g protein, 11% calcium

## REDUCED-FAT TUNA WRAP

If your sandwich wrap looks bigger than 10", or a bit wider than a piece of paper, leave some of the wrap behind. Every extra inch adds about 25 calories.

| | calories |
|---|---|
| Flour tortilla, one 10" | 220 |
| Reduced-fat tuna salad, ½ cup | 130 |
| Shredded lettuce, ¼ cup | 5 |
| Sliced olives, 2 Tbsp | 20 |
| Coleslaw, ¼ cup | 50 |

**425 calories,** 16 g fat, 3 g saturated fat, 1,173 mg sodium, 50 g carbohydrate, 5 g fiber, 19 g protein, 12% calcium

## OLIVE GARDEN GRILLED CHICKEN SPIEDINI
★ ★

The grilled chicken skewers in this dish make it lower in fat than the other Italian specialties on the menu.

| | calories |
|---|---|
| Olive Garden Grilled Chicken Spiedini, 1 | 380 |

**380 calories,** 12 g fat, 2 g saturated fat, 835 mg sodium, 21 g carbohydrate, 8 g fiber, protein n/a, calcium n/a

## CHICKEN FAJITA
★ ★

Fajitas usually are served with smaller-size tortillas, perfect for putting together a 400-calorie meal. Ask for lettuce leaves on the side so that you can make a few tortilla-free wraps.

| | calories |
|---|---|
| Flour tortilla, one 7½" | 140 |
| Grilled chicken breast, 3 oz | 110 |
| Grilled bell peppers and onions, ½ cup | 90 |
| Salsa, 2 Tbsp | 10 |
| Guacamole, 2 Tbsp | 40 |

**390 calories,** 15 g fat, 2 g saturated fat, 1,400 mg sodium, 36 g carbohydrate, 4 g fiber, 27 g protein, 8% calcium

## OLIVE GARDEN CHEESE RAVIOLI WITH MEAT SAUCE

Here's a classic Italian dish to enjoy.

| | calories |
|---|---|
| Olive Garden Cheese Ravioli with Meat Sauce, ½ order | 400 |

**400 calories,** 14 g fat, 7 g saturated fat, 755 mg sodium, 44 g carbohydrate, 6 g fiber, protein n/a, calcium n/a

## DENNY'S GRILLED SHRIMP SKEWERS
★

Shrimp usually is a safe bet, and grilled is lower in calories than fried or sautéed in lots of oil or butter.

| | calories |
|---|---|
| Denny's Shrimp Skewers, 2 | 180 |
| Denny's Vegetable Rice Pilaf, 5 oz | 200 |
| Tomato, 2 slices | 10 |

**390 calories,** 10 g fat, 2 g saturated fat, 1,143 mg sodium, 39 g carbohydrate, 2 g fiber, 33 g protein, calcium n/a

## BOB EVANS POTATO-CRUSTED FLOUNDER
★

Flounder and other white fish tend to be lower in calories because they're so low in fat. Check out the menu for vegetable and fruit side dishes to pair with your fish.

| | calories |
|---|---|
| Bob Evans Potato-Crusted Flounder, 1 | 250 |
| Bob Evans Glazed Baby Carrots, 1 | 80 |
| Bob Evans Fresh Fruit Dish, 1 | 70 |

**400 calories,** 20 g fat, 5 g saturated fat, 657 mg sodium, 40 g carbohydrate, 5 g fiber, 19 g protein, calcium n/a

## RED ROBIN GRILLED SALMON BURGER
★ ★

Red Robin portions are so generous that we had to order this burger without the bun. We topped it off with veggies and avocado to hit our 400-calorie limit. Our other option was to order the Grilled Salmon Burger right off the menu and then eat just half.

| | calories |
|---|---|
| Red Robin Grilled Salmon patty with lettuce, balsamic-marinated tomato, onion, fajita veggies, and avocado, 1 | 400 |

**400 calories,** 26 g fat, saturated fat n/a, 363 mg sodium, 16 g carbohydrates, 6 g fiber, 31 g protein, calcium n/a

## P.F. CHANG'S GINGER CHICKEN WITH BROCCOLI
★

Chinese restaurants are the ultimate in family-style dining. Claim a couple dumplings as your appetizer and then enjoy a small portion of an entrée like ginger chicken.

| | calories |
|---|---|
| P.F. Chang's Ginger Chicken with Broccoli, 1 cup | 280 |
| P.F. Chang's Steamed Shrimp Dumplings, 2 | 120 |

**400 calories,** 15 g fat, 2 g saturated fat, 1,198 mg sodium, 37 g carbohydrate, 34 g protein, fiber n/a, calcium n/a

## TACO SALAD
★ ★ ★

Between the shell and high-fat toppings like cheese, sour cream, and guacamole, a taco salad is one of the highest-calorie choices. Here, we included just small portions of some of the higher-calorie fixings.

| | calories |
|---|---|
| Taco salad, no shell | |
| Shredded lettuce, 2 cups | 10 |
| Diced tomato, ¼ cup | 10 |
| Ground beef, ¼ cup cooked | 60 |
| Refried beans, ¼ cup | 50 |
| Guacamole, 2 Tbsp | 60 |
| Grated cheese, 2 Tbsp | 60 |
| Salsa, 2 Tbsp | 10 |
| Tortilla chips, 10 chips (1 oz) | 140 |

**400 calories,** 21 g fat, 6 g saturated fat, 854 mg sodium, 37 g carbohydrate, 9 g fiber, 16 g protein, 23% calcium

## ATLANTA BREAD COMPANY ROASTED TURKEY ON NINE GRAIN BREAD
★

You may want a smear of mustard to complement the lettuce, tomato, and red onion on this sandwich, but say no to the side salads and chips.

| | calories |
|---|---|
| Atlanta Bread Company Roasted Turkey on Nine Grain Bread with lettuce, tomato, and onion (no mayo), 1 | 390 |

**390 calories,** 6 g fat, 2 g saturated fat, 1,243 mg sodium, 55 g carbohydrate, 6 g fiber, 30 g protein, 20% calcium

## BLACKENED CHICKEN BREAST
★ ★

Blackened entrées, typically fish or chicken, are coated in peppery seasoning and then sautéed or grilled over high heat, adding few extra calories.

| | calories |
|---|---|
| Shrimp cocktail, 3 shrimp with 2 Tbsp cocktail sauce | 50 |
| Blackened chicken breast, 3 oz cooked | 140 |
| Rice pilaf, ½ cup | 140 |
| Asparagus, 5 spears | 20 |
| Strawberries, 1 cup | 50 |

**400 calories,** 7 g fat, 1 g saturated fat, 907 mg sodium, 46 g carbohydrate, 6 g fiber, 36 g protein, 7% calcium

BLACKENED CHICKEN BREAST
400

## LOBSTER

★ ★ ★

Yes, you really can have a lobster dinner without looking like you're on a diet. Dipping your lobster in melted butter is out, of course, since a little cup of it can top 400 calories. So pick a restaurant that does a really good job with this favorite, or try making your own at home.

| | calories |
|---|---|
| Lobster,  1 lb lobster (4 oz meat) | 110 |
| Baked potato, 1 medium with 1 tsp butter | 190 |
| Broccoli, 1 cup, with garlic and ½ teaspoon olive oil | 40 |
| Raspberries, 1 cup | 60 |

**400 calories,** 7 g fat, 2 g saturated fat, 452 mg sodium, 57 g carbohydrates, 14 g fiber, 30 g protein, 16% calcium

## GRILLED MAHI-MAHI

★ ★

While mahi-mahi is also known as dolphin fish, it is not at all related to dolphins and porpoises. Mahi-mahi has a thicker fillet and firmer texture than other white-flesh fish like sole and flounder.

| | calories |
|---|---|
| Grilled mahi-mahi, 4 oz | 120 |
| Whole wheat roll, medium, with 1 tsp butter | 130 |
| Broccoli, 1 cup sautéed in 1 tsp olive oil | 70 |
| Cappuccino, 16 oz, made with 8 oz fat-free milk | 80 |

**400 calories,** 15 g fat, 6 g saturated fat, 381 mg sodium, 29 g carbohydrate, 5 g fiber, 27 g protein, 20% calcium

## SUSHI

★

To get the most out of your meal, stick with rolls that aren't "spicy," since it usually refers to a peppery mayo spread. If you prefer more fish, order sashimi and limit yourself to about ⅔ cup of rice.

| | calories |
|---|---|
| Miso soup, 1 cup | 40 |
| California roll (real or mock crabmeat) or salmon roll, 4 pieces | 150 |
| Spicy tuna roll, 4 pieces | 140 |
| Orange wedges, 8 | 70 |

**400 calories,** 7.5 g fat, 0.5 g saturated fat, 1025 mg sodium, 69 g carbohydrate, 6 g fiber, 14 g protein, calcium n/a

## FAZOLI'S BAKED SPAGHETTI

★

Italian restaurants usually have different salads and vegetables on their menu, making it easier to round out your meal. As with most Italian restaurants, portions are meant to be shared with the family.

| | calories |
|---|---|
| Fazoli's Baked Spaghetti, ½ order | 320 |
| Fazoli's Caesar Side Salad, 1 | 40 |
| Fazoli's Lite Ranch Dressing, 1 Tbsp | 40 |

**400 calories,** 17 g fat, 8 g saturated fat, 902 mg sodium, 45 g carbohydrate, 6 g fiber, 19 g protein, 33% calcium

CHINESE BUFFET
420

## HOLIDAY BUFFET, WITH SECONDS
★ ★

Wait at least 20 minutes after finishing your first plate before deciding whether to go back for seconds to determine whether you're really still hungry.

| | calories |
|---|---|
| Bocconcini and cherry tomato skewers, 2 | 100 |
| Roast turkey breast, two 1-oz slices | 80 |
| Turkey gravy, 1 Tbsp | 10 |
| Wild rice pilaf, ¼ cup | 70 |
| Steamed broccoli, ½ cup | 30 |
| Fruit salad, ½ cup | 50 |
| *Seconds* | |
| Roast turkey breast, one 1-oz slice | 40 |
| Turkey gravy, 1 tsp | 5 |
| Wild rice/brown rice pilaf, 2 Tbsp | 40 |

**425 calories,** 12 g fat, 5 g saturated fat, 507 mg sodium, 41 g carbohydrate, 6 g fiber, 36 g protein, 7% calcium

## P.F. CHANG'S STIR-FRIED BUDDHA'S FEAST
★

Dishes named for Buddha usually have an assortment of vegetables and sometimes tofu.

| | calories |
|---|---|
| P.F. Chang's Stir-Fried Buddha's Feast, 1 cup | 190 |
| Brown rice, ½ cup cooked | 110 |
| P.F. Chang's Garlic Snap Peas, small | 100 |

**400 calories,** 9 g fat, saturated fat n/a, 1,227 mg sodium, 63 g carbohydrate, fiber n/a, 17 g protein, calcium n/a

## CHINESE BUFFET
★

Fat is not very satiating, and that's part of the reason that you might be hungry an hour after eating Chinese food . . . even though you've had more than enough calories. To eat the 400-calorie way, have a ½-cup portion of one item and three ¼-cup portions of three other dishes.

| | calories |
|---|---|
| Beef and broccoli, ½ cup | 110 |
| Fried rice, ¼ cup | 100 |
| Pork lo mein, ¼ cup | 80 |
| Sweet and sour chicken, ¼ cup | 100 |
| Fortune cookie, 1 | 30 |

**420 calories,** 9.5 g fat, 2 g saturated fat, 1242 mg sodium, 56 g carbohydrate, 3 g fiber, 20 g protein, 3% calcium

## MEXICAN VEGETARIAN
★ ★

Refried beans are often cooked with lard. Ask for refried beans that are not made with lard.

| | calories |
|---|---|
| Corn tortillas, two 6" tortillas | 110 |
| Refried black beans, ½ cup | 110 |
| Salsa, ¼ cup | 20 |
| Grated jack cheese, 2 Tbsp | 50 |
| Guacamole, ¼ cup | 110 |

**400 calories,** 17 g fat, 5 g saturated fat, 955 mg sodium, 50 g carbohydrate, 15 g fiber, 15 g protein, 23% calcium

## BUFFET MEAL WITH DESSERT

Three rules to remember when you're eating from a buffet—take small portions, eat only when you're truly hungry, and stand out of reach of the buffet table.

| | calories |
|---|---:|
| Caesar salad, ½ cup | 150 |
| Tortellini salad, ¼ cup | 100 |
| Spiral ham, 6 thin slices, about 2 oz | 60 |
| Chocolate layer cake, 4 bites, about 1 oz | 100 |

**410 calories,** 26 g fat, 6 g saturated fat, 1,200 mg sodium, 26 g carbohydrate, 2 g fiber, 17 g protein, 10% calcium

## BUFFET MEAL WITH A COCKTAIL
★

In this meal, the martini takes up almost half the calories. Shrimp and other raw-bar seafood items are mostly protein and don't have many calories unless they're served with high-fat sauces.

| | calories |
|---|---:|
| Martini, 3 oz | 170 |
| Shrimp cocktail, 2 shrimp with 2 Tbsp cocktail sauce | 20 |
| Flank steak, 5 thin slices (about 3 oz total) | 160 |
| Roasted potatoes, ⅓ cup | 60 |

**410 calories,** 9 g fat, 3.5 g saturated fat, 343 mg sodium, 10 g carbohydrate, 1 g fiber, 27 g protein, 2% calcium

# SNACKS/DESSERTS

## HORS D'OEUVRES MEAL

Compared with other alcoholic beverages, champagne is among the lowest in calories. At a party with passed hors d'oeuvres, try to limit yourself to 10 bites of a combo of heavier foods like the egg roll and fruit or veggie dishes like the melon and prosciutto. Plain veggies are free!

| | calories |
|---|---:|
| Champagne, 5 oz | 110 |
| Spiral ham, 3 thin slices, with 1 Tbsp Dijon mustard on a small roll | 110 |
| Baby carrots, 10, with 1 Tbsp fat-free ranch dressing | 50 |
| Honeydew wrapped in prosciutto, 3 pieces | 90 |
| Mini egg roll, 1 | 40 |

**400 calories,** 7.5 g fat, 2 g saturated fat, 1,565 mg sodium, 40 g carbohydrate, 4 g fiber, 19 g protein, 12% calcium

## HORS D'OEUVRES CELEBRATION MEAL

Calories in mixed drinks add up quickly, leaving few calories for typical passed hors d'oeuvres.

| | calories |
|---|---:|
| Cosmo, 5 oz | 250 |
| Crab cake, 1 mini | 30 |
| Cheese soufflé, 1 mini | 60 |
| Scallop wrapped in bacon, 1 | 50 |

**390 calories,** 7 g fat, 5 g saturated fat, 267 mg sodium, 25 g carbohydrate, 0 g fiber, 7 g protein, 4% calcium

## T.G.I. FRIDAY'S CHOCOLATE PEANUT BUTTER PIE

★

Should this dish earn a star for good fats since it's chock-full of peanut butter and chocolate, or does its high calorie count undo any positive nutritional content? You be the judge. By the way, this is one of the lower-calorie dessert picks at Friday's!

| | calories |
|---|---|
| T.G.I. Friday's Chocolate Peanut Butter Pie, ½ slice | 390 |

**390 calories,** fat n/a, saturated fat n/a, sodium n/a, carbohydrate n/a, fiber n/a, protein n/a, calcium n/a

## CHEESECAKE FACTORY

★ ★ ★ ★

Back in the day, Cheesecake Factory's one store in Beverly Hills was as well known for its salad bar as for its delicious and modestly sized` pieces of cheesecake. Today, 400 calories won't buy you a slice, so order your cheesecake with extra spoons for sharing.

| | calories |
|---|---|
| Cheesecake Factory Fresh Strawberry Cheesecake, ½ slice | 370 |

**370 calories,** fat n/a, saturated fat n/a, sodium n/a, carbohydrate n/a, fiber n/a, protein n/a, calcium n/a

CHEESECAKE FACTORY FRESH STRAWBERRY CHEESECAKE
370

# 400 CALORIE STEAKHOUSE

*BIG* IS THE WORD THAT COMES to mind when we think steakhouse. A big steak hanging over the edge of the plate, a big baked potato, a big dessert. Big calories. But it doesn't have to be that way.

## FIXES

**1** If you're starting with starters, stick with selections from the raw bar or a seafood cocktail. Shellfish, shrimp, and white-flesh fish are extremely lean and low in calories.

**2** Salads are a smart pick, but you may want to share since they're large enough to be a meal. Always order dressing on the side and limit yourself to a tablespoon max, or sprinkle with a bit of oil plus naturally calorie-free vinegar.

**3** Don't let them call you a wimp for ordering the petite or ladies'-size steak. You'll still get more than 400 calories' worth.

**4** Consider seafood entrées like broiled salmon, king crab legs, steamed lobster, and grilled shrimp—they're a leaner alternative, although portions are still way too big.

**5** To come close to 400 calories, limit yourself to half or two-quarter portions of steak, one side dish, and one appetizer.

**FIND THE FAT**
Only 2% of all cuts of beef are labeled "prime," meaning that they are the most highly marbled, and highest in fat and calories. The prime designation adds 100 calories to a 5¾-ounce rib eye steak.

**FILET MIGNON**
4 OZ
**250 calories**
+ 4-OZ BAKED POTATO WITH 1 PAT OF BUTTER
**130 calories**
+ 8 ASPARAGUS SPEARS
30 calories

**410 CALORIES**

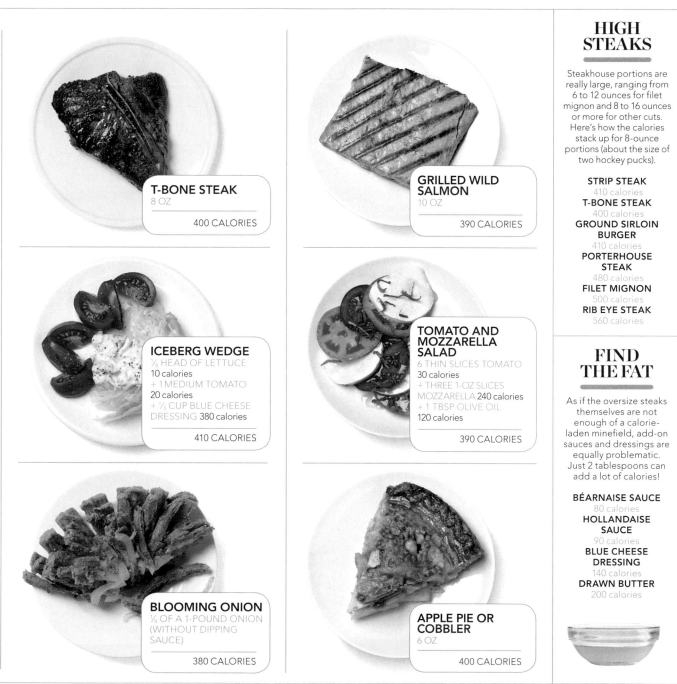

### T-BONE STEAK
8 OZ

400 CALORIES

### GRILLED WILD SALMON
10 OZ

390 CALORIES

### ICEBERG WEDGE
⅓ HEAD OF LETTUCE
10 calories
+ 1 MEDIUM TOMATO
20 calories
+ ⅓ CUP BLUE CHEESE DRESSING 380 calories

410 CALORIES

### TOMATO AND MOZZARELLA SALAD
6 THIN SLICES TOMATO
30 calories
+ THREE 1-OZ SLICES MOZZARELLA 240 calories
+ 1 TBSP OLIVE OIL
120 calories

390 CALORIES

### BLOOMING ONION
¼ OF A 1-POUND ONION (WITHOUT DIPPING SAUCE)

380 CALORIES

### APPLE PIE OR COBBLER
6 OZ

400 CALORIES

## HIGH STEAKS

Steakhouse portions are really large, ranging from 6 to 12 ounces for filet mignon and 8 to 16 ounces or more for other cuts. Here's how the calories stack up for 8-ounce portions (about the size of two hockey pucks).

**STRIP STEAK**
410 calories
**T-BONE STEAK**
400 calories
**GROUND SIRLOIN BURGER**
410 calories
**PORTERHOUSE STEAK**
480 calories
**FILET MIGNON**
500 calories
**RIB EYE STEAK**
560 calories

## FIND THE FAT

As if the oversize steaks themselves are not enough of a calorie-laden minefield, add-on sauces and dressings are equally problematic. Just 2 tablespoons can add a lot of calories!

**BÉARNAISE SAUCE**
80 calories
**HOLLANDAISE SAUCE**
90 calories
**BLUE CHEESE DRESSING**
140 calories
**DRAWN BUTTER**
200 calories

# FIXES

1 Ask about the size of dishes. Many restaurants serve enough for two to four people.

2 When selecting your main dish, ask for appetizer-size or half-size portions, if they're available.

3 Keep pasta portions to the size of your fist and protein portions to the size of your palm.

4 For a side dish, choose salad with oil and vinegar on the side rather than sautéed vegetables. The veggies are prepared with lots of oil.

5 Request red sauce rather than pink or white. The lighter the color of the sauce, the more cream it contains.

## ANTIPASTO PLATE
⅛ CUP PEPPERONCINI
10 calories
+ 3 PIECES MARINATED ARTICHOKE HEARTS
90 calories
+ 3 THIN SLICES PROSCIUTTO
50 calories
+ 5 SLICES PEPPERONI
50 calories
+ 1 OZ PROVOLONE CHEESE
100 calories
+ 5 KALAMATA-SIZE OLIVES
50 calories
+ MEDIUM SLICE (⅔ OZ) ITALIAN BREAD
50 calories

400 CALORIES

# 400 CALORIE ITALIAN

IF YOU VISIT ITALY, YOU'LL NOTICE plenty of thin Italians, which means it is possible to love Italian food without love handles. The challenge is portion size. The pasta course in Italy is small, almost like an appetizer. In the United States, it's big enough to feed Nonna, Nonno, Mamma, Papa, and all the kids. Keep your pasta portion to no bigger than your fist to come close to 400 calories.

**FIND THE FAT**
Italian meatballs are not known for being lean and they often are made with grated Parmesan cheese.

## SPAGHETTI AND MEATBALLS
1 CUP SPAGHETTI
220 calories
+ TWO 1-OZ MEATBALLS
90 calories
+ ½ CUP TOMATO SAUCE 80 calories

390 CALORIES

## PENNE ALLA VODKA
1 CUP PENNE
210 calories
+ ½ CUP VODKA SAUCE
140 calories

**350 CALORIES**

## MEAT LASAGNA
10 OZ

**420 CALORIES**

## VEAL MARSALA
5 OZ

**390 CALORIES**

## LINGUINE WITH WHITE CLAM SAUCE
1 CUP LINGUINE
210 calories
+ 5 TBSP WHITE CLAM SAUCE 190 calories

**400 CALORIES**

## FRIED CALAMARI
8 OZ (ABOUT 1½ CUPS)
(NO SAUCE)

**400 CALORIES**

## MOZZARELLA STICKS
4 STICKS 300 calories
+ 6 TBSP MARINARA SAUCE 90 calories

**390 CALORIES**

# WHAT ADDS 100 CALORIES?

Each of these adds
100 calories:
2½ TSP OLIVE OIL
10 OLIVES
½ PIECE GARLIC BREAD
1 OZ PROVOLONE
CHEESE
1½ TBSP ITALIAN SALAD
DRESSING
½ CUP SAUTÉED
SPINACH

# FIND THE FAT

Standard red sauce and red
clam sauce are the only
sauces without extra fat and
calories. Here's what a
½-cup portion will cost you.

**RED OR RED CLAM SAUCE**
60 calories
**MARINARA SAUCE**
110 calories
**VODKA SAUCE**
140 calories
**RED SAUCE WITH SAUSAGE**
150 calories
**ALFREDO SAUCE**
180 calories
**WHITE CLAM SAUCE**
300 calories

# FIXES

**1** Get the basket of tortilla chips off the table. It's hard to stop eating these amazingly high-calorie freebies, especially when you're hungry.

**2** If you want a margarita, skip a meal. The margarita takes up almost a full meal's worth of calories.

**3** Order à la carte rather than having a full meal—a meal with an entrée, sides of rice and beans, and calorie-laden toppings like sour cream and cheese can easily hit 1,000 calories or more.

**4** Limit yourself to one high-fat topping—cheese, sour cream, or guacamole—and order your meal without the others. Our pick is guacamole for its good fats and abundance of nutrients.

**5** Use vegetable-based salsas like pico de gallo, classic tomato salsa, tomatillo salsa, and roasted vegetable salsa as universal toppings. They're much lower in calories than salad dressing, sour cream, and other higher-fat fare. Corn and black bean salsas are slightly higher in calories, with about 20 calories in 2 tablespoons, but still are a nutrition bargain.

**FIND THE FAT**
Taco salads might seem like a great healthy option, but beware of the fried tortilla bowls that hold them. They are surprisingly high in calories—almost 400 calories at one national chain.

### CHEESE QUESADILLA
⅛ OF AN 8" CHEESE QUESADILLA (ANY TYPE OF CHEESE)

**410 CALORIES**

### TOSTADA SALAD
½ OF A TOSTADA SALAD WITH REFRIED BEANS, BABY GREENS, HEARTS OF ROMAINE, JACK AND CHEDDAR CHEESES, FRESH GUACAMOLE, CHICKEN, TORTILLA STRIPS, AND SOUR CREAM IN A TORTILLA BOWL

**390 CALORIES**

### BURRITO PLATE
1 3-OZ BEAN AND CHEESE BURRITO
190 calories
+ 1 CUP RICE AND BEANS
260 calories

**450 CALORIES**

### TORTILLA CHIPS WITH GUACAMOLE
20 TORTILLA CHIPS 290 calories
+ ⅓ CUP GUACAMOLE
110 calories

**400 CALORIES**

## 400 *CALORIE* MEXICAN

AUTHENTIC MEXICAN FOOD IS MUCH LEANER than its American interpretation—our Mexican food often is piled with beans, sour cream, and other high-fat toppings. Not to mention the *grande* portions we've come to expect. Stick with veggies and grilled items.

### FAJITAS

1 6" CORN TORTILLA 50 calories
+ 3 OZ GRILLED FAJITA STEAK 170 calories
+ 1 CUP GRILLED ONIONS AND PEPPERS 200 calories

420 CALORIES

### CHILE RELLENO
5 OZ

370 CALORIES

### SHRIMP TACOS
2

400 CALORIES

### FROZEN MARGARITA
12 OZ

370 CALORIES

## TOPPINGS

**1 JALAPEÑO CHILE PEPPER**
5 calories
**2 TBSP CHOPPED TOMATOES**
5 calories
**¼ CUP SHREDDED LETTUCE**
5 calories
**2 TBSP PICO DE GALLO**
10 calories
**2 TBSP SALSA**
10 calories
**2 TBSP SLICED OLIVES**
20 calories

## THE TORTILLA WEIGH-IN

If you've ever made a wrap or a burrito, you know that it takes a big tortilla—with a lot of calories—to hold all the filling.

**5" CORN TORTILLA**
**⅔ OZ**
50 calories
**5" FLOUR TORTILLA**
**⅔ OZ**
80 calories
**7½" FLOUR TORTILLA**
**1½ OZ**
140 calories
**10" FLOUR TORTILLA**
**2½ OZ**
220 calories
**12" FLOUR TORTILLA**
**4 OZ**
280 calories

## SMART STARTERS

Enjoy a cup of soup or a couple of steamed dumplings as a smart start to your Chinese meal.

**1 CUP EGG DROP SOUP**
70 calories

**1 CUP HOT AND SOUR SOUP**
80 calories

**2 STEAMED VEGETABLE DUMPLINGS**
110 calories

**1 CUP WONTON SOUP**
150 calories

### SPOT THE SUGAR
Many popular Chinese sauces, including brown sauce, sweet and sour sauce, hoisin sauce, duck sauce, and plum sauce, get almost all their calories from sugar, up to 5 teaspoons per ¼ cup.

**WHITE RICE**
2 CUPS

380 CALORIES

# 400 CALORIE CHINESE

EATING CHINESE FOOD IN A 400-CALORIE way can be challenging. Dishes are filled with veggies but also cooked in oil. And it's hard to use your stomach as a guide—lots of people complain that they're hungry an hour after eating a Chinese meal.

**⅔ CUP GENERAL TSAO'S CHICKEN**
390 calories

**2½ CHICKEN LETTUCE WRAPS**
(4 OZ EACH)
380 calories

**2¼ EGG ROLLS**
390 Calories

**2½ CUPS STEAMED BUDDHA'S DELIGHT**
400 calories

**1½ CUPS KUNG PAO SHRIMP**
390 calories

**1⅓ CUPS VEGETABLE LO MEIN**
390 calories

**1⅓ CUPS VEGETABLE FRIED RICE**
390 calories

**1⅛ CUPS BEEF WITH BROCCOLI**
390 calories

**1¾ CUP BROWN RICE**
410 calories

# FIXES

**1** Start with a cup of soup. Soups can help tame your appetite and are relatively low in calories.

**2** Request an order of steamed vegetables to mix in with other dishes and make them larger and more satisfying.

**3** Choose one entrée and eat just half, since many have enough calories for at least two meals. Seafood and fish entrées generally are lower in fat and calories than chicken or beef dishes.

**4** Eat only half a cup of rice (white or brown). Fried rice—with about twice the calories of plain rice—takes the place of an entrée plus rice. Use the Chinese teacups on your table as a handy portion guide; a teacup holds about half a cup.

**5** Beware of the following words on the menu, which signal foods cooked with lots of added fat or sugar: crispy, kung pao, pan-fried, General Tso's, sweet and sour.

# FIXES

**1** Begin your meal with a vegetable salad or a bowl of miso soup. But go easy on the carrot-ginger dressing, since it has a fair amount of oil.

**2** In general, each piece of a sushi roll weighs about 1 ounce, with the exception of large rolls like futomaki that weigh two or three times as much. Figure about ½ ounce per piece of sashimi. The larger hand roll (temaki), a combination of rice and fish in a seaweed "cone," measures about 4 ounces.

**3** Order a combination of sushi and sashimi for the smartest use of 400 calories. Most of the calories in sushi come from the rice, which contains sugar.

**4** Limit the number of sushi pieces with *spicy* (made with mayo) or *tempura* (breaded and fried) in their name.

**5** Figure on about 8 pieces of sushi plus a veggie starter for your 400-calorie meal. For sashimi, 2 pieces equal 1 piece of sushi.

## 400 CALORIE SUSHI

IT'S EASY TO EAT IN A 400-calorie way at a sushi restaurant—menu items are small and most don't contain a lot of calorie-adding fats.

## ROLLS

**1 PIECE CALIFORNIA ROLL**
40 calories

**1 PIECE CUCUMBER ROLL**
40 calories

**1 PIECE TUNA ROLL**
40 calories

**1 HAND ROLL (TEMAKI)**
120 calories

**1 PIECE PHILADELPHIA ROLL**
50 calories

**1 PIECE SPICY SALMON ROLL**
50 calories

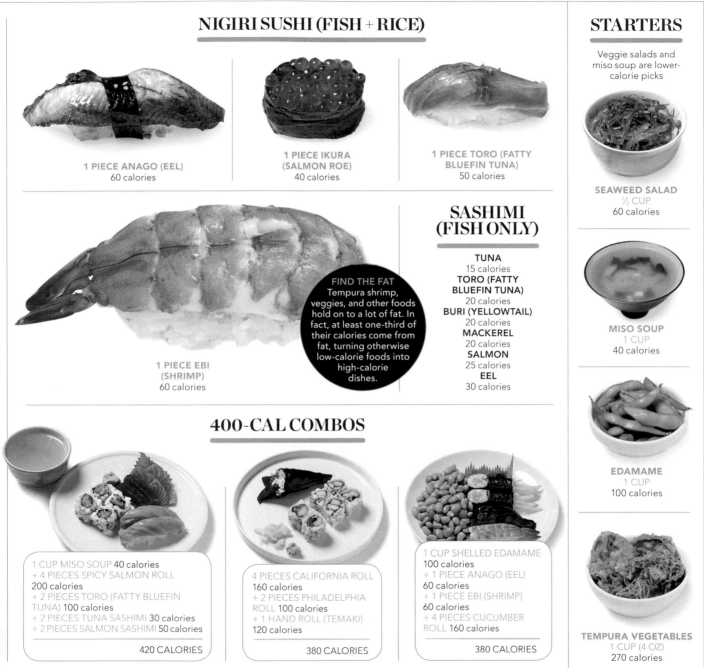

# NIGIRI SUSHI (FISH + RICE)

**1 PIECE ANAGO (EEL)**
60 calories

**1 PIECE IKURA (SALMON ROE)**
40 calories

**1 PIECE TORO (FATTY BLUEFIN TUNA)**
50 calories

**1 PIECE EBI (SHRIMP)**
60 calories

**FIND THE FAT**
Tempura shrimp, veggies, and other foods hold on to a lot of fat. In fact, at least one-third of their calories come from fat, turning otherwise low-calorie foods into high-calorie dishes.

## SASHIMI (FISH ONLY)

**TUNA**
15 calories
**TORO (FATTY BLUEFIN TUNA)**
20 calories
**BURI (YELLOWTAIL)**
20 calories
**MACKEREL**
20 calories
**SALMON**
25 calories
**EEL**
30 calories

## STARTERS

Veggie salads and miso soup are lower-calorie picks

**SEAWEED SALAD**
½ CUP
60 calories

**MISO SOUP**
1 CUP
40 calories

**EDAMAME**
1 CUP
100 calories

**TEMPURA VEGETABLES**
1 CUP (4 OZ)
270 calories

## 400-CAL COMBOS

1 CUP MISO SOUP **40 calories**
+ 4 PIECES SPICY SALMON ROLL **200 calories**
+ 2 PIECES TORO (FATTY BLUEFIN TUNA) **100 calories**
+ 2 PIECES TUNA SASHIMI **30 calories**
+ 2 PIECES SALMON SASHIMI **50 calories**

**420 CALORIES**

4 PIECES CALIFORNIA ROLL **160 calories**
+ 2 PIECES PHILADELPHIA ROLL **100 calories**
+ 1 HAND ROLL (TEMAKI) **120 calories**

**380 CALORIES**

1 CUP SHELLED EDAMAME **100 calories**
+ 1 PIECE ANAGO (EEL) **60 calories**
+ 1 PIECE EBI (SHRIMP) **60 calories**
+ 4 PIECES CUCUMBER ROLL **160 calories**

**380 CALORIES**

# 9.
## QUICK
## FIX
### & No-Cook

# BREAKFAST

## CHEERIOS
★ ★ ★

We added the walnuts and apple to make this a more filling meal. Use the nuts on top of your cereal or enjoy them with the apple as a second course.

|  | calories |
|---|---|
| Cheerios, 1 cup | 100 |
| Low-fat or fat-free milk, ¾ cup | 80 |
| Blueberries, ½ cup | 40 |
| Walnuts, 2 Tbsp | 80 |
| Apple, 1 small | 80 |

**380 calories,** 12 g fat, 2 g saturated fat, 277 mg sodium, 62 g carbohydrate, 10 g fiber, 11 g protein, 32% calcium

## FIBER ONE HONEY CLUSTERS
★ ★

We picked this superhigh-fiber cereal for its staying power. It's okay to swap to a different type of nut if you prefer.

|  | calories |
|---|---|
| Fiber One Honey Clusters, 1 cup | 160 |
| Sliced banana, ½ medium | 50 |
| Chopped walnuts, 2 Tbsp | 100 |
| Low-fat or fat-free milk, 1 cup | 100 |

**410 calories,** 13.5 g fat, 2.5 g saturated fat, 390 mg sodium, 70 g carbohydrate, 16 g fiber, 16 g protein, 40% calcium

## STAR SYSTEM

★ PROTEIN
★ FIBER
★ GOOD FATS
★ FRUITS/VEGGIES

## MUESLI
★ ★ ★

Muesli is a combination of oats, seeds, and dried fruit that is popular in Europe. You can eat it as is or cook it to make a hot cereal.

|  | calories |
|---|---|
| Muesli, five-grain, ½ cup | 140 |
| Plain low-fat yogurt, ¾ cup | 120 |
| Frozen blueberries, thawed, 1 cup | 80 |
| Sliced almonds, 2 Tbsp | 70 |

**410 calories,** 12 g fat, 3 g saturated fat, 184 mg cholesterol, 65 g carbohydrate, 8 g fiber, 17 g protein, 40% calcium

## BREAKFAST TRAIL MIX
★ ★

To make this breakfast trail mix, combine the cereal and nuts ahead of time and be sure to make extra for the family. Add the cranberries and raisins just before eating so that their natural moisture doesn't make the cereal soggy.

|  | calories |
|---|---|
| Barbara's Bakery Puffins, Cinnamon, ⅔ cup | 100 |
| Peanuts, 1 Tbsp | 50 |
| Slivered almonds, 1 Tbsp | 40 |
| Dried cranberries, 2 Tbsp | 50 |
| Raisins, 2 Tbsp | 50 |
| Steamed low-fat milk with sugar-free vanilla syrup, 1 cup | 100 |

**390 calories,** 10.5 g fat, 2.5 g saturated fat, 259 mg sodium, 68 g carbohydrate, 10 g fiber, 14 g protein, 29% calcium

FIBER ONE
HONEY
CLUSTERS
410

BREAKFAST
TRAIL MIX
390

MUESLI
410

## GET MORE...

Looking to get the fewest calories from your tablespoon of almonds? Go with sliced, because they're the least dense. They have 33 calories in each tablespoon, compared to 39 calories for slivered and 51 for whole.

AMY'S
ORGANIC
MULTI-GRAIN
HOT CEREAL
BOWL
390

## AMY'S ORGANIC MULTI-GRAIN HOT CEREAL BOWL
★ ★

This is an easy meal to enjoy at work or when you're short on time—just add water and cook according to directions. Spread the almond butter on the apple slices, wrap them up, and take them with you.

| | calories |
|---|---|
| Amy's Organic Multi-Grain Hot Cereal Bowl, 1 | 190 |
| Sliced apple, 1 medium | 100 |
| Almond butter, 1 Tbsp | 100 |

**390 calories,** 11 g fat, 1 g saturated fat, 372 mg sodium, 68 g carbohydrate, 9 g fiber, 6 g protein, 7% calcium

## OATMEAL
★

Instant oats are cut into smaller flakes and have added salt to help them cook faster. For a heartier flavor and texture, switch to old-fashioned or even steel-cut oats.

| | calories |
|---|---|
| Instant oatmeal, 1 cup cooked | 160 |
| Chopped walnuts, 2 Tbsp | 100 |
| Raisins, 2 Tbsp | 50 |
| Latte made with ¾ cup low-fat milk | 80 |

**390 calories,** 15 g fat, 2.5 g saturated fat, 200 mg sodium, 53 g carbohydrate, 6 g fiber, 15 g protein, 45% calcium

## MILK RICE BREAKFAST PUDDING
★

A quick hot breakfast for a cold morning, this is a good way to use up leftover brown rice. Whisk together the rice, milk, egg, and vanilla extract in a bowl and microwave three times for 45 seconds, stirring after each 45 seconds. Watch carefully to avoid boiling over. Stir in fruit and pecans before serving.

| | calories |
|---|---|
| Cooked brown rice, ⅔ cup | 150 |
| Low-fat or fat-free milk, ¾ cup | 80 |
| Egg, 1 large | 80 |
| Vanilla extract, ½ tsp | 5 |
| Chopped dried fruit, 2 Tbsp | 60 |
| Chopped pecans, 1 Tbsp | 50 |

**425 calories,** 13 g fat, 3 g saturated fat, 183 mg sodium, 54 g carbohydrate, 4 g fiber, 16 g protein, 25% calcium

## WHOLE GRAIN TOAST
★ ★ ★

We like the extra fiber provided by this hearty bread. Slice the cheese into thin pieces so that it can soften or melt.

| | calories |
|---|---|
| Pepperidge Farm Whole Grain Double Fiber Bread, 2 slices | 200 |
| Laughing Cow Mini Babybel Light, 2 rounds | 100 |
| Fruit salad, 1 cup | 100 |

**400 calories,** 10 g fat, 3 g saturated fat, 661 mg sodium, 67 g carbohydrate, 15 g fiber, 21 g protein, 50% calcium

### FUN FACT...

The link between oats and a healthy heart is so strong that oats were among the first foods whose manufacturers were granted permission to state health claims on package labels.

## BAGEL WITH HUMMUS
★

This savory breakfast may strike you as unusual, but folks in the Middle East eat this way all the time. Seek out a 4" bagel, which will weigh about 3 ounces. Many bagel shop bagels are close to twice that weight, and twice the calories.

|  | calories |
|---|---|
| Plain bagel, 4" | 290 |
| Sabra Classic Hummus, 2 Tbsp | 70 |
| Sliced cucumber, ¼ cup | 5 |
| Sliced tomato, ¼ cup | 10 |
| Cantaloupe, ½ cup | 25 |

**400 calories,** 8 g fat, 1 g saturated fat, 696 mg sodium, 70 g carbohydrate, 4 g fiber, 13 g protein, 3% calcium

## BAGEL WITH CREAM CHEESE
★

These portion-controlled bagels eliminate the guesswork about how much to eat. Light cream cheese doesn't supply a lot of nutrition, so feel free to use another spread that provides similar calories.

|  | calories |
|---|---|
| Lender's Wheat Bagel, 1 | 210 |
| Light cream cheese, 2 Tbsp | 70 |
| Banana, ½ medium | 50 |
| Fat-free flavored yogurt, 6 oz | 80 |

**410 calories,** 6 g fat, 3 g saturated fat, 650 mg sodium, 72 g carbohydrate, 8 g fiber, 18 g protein, 29% calcium

## ENGLISH MUFFIN WITH NUT BUTTER
★ ★ ★

Nut butters deliver good fats and also are highly satiating. Keep them in the fridge to maintain their fresh flavor, but bring to room temperature before spreading.

|  | calories |
|---|---|
| Toasted whole wheat English muffin, 1 | 130 |
| Peanut or almond butter, 4 tsp | 130 |
| Sliced banana, ½ medium | 50 |
| Low-fat or fat-free milk, 1 cup | 100 |

**410 calories,** 15 g fat, 4 g saturated fat, 520 mg sodium, 56 g carbohydrate, 7 g fiber, 20 g protein, 50% calcium

## ENGLISH MUFFIN WITH CHEESE
★

Cut the cheese into small pieces and whisk with the egg before microwaving to add flavor and creaminess. Microwave 15 seconds at a time until firm to avoid overcooking, lightly covering the bowl in case the egg splatters.

|  | calories |
|---|---|
| Pepperidge Farm 100% Whole Wheat English Muffin | 140 |
| Microwave scrambled egg, 1 large | 80 |
| Laughing Cow Light French Onion Wedge, 1 wedge | 40 |
| Stonyfield Farm Wild Berry Smoothie, 6 oz | 140 |

**400 calories,** 10.5 g fat, 4.5 g saturated fat, 622 mg sodium, 50 g carbohydrate, 3 g fiber, 21 g protein, 36% calcium

## FUN FACT...

Butter and peanut butter have about the same number of calories, but that's where their similarities end. Research shows that peanut butter, and peanuts as well, are satiating and can help lower blood cholesterol when they're substituted for other high-fat foods.

## ENGLISH MUFFIN WITH BUTTER
★ ★ ★

Whipped butter is easier to spread than regular butter and has fewer calories per teaspoon because it also contains air. Mix the honey and strawberries with the yogurt.

|  | calories |
|---|---|
| Toasted whole wheat English muffin, 1 | 130 |
| Whipped butter, 2 tsp | 50 |
| Plain low-fat or fat-free yogurt, 1 cup | 150 |
| Sliced strawberries, 1 cup | 50 |
| Honey, 1 tsp | 20 |

**400 calories,** 11 g fat, 6 g saturated fat, 537 mg sodium, 62 g carbohydrate, 8 g fiber, 20 g protein, 65% calcium

## BOB'S RED MILL HOT CEREAL
★ ★

Cooking the cereal in milk instead of water adds creaminess and body. If you prefer not to fuss with cooking dried apricots, you can substitute apricots canned in juice.

|  | calories |
|---|---|
| Bob's Red Mill 7 Grain or 10 Grain Hot Cereal, ¼ cup | 140 |
| Low-fat or fat-free milk, 1 cup | 100 |
| Pecans, 2 Tbsp | 90 |
| Dried apricot halves, cooked, ¼ cup | 50 |

**380 calories,** 12.5 g fat, 2.5 g saturated fat, 114 mg sodium, 55 g carbohydrate, 8 g fiber, 16 g protein, 33% calcium

ENGLISH MUFFIN WITH BUTTER
400

BOB'S RED MILL HOT CEREAL
380

BAGEL EGG SANDWICH
410

## RAISIN BRAN MUFFIN
★ ★

Take out your 400 Calorie Lens—a 2-ounce muffin is about the size of a standard cake mix cupcake. Plunk your favorite muffin on the scale to see how it measures up. In this meal, you can spread jam on the muffin or mix it into the combo of yogurt, wheat germ, and berries.

| | calories |
|---|---|
| Raisin bran muffin, 2 oz | 150 |
| All-fruit strawberry jam, 2 tsp | 20 |
| Plain low-fat yogurt, ¾ cup | 120 |
| Wheat germ, 1 Tbsp | 30 |
| Mixed berries, 1 cup | 100 |

**420 calories,** 6.5 g fat, 2.5 g saturated fat, 393 mg sodium, 75 g carbohydrate, 14 g fiber, 18 g protein, 40% calcium

## CORN MUFFIN TOP
★ ★ ★

Pick whichever flavor Vita Top you like, since all are 100 calories. If you prefer a different brand, look for a muffin top that weighs about 1½ ounces.

| | calories |
|---|---|
| Golden Corn VitaTop, 1 | 100 |
| Low-fat cottage cheese, ½ cup | 80 |
| Mango, 1 cup | 110 |
| Latte made with ¾ cup low-fat milk | 80 |

**370 calories,** 4.5 g fat, 2 g saturated fat, 682 mg sodium, 65 g carbohydrate, 9 g fiber, 25 g protein, 29% calcium

## BAGEL EGG SANDWICH
★ ★

You can get rid of at least an ounce of bagel—80 to 100 calories—by scooping out (and not eating) the insides of your bagel. Plus you'll be able to fit more fillings without creating a sandwich that is too tall for you to bite.

| | calories |
|---|---|
| Whole wheat bagel, hollowed out, 4" | 230 |
| Hard-boiled egg, 1 | 80 |
| Miracle Whip Light, 1 Tbsp | 40 |
| Lettuce, 2 leaves | 10 |
| Tomato, 2 slices | 10 |
| Large coffee with 3 oz low-fat milk | 40 |

**410 calories,** 11 g fat, 3 g saturated fat, 640 mg sodium, 55 g carbohydrate, 8 g fiber, 20 g protein, 25% calcium

MUFFIN TOPS aren't lower in calories—an ounce of muffin is about 70 calories regardless of where it comes from—but they're perfect if you prefer the texture of crust over the softness of insides.

## ALL-IN-ONE SMOOTHIE
★ ★ ★

This smoothie is quick, filling, and really delicious, and the frozen fruit adds slushiness.

| | calories |
|---|---|
| Low-fat or fat-free milk, 1 cup | 100 |
| Banana (peel, slice, and freeze the night before), small | 90 |
| Frozen berries, ½ cup | 30 |
| Old-fashioned oats, ¼ cup | 80 |
| Peanut butter, 1 Tbsp | 90 |

**390 calories,** 13 g fat, 3.5 g saturated fat, 180 mg sodium, 59 g carbohydrate, 9 g fiber, 17 g protein, 30% calcium

## CRUNCHY YOGURT PARFAIT
★ ★

For a parfait look, use half the yogurt, bar, and banana for the first layers, repeat, and top with honey. Because it's extra thick, Greek yogurt is higher in calories (it's okay to swap for a different yogurt with similar calories).

| | calories |
|---|---|
| Chobani Plain 2% Greek Yogurt, 6-oz container | 130 |
| Chex Mix Bar, Chocolate Chunk, 1 bar, crumbled | 140 |
| Banana, 1 medium | 110 |
| Honey, 1 tsp | 20 |

**400 calories,** 6.5 g fat, 2 g saturated fat, 205 mg sodium, 66 g carbohydrate, 5 g fiber, 20 g protein, 20% calcium

## PUMPED-UP FRUIT SALAD
★ ★ ★

This colorful breakfast combines five different fruits—substitute frozen strawberries if fresh are not in season—with cottage cheese and nuts. It's okay to substitute a different 40- to 70-calorie beverage for the hot cocoa.

| | calories |
|---|---|
| Banana, ½ medium | 60 |
| Strawberries, ½ cup | 30 |
| Kiwifruit, 1 medium | 50 |
| Cubed cantaloupe, 1 cup | 50 |
| 1% low-fat cottage cheese with pineapple, ½ cup | 120 |
| Chopped pistachios, 2 tsp | 30 |
| Sugar-free hot cocoa, 1 packet | 50 |

**390 calories,** 4.5 g fat, 1 g saturated fat, 508 mg sodium, 70 g carbohydrate, 9 g fiber, 18 g protein, 44% calcium

**IF YOU'RE** not a cottage cheese lover, have yogurt instead—plain, Greek, flavored, or diet to total 120 calories—or add a couple tablespoons of nuts.

CRUNCHY YOGURT PARFAIT **400**

MARGHERITA SALAD 390

CHILI BAKED POTATO 390

# LUNCH/DINNER

### ASIAN-STYLE SOUP
★ ★ ★

To make this quick meal, bring the broth to a simmer, add the spinach, tofu, and noodles, and simmer until the noodles are cooked. Japanese seaweed-sesame seasoning mix adds flavor without calories.

| | calories |
|---|---|
| Low-sodium chicken or vegetable broth, or miso soup, 1 cup | 40 |
| Baby spinach, 1 cup | 10 |
| Silken tofu, 3 oz (about ¼ box) | 50 |
| Soba noodles, 2 oz | 190 |
| Low-fat frozen yogurt, ½ cup | 110 |

**400 calories,** 7.5 g fat, 3 g saturated fat, 619 mg sodium, 61 g carbohydrate, 9 g fiber, 20 g protein, 16% calcium

### CHILI BAKED POTATO
★ ★

This meal offers a perfect opportunity to check out that baked-potato option on your microwave. Scrub the potato well, set the microwave to cook one potato, and you're ready to go.

| | calories |
|---|---|
| Potato, 1 medium | 160 |
| Canned vegetarian chili, ½ cup | 90 |
| Grated reduced-fat Cheddar cheese, 2 Tbsp | 40 |
| 100-calorie ice cream sandwich, 1 | 100 |

**390 calories,** 6.5 g fat, 3 g saturated fat, 537 mg sodium, 72 g carbohydrate, 8 g fiber, 15 g protein, 32% calcium

## VEGETABLE MEDLEY SALAD
★ ★ ★

Mrs. Dash, McCormick, Penzeys, and others have a large and growing selection of salt-free seasoning blends that add a nice flavor accent to salads. Draining and rinsing canned beans removes more than half of their sodium.

|  | calories |
|---|---|
| Romaine or other lettuce mix, 2 cups | 20 |
| Canned chickpeas, rinsed and drained, ½ cup | 140 |
| Alpine Lace Swiss cheese, cut into thin strips, one ½-oz slice | 45 |
| Tomato, cut into wedges, 1 medium | 20 |
| Sliced cucumber, ¼ cup | 5 |
| Plain croutons, ½ cup | 60 |
| Mrs. Dash Tomato Basil Garlic Seasoning Blend, few shakes | 0 |
| Olive oil, 2 tsp, mixed with 1 Tbsp balsamic vinegar | 90 |

**380 calories,** 16 g fat, 4.5 g saturated fat, 290 mg sodium, 51 g carbohydrate, 10 g fiber, 16 g protein, 30% calcium

## MARGHERITA SALAD
★

Use only fresh basil—dried has a totally different flavor—and the best Parmesan you can find.

|  | calories |
|---|---|
| Bocconcini or fresh mozzarella, 2 oz | 150 |
| Sliced tomato, 1 medium | 20 |
| Fresh basil, slivered, 2 Tbsp | 0 |
| Olive oil, 2 tsp, mixed with 1 Tbsp balsamic vinegar | 90 |
| Mesclun lettuce, 2 cups | 20 |
| Grated Parmesan, ½ oz | 60 |
| Italian bread, ⅔ oz slice | 50 |

**390 calories,** 27 g fat, 12 g saturated fat, 284 mg sodium, 21 g carbohydrate, 4 g fiber, 14 g protein, 27% calcium

## BEET, BLUE CHEESE, AND WALNUT SALAD
★ ★ ★

This elegant and hearty salad features a flavorful orange dressing.

|  | calories |
|---|---|
| Shredded romaine, 2 cups | 20 |
| Cubed beets, 2 medium | 40 |
| Blue cheese, 2 Tbsp | 60 |
| Walnut halves, 2 Tbsp | 80 |
| Pear, 1 medium | 100 |
| Olive oil, 1 tsp, mixed with 1 tsp walnut oil, 2 Tbsp orange juice, and salt and pepper | 95 |

**395 calories,** 23 g fat, 5 g saturated fat, 320 mg sodium, 46 g carbohydrate, 10 g fiber, 9 g protein, 15% calcium

FRESH MOZZARELLA is lower in calories than regular because it has more moisture. Dice into small pieces to help spread it throughout the salad.

## GREEK SALAD

★ ★ ★

Canned black olives are a suitable substitute for the kalamatas.

| | calories |
|---|---|
| Chopped romaine lettuce, 2 cups | 20 |
| Tomato, 1 medium, cut into wedges | 20 |
| Kalamata olives, 5 | 50 |
| Stuffed grape leaves, 3 | 120 |
| Reduced-fat feta cheese, ¼ cup | 70 |
| Olive oil, 1 tsp, mixed with ½ Tbsp red vinegar | 40 |
| Dried oregano, ½ tsp | 0 |
| Whole wheat pita, ½ medium | 90 |

**410 calories,** 22 g fat, 5 g saturated fat, 1,299 mg sodium, 42 g carbohydrate, 8 g fiber, 14 g protein, 16% calcium

GREEK
SALAD
410

## CHEF'S SALAD

★ ★ ★

You may prefer to double up on one of the meats.

| | calories |
|---|---|
| Mixed greens, 2 cups | 20 |
| Turkey, ham, and roast beef, cut into thin strips, 1 oz each | 120 |
| Sliced olives, 5 | 50 |
| Diced tomato, 1 medium | 20 |
| Diced bell pepper, ½ medium | 10 |
| Sliced almonds, 1 Tbsp | 30 |
| Olive oil, 1 tsp, mixed with 1 Tbsp balsamic vinegar | 50 |
| 100-calorie pack of cookies of your choice | 100 |

**400 calories,** 19.5 g fat, 3.5 g saturated fat, 1,134 mg sodium, 35 g carbohydrate, 5 g fiber, 24 g protein, 8% calcium

## ITALIAN TUNA SALAD

★ ★ ★ ★

Rinsing the tuna and beans gets rid of extra salt.

| | calories |
|---|---|
| Arugula, 2 cups | 10 |
| Canned light tuna, packed in water, rinsed and drained, ½ cup (about 3 oz) | 90 |
| Canned cannellini or white beans, rinsed and drained, ½ cup | 100 |
| Kalamata olives, 7 | 70 |
| Roasted red bell pepper, ½ cup | 40 |
| Minced garlic, 1 tsp | 0 |
| Olive oil, 2 tsp | 80 |
| Lemon juice, 2 tsp | 5 |

**395 calories,** 18 g fat, 2.5 g saturated fat, 1,220 mg sodium, 30 g carbohydrate, 7 g fiber, 28 g protein, 15% calcium

CHEF'S
SALAD
400

THE
COMBINATION
of olives, olive oil,
and almonds packs
a triple punch
of healthy mono-
unsaturated
fats.

## QUICK TUNA SALAD
★ ★

What could be easier than opening up a bag filled with greens, pineapple, snow peas, carrots, and crunchy toppings? Your local market may have other salad combos that can give this dish a different twist.

calories

| | |
|---|---|
| Dole Asian Island Crunch Salad Kit, 1½ cups | 130 |
| Light tuna, packed in water, in pouch, 3 oz | 90 |
| Newman's Own Low Fat Family Recipe Italian Dressing, 2 Tbsp | 60 |
| Bagel, hollowed out, one-half 4 oz | 120 |

**400 calories,** 11 g fat, 1 g saturated fat, 1340 mg sodium, 45 g carbohydrate, 3 g fiber, 28 g protein, 6% calcium

## SPINACH SALAD
★ ★

Dice the egg and break the tuna and cheese into small pieces to give every bite of salad a burst of flavor. Use any salad dressing spray or switch to balsamic vinegar.

calories

| | |
|---|---|
| Spinach, 2 cups | 15 |
| Light tuna, packed in water, drained and rinsed, ¼ cup | 50 |
| Hard-cooked egg, 1 | 80 |
| Crumbled blue cheese, 2 Tbsp | 60 |
| Salad dressing spray, 10 sprays | 10 |
| Whole wheat English muffin, 1 | 130 |
| Sweet iced tea, 1 cup | 60 |

**405 calories,** 12 g fat, 5 g saturated fat, 887 mg sodium, 46 g carbohydrate, 6 g fiber, 27 g protein, 35% calcium

## ASIAN CHICKEN SALAD
★ ★ ★ ★

For a change of pace, try this salad with raw spinach in place of field greens and peanuts rather than sunflower seeds. Salad dressing sprays add a lot of flavor with very few calories.

calories

| | |
|---|---|
| Field greens, 2 cups | 20 |
| Cooked chicken breast strips, ½ cup | 120 |
| Sunflower seeds, 2 Tbsp | 90 |
| Shelled edamame, ¼ cup | 50 |
| Sliced water chestnuts, ¼ cup | 30 |
| Newman's Own Asian Sesame Natural Salad Mist, 10 sprays | 10 |
| Rice crackers, 6 | 110 |

**430 calories,** 16 g fat, 1 g saturated fat, 630 mg sodium, 38 g carbohydrate, 11 g fiber, 32 g protein, 8% calcium

## ALMOND JOY SANDWICH
★ ★ ★

This sandwich is even tastier if you warm it in a pan or wrap it in foil to heat in the oven. Allow the almond butter to come to room temperature for easier spreading. Have the cantaloupe on the side.

calories

| | |
|---|---|
| Whole wheat bread, 2 slices | 140 |
| Almond butter, 1 Tbsp | 100 |
| Sliced almonds, 1 Tbsp | 30 |
| Shredded coconut, 1 Tbsp | 30 |
| Chocolate syrup, 2 tsp | 40 |
| Cubed cantaloupe, 1 cup | 50 |

**390 calories,** 16 g fat, 3.5 g saturated fat, 385 mg sodium, 52 g carbohydrate, 7 g fiber, 13 g protein, 13% calcium

## FUN FACT...

To stretch out your drink calories, mix half sweetened iced tea and half unsweetened iced tea, or combine unsweetened iced tea with an equal amount of sugar-sweetened lemonade. If you want to add a drink with calories to a meal, you'll need to cut something out. And if you prefer to ditch the drink calories in a meal, you can add extra calories in food.

QUICK TUNA
SALAD
400

ASIAN
CHICKEN
SALAD
430

SPINACH
SALAD
405

GRILLED
CHEESE
SANDWICH
410

## GRILLED CHEESE SANDWICH

No nutrition stars, but a whole lot of fun. Use a nonstick pan or cooking spray to grill the sandwich without a lot of extra fat, placing a pot lid on top of the sandwich to trap the heat.

| | calories |
|---|---|
| White bread, 2 slices | 130 |
| American cheese, 2 slices | 140 |
| Unsalted butter, 1 tsp | 30 |
| Chips Ahoy cookies, 2 | 110 |

**410 calories,** 21 g fat, 11 g saturated fat, 942 mg sodium, 43 g carbohydrate, 2 g fiber, 13 g protein, 32% calcium

## QUICK PANINI
★ ★

A small cast-iron pan or heavy pot lid can press down the sandwich panini-style if you don't have a panini grill. Or cook the sandwich in your waffle iron instead. Enjoy the soup as a side dish.

| | calories |
|---|---|
| Pepperidge Farm Whole Grain Double Fiber Bread, 2 slices | 200 |
| Sliced tomato, 4 slices | 10 |
| Cabot 50% Reduced Fat Pepper Jack Cheese, 1 oz | 70 |
| Campbell's Soup at Hand 25% Less Sodium Classic Tomato, 1 | 120 |

**400 calories,** 7.5 g fat, 3 g saturated fat, 1173 mg sodium, 72 g carbohydrate, 15 g fiber, 20 g protein, 30% calcium

## GRILLED VEGGIE WRAP
★ ★

Cook up extra veggies the next time you fire up the grill or pick up grilled veggies at the deli counter of your market. If the veggies look shiny, they're too oily, so blot them with paper towels to degrease.

| | calories |
|---|---|
| Whole wheat tortilla, one 7" | 120 |
| Soft goat cheese, 1 oz (2 Tbsp) | 80 |
| Grilled red bell pepper, ¼ medium | 10 |
| Grilled portobello mushroom, 1 slice | 20 |
| Grilled red onion, 1 slice | 10 |
| Grilled zucchini, ¼ cup | 5 |
| Olive oil used for grilling, 1 Tbsp | 120 |
| Fruit salad, ½ cup | 50 |

**415 calories,** 21 g fat, 6 g saturated fat, 390 mg sodium, 54 g carbohydrate, 7 g fiber, 13 g protein, 8% calcium

## FUN FACT...

The cheese case has plenty of lower-fat options that melt well and taste good. For the panini and grilled cheese sandwiches, use any reduced-fat or shredded cheese that melts well—Cheddar, mozzarella, Swiss, even cheese wedges like The Laughing Cow.

GRILLED VEGGIE WRAP
415

GRILLED CHICKEN AND PESTO SANDWICH
410

TURKEY, APPLE, AND ASIAGO CHEESE SANDWICH
410

### GRILLED CHICKEN AND PESTO SANDWICH
★ ★ ★

Pesto gets most of its calories from olive oil and nuts, two sources of good fats. Enjoy broccoli on the side with the fat-free ranch.

|  | calories |
| --- | --- |
| Whole grain bread, 2 slices | 140 |
| Grilled chicken breast, 3 oz | 140 |
| Pesto, 1 Tbsp | 80 |
| Tomato slices, 2 slices | 10 |
| Broccoli florets, 1 cup | 20 |
| Fat-free ranch dressing, 1 Tbsp | 20 |

**410 calories,** 13 g fat, 4 g saturated fat, 527 mg sodium, 33 g carbohydrate, 7 g fiber, 39 g protein, 22% calcium

### TURKEY, APPLE, AND ASIAGO CHEESE SANDWICH
★ ★ ★

Hollowing out the roll gets rid of a few calories and makes more room for fillings. We prefer fresh turkey breast to deli turkey because it tends to be less salty.

|  | calories |
| --- | --- |
| Whole wheat roll, hollowed out, 1 medium | 110 |
| Fresh turkey breast, 2 oz | 80 |
| Asiago cheese, 1-oz slice | 110 |
| Sliced apple, ½ small | 40 |
| Chutney, 1 Tbsp | 30 |
| Lettuce, 2 leaves | 10 |
| Sliced almonds, 1 Tbsp | 30 |

**410 calories,** 15 g fat, 6 g saturated fat, 511 mg sodium, 41 g carbohydrate, 7 g fiber, 28 g protein, 29% calcium

## ENGLISH MUFFIN PIZZA

★

To make, split the English muffin and spread each half with half the sauce, cheeses, and Italian seasoning. Then bake or broil until the cheese bubbles. Toss the salad with the olive oil first to coat the leaves and help spread the lemon flavor.

| | calories |
|---|---:|
| English muffin, 1 | 130 |
| Marinara sauce, 2 Tbsp | 30 |
| Part-skim mozzarella, ¼ cup | 90 |
| Grated Parmesan cheese, 2 Tbsp | 40 |
| Italian seasoning, ½ tsp | 0 |
| Green salad, 2 cups | 20 |
| Olive oil mixed with lemon juice, 2 tsp each | 80 |

**390 calories,** 20 g fat, 7 g saturated fat, 726 mg sodium, 37 g carbohydrate, 5 g fiber, 18 g protein, 42% calcium

## GRILLED SALMON SANDWICH

★ ★ ★

Dill is a perfect flavor partner for salmon. Mix it with plain yogurt rather than sour cream.

| | calories |
|---|---:|
| 100% whole wheat bread, 2 slices | 140 |
| Grilled salmon, 3 oz | 180 |
| Plain yogurt, 2 Tbsp, mixed with 1 tsp fresh dill | 20 |
| Deli mustard, 1 tsp | 5 |
| Lettuce , 2 leaves | 10 |
| Tomato, 2 slices | 10 |
| Deli three-bean salad, ⅓ cup | 60 |

**425 calories,** 16 g fat, 3 g saturated fat, 715 mg sodium, 35 g carbohydrate, 7 g fiber, 30 g protein, 14% calcium

ENGLISH MUFFIN PIZZA
390

GRILLED SALMON SANDWICH
425

## DELI SANDWICH

★ ★

Try different types of turkey breast—peppercorn, mesquite, hickory, honey, jalapeño chile—to make your sandwich more interesting.

| | calories |
|---|---|
| Whole wheat bread, 2 slices | 140 |
| Lean roast beef, two 1-oz slices | 120 |
| Deli turkey breast, two 1-oz slices | 60 |
| Lettuce, 2 leaves | 10 |
| Tomato, 2 slices | 10 |
| Deli mustard, 1 tsp | 5 |
| Fresh fruit salad, ½ cup | 50 |

**395 calories,** 8 g fat, 2.5 g saturated fat, 980 mg sodium, 44 g carbohydrate, 7 g fiber, 35 g protein, 8% calcium

## LAYERED TURKEY SANDWICH

★ ★

Sports drinks have about half the sugar and calories of soft drinks and can help quench your thirst after high-intensity activities.

| | calories |
|---|---|
| Whole wheat bread, 2 slices | 140 |
| Turkey breast, 3 oz | 120 |
| Roasted bell peppers, 1 oz | 15 |
| Alfalfa sprouts, 2 Tbsp | 0 |
| Provolone cheese, ½ oz | 50 |
| Dijon mustard, 1 tsp | 5 |
| Green salad with balsamic vinegar, 1 cup | 10 |
| Gatorade, 1 cup | 60 |

**400 calories,** 7 g fat, 3 g saturated fat, 760 mg sodium, 43 g carbohydrate, 6 g fiber, 38 g protein, 20% calcium

## SCANDINAVIAN SANDWICH

★ ★ ★

Although much of our salmon now comes from Chile, the Scandinavian countries are among the originators of smoked salmon. Smoked salmon holds up well in the freezer, so buy extra to keep on hand.

| | calories |
|---|---|
| Wasa Fiber Rye, 4 slices | 120 |
| Light cream cheese, 2 Tbsp | 50 |
| Smoked salmon, 3 oz | 130 |
| Vinegar-marinated cucumber salad, ½ cup | 20 |
| Sorbet, ½ cup | 80 |

**400 calories,** 12 g fat, 6 g saturated fat, 769 mg sodium, 57 g carbohydrate, 9 g fiber, 20 g protein, 13% calcium

SCANDINAVIAN
SANDWICH
400

## HAM SANDWICH
★ ★ ★

Today's pigs are skinnier than their relatives from a generation or two ago, so deli ham is much less fatty, especially when you buy brands that are labeled "lean."

| | calories |
|---|---|
| Lean deli ham, 3 oz | 90 |
| Alpine Lace Swiss cheese, one ½-oz slice | 45 |
| Deli mustard, 1 tsp | 5 |
| Rye bread, 2 slices | 170 |
| Lettuce , 2 leaves | 10 |
| Tomato, 2 slices | 10 |
| Orange, 1 medium | 70 |

**400 calories,** 8 g fat, 3 g saturated fat, 1,167 mg sodium, 54 g carbohydrate, 8 g fiber, 25 g protein, 25% calcium

## FALAFEL SANDWICH
★ ★

The international aisle of your market may stock falafel mix, and some markets carry falafel ready-made and frozen. To make the tahini sauce, use ½ tablespoon of tahini thinned with a teaspoon of lemon juice and a teaspoon of water. Hot sauce is optional.

| | calories |
|---|---|
| Whole wheat pita, 1 pita | 170 |
| Falafel balls, 2 | 110 |
| Tahini sauce, 1⅔ Tbsp | 50 |
| Shredded lettuce, ¼ cup | 5 |
| Chopped tomato, 2 Tbsp | 5 |
| Honeydew, 1 cup | 60 |

**400 calories,** 12 g fat, 2 g saturated fat, 479 mg sodium, 65 g carbohydrate, 7 g fiber, 13 g protein, 5% calcium

## QUICK BAKED ZITI
★ ★

Put the ziti in a bowl and mix in the sauce. Top with the cheeses and microwave until hot. While it's cooking, quickly put together a spinach salad.

| | calories |
|---|---|
| Cooked whole wheat ziti, 1 cup | 170 |
| Pasta sauce, ½ cup | 80 |
| Part-skim ricotta cheese, ¼ cup | 70 |
| Part-skim mozzarella, 2 Tbsp | 40 |
| Grated Parmesan cheese, 1 Tbsp | 20 |
| Spinach leaves, 2 cups | 15 |
| Sliced mushrooms, ½ cup | 10 |
| Salad dressing spray, 10 sprays | 10 |

**415 calories,** 14 g fat, 6 g saturated fat, 890 mg sodium, 55 g carbohydrate, 6 g fiber, 25 g protein, 45% calcium

## HOT MACARONI TUNA
★ ★

Just mix together all the ingredients, cover, and cook in the microwave for about 1 minute or in the oven.

| | calories |
|---|---|
| Cooked macaroni, ⅔ cup | 150 |
| Grated reduced-fat cheddar cheese, ¼ cup | 80 |
| Light tuna, packed in water, rinsed and drained, ½ cup (about 3 oz) | 90 |
| Diced tomato, 1 medium | 20 |
| Finely chopped red onion, 2 Tbsp | 10 |
| Miracle Whip Light, 1 Tbsp | 40 |

**390 calories,** 11 g fat, 4.5 g saturated fat, 630 mg sodium, 39 g carbohydrate, 4 g fiber, 33 g protein, 45% calcium

## PASTA, PEPPERS, SAUSAGE, AND SAUCE

★ ★

We keep extra cooked pasta in the fridge for quick microwaveable meals like this one.

| | calories |
|---|---:|
| Cooked spaghetti, ⅔ cup | 150 |
| Sliced cooked smoked low-fat sausage, ½ cup (about 3 oz) | 90 |
| Marinara sauce, ½ cup | 110 |
| Red bell pepper, 1 medium | 40 |

**390 calories,** 7 g fat, 2 g saturated fat, 1,210 mg sodium, 64 g carbohydrate, 8 g fiber, 16 g protein, 6% calcium

## 90% LEAN BURGER

★

Ground beef usually is marked with its percentage of leanness; 90% lean has enough fat to be grilled without becoming overly dry.

| | calories |
|---|---:|
| 90% lean cooked hamburger, one 3-oz patty | 180 |
| Hamburger bun, 1 | 120 |
| Tomato, 1 medium slice | 5 |
| Lettuce, 1 leaf | 5 |
| Ketchup, 1 Tbsp | 20 |
| Pickle slices, 2 | 0 |
| Potato salad, ¼ cup | 80 |

**410 calories,** 15 g fat, 5 g saturated fat, 806 mg sodium, 37 g carbohydrate, 2 g fiber, 27 g protein, 8% calcium

PASTA, PEPPERS, SAUSAGE, AND SAUCE
390

90% LEAN BURGER
410

## TOFU RICE BOWL
★

The next time your 400 Calorie Lens says that the Chinese restaurant served too big a portion of rice, pack up the extras and make this meal for a quick microwave lunch or dinner.

| | calories |
|---|---|
| Leftover brown rice, ⅔ cup | 150 |
| Extra-firm tofu, 4 oz | 100 |
| Thai-style frozen vegetables, ¾ package | 30 |
| Mrs. Dash Spicy Teriyaki 10-Minute Marinade, 1 Tbsp | 25 |
| Fat-free chocolate pudding snack, 1 | 90 |

**395 calories,** 9 g fat, 2 g saturated fat, 171 mg sodium, 62 g carbohydrate, 4 g fiber, 17 g protein, 27% calcium

## CHICKEN BREAST "STIR-FRY"
★ ★ ★

We use the term *stir-fry* loosely—you can make this meal just as quickly in the microwave. Cut the chicken into strips so that it's done when the vegetables are.

| | calories |
|---|---|
| Chicken breast fillet, 4 oz raw | 120 |
| Frozen Asian mixed vegetables, 2 cups | 50 |
| Low-sodium soy sauce, 2 tsp | 10 |
| Sesame oil, 1 tsp | 40 |
| Brown rice, ⅔ cup cooked | 150 |

**370 calories,** 8 g fat, 1.5 g saturated fat, 450 mg sodium, 46 g carbohydrate, 7 g fiber, 31 g protein, 6% calcium

## CHICKEN QUESADILLA
★ ★ ★ ★

If you can't fit all the chicken, salsa, and cheese onto half a tortilla, either make your quesadilla open-face or put the extras on your salad.

| | calories |
|---|---|
| Whole wheat tortilla, one 7" | 120 |
| Cooked chicken breast, ½ cup | 120 |
| Salsa, 2 Tbsp | 10 |
| Shredded cheese, 2 Tbsp | 50 |
| Mixed greens, 2 cups | 20 |
| Avocado, mashed, 2 Tbsp | 50 |
| Salad dressing spray, 10 sprays | 10 |
| Raspberries, ½ cup | 30 |

**410 calories,** 12 g fat, 4 g saturated fat, 737 mg sodium, 48 g carbohydrate, 11 g fiber, 33 g protein, 22% calcium

## GRILLED SALMON
★ ★ ★

This meal is quicker than it sounds—brush the salmon with the marinade (we picked Mrs. Dash because it's low in sodium) and bake or broil until done. Meanwhile, quickly sauté the spinach and garlic together in a bit of oil.

| | calories |
|---|---|
| Salmon fillet, 4 oz raw, brushed with 1 tsp Mrs. Dash Spicy Teriyaki 10-Minute Marinade | 250 |
| Brown rice, ½ cup cooked | 110 |
| Spinach, 2 cups, sautéed with 1 minced clove garlic in 1 tsp peanut oil | 60 |

**420 calories,** 21 g fat, 4.5 g saturated fat, 120 mg sodium, 26 g carbohydrate, 3 g fiber, 28 g protein, 8% calcium

SALMON OFFERS great balance between monounsaturated fatty acids and flavor; other high-MUFA fish like sardines and mackerel don't appeal to as many palates. You can even find grill-worthy frozen salmon burgers at places like Trader Joe's.

## PISTACHIO TILAPIA

★ ★ ★ ★

You can use any whitefish fillet for this quick meal. Place the fish in a nonstick pan, press the pistachios on top, and bake until the flesh is cooked. While the fish is in the oven, prepare the potato and vegetables.

| | calories |
|---|---|
| Tilapia, 4 oz raw | 110 |
| Chopped lightly salted pistachios, 2 Tbsp | 90 |
| Microwaved potato, 1 medium | 160 |
| Frozen veggies, 1 cup | 40 |

**400 calories,** 9 g fat, 1.5 g saturated fat, 180 mg sodium, 48 g carbohydrate, 8 g fiber, 32 g protein, 8% calcium

## PANTRY DINNER

★ ★ ★

The fish, rice, and veggies all can be microwaved for quick heating and less cleanup. The veggie portion below is twice the size of the portion recommended on the bag, in order to make the meal more filling and award it a fruit/veggie star.

| | calories |
|---|---|
| Gorton's Frozen Salmon Fillet, 4 oz | 100 |
| Uncle Ben's Ready Rice Whole Grain Brown, ½ cup cooked | 110 |
| Green Giant Broccoli & Carrots (19-oz bag), 2½ cups frozen | 80 |
| Nabisco Ginger Snaps, 4 cookies | 120 |

**410 calories,** 8 g fat, 0.5 g saturated fat, 868 mg sodium, 59 g carbohydrates, 5 g fiber, 23 g protein, 8% calcium

SHRIMP TERIYAKI NOODLE BOWL 390

## SHRIMP TERIYAKI NOODLE BOWL

★ ★ ★

This meal cooks up in minutes in either the microwave or a pot on the stove. Use any fresh or frozen vegetables you like.

| | calories |
|---|---|
| Frozen shrimp, 4 oz | 120 |
| Low-sodium teriyaki sauce, 2 Tbsp | 30 |
| Cooked whole wheat spaghetti, 1 cup | 170 |
| Frozen broccoli, 1 cup | 40 |
| Sliced water chestnuts, ¼ cup | 30 |

**390 calories,** 3.5 g fat, 1 g saturated fat, 856 mg sodium, 58 g carbohydrate, 14 g fiber, 37 g protein, 18% calcium

# SNACKS/DESSERTS

## CHEESE AND CRACKERS

If you prefer to do without the wine, add three more crackers and a small apple.

| | calories |
|---|---|
| Cheddar cheese, 1 oz | 110 |
| Brie cheese, 1 oz | 100 |
| Reduced Fat Triscuits, 4 | 70 |
| White wine, 5 oz | 120 |

**400 calories,** 19 g fat, 11 g saturated fat, 453 mg sodium, 16 g carbohydrate, 2 g fiber, 15 g protein, 27% calcium

## BAR FOOD
★

You can have another eight pretzels if you switch to light beer.

| | calories |
|---|---|
| Small pretzel twists, 8 pretzels | 50 |
| Mixed nuts, ¼ cup | 200 |
| Beer, 12 oz | 150 |

**400 calories,** 18 g fat, 2.5 g saturated fat, 516 mg sodium, 32 g carbohydrate, 4 g fiber, 9 g protein, 4% calcium

## PITA CHIPS
★ ★

Hummus is available in several different flavors, all with about the same calories per serving. You can quadruple this meal, or upsize it even more, to serve at a party.

| | calories |
|---|---|
| Whole wheat pita chips, 12 chips | 140 |
| Hummus, ¼ cup | 100 |
| Olives, 10 | 100 |
| Baby carrots, 10 | 40 |

**380 calories,** 21 g fat, 2 g saturated fat, 1,264 mg sodium, 39 g carbohydrate, 9 g fiber, 11 g protein, 11% calcium

## PEANUT BUTTER PRETZELS
★

Peanut butter is highly satiating so it makes a good go-to snack to keep hunger at bay.

| | calories |
|---|---|
| Peanut butter pretzels, 22 (2 oz) | 300 |
| Low-fat or fat-free milk, 1 cup | 100 |

**400 calories,** 18.5 g fat, 6 g saturated fat, 567 mg sodium, 40 g carbohydrate, 2 g fiber, 18 g protein, 29% calcium

## FUN FACT...

Supermarket dairy and freezer cases are filled with fun desserts of about 100 calories, including puddings, ice cream bars, and single-serve cups of ice cream. Sometimes it's better to pay a bit more for a one-time treat than to have to resist a big carton of ice cream every time you open the freezer door.

CHEESE AND
CRACKERS
400

HONEY
WHEAT
PRETZELS
420

NACHOS
400

## HONEY WHEAT PRETZELS

★

Honey wheat pretzels have become so popular that stores stock their own generic brands. Despite the word *wheat* in their name, they don't have much fiber.

| | calories |
|---|---|
| Honey wheat pretzels, 8 | 110 |
| Almond butter, 2 Tbsp | 200 |
| Cranberry-raspberry juice drink, 1 cup | 110 |

**420 calories,** 19 g fat, 2 g saturated fat, 560 mg sodium, 55 g carbohydrate, 2 g fiber, 7 g protein, 8% calcium

## NACHOS

You probably suspected that margaritas and other blended drinks are high in calories, and they are. Skip the margarita and you can enjoy twice as many nachos, with calories to spare for some guacamole.

| | calories |
|---|---|
| Blue corn tortilla chips, 10 chips | 90 |
| Salsa, ¼ cup | 20 |
| Shredded reduced-fat Mexican four cheese, 2 Tbsp | 40 |
| Margarita, 4 oz | 250 |

**400 calories,** 7.5 g fat, 2 g saturated fat, 550 mg sodium, 32 g carbohydrate, 2 g fiber, 6 g protein, 23% calcium

## BAGEL BITES

★

Bagel Bites make a pretty quick meal, and this meal even earns a fiber star from the soup.

| | calories |
|---|---|
| Bagel Bites Three Cheese, 4 pieces | 210 |
| Healthy Choice Minestrone Soup, 1 cup | 200 |

**410 calories,** 8 g fat, 3 g saturated fat, 870 mg sodium, 70 g carbohydrate, 7 g fiber, 16 g protein, 18% calcium

## RICE CAKES

★

On one hand, rice cakes seem so 1980s. On the other hand, they're great for crunch without too many calories. If your market makes its own rice cakes on-site, give them a try. They have a stronger toasted flavor than packaged rice cakes do.

| | calories |
|---|---|
| Rice cakes, 4 | 140 |
| The Laughing Cow Mini Babybel Bonbel, 2 rounds | 140 |
| Low-sodium tomato juice, 6 oz | 40 |
| Grapes, ½ cup | 60 |

**380 calories,** 14 g fat, 8.5 g saturated fat, 494 mg sodium, 52 g carbohydrate, 4 g fiber, 14 g protein, 33% calcium

BAGEL
BITES
410

RICE
CAKES
380

## CHIPS AND DIP
★ ★

You can have just tomatoes or enjoy a variety of raw veggies, including broccoli, cauliflower, celery, mushrooms, and baby carrots. It's virtually impossible to eat too many vegetables.

| | calories |
|---|---|
| SunChips, 16 chips | 140 |
| Onion dip, ¼ cup | 100 |
| Cherry tomatoes, 20 | 60 |
| White wine, 5 oz | 120 |

**420 calories,** 17 g fat, 5 g saturated fat, 577 mg sodium, 40 g carbohydrate, 8 g fiber, 7 g protein, 5% calcium

## CHIPS AND QUICK GUACAMOLE
★ ★

Make your own quick guacamole by mixing together the salsa and avocado. And keep these portions in mind if you're having chips and guacamole at someone's house or at a restaurant.

| | calories |
|---|---|
| Tortilla chips, 2 oz (about 20) | 280 |
| Salsa, ¼ cup | 20 |
| Mashed avocado, ¼ cup | 100 |

**400 calories,** 22 g fat, 3 g saturated fat, 630 mg sodium, 46 g carbohydrate, 8 g fiber, 7 g protein, 10% calcium

## POPCORNS

If you prefer, switch to a calorie-free beverage and you can enjoy an extra cup of Cheddar popcorn.

| | calories |
|---|---|
| Reduced-fat Cheddar popcorn, 2 cups | 90 |
| Regular microwave popcorn, 3 cups | 190 |
| Regular cola, 1 cup | 100 |

**380 calories,** 18 g fat, 3 g saturated fat, 541 mg sodium, 54 g carbohydrate, 5 g fiber, 5 g protein, 2% calcium

## POPCORN TRAIL MIX
★

Toss this together right before you're ready to eat it or serve it at a party so that the raisins don't make the popcorn soggy.

| | calories |
|---|---|
| Microwave light butter popcorn, 6 cups | 90 |
| Grated Parmesan, 2 Tbsp | 40 |
| Unsalted cashew pieces, 2 Tbsp | 100 |
| Raisins, 2 Tbsp | 50 |
| Light beer, 12 oz | 100 |

**380 calories,** 11 g fat, 3.5 g saturated fat, 380 mg sodium, 50 g carbohydrate, 4 g fiber, 11 g protein, 15% calcium

## FUN FACT...

For the same calories in a 12-ounce bottle of beer, you can have 1½ bottles of light beer, about 6 ounces of wine, ⅔ bottle (about 1 cup) of hard lemonade, or 1½ bottles of light hard lemonade.

CHIPS
AND DIP
420

POPCORN
TRAIL MIX
380

## OREOS

Compare the calories of other sandwich cookies if you want to swap out the Oreos, but who would?

|  | calories |
|---|---|
| Oreos, 5 | 270 |
| Low-fat or fat-free milk, 1 cup | 100 |

**370 calories,** 14 g fat, 4 g saturated fat, 407 mg sodium, 52 g carbohydrate, 2 g fiber, 10 g protein, 29% calcium

## VANILLA WAFERS
★

This is one take on milk and cookies, where you make your own sandwich cookies filled with Nutella, a hazelnut-chocolate spread that tastes so good and even earns a good-fats star.

|  | calories |
|---|---|
| Vanilla wafers, 8 | 130 |
| Nutella, 1 Tbsp | 100 |
| Banana, ½ medium | 50 |
| Low-fat or fat-free milk, 1 cup | 100 |

**380 calories,** 13 g fat, 8 g saturated fat, 209 mg sodium, 60 g carbohydrate, 3 g fiber, 11 g protein, 33% calcium

OREOS
370

## MICROWAVE S'MORES

★

To make, place two graham cracker squares on a microwaveable plate, top each with chocolate, press a marshmallow on top, and microwave for 10 to 15 seconds. Turn off the microwave as soon as you see the marshmallow puffing up so that it doesn't burn.

| | calories |
|---|---|
| Graham crackers, 4 squares | 120 |
| Dark chocolate, two ½-oz squares | 150 |
| Marshmallows, 2 large | 50 |
| Low-fat or fat-free milk, ¾ cup | 80 |

**400 calories,** 14 g fat, 8 g saturated fat, 261 mg sodium, 59 g carbohydrate, 3 g fiber, 10 g protein, 22% calcium

## MICROWAVE "BANANAS FOSTER"

★ ★

This dessert traditionally is made with much more butter and sugar, but the flavor is just as good the 400-calorie way. Slice the banana and place in a microwave-proof bowl with the butter, sugar, and pecans. Microwave until the butter and sugar bubble, less than a minute, and enjoy with a scoop of ice cream.

| | calories |
|---|---|
| Banana, 1 medium | 110 |
| Unsalted butter, 1 tsp | 30 |
| Brown sugar, 2 tsp | 20 |
| Chopped pecans, 2 Tbsp | 90 |
| Vanilla ice cream, ½ cup | 140 |

**390 calories,** 21 g fat, 8 g saturated fat, 56 mg sodium, 50 g carbohydrate, 5 g fiber, 5 g protein, 10% calcium

MICROWAVE S'MORES
400

MICROWAVE "BANANAS FOSTER"
390

FROZEN
YOGURT
SUNDAE
410

## FROZEN YOGURT SUNDAE
★

Premium brands of frozen yogurt sometimes are worth the extra calories they have because they come in so many fun flavors.

| | calories |
|---|---|
| Premium frozen yogurt, ½ cup | 200 |
| Strawberries, ½ cup | 30 |
| Slivered almonds, 2 Tbsp | 80 |
| Mini chocolate chips, 2 Tbsp | 100 |

**410 calories,** 18 g fat, 7 g saturated fat, 60 mg sodium, 54 g carbohydrate, 5 g fiber, 13 g protein, 30% calcium

## CUPCAKE

Big cupcakes covered in frosting well exceed the 400-calorie threshold. The good news is that some bakeries still make cupcakes of a reasonable size, and you can eat just a small amount of the frosting to bring the calories in line.

| | calories |
|---|---|
| Yellow cupcake, 2.5 oz, with 2 Tbsp chocolate frosting | 380 |

**380 calories,** 17 g fat, 5 g saturated fat, 334 mg sodium, 55 g carbohydrate, 2 g fiber, 4 g protein, 4% calcium

## POUND CAKE
★ ★

This sweet treat is particularly good in the summer when raspberries are in season. If fresh raspberries aren't available, defrost frozen berries.

| | calories |
|---|---|
| Pound cake, one 2-oz slice | 220 |
| Raspberries, 1 cup | 60 |
| Fresh whipped cream, ¼ cup | 100 |

**380 calories,** 22 g fat, 10 g saturated fat, 239 mg sodium, 45 g carbohydrate, 9 g fiber, 5 g protein, 9% calcium

## PUDDING PARFAIT
★ ★ ★

Use your favorite flavor of instant pudding or substitute a ready-to-eat pudding cup with the same number of calories.

| | calories |
|---|---|
| Instant vanilla sugar-free pudding made with ½ cup low-fat milk | 80 |
| Frozen berries, 1 cup | 60 |
| Low-fat granola, ⅓ cup | 130 |
| Chopped walnuts, 2 Tbsp | 100 |
| Cool Whip Lite, 2 Tbsp | 20 |

**390 calories,** 14 g fat, 3 g saturated fat, 440 mg sodium, 60 g carbohydrate, 7 g fiber, 10 g protein, 20% calcium

## FUN FACT...

Whipped toppings don't vary as much in calories per tablespoon as you might expect:
**COOL WHIP FREE**
8 calories
**PRESSURIZED WHIPPED CREAM**
9 calories
**COOL WHIP LITE**
10 calories
**COOL WHIP**
13 calories
**COOL WHIP EXTRA CREAMY**
13 calories
**FRESH WHIPPED CREAM**
26 calories

DARK
CHOCOLATE
390

## DARK CHOCOLATE
★

When only dark chocolate will do, pick the best chocolate you can find.

| | calories |
|---|---|
| Dark chocolate candy bar, 2.6 oz | 390 |

**390 calories,** 24 g fat, 14 g saturated fat, 3 mg sodium, 44 g carbohydrate, 6 g fiber, 4 g protein, 3% calcium

## PB AND BANANA ON CARAMEL CAKES
★

Caramel cakes usually are made from puffed corn rather than rice, giving them a Cracker Jack–like flavor. We added peanut butter for staying power.

| | calories |
|---|---|
| Caramel cakes, 4 | 200 |
| Peanut butter, 4 tsp | 130 |
| Banana, ½ medium | 50 |

**380 calories,** 11 g fat, 2.5 g saturated fat, 220 mg sodium, 62 g carbohydrate, 3 g fiber, 10 g protein, 2% calcium

## BIRTHDAY CAKE

Almost all cakes are high in calories, so take just a small piece (about the size of a hockey puck) along with a small scoop of ice cream and eat slowly.

| | calories |
|---|---|
| Chocolate mousse cake, 3 oz | 330 |
| Vanilla ice cream, ¼ cup | 70 |

**400 calories,** 20 g fat, 10 g saturated fat, 190 mg sodium, 52 g carbohydrate, 2 g fiber, 4 g protein, 4% calcium

## PEANUT BUTTER CUPS
★

Look in the candy aisle for Halloween-size peanut butter cups and small boxes of chocolate-covered peanuts. You'll find nutrition info on the outside of the bag, but not on the small cups or boxes.

| | calories |
|---|---|
| Mini peanut butter cups, 5 | 180 |
| Candy coated peanuts, 20 | 210 |

**390 calories,** 21 g fat, 8 g saturated fat, 130 mg sodium, 43 g carbohydrate, 2 g fiber, 8 g protein, 7% calcium

# 400 CALORIE MUFFIN

MUFFINS COME IN ALL SHAPES and sizes, so gauging calories can be confusing.

### MUFFIN
**4 OZ** (about the size of a tennis ball)
**360 calories**

Standard-size muffins, like the ones you'd bake at home, are difficult to find on the go.

### MINI MUFFINS
**5 OZ** (1 oz each)
**400 calories**

These minis average about 80 calories apiece, so limit yourself to five—or four if they contain chocolate chips or nuts. Each one is about the size of 2 large marbles.

### MUFFIN TOPS
**375 calories**

You're getting only part of a muffin, but you're taking in more than half of a meal's worth of calories.

### OVERSIZE MUFFINS
**⅔ MUFFIN (4 OZ)**
**415 calories**

These gigantic specimens (about the size of a softball) are the norm! At chains like Dunkin' Donuts and Au Bon Pain, you'll be hard-pressed to find a choice under 450 calories. Eat half and pair it with about 100 calories of something more nutritious and satisfying, such as fruit, dairy, or lean protein.

# FIXES

**1** Supersize portions are standard at most chain bakeries, so you'll need to save a portion for later if you want to stick to 400 calories. If you can't resist the temptation, it's smarter to bake these treats at home in regular tins for instant portion control.

**2** Choose flavors that contain fiber (oat bran instead of corn) to stay satisfied longer, and remember that the calories in ingredients like chocolate chips and nuts can add up quickly.

**3** Be aware that "low-fat" doesn't equal "low-calorie." Reduced-fat muffins often contain additional sugar to compensate for the chewier texture.

**4** Make your favorite recipe using applesauce or plain yogurt in place of half the fat. You'll save about 90 calories per tablespoon.

**5** Pair a small muffin with foods that enhance fullness, like yogurt and fruit.

# 400 *CALORIE* SANDWICH

SANDWICHES GIVE YOU MORE FLEXIBILITY THAN almost any other type of food. To stay within 400 calories, you'll need to make smart picks for every component of the sandwich.

### DECONSTRUCTED SANDWICH

1 SLICE WHOLE WHEAT BREAD
**70 CALORIES**

2 THICK TOMATO SLICES
**10 CALORIES**

ROASTED RED BELL PEPPERS, 1 OZ
**15 CALORIES**

SLICED OLIVES, 1 TBSP
**10 CALORIES**

ALPINE LACE SWISS CHEESE, 1 OZ
**90 CALORIES**

TURKEY BREAST, 2 OZ
**60 CALORIES**

AVOCADO SLICES, ¼ AVOCADO
**80 CALORIES**

2 DILL PICKLE SLICES
**5 CALORIES**

1 LETTUCE LEAF
**5 CALORIES**

HONEY MUSTARD, 1 TSP
**10 CALORIES**

1 SLICE WHOLE WHEAT BREAD
**70 CALORIES**

**TOTAL = 425 CALORIES**

## BREADS

2 SLICES WHITE BREAD
130 calories

2 SLICES WHOLE
WHEAT BREAD
140 calories

6½" WHOLE WHEAT
PITA
170 calories

2 SLICES RYE BREAD
170 calories

KAISER ROLL
170 calories

½ SUBMARINE/
HOAGIE ROLL
190 calories

10" WRAP
220 calories

2 SLICES SOURDOUGH
BREAD
260 calories

## SPREADS

2 TSP DIJON OR DELI
MUSTARD
10 calories

2 TSP HONEY
MUSTARD
25 calories

1 TBSP ITALIAN
DRESSING
40 calories

1 TBSP TAPENADE
40 calories

1 TBSP LIGHT MAYO
50 calories

2 TBSP HUMMUS
50 calories

1 TBSP THOUSAND
ISLAND DRESSING
60 calories

1 TBSP PESTO
80 calories

1 TBSP MAYONNAISE
100 calories

## FILLINGS

1 SLICE BACON
45 calories

1 OZ PROSCIUTTO
60 calories

⅔ OZ SLICE
AMERICAN CHEESE
70 calories

3 OZ TURKEY BREAST,
HAM, ROAST BEEF,
OR TURKEY HAM
90 calories

1 OZ SWISS,
CHEDDAR, JACK, OR
PROVOLONE CHEESE
100 calories

3 OZ CHICKEN
BREAST CUTLET
140 calories

½ CUP GRILLED
VEGETABLES
140 calories

3 OZ BEEF SALAMI
220 calories

½ CUP EGG,
SEAFOOD, CHICKEN,
OR TUNA SALAD
230–260 calories

3 OZ BOLOGNA
269 calories

3 OZ PORK SALAMI
360 calories

3 OZ PEPPERONI
420 calories

## FIXES

1 A slice of bread should be about the thickness of your pointer finger. For sandwiches on rolls, hollow out the insides whenever possible to save close to 100 calories.

2 Meat or protein fillings should be no more than half to three-quarters the thickness of your finger.

3 Fill your sandwich with veggies to add volume and make it more satisfying.

4 Don't let someone else put a spread on your bread, especially mayo, butter, or other high-fat spreads. They're likely to use too much.

5 If you're not sure if your bread has a lot of calories, get rid of the top half and enjoy your sandwich open faced.

## TOPPINGS

2 DILL PICKLE SLICES
5 calories

1 THICK TOMATO SLICE
5 calories

1 LEAF LETTUCE
5 calories

2 THIN RED ONION
SLICES
10 calories

1 OZ ROASTED RED
BELL PEPPERS
15 calories

1 HOT PEPPER
20 calories

2 TBSP SLICED OLIVES
20 calories

# 400 *CALORIE* PASTA

PASTA COMES IN ALL SHAPES AND sizes and includes Asian noodles made with rice and buckwheat flours. In general, a 400-calorie portion of pasta starts off with 4 ounces of dried.

| SPAGHETTI | | | |
|---|---|---|---|
| |  | | |
| # OF 400-CAL SERVINGS | ONE (¼ box) | TWO (½ box) | FOUR (1 box) |
| DRY | 4 oz | 8 oz | 16 oz |
| DIAMETER | ¾" to 1" | 1¼" to 1½" | 1¾" to 2" |
| COOKED | 2 cups | 4 cups | 8 cups |

# PICK YOUR PASTA: HERE'S WHAT 400 CALORIES LOOKS LIKE (COOKED, NO SAUCE)

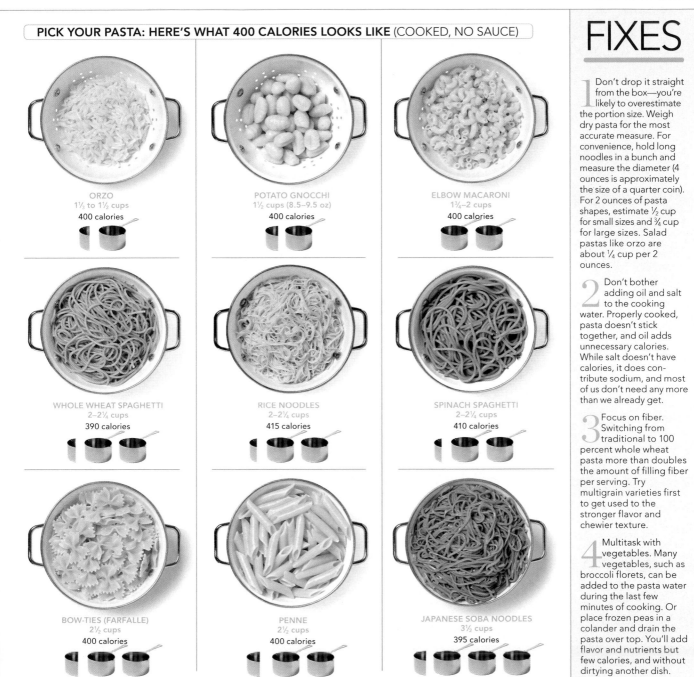

**ORZO**
1⅓ to 1½ cups
400 calories

**POTATO GNOCCHI**
1½ cups (8.5–9.5 oz)
400 calories

**ELBOW MACARONI**
1¾–2 cups
400 calories

**WHOLE WHEAT SPAGHETTI**
2–2¼ cups
390 calories

**RICE NOODLES**
2–2¼ cups
415 calories

**SPINACH SPAGHETTI**
2–2¼ cups
410 calories

**BOW-TIES (FARFALLE)**
2½ cups
400 calories

**PENNE**
2½ cups
400 calories

**JAPANESE SOBA NOODLES**
3½ cups
395 calories

# FIXES

1. Don't drop it straight from the box—you're likely to overestimate the portion size. Weigh dry pasta for the most accurate measure. For convenience, hold long noodles in a bunch and measure the diameter (4 ounces is approximately the size of a quarter coin). For 2 ounces of pasta shapes, estimate ½ cup for small sizes and ¾ cup for large sizes. Salad pastas like orzo are about ¼ cup per 2 ounces.

2. Don't bother adding oil and salt to the cooking water. Properly cooked, pasta doesn't stick together, and oil adds unnecessary calories. While salt doesn't have calories, it does contribute sodium, and most of us don't need any more than we already get.

3. Focus on fiber. Switching from traditional to 100 percent whole wheat pasta more than doubles the amount of filling fiber per serving. Try multigrain varieties first to get used to the stronger flavor and chewier texture.

4. Multitask with vegetables. Many vegetables, such as broccoli florets, can be added to the pasta water during the last few minutes of cooking. Or place frozen peas in a colander and drain the pasta over top. You'll add flavor and nutrients but few calories, and without dirtying another dish.

# 10.
# BREAKFAST & BRUNCH RECIPES

# Many Ways Granola

**PREP TIME:** 5 MINUTES / **COOK TIME:** 2 HOURS / MAKES 4 SERVINGS

PACKAGED GRANOLA IS REALLY HIGH IN CALORIES FROM OIL AND SWEETENERS. WE LIGHTENED UP OUR VERSION BY USING JUST A TOUCH OF OIL AND HONEY. CHOOSE YOUR FAVORITE NUTS AND DRIED FRUITS.

## MAKE IT A MEAL

½ cup 1% cottage cheese
**80 CALORIES**

2 tablespoons walnut halves
**80 CALORIES**

½ medium apple, chopped
**50 CALORIES**

# 410
## CALORIES PER MEAL
★ ★ ★

## STAR SYSTEM

★ PROTEIN
★ FIBER
★ GOOD FATS
★ FRUITS/VEGGIES

- 1 cup old-fashioned oats
- ¼ cup sliced almonds, chopped pecans, chopped walnuts, or chopped mixed nuts
- ½ tablespoon ground cinnamon or pumpkin pie spice
- ½ teaspoon ground ginger or nutmeg (optional)
- 1 tablespoon vegetable or sesame oil
- 1 tablespoon honey or maple syrup
- ½ tablespoon maple syrup
- ¼ cup raisins, dried cranberries, or chopped dried fruit

1. **PREHEAT** the oven to 250°F. Coat a baking sheet with cooking spray or line with a silicone baking sheet or parchment paper.

2. **COMBINE** the oats, nuts, cinnamon or pumpkin pie spice, and ginger (if desired) in a small bowl. Stir in the oil, honey, and syrup. Mix thoroughly. Put the mixture on the baking sheet and bake for approximately 2 hours.

3. **REMOVE** from the oven and cool. Add the dried fruit. Place in an airtight container.

**PER SERVING** (1 serving = ½ cup)

| Calories | Total Fat | Saturated Fat | Sodium | Carbohydrate | Dietary Fiber | Protein | Calcium |
|----------|-----------|---------------|--------|--------------|---------------|---------|---------|
| 200 | 8 g | 0 g | 0 mg | 30 g | 4 g | 5 g | 4% |

# Toasted Barley-Almond Cereal with Roasted Fruit

**PREP TIME:** 5 MINUTES/ **COOK TIME:** 50 MINUTES/ MAKES 4 SERVINGS

BARLEY IS HIGH IN SOLUBLE FIBER, THE TYPE OF FIBER LINKED TO A HEALTHY HEART. SOME PEOPLE PREFER THEIR BARLEY FIRM, WHILE OTHERS LIKE IT AFTER IT HAS "GIVEN UP ITS STARCH" AND DEVELOPED A CONSISTENCY MORE LIKE OATMEAL. YOU DECIDE. WHEN ROASTING THE DRIED FRUIT, WATCH IT CAREFULLY TO PREVENT BURNING. THE ROASTED FRUIT WILL LOOK ALMOST LIKE JEWELS ON TOP OF THE CEREAL.

1 cup pearl barley

½ cup slivered almonds

2 cups water

1 can (15 ounces) fruit cocktail in juice or ½ cup mixed chopped dried fruits (raisins, cranberries, pineapple, etc.), soaked for 1 hour in warm water

1 teaspoon unsalted butter, cut into small pieces

1 teaspoon honey

1. PREHEAT the oven to 425°F. Coat a small baking sheet with cooking spray.

2. HEAT a large saucepan over medium heat. Add the barley and almonds. Toast until lightly browned and aromatic, about 10 minutes. Add the water and cover. Cook until done, 30 minutes for al dente or up to 40 minutes for soft.

3. DRAIN the canned or soaked dried fruit while the barley cooks. Combine with the butter and honey. Place on a baking sheet and roast until lightly browned, 20 minutes for the fruit cocktail or 10 minutes for the dried fruit.

4. TOP the cereal with the roasted fruits. Serve.

## MAKE IT A MEAL

1 cup low-fat or fat-free milk
100 CALORIES

### 400
CALORIES PER MEAL
★ ★

**PER SERVING** (1 serving = 1 cup)

| Calories | Total Fat | Saturated Fat | Sodium | Carbohydrate | Dietary Fiber | Protein | Calcium |
|----------|-----------|---------------|--------|--------------|---------------|---------|---------|
| 300 | 8 g | 1 g | 10 mg | 52 g | 11 g | 8 g | 6% |

# Red, White, and Blueberry Muffins

**PREP TIME:** 10 MINUTES/ **COOK TIME:** 20 MINUTES/ MAKES 12 MUFFINS

WE CUT DOWN ON THE SUGAR IN THIS RECIPE BECAUSE THE STRAWBERRY YOGURT ADDS SWEETNESS. VANILLA YOGURT WOULD BE JUST AS GOOD.

## MAKE IT A MEAL

1 container
(6 ounces) 80-calorie
light yogurt
**80 CALORIES**

1 medium banana
**110 CALORIES**

Tea with 2 ounces
low-fat milk
**25 CALORIES**

## 395

**CALORIES
PER MEAL**
★

| | |
|---|---|
| 2 | cups all-purpose flour |
| ½ | cup sugar |
| 1 | tablespoon baking powder |
| ½ | teaspoon salt |
| ½ | teaspoon ground cinnamon |
| 2 | eggs |
| 1 | cup strawberry blended yogurt |
| ¼ | cup buttermilk |
| ¼ | cup melted butter |
| ½ | teaspoon almond extract |
| 1 | cup frozen raspberries, blackberries, and blueberries |

1. **PREHEAT** the oven to 400°F. Coat a 12-cup (3½" to 4" diameter) muffin pan with cooking spray.

2. **COMBINE** the flour, sugar, baking powder, salt, and cinnamon in a large bowl.

3. **WHISK** together the eggs, yogurt, buttermilk, butter, and almond extract in a medium bowl.

4. **FOLD** the egg mixture into the flour mixture, until just mixed. Gently fold in the frozen berries.

5. **SPOON** into the muffin pan. Bake for 15 to 20 minutes, or until a wooden pick inserted into the center of a muffin comes out clean.

**PER SERVING** (1 serving = 1 muffin)

| Calories | Total Fat | Saturated Fat | Sodium | Carbohydrate | Dietary Fiber | Protein | Calcium |
|---|---|---|---|---|---|---|---|
| 180 | 5 g | 3 g | 250 mg | 30 g | 1 g | 4 g | 10% |

# Banana Walnut Bread

**PREP TIME:** 10 MINUTES/ **COOK TIME:** 45 MINUTES/ MAKES 12 SERVINGS

WHEN BANANAS BECOME OVERRIPE, PEEL THEM AND PUT THEM IN A RESEALABLE PLASTIC BAG IN THE FREEZER. THEY'RE PERFECT FOR THIS RECIPE OR FOR A SMOOTHIE.

- 1 cup all-purpose flour
- 1 cup whole wheat flour
- 2 teaspoons baking powder
- 1 teaspoon ground cinnamon
- ½ teaspoon baking soda
- ½ teaspoon salt
- 3 very ripe medium bananas, mashed
- 2 large eggs
- ½ cup brown sugar
- ½ cup plain low-fat or fat-free yogurt
- ¼ cup canola or vegetable oil
- 1 teaspoon vanilla extract
- ½ cup chopped walnuts

1. **PREHEAT** the oven to 350°F. Coat a 9" × 5" loaf pan with cooking spray or use a nonstick pan.

2. **COMBINE** the all-purpose flour, whole wheat flour, baking powder, cinnamon, baking soda, and salt in a large bowl. Mix together the bananas, eggs, brown sugar, yogurt, oil, and vanilla extract in a medium bowl until well blended. Add to the dry ingredients. Stir just enough to combine. Add the walnuts and stir to combine. Avoid overmixing.

3. **POUR** the batter into the pan. Bake for 45 minutes, or until the top is browned and a wooden pick comes out clean when inserted in the middle of the loaf. Cool before slicing.

## MAKE IT A MEAL

1 tablespoon light cream cheese
**40 CALORIES**

½ cup fruit salad
**50 CALORIES**

Latte made with ¾ cup low-fat milk
**80 CALORIES**

# 400
**CALORIES PER MEAL**
★ ★

**PER SERVING** (1 serving = 1 slice 3/4" thick)

| Calories | Total Fat | Saturated Fat | Sodium | Carbohydrate | Dietary Fiber | Protein | Calcium |
|----------|-----------|---------------|--------|--------------|---------------|---------|---------|
| 230 | 9 g | 1 g | 250 mg | 33 g | 3 g | 5 g | 8% |

## MAKE IT A MEAL

¼ cup part-skim
ricotta
**70 CALORIES**

1 cup strawberries
**50 CALORIES**

1 tablespoon sliced
almonds
**30 CALORIES**

Latte made with
¾ cup low-fat milk
**80 CALORIES**

# 390

## CALORIES
PER MEAL
★ ★

# Chocolate Chip Scones

**PREP TIME:** 10 MINUTES/ **COOK TIME:** 15 MINUTES/ MAKES 8 SERVINGS

MAKE THESE AHEAD AND FREEZE SO THAT THEY'RE HANDY FOR A QUICK BREAKFAST. TO GIVE THEM A FANCIER LOOK, BRUSH WITH A BEATEN EGG AND SPRINKLE WITH DECORATING SUGAR BEFORE BAKING.

- ½ cup whole wheat flour
- ½ cup all-purpose flour
- ½ cup old-fashioned oats
- 3 tablespoons sugar
- 1 teaspoon baking powder
- ¼ teaspoon baking soda
- ½ teaspoon ground cinnamon
- 2 tablespoons unsalted butter
- ¼ cup plain low-fat or fat-free yogurt
- 1 egg
- ¼ teaspoon vanilla extract
- ¼ cup mini chocolate chips

1. **PREHEAT** the oven to 400°F.

2. **MIX** together the whole wheat flour, all-purpose flour, oats, sugar, baking powder, baking soda, and cinnamon in a food processor. With the processor running, add small cubes of butter one at a time. Process until the mixture looks crumbly. Add the yogurt, egg, and vanilla extract. Process just until well mixed. Add the chocolate chips. Process for about 10 seconds.

3. **PLACE** the dough on a lightly floured cutting board. Knead lightly to finish combining all the ingredients. Form into a ball, flatten into an 8" circle (½" thick) with your hands or a floured rolling pin, and cut into 8 wedges. Coat a baking sheet with cooking spray or use a nonstick baking sheet. Place the 8 wedges on the baking sheet.

4. **BAKE** for approximately 12 to 15 minutes, until lightly browned.

Variations: Use raisins, chopped dried apricots, dried cranberries, dried blueberries, or dried cherries in place of the chocolate chips.

**PER SERVING** (1 serving = 1 scone)

| Calories | Total Fat | Saturated Fat | Sodium | Carbohydrate | Dietary Fiber | Protein | Calcium |
|---|---|---|---|---|---|---|---|
| 160 | 6 g | 3 g | 115 mg | 24 g | 2 g | 4 g | 6% |

# Fruity Bran Muffins

**PREP TIME:** 5 MINUTES/ **COOK TIME:** 15 MINUTES/ MAKES 10 MUFFINS

BRAN MUFFINS CAN BE QUITE DRY, BUT NOT THESE. THEY'RE FILLED WITH DRIED FRUIT TO HELP THEM STAY MOIST. SPREADING THEM WITH PEANUT BUTTER ADDS STAYING POWER.

## MAKE IT A MEAL

1 tablespoon
peanut butter
**90 CALORIES**

Latte made with
¾ cup low-fat milk
**80 CALORIES**

# 390
**CALORIES PER MEAL**
★

- 1½ cups raisin bran cereal
- ½ cup low-fat or fat-free milk
- ½ cup low-fat plain yogurt
- ½ cup whole wheat flour
- ½ cup all-purpose flour
- 1 teaspoon baking soda
- ½ teaspoon baking powder
- ½ teaspoon salt
- ½ teaspoon ground cinnamon
- 1 large egg
- ¼ cup vegetable oil
- ¼ cup molasses
- ¼ cup brown sugar
- ¼ cup raisins
- ¼ cup dried cranberries
- ¼ cup chopped dried dates

1. **PREHEAT** the oven to 400°F. Prepare a 12-muffin pan with muffin liners or cooking spray.

2. **PUT** the cereal, milk, and yogurt in a medium bowl. Stir to combine.

3. **STIR** together the whole wheat flour, all-purpose flour, baking soda, baking powder, salt, and cinnamon in a large bowl.

4. **ADD** the egg, oil, molasses, and brown sugar to the cereal mixture. Stir well until the cereal breaks up and the ingredients are well mixed. Add to the flour mixture. Stir until combined. Stir in the raisins, cranberries, and dates.

5. **PLACE** ¼ cup of the batter into each of 10 muffin cups. Bake for 15 minutes, or until a wooden pick inserted into the center of a muffin comes out clean. Avoid overbaking.

**PER SERVING** (1 serving = 1 muffin)

| Calories | Total Fat | Saturated Fat | Sodium | Carbohydrate | Dietary Fiber | Protein | Calcium |
|---|---|---|---|---|---|---|---|
| 220 | 7 g | 1 g | 340 mg | 37 g | 3 g | 4 g | 8% |

# Smoky Cheesy Grits

**PREP TIME:** 5 MINUTES + OVERNIGHT REFRIGERATION/ **COOK TIME:** 27 MINUTES/ MAKES 4 SERVINGS

THIS RECIPE SHOULD BE PREPARED THE NIGHT BEFORE, OR EARLY IN THE MORNING FOR A MIDDAY BRUNCH. TURKEY BACON IS LEANER THAN TRADITIONAL BACON, AND FRESH MOZZARELLA IS A BIT LOWER IN CALORIES THAN THE CHEDDAR CHEESE THAT IS TYPICALLY PAIRED WITH GRITS.

2¼  cups water
     Pinch of salt
½   cup grits (not instant)
4   slices (1 ounce each) turkey bacon
½   cup grated smoked fresh mozzarella cheese

1. **PLACE** the water in a small saucepan. Add the salt and bring to a boil. Pour the grits into the water in a thin stream, whisking to prevent clumping. Reduce the heat. Simmer the grits until fully cooked, about 12 minutes, stirring occasionally.

2. **COOK** the turkey bacon according to package directions. Drain on paper towels and chop. Coat an 8" × 3" loaf pan with cooking spray.

3. **STIR** the bacon and cheese into the grits until well mixed. Spoon the grits into the the loaf pan, cover, and refrigerate at least 4 hours or overnight.

4. **CUT** the grits into 8 slices in the morning. Place on foil or a nonstick baking sheet. Broil until lightly browned on one side, about 5 minutes. Turn the slices over and broil on the other side for about 5 minutes, or until lightly browned.

## MAKE IT A MEAL

2 eggs, scrambled or fried in a nonstick pan
**150 CALORIES**

½ cup fruit salad
**50 CALORIES**

# 420
**CALORIES PER MEAL**
★

**PER SERVING** (1 serving = ¾ cup)

| Calories | Total Fat | Saturated Fat | Sodium | Carbohydrate | Dietary Fiber | Protein | Calcium |
|----------|-----------|---------------|--------|--------------|---------------|---------|---------|
| 220 | 11 g | 5 g | 690 mg | 16 g | 0 g | 13 g | 8% |

# Creamy One-Dish Breakfast Oats

**PREP TIME:** 1 MINUTE/ **COOK TIME:** 4 MINUTES/ MAKES 1 SERVING

WE CHOSE OLD-FASHIONED OATS FOR THEIR CHEWY TEXTURE. TUCK THIS INTO A 16-OUNCE WIDE-MOUTHED INSULATED CONTAINER TO BRING TO WORK WITH YOU.

½ cup old-fashioned oats
1 cup low-fat or fat-free milk
1 tablespoon raisins
2 tablespoons chopped pecans

COMBINE the oats, milk, raisins, and pecans in a microwaveable bowl. Microwave for 30 seconds at a time for 2 to 4 minutes, or until the oats are softened to taste. Stir between heatings. Watch carefully, because the oatmeal may overflow.

## 380
**CALORIES
PER MEAL**
★

**PER SERVING** (1 serving = 1¼ cup)

| Calories | Total Fat | Saturated Fat | Sodium | Carbohydrate | Dietary Fiber | Protein | Calcium |
|----------|-----------|---------------|--------|--------------|---------------|---------|---------|
| 380 | 16 g | 3 g | 110 mg | 49 g | 6 g | 15 g | 30% |

# Hearty Waffles

**PREP TIME:** 5 MINUTES/ **COOK TIME:** 20 MINUTES (DEPENDING ON THE WAFFLE IRON)/ MAKES 4 SERVINGS

ALTHOUGH THIS MEAL DOESN'T EARN A STAR, IT IS FILLED WITH NUTRIENTS FROM THE OATS AND WHOLE WHEAT FLOUR.

½ cup old-fashioned oats

½ cup whole wheat flour

⅓ cup all-purpose flour

2 teaspoons baking powder

½ teaspoon salt

2 tablespoons brown sugar

2 teaspoons ground cinnamon

½ teaspoon ground nutmeg

1½ cups low-fat milk

2 eggs

½ teaspoon vanilla extract

1 cup fresh blueberries

4 tablespoons maple syrup

1. **BLEND** together the oats, whole wheat flour, all-purpose flour, baking powder, and salt in a medium bowl until powdery. Add the sugar, cinnamon, nutmeg, milk, eggs, and vanilla extract. Blend until smooth.

2. **HEAT** a waffle iron and coat well with cooking spray. Cook the waffles in the waffle iron.

3. **SERVE** each waffle with ¼ cup blueberries and 1 tablespoon maple syrup.

## MAKE IT A MEAL

Latte made with ¾ cup low-fat milk
**80 CALORIES**

# 380

**CALORIES PER MEAL**

**PER SERVING** (1 serving = 1 waffle)

| Calories | Total Fat | Saturated Fat | Sodium | Carbohydrate | Dietary Fiber | Protein | Calcium |
|----------|-----------|---------------|--------|--------------|---------------|---------|---------|
| 300 | 5 g | 2 g | 470 mg | 56 g | 5 g | 11 g | 30% |

# Cinnamon Raisin French Toast with Maple Apple Topping

**PREP TIME:** 10 MINUTES/ **COOK TIME:** 25 MINUTES/ MAKES 4 SERVINGS

BAKED FRENCH TOAST IS MUCH LESS LABOR INTENSIVE THAN REGULAR FRENCH TOAST, AND IT USES LESS FAT. TRY TOPPING WITH PEACHES WHEN THEY'RE IN SEASON IN PLACE OF APPLES.

- 2 eggs
- 2 egg whites
- ¾ cup low-fat milk
- 1 tablespoon sugar
- ½ teaspoon vanilla extract
- ½ teaspoon ground cinnamon
- 8 slices cinnamon raisin bread (80 calories per slice), cut diagonally in half
- 1 teaspoon unsalted butter
- 1 tablespoon maple syrup
- 2 medium-large apples (about ¾ pound total), sliced thin
- 2 tablespoons water
- 4 tablespoons sliced almonds

1. **PREHEAT** the oven to 350°F. Coat a 13" × 9" baking pan with cooking spray.

2. **WHISK** together the eggs, egg whites, milk, sugar, vanilla extract, and cinnamon in a medium bowl. Pour into the prepared pan. Arrange the bread slices in the pan and press gently to help them soak up the liquid. Cover with foil and bake for 15 minutes. Remove the foil and bake for 10 minutes, or until the bread is firm and lightly browned.

3. **MEANWHILE,** coat a skillet with cooking spray and place over medium heat. When the skillet is hot, add the butter and syrup and swirl to combine. Add the apples and water. Cover and simmer until the apples are soft, about 10 minutes. Uncover and simmer for 1 minute, or until most of the liquid evaporates.

4. **SERVE** 4 French toast triangles topped with one-quarter of the apple mixture and 1 tablespoon of the almonds.

## MAKE IT A MEAL

1 cup low-fat milk
**80 CALORIES**

# 380
**CALORIES PER MEAL**

**PER SERVING** (1 serving = 4 triangles)

| Calories | Total Fat | Saturated Fat | Sodium | Carbohydrate | Dietary Fiber | Protein | Calcium |
|---|---|---|---|---|---|---|---|
| 300 | 9 g | 3 g | 290 mg | 46 g | 5 g | 12 g | 15% |

# Apple Pudding Pancake

**PREP TIME:** 10 MINUTES/ **COOK TIME:** 35 MINUTES/ MAKES 4 SERVINGS

THIS GERMAN-STYLE PANCAKE HAS A CREAMY CONSISTENCY THAT REMINDS US OF PUDDING AND PAIRS WELL WITH GREEK YOGURT. TRY THIS RECIPE WITH PEARS OR BLUEBERRIES FOR A DIFFERENT FLAVOR.

| 2 | medium Golden Delicious or other apples suitable for cooking |
| ¾ | cup all-purpose flour |
| 4 | eggs |
| 1 | cup low-fat or fat-free milk |
| ¼ | cup + 1 tablespoon sugar |
| ½ | teaspoon vanilla extract |
| 1 | tablespoon ground cinnamon |

1. **PREHEAT** the oven to 425°F. Coat a large ovenproof skillet with cooking spray.

2. **GRATE** the apples coarsely (with or without peel). Place in a strainer to drain the excess liquid.

3. **PLACE** the flour, eggs, milk, ¼ cup sugar, and vanilla extract in a blender. Blend until very smooth. Pour into the skillet. Gently press any excess water out of the grated apples and spread them on top of the batter. Sprinkle with the cinnamon and remaining sugar.

4. **BAKE** for 30 to 35 minutes, or until the pancake is golden and firm on top. Bake for 5 minutes longer if you prefer a firmer consistency.

## MAKE IT A MEAL

1 teaspoon honey
**20 CALORIES**

3 ounces Chobani 2% Plain Greek Yogurt
**70 CALORIES**

# 390
**CALORIES PER MEAL**
★

**PER SERVING** (1 serving = ¼ of one 10"–12" diameter pancake)

| Calories | Total Fat | Saturated Fat | Sodium | Carbohydrate | Dietary Fiber | Protein | Calcium |
|----------|-----------|---------------|--------|--------------|---------------|---------|---------|
| 300 | 6 g | 2 g | 100 mg | 51 g | 4 g | 11 g | 15% |

# Cornmeal Pancakes

**PREP TIME:** 5 MINUTES/ **COOK TIME:** 15 MINUTES/ MAKES 4 SERVINGS

USE REGULAR OR COARSE STONE-GROUND CORNMEAL, DEPENDING ON THE TEXTURE YOU LIKE. BLUEBERRIES ARE AMONG THE MOST ANTIOXIDANT-RICH FRUITS.

- ½ cup yellow or white cornmeal
- ½ cup all-purpose flour
- ½ tablespoon baking powder
- ¼ teaspoon salt
- ¾ cup low-fat or fat-free milk
- 1 large egg
- 2 tablespoons vegetable oil
- 2 tablespoons honey
- ½ teaspoon vanilla extract

1. **COMBINE** the cornmeal, flour, baking power, and salt in a large bowl, preferably one with a pour spout. Add the milk, egg, oil, honey, and vanilla extract. Stir well to combine.

2. **HEAT** a pancake griddle or large skillet over medium heat. Coat with cooking spray. Pour the batter to make 4" pancakes, about ¼ cup each. Cook the pancakes until the bubbles on top have popped and the top appears firm but not dry. Flip the pancakes and cook until the underside is done.

## MAKE IT A MEAL

1 cup frozen blueberries, warmed
**80 CALORIES**

6 ounces light blueberry yogurt
**80 CALORIES**

400
**CALORIES PER MEAL**
★

**PER SERVING** (1 serving = 2 pancakes)

| Calories | Total Fat | Saturated Fat | Sodium | Carbohydrate | Dietary Fiber | Protein | Calcium |
|----------|-----------|---------------|--------|--------------|---------------|---------|---------|
| 240 | 9 g | 2 g | 370 mg | 35 g | 2 g | 6 g | 15% |

# Lox, Eggs, and Onions

**PREP TIME:** 5 MINUTES/ **COOK TIME:** 8 MINUTES/ MAKES 4 SERVINGS

THIS RECIPE WORKS EQUALLY WELL WITH WHOLE EGGS, EGG WHITES, OR EGG SUBSTITUTE. SOME TYPES OF SMOKED SALMON, ALSO CALLED LOX, ARE SALTIER THAN OTHERS, SO COMPARE LABELS.

## MAKE IT A MEAL

½ hollowed-out
4½" bagel
**120 CALORIES**

6 ounces
orange juice
**80 CALORIES**

# 400
**CALORIES
PER MEAL**
★ ★ ★

1 teaspoon olive oil

1 medium yellow onion, finely chopped

4 ounces smoked salmon, sliced into thin strips

4 large eggs or 8 egg whites or 1 cup egg substitute

2 tablespoons low-fat or fat-free milk

4 tablespoons sliced scallions

4 tablespoons sliced roasted red bell peppers

**1. HEAT** a large skillet coated with cooking spray over medium heat. Add the olive oil. Add the onion and cook for 1 minute. Add the smoked salmon and cook for about 2 minutes, or until the salmon begins to turn opaque and lighter in color. Whisk together the eggs and milk and add to the skillet. Cook until the eggs are firm and almost dry, about 5 minutes, stirring to heat evenly.

**2. TOP** each serving with 1 tablespoon each of the scallions and peppers.

**PER SERVING** (1 serving = ¾ cup)

| Calories | Total Fat | Saturated Fat | Sodium | Carbohydrate | Dietary Fiber | Protein | Calcium |
|---|---|---|---|---|---|---|---|
| 200 | 9 g | 3 g | 130 mg | 4 g | 1 g | 24 g | 6% |

# Western Frittata

**PREP TIME:** 5 MINUTES/ **COOK TIME:** 10 MINUTES/ MAKES 1 SERVING

THE KEY TO SUCCESS WITH FRITTATAS, OMELETS, AND EVEN SCRAMBLED EGGS IS TO MAKE SURE THAT THE PAN IS WELL COATED TO PREVENT STICKING. USING EGG SUBSTITUTE CUTS OUT 80 CALORIES, SO FEEL FREE TO ADD ANOTHER SLICE OF TOAST.

½  tablespoon olive oil

½  cup chopped onion

½  cup chopped green bell pepper

2  large eggs or ½ cup egg substitute

2  tablespoons low-fat or fat-free milk

2  tablespoons grated Parmesan or Parmigiano-Reggiano cheese

2  tablespoons salsa

1. **HEAT** a small ovenproof skillet coated with cooking spray over medium heat. Add the oil. Cook the onion and pepper until lightly browned, 5 to 7 minutes.

2. **WHISK** together the eggs and milk. Add to the skillet. Stir to distribute the onion and pepper. Cook for 1 minute without stirring. Remove the skillet from the heat.

3. **SPRINKLE** the egg mixture with the cheese. Broil until the cheese browns and the top of the frittata is firm, about 1 to 2 minutes.

4. **SLICE** into 4 wedges. Top each wedge with a dollop of salsa.

## MAKE IT A MEAL

1 slice whole wheat toast
**70 CALORIES**

½ grapefruit
**50 CALORIES**

# 400
**CALORIES PER MEAL**
★ ★ ★

**PER SERVING** (1 serving = 4 wedges)

| Calories | Total Fat | Saturated Fat | Sodium | Carbohydrate | Dietary Fiber | Protein | Calcium |
|----------|-----------|---------------|--------|--------------|---------------|---------|---------|
| 280 | 17 g | 6 g | 500 mg | 16 g | 3 g | 19 g | 25% |

# Eggs and Sausage Omelet with Tomatoes and Peppers

**PREP TIME:** 10 MINUTES/ **COOK TIME:** 10 MINUTES/ MAKES 1 SERVING

THIS RECIPE ALSO CAN BE MADE WITH 5 EGG WHITES OR THE EQUIVALENT IN LIQUID EGG WHITES. IF BLUE-BERRIES ARE NOT IN SEASON, SUBSTITUTE FROZEN BERRIES OR FRESH FRUIT SALAD.

## 380
### CALORIES PER MEAL
★ ★ ★

- 1 teaspoon olive oil
- ½ small red bell pepper, finely chopped
- ½ small red onion, finely chopped
- 1½ ounces turkey kielbasa, finely chopped
- 1 clove garlic, minced
- 1 plum tomato, seeded and finely chopped
- 2 teaspoons thinly sliced fresh basil
- ⅔ cup fat-free egg substitute
- ⅛ teaspoon salt
- ⅛ teaspoon freshly ground black pepper
- 1 slice whole wheat bread, toasted
- 1 cup fresh blueberries

1. HEAT ½ teaspoon of the oil in a medium nonstick skillet over medium-high heat. Add the bell pepper, onion, kielbasa, and garlic. Cook, stirring occasionally, until the onion and kielbasa start to brown, about 4 to 5 minutes.

2. ADD the tomato and cook until wilted, 2 minutes. Remove from the heat. Stir in 1 teaspoon of the basil and transfer to a bowl. Return the skillet to the stove and heat the remaining ½ teaspoon oil over medium-high heat.

3. COMBINE the egg substitute, salt, and black pepper in a small bowl. Pour the mixture into the skillet and cook until almost set, 2 minutes. Top with the bell pepper mixture and cook for 1 minute, or until cooked through.

4. FOLD the omelet in half and slide onto a plate. Top with the remaining 1 teaspoon basil. Serve with the whole wheat toast and blueberries.

**PER SERVING** (1 serving = 1 omelet)

| Calories | Total Fat | Saturated Fat | Sodium | Carbohydrate | Dietary Fiber | Protein | Calcium |
|----------|-----------|---------------|----------|--------------|---------------|---------|---------|
| 380 | 10 g | 2 g | 1,140 mg | 46 g | 8 g | 28 g | 10% |

# Huevos Rancheros Burritos

**PREP TIME:** 5 MINUTES/ **COOK TIME:** 5 MINUTES/ MAKES 4 SERVINGS

PAIRING THIS BRUNCH WITH A BLOODY MARY MAKES FOR A FESTIVE MEAL. IF YOU PREFER—AND TO EARN A FRUIT/VEGGIE STAR—SERVE WITH PLAIN TOMATO JUICE AND A SMALL FRUIT SALAD.

## MAKE IT A MEAL

6 ounces
Bloody Mary
**120 CALORIES**

# 390
**CALORIES
PER MEAL**

- 4 medium (7" diameter or 2 ounces each) whole wheat tortillas
- 6 large eggs
- 4 tablespoons low-fat or fat-free milk
- 4 tablespoons thinly sliced scallions
- 4 tablespoons finely chopped cilantro
- 4 tablespoons shredded Mexican four-cheese blend
- 8 tablespoons salsa

1. **PREHEAT** the oven to 250°F. Wrap the tortillas in foil and place in the oven.

2. **WHISK** the eggs and milk in a medium bowl. Heat a large nonstick or standard skillet coated with cooking spray over medium-low heat. When the skillet is hot, pour in the eggs and scramble.

3. **REMOVE** the tortillas from the oven and place on 4 plates. Divide the egg mixture among the tortillas. Top each tortilla with 1 tablespoon each of the scallions, cilantro, cheese, and salsa. Fold the tortilla over the filling. Top each burrito with an additional tablespoon of salsa.

**PER SERVING** (1 serving = 1 burrito)

| Calories | Total Fat | Saturated Fat | Sodium | Carbohydrate | Dietary Fiber | Protein | Calcium |
|----------|-----------|---------------|--------|--------------|---------------|---------|---------|
| 270 | 11 g | 4 g | 630 mg | 36 g | 4 g | 17 g | 15% |

# Breakfast Pocket to Go

**PREP TIME:** 5 MINUTES/ **COOK TIME:** 5 MINUTES/ MAKES 1 SERVING

WE CHOSE A WEIGHT WATCHERS PITA BECAUSE IT IS PARTICULARLY HIGH IN SATIATING FIBER AND PROTEIN FOR ITS REASONABLE NUMBER OF CALORIES. ANY VEGGIES WORK IN THIS RECIPE; JUST CUT THEM SMALL SO THEY COOK UP QUICKLY.

- 1 teaspoon olive oil
- 1 tablespoon chopped onion
- 6 cherry tomatoes, halved
- 1 cup baby spinach leaves
- 3 medium button or cremini mushrooms, sliced
- ⅛ teaspoon salt
- ⅛ teaspoon freshly ground black pepper
- 2 large eggs
- 2 tablespoons low-fat milk
- 1 whole wheat pita (6" diameter), cut in half and warmed (we used Weight Watchers)
- 1 tablespoon guacamole
- 1 tablespoon shredded reduced-fat Cheddar cheese

1. **COAT** a skillet with cooking spray and add the oil. Place over medium heat, add the onion, and cook until it softens, about 1 minute. Add the tomatoes, spinach, mushrooms, salt, and pepper and cook until soft, about 2 minutes. Remove the vegetables from the skillet and place in a bowl.

2. **PLACE** the skillet over medium-low heat. Whisk together the eggs and milk, transfer to the skillet, and scramble until cooked, 1 to 2 minutes.

3. **SPREAD** the inside of each pita half with guacamole. Fill each half with the egg and vegetables. Top with the cheese.

MAKE IT
A MEAL

½ cup strawberries
30 CALORIES

400

**CALORIES
PER MEAL**

★ ★ ★ ★

**PER SERVING** (1 serving = 2 breakfast pockets)

| Calories | Total Fat | Saturated Fat | Sodium | Carbohydrate | Dietary Fiber | Protein | Calcium |
|---|---|---|---|---|---|---|---|
| 370 | 18 g | 5 g | 620 mg | 37 g | 13 g | 26 g | 20% |

# Layered Mediterranean Breakfast Bake

**PREP TIME:** 25 MINUTES/ **COOK TIME:** 40 MINUTES/ MAKES 4 SERVINGS

THIS PRETTY BREAKFAST DISH CAN BE DOUBLED OR TRIPLED TO SERVE TO GUESTS. FOR A DIFFERENT FLAVOR, SWITCH TO SMOKED MOZZARELLA CHEESE.

1    medium zucchini, coarsely grated

¼    teaspoon salt

1    teaspoon olive oil

1½    cups sliced scallions

1    clove garlic, minced

½    cup crumbled reduced-fat feta cheese

1⅓    cups part-skim ricotta cheese

½    teaspoon freshly ground black pepper

¼    cup slivered sun-dried tomatoes

4    large eggs

1    teaspoon McCormick Perfect Pinch Salt Free Italian seasoning

1    jar (12 ounces) roasted red bell peppers, drained, rinsed, and cut into strips

½    cup shredded part-skim mozzarella cheese

1    tablespoon grated Parmesan cheese

1. **PREHEAT** the oven to 400°F. Place the zucchini in a small bowl and sprinkle with the salt. Coat a 2½-quart baking dish with cooking spray.

2. **HEAT** the oil in a large nonstick skillet or a skillet coated with cooking spray over medium heat. Add the scallions and garlic. Cook for 2 to 3 minutes, or until tender. Add the feta and cook for 1 minute, or until almost melted. Transfer to a large bowl and stir in the ricotta and ¼ teaspoon black pepper.

3. **HEAT** the skillet coated with cooking spray over medium heat. Squeeze extra moisture out of the zucchini, add the zucchini to the skillet, and cook for 2 minutes, stirring occasionally. Season with the remaining ¼ teaspoon black pepper and spread on the bottom of the baking dish. Top the zucchini with the ricotta mixture. Top the ricotta with the tomatoes. Whisk the eggs and Italian seasoning in a small bowl. Pour on top of the tomatoes. Top with the roasted peppers. Sprinkle with the mozzarella and Parmesan.

4. **BAKE** for 40 minutes, or until bubbly.

## MAKE IT A MEAL

1-ounce mini corn muffin
**90 CALORIES**

# 420
**CALORIES PER MEAL**
★ ★

**PER SERVING** (1 serving = one 4" square)

| Calories | Total Fat | Saturated Fat | Sodium | Carbohydrate | Dietary Fiber | Protein | Calcium |
|---|---|---|---|---|---|---|---|
| 330 | 18 g | 9 g | 930 mg | 16 g | 3 g | 26 g | 45% |

# Greek-Style Yogurt with Apricots, Honey, and Crunch

**PREP TIME:** 5 MINUTES/ MAKES 1 SERVING

THIS RECIPE CALLS FOR MAKING YOUR OWN GREEK YOGURT SO THAT YOU CAN MAKE IT AS THICK AS YOU LIKE. YOU CAN SUBSTITUTE COMMERCIAL 0% FAT GREEK YOGURT AND SWITCH TO DIFFERENT NUTS AND CEREAL TO SUIT YOUR TASTES.

**390**

**CALORIES
PER MEAL**

★ ★

- 1 cup plain fat-free yogurt
- 5 canned apricot halves in juice, thinly sliced
- 4 tablespoons Grape-Nuts cereal
- 1 tablespoon slivered almonds
- 1 teaspoon honey

1. **TO MAKE** Greek yogurt: Place the plain yogurt in a paper coffee filter and gold coffee strainer or a very fine mesh strainer over a bowl. Whey will drain out of the yogurt into the bowl, leaving thicker yogurt. Refrigerate for at least 1 hour, longer for thicker yogurt.

2. **SPOON** about half of the yogurt into a parfait glass. Top with 2 tablespoons each of the apricots and cereal. Repeat. Top each with half the almonds and honey.

**PER SERVING** (1 serving = 1 parfait)

| Calories | Total Fat | Saturated Fat | Sodium | Carbohydrate | Dietary Fiber | Protein | Calcium |
|----------|-----------|---------------|--------|--------------|---------------|---------|---------|
| 390 | 5 g | 0.5 g | 370 mg | 72 g | 6 g | 20 g | 50% |

# Peanut Butter Breakfast Shake

**PREP TIME:** 5 MINUTES/ MAKES 1 SERVING

LIGHT YOGURT ADDS TEXTURE AND CREAMINESS TO THIS QUICK AND FILLING SHAKE. TO MAINTAIN ITS SLUSHINESS, POUR INTO AN INSULATED COFFEE CUP.

1 cup light vanilla yogurt (110 calories per cup)

½ medium banana (peeled, sliced, and frozen ahead of time)

¼ cup low-fat or fat-free milk

1 tablespoon peanut butter

PLACE the yogurt, banana, milk, and peanut butter in a blender. Blend until smooth.

## MAKE IT A MEAL

Pepperidge Farm Brown Sugar Cinnamon Mini Bagel
**120 CALORIES**

410
**CALORIES PER MEAL**
★

**PER SERVING** (1 serving = 1 shake)

| Calories | Total Fat | Saturated Fat | Sodium | Carbohydrate | Dietary Fiber | Protein | Calcium |
|----------|-----------|---------------|--------|--------------|---------------|---------|---------|
| 290 | 9 g | 2 g | 230 mg | 41 g | 2 g | 14 g | 45% |

# 11.
## SOUP, SALAD & SANDWICH RECIPES

# Creamy Vegetable Soup

**PREP TIME:** 15 MINUTES/ **COOK TIME:** 35 MINUTES/ MAKES 6 SERVINGS

THE CANNELLINI BEANS GIVE THIS SOUP A CREAMY CONSISTENCY WITHOUT USING MILK OR CREAM. FEEL FREE TO VARY THE VEGETABLES, DEPENDING ON WHAT YOU HAVE HANDY. FROZEN VEGGIES ALSO WORK WELL.

## MAKE IT A MEAL

Toasted whole wheat English muffin
**130 CALORIES**

So Delicious Mini or other 80–100-calorie ice cream sandwich
**90 CALORIES**

## 390
**CALORIES PER MEAL**
★ ★

## STAR SYSTEM
★ PROTEIN
★ FIBER
★ GOOD FATS
★ FRUITS/VEGGIES

| | |
|---|---|
| 1 | tablespoon olive oil |
| 1 | cup chopped onion |
| 1 | cup sliced mushrooms |
| 1½ | cups broccoli florets |
| 1½ | cups cauliflower florets |
| 1 | medium potato, peeled and cubed |
| 1 | can (14–19 ounces) cannellini or white beans, rinsed and drained |
| 4 | cups low-sodium chicken or vegetable broth |
| 1 | teaspoon McCormick Salt Free Original Perfect Pinch seasoning |
| 8 | tablespoons grated reduced-fat Cheddar cheese |

**1. HEAT** the oil in a medium pot over medium heat. Add the onion and mushrooms. Cook until soft, stirring frequently, about 5 minutes.

**2. ADD** the broccoli, cauliflower, potato, beans, broth, and seasoning. Cook, covered, for 30 minutes. Remove from the heat.

**3. PUREE** the mixture until smooth using an immersion blender, or allow to reach lukewarm temperature and puree in a blender.

**4. SPRINKLE** with 2 tablespoons cheese per serving.

**PER SERVING** (1 serving = 2 cups)

| Calories | Total Fat | Saturated Fat | Sodium | Carbohydrate | Dietary Fiber | Protein | Calcium |
|---|---|---|---|---|---|---|---|
| 170 | 6 g | 3 g | 270 mg | 20 g | 4 g | 11 g | 25% |

# White Bean and Escarole Soup

**PREP TIME:** 20 MINUTES/ **COOK TIME:** 28 MINUTES/ MAKES 4 SERVINGS

THIS RECIPE WAS INSPIRED BY AN ITALIAN CLASSIC. YOU CAN CREATE A COMPLETELY DIFFERENT DISH BY SWAPPING THE GREENS FOR SPINACH OR KALE AND CHOOSING A DIFFERENT CHEESE.

1   head escarole, about 1 pound

4   teaspoons olive oil

1   cup chopped onion

2   cloves garlic, minced

4   cups Health Valley Fat Free Vegetable Broth or other reduced-sodium broth

2   cans (12–15 ounces each) cannellini beans, rinsed and drained

4   slices firm Italian bread, ½" each

1   clove garlic, halved

4   tablespoons Parmesan cheese

**1. PLACE** the escarole leaves in a large bowl of cold water and swish around to remove dirt. Remove the leaves, place in a colander, rinse well with water, and drain well. Cut into thin slices.

**2. HEAT** 2 teaspoons of the oil in a medium pot over medium heat. Add the onion and garlic and cook until soft, about 3 minutes. Add the broth, raise the heat to bring to a boil, and then lower the heat to medium-low. Add the escarole and beans, cover, and simmer for 25 minutes.

**3. WHILE** the soup is cooking, rub both sides of the bread slices with cut garlic. Brush the slices on both sides with the remaining 2 teaspoons olive oil and toast until crisp. Top each slice with 1 tablespoon Parmesan. Just before serving, broil the bread slices until the cheese begins to melt.

**4. LADLE** the soup into 4 bowls and top each with a slice of bread.

## MAKE IT A MEAL

1 slice
angel food cake
70 CALORIES

½ cup frozen berries
30 CALORIES

# 380
**CALORIES
PER MEAL**
★ ★

**PER SERVING** (1 serving = 1½ cups)

| Calories | Total Fat | Saturated Fat | Sodium | Carbohydrate | Dietary Fiber | Protein | Calcium |
|----------|-----------|---------------|--------|--------------|---------------|---------|---------|
| 280 | 7 g | 2 g | 680 mg | 41 g | 11 g | 11 g | 20% |

# Spicy Black Bean Soup

**PREP TIME:** 10 MINUTES + OVERNIGHT SOAKING/
**COOK TIME:** 8 HOURS UNATTENDED/ MAKES 6 SERVINGS

DRIED BEANS WORK WELL IN THIS SLOW-COOKER RECIPE BECAUSE VERY GENTLE HEATING HELPS THE BEANS HOLD THEIR SHAPE. CHOOSE ANY TYPE OF SALSA TO SUIT YOUR TASTE.

1½ cups dried black beans, covered with cold water and soaked overnight

5 cups water

1 cup chopped yellow onion

1 cup mild, medium, or hot salsa

½ pound red potatoes, chopped

2 cloves garlic, minced

½ teaspoon sea salt

⅛ teaspoon smoked black pepper (optional)

6 tablespoons shredded Mexican four-cheese blend

6 tablespoons plain low-fat yogurt

6 tablespoons finely chopped cilantro

**1. DRAIN** the beans in the morning. Place in a slow cooker with the water, onion, salsa, potatoes, and garlic. Cover and cook on low for 8 hours, or until the beans are soft.

**2. SEASON** with the salt and, if desired, black pepper. Serve topped with 1 tablespoon each cheese, yogurt, and cilantro.

## MAKE IT A MEAL

2 warmed corn tortillas
**120 CALORIES**

Small green salad with 10 salad dressing sprays
**30 CALORIES**

# 390
**CALORIES
PER MEAL**
★ ★

**PER SERVING** (1 serving = 1½ cups)

| Calories | Total Fat | Saturated Fat | Sodium | Carbohydrate | Dietary Fiber | Protein | Calcium |
|---|---|---|---|---|---|---|---|
| 240 | 4 g | 2 g | 500 mg | 40 g | 12 g | 14 g | 15% |

# Greek-Style Lentil Soup with Crispy Olives

**PREP TIME:** 15 MINUTES/ **COOK TIME:** 50 MINUTES/ MAKES 4 SERVINGS

THIS DISH IS SO HIGH IN FIBER THAT IT SUPPLIES CLOSE TO YOUR DAILY RECOMMENDATION IN JUST ONE BOWL. THE CRISPY OLIVES ADD AN UNUSUAL TOUCH, PLUS GOOD FATS.

## MAKE IT A MEAL

Weight Watchers 100% Whole Wheat Pita Pocket Bread **100 CALORIES**

# 390

**CALORIES PER MEAL**

★ ★ ★ ★

| | |
|---|---|
| ½ | pound brown lentils, picked over and rinsed |
| 4½ | cups water |
| 3 | cloves garlic, minced |
| 2 | medium carrots, cut into ¼" pieces |
| 2 | medium onions, chopped |
| 1 | medium rib celery, chopped |
| 1 | teaspoon dried thyme, crushed |
| 1 | teaspoon freshly ground black pepper |
| 1 | teaspoon dried oregano, crushed |
| ½ | teaspoon dried rosemary, crushed |
| ¾ | cup tomato puree |
| 1 | teaspoon salt |
| ⅛ | teaspoon ground cinnamon |
| ¼ | cup chopped green olives |
| 2 | teaspoons cornstarch |
| 4 | tablespoons plain low-fat or fat-free yogurt |

**1. COMBINE** the lentils, water, garlic, carrots, onions, celery, thyme, pepper, oregano, and rosemary in a large saucepan or Dutch oven. Bring to a boil over high heat. Reduce the heat to low and cover. Simmer, stirring occasionally, for 30 minutes, or until the lentils are tender. Stir in the tomato puree, salt, and cinnamon. Simmer for 20 minutes to blend the flavors.

**2. WHILE** the soup cooks, preheat the oven to 400°F. Blot the olives with a paper towel to remove excess moisture. Place in a small bowl and sprinkle with the cornstarch, tossing gently to cover evenly. Place on a piece of heavy-duty foil or a small baking sheet and bake until crisp, about 10 minutes.

**3. TOP** each bowl of soup with 1 tablespoon yogurt and 2 teaspoons olives.

**PER SERVING** (1 serving = 1½ cups)

| Calories | Total Fat | Saturated Fat | Sodium | Carbohydrate | Dietary Fiber | Protein | Calcium |
|---|---|---|---|---|---|---|---|
| 290 | 3 g | 0 g | 980 mg | 51 g | 20 g | 17 g | 10% |

# Italian Egg Drop Soup

**PREP TIME:** 10 MINUTES/ **COOK TIME:** 25 MINUTES/ MAKES 4 SERVINGS

FOR A HEAVIER EGG DROP, WHISK THE PARMESAN CHEESE WITH THE EGGS BEFORE ADDING TO THE SOUP.

6 cups reduced-sodium chicken broth or vegetable broth

2 carrots, finely chopped

1 small onion, finely chopped

1 cup spinach, cut into thin strips

½ cup ditalini or other small-cut pasta

3 eggs

4 tablespoons grated Parmesan cheese

**1. POUR** 5½ cups of the broth into a medium saucepan over medium-high heat. Add the carrots, onion, and spinach. Bring to a boil. Reduce the heat to low, cover, and simmer for 10 minutes.

**2. ADD** the pasta to the soup. Cook according to the package directions.

**3. WHISK** together the eggs and remaining ½ cup broth. Bring the soup to a boil. Whisk in the egg mixture, stirring constantly. The egg should form fine strands.

**4. TOP** each bowl with 1 tablespoon Parmesan cheese.

## MAKE IT A MEAL

½ cup cooked spaghetti with ⅓ cup pasta sauce, 2 ounces cooked lean ground turkey
**240 CALORIES**

# 420
**CALORIES
PER MEAL**
★ ★

**PER SERVING** (1 serving = 2 cups)

| Calories | Total Fat | Saturated Fat | Sodium | Carbohydrate | Dietary Fiber | Protein | Calcium |
|---|---|---|---|---|---|---|---|
| 180 | 6 g | 3 g | 370 mg | 17 g | 2 g | 15 g | 18% |

# Amy's Minestrone Soup

**PREP TIME:** 15 MINUTES/ **COOK TIME:** 43 MINUTES/ MAKES 8 SERVINGS

AMY, THE MOTHER OF ONE OF MINDY'S NEIGHBORS, WAS FAMOUS FOR HER MINESTRONE SOUP, AND HER DAUGHTER WAS KIND ENOUGH TO LET US PUT OUR 400 CALORIE LENS TO THE RECIPE. PAIR THIS WITH A SALAD FOR A TRULY SATISFYING MEAL.

- 1 pound sweet Italian chicken sausage, cut into 1" pieces
- 2 cloves garlic, minced
- 1 medium yellow onion, chopped
- 2 medium ribs celery, chopped
- 1 medium carrot, chopped
- 4 cups water
- 1 can (16 ounces) reduced-sodium chicken broth
- 1 can (6 ounces) tomato paste
- 1 can (14–19 ounces) kidney beans, rinsed and drained
- 1 can (15–16 ounces) no-salt-added corn, drained
- ½ cup fresh or frozen green beans
- 3 tablespoons dried pearl barley

  Salt and freshly ground black pepper
- 1 cup ditalini pasta
- 4 tablespoons grated Parmesan cheese

**1. HEAT** a large pot over medium heat. Add the sausage and cook until no longer pink, stirring occasionally, about 10 minutes. Remove the sausage from the pot and pour off the liquid and fat.

**2. RETURN** the pot to the stove. Add the garlic, onion, celery, and carrot. Cook until soft, about 3 minutes. Add the water, broth, tomato paste, kidney beans, corn, green beans, and barley. Add the salt and pepper. Increase the heat to high and bring to a boil. Reduce the heat to medium-low, cover, and simmer for 20 minutes.

**3. ADD** the pasta and stir. Cook until the pasta is done, about 10 minutes.

**4. SPRINKLE** each serving with ½ tablespoon Parmesan cheese.

## MAKE IT A MEAL

Small green salad with 1 teaspoon finely chopped walnuts, 10 salad dressing sprays
**40 CALORIES**

# 380
**CALORIES PER MEAL**
★ ★ ★

**PER SERVING** (1 serving = 2 cups)

| Calories | Total Fat | Saturated Fat | Sodium | Carbohydrate | Dietary Fiber | Protein | Calcium |
|----------|-----------|---------------|--------|--------------|---------------|---------|---------|
| 340 | 7 g | 2 g | 700 mg | 47 g | 7 g | 22 g | 6% |

# Slow-Cooker Split Pea Soup

**PREP TIME:** 10 MINUTES/ **COOK TIME:** 9 HOURS/ MAKES 8 SERVINGS

A FILLING DINNER ON A COLD WINTER DAY, THIS DISH CAN COOK WHILE YOU'RE AT WORK OR RUNNING AN ERRAND. IT ALSO CAN BE PREPARED ON THE STOVE TOP IN ABOUT 1 HOUR.

## MAKE IT A MEAL

Open-faced turkey
sandwich with
1 slice whole wheat
bread, 2 ounces deli
turkey breast,
1 teaspoon mustard,
2 tomato slices,
2 lettuce leaves
**150 CALORIES**

# 385

## CALORIES
## PER MEAL
★ ★ ★

1 pound dried split green peas

3 ribs celery, chopped

2 cloves garlic, minced

1 large yellow onion, chopped

3 medium carrots, chopped

½ cup chopped fresh parsley

2 teaspoons herbes de Provence, 1 tablespoon dried thyme, or 1 tablespoon curry powder

2 bay leaves

1 teaspoon sea salt

Freshly ground black pepper or smoked black pepper

2 teaspoons liquid smoke seasoning

4 cups vegetable broth

4 cups water

**1. COMBINE** the peas, celery, garlic, onion, carrots, parsley, herbs, bay leaves, sea salt, pepper, liquid smoke seasoning, broth, and water in a slow cooker.

**2. COOK** on low for 8 to 9 hours or on high for 4 to 5 hours, until the peas are completely cooked and softened. Remove the bay leaves before serving.

**PER SERVING** (1 serving = 1½ cups)

| Calories | Total Fat | Saturated Fat | Sodium | Carbohydrate | Dietary Fiber | Protein | Calcium |
|---|---|---|---|---|---|---|---|
| 230 | 1 g | 0 g | 360 mg | 41 g | 16 g | 15 g | 6% |

# Roasted Chicken Soup

**PREP TIME:** 10 MINUTES/ **COOK TIME:** 1 HOUR 23 MINUTES/ MAKES 4 SERVINGS

A TWIST ON TRADITIONAL CHICKEN SOUP, THIS RECIPE CALLS FOR ROASTING THE VEGETABLES TO BRING OUT THEIR SWEETNESS AND ROASTING THE CHICKEN TO GIVE IT A FIRMER TEXTURE.

- 6 ounces extra-wide egg noodles
- 1 tablespoon olive oil
- 2 medium onions, chopped
- 3 carrots, chopped
- 3 ribs celery, chopped
- 1 parsnip, chopped
- 1 pound bone-in skin-on chicken breast halves
- 6 cups fat-free reduced-sodium chicken broth
- 5 sprigs fresh parsley
- 1 teaspoon fresh thyme leaves
- 8 ounces tomatoes, seeded and chopped
- ¼ teaspoon freshly ground black pepper

**1. PREHEAT** the oven to 425°F. Coat 2 baking sheets with cooking spray.

**2. BRING** a large pot of lightly salted water to a boil over high heat. Add the noodles and cook according to package directions; drain and reserve.

**3. COMBINE** the oil, onions, carrots, celery, and parsnip in a bowl. Spread out on the first baking sheet. Set the chicken on the second baking sheet. Place both baking sheets in the oven. Roast the vegetables, tossing occasionally, until browned, about 35 minutes. Transfer the vegetables to a large pot. Pour some chicken broth onto the baking sheet and scrape up any browned bits. Add to the pot. Roast the chicken until a thermometer inserted into the thickest portion registers 170°F, about 22 to 25 minutes. Transfer the chicken to a cutting board and let stand until cool enough to handle, about 5 minutes. Remove the chicken from the bones. Discard the skins and add the bones to the pot with the vegetables. Pull the chicken into strips and reserve.

**4. ADD** the remaining broth, parsley, and thyme to the pot. Bring to a boil over medium-high heat. Reduce the heat to medium-low and cover. Simmer for 30 minutes. Remove the bones and discard. Stir in the tomatoes and pepper. Return to a simmer and cook over medium-low heat until the tomatoes are wilted, about 5 minutes. Stir in the reserved noodles and chicken. Cook for 2 to 3 minutes longer, or until heated through.

## MAKE IT A MEAL

Small salad with 1 cup lettuce, 1 teaspoon olive oil, ½ teaspoon vinegar **50 CALORIES**

# 420
**CALORIES PER MEAL**
★ ★ ★ ★

**PER SERVING** (1 serving = 2 cups)

| Calories | Total Fat | Saturated Fat | Sodium | Carbohydrate | Dietary Fiber | Protein | Calcium |
|---|---|---|---|---|---|---|---|
| 370 | 8 g | 2 g | 790 mg | 48 g | 6 g | 26 g | 8% |

# Thai Chicken Lime Coconut Soup

**PREP TIME:** 15 MINUTES/ **COOK TIME:** 30 MINUTES/ MAKES 4 SERVINGS

ALTHOUGH COCONUT MILK IS HIGH IN FAT AND CALORIES, A BIT OF LIGHT COCONUT MILK ADDS GREAT FLAVOR WITHOUT PUSHING CALORIES WAY UP.

## 420
**CALORIES PER MEAL**
★ ★

- 4 cups low-sodium chicken broth
- 2 cups water
- 3 cloves garlic, finely minced
- 2 scallions, white parts and ½ of green parts thinly sliced into rounds
- 1 2" piece lemongrass
- 1 1" piece fresh ginger, finely chopped
  Juice and grated peel of 1 lime
- 1 tablespoon reduced-sodium soy sauce
- 1 teaspoon anchovy paste or 4 tablespoons fish sauce
- 2 Thai chile peppers (optional)
- 1 pound boneless, skinless chicken thighs, cut into 1" chunks
- 2 carrots, cut into 2" julienne (about 1½ cups)
- 1 cup chopped spinach or bok choy
- 1 cup enoki or sliced button mushrooms
- 8 ounces fresh or 6 ounces dried vermicelli
- ½ cup canned light coconut milk
- 4 tablespoons chopped fresh cilantro

**1. COMBINE** the broth, water, garlic, scallions, lemongrass, ginger, lime juice and peel, soy sauce, anchovy paste or fish sauce, and chilies (if desired) in a large pot. Cover and bring to a boil over medium heat.

**2. ADD** the chicken and carrots, spinach, and mushrooms. Bring to a boil. Reduce the heat and cover. Simmer for 20 minutes.

**3. STIR** in the vermicelli and coconut milk. Simmer until the vermicelli is cooked, about 5 minutes for fresh and 10 minutes for dried.

**4. SERVE** topped with 1 tablespoon cilantro each.

**PER SERVING** (1 serving = 2 cups)

| Calories | Total Fat | Saturated Fat | Sodium | Carbohydrate | Dietary Fiber | Protein | Calcium |
|----------|-----------|---------------|--------|--------------|---------------|---------|---------|
| 420 | 13 g | 5 g | 470 mg | 44 g | 4 g | 34 g | 6% |

# Chicken and Sausage Gumbo

**PREP TIME:** 10 MINUTES/ **COOK TIME:** 38 MINUTES/ MAKES 4 SERVINGS

CLASSIC GUMBO REQUIRES THREE KEY INGREDIENTS—CELERY, GREEN BELL PEPPER, AND ONIONS. OKRA ALSO IS TRADITIONAL, BUT ITS VISCOUS TEXTURE DOESN'T APPEAL TO EVERYONE. INSTEAD OF HAM, THIS RECIPE CALLS FOR EQUALLY FLAVORFUL BUT MUCH LEANER TURKEY KIELBASA.

**380**
**CALORIES**
**PER MEAL**
★ ★

- 1 tablespoon olive oil
- 4 ounces turkey kielbasa, sliced
- 1 large onion, chopped
- 1 large green bell pepper, chopped
- 2 ribs celery, chopped
- 3 cloves garlic, minced
- ¼ teaspoon dried thyme
- 2 tablespoons all-purpose flour
- 1 can (14.5 ounces) reduced-sodium fat-free chicken broth
- 1 can (14.5 ounces) unsalted diced tomatoes
- 12 ounces boneless, skinless chicken thighs, trimmed, cut into 1" pieces
- ½ teaspoon hot pepper sauce
- 3 scallions, chopped
- 2 cups hot cooked brown rice

**HEAT** the oil in a nonstick Dutch oven over medium-high heat. Add the kielbasa, onion, bell pepper, celery, garlic, and thyme. Cook, stirring occasionally, until crisp-tender, 6 to 7 minutes. Stir in the flour and cook for 1 minute. Add the broth, tomatoes, chicken, and hot pepper sauce. Bring to a boil. Reduce the heat to medium and simmer, partially covered, until thickened and the chicken is cooked through, about 28 to 30 minutes. Remove from the heat and stir in the scallions. Serve over the brown rice.

**PER SERVING** (1 serving = 1½ cups gumbo, ½ cup rice)

| Calories | Total Fat | Saturated Fat | Sodium | Carbohydrate | Dietary Fiber | Protein | Calcium |
|----------|-----------|---------------|--------|--------------|---------------|---------|---------|
| 380 | 13 g | 3 g | 590 mg | 37 g | 5 g | 25 g | 6% |

# Chicken Corn Chowder

**PREP TIME:** 10 MINUTES/ **COOK TIME:** 30 MINUTES/ MAKES 4 SERVINGS

CORN CHOWDER IS AT ITS BEST IN THE LATE SUMMER, AT THE HEIGHT OF CORN SEASON. FOR THE REST OF THE YEAR, KEEP A BAG OF FROZEN KERNELS AT HAND IN THE FREEZER.

- 2 teaspoons olive oil
- 4 cups fresh or frozen and thawed corn kernels
- 1 medium onion, chopped
- ½ teaspoon dried thyme
- 2 cups fat-free reduced-sodium chicken broth
- 2 cups low-fat milk
- 3 tablespoons all-purpose flour
- 2 teaspoons sugar
- 2 cups cubed cooked chicken breast (about 10 ounces)
- ¼ teaspoon salt
- ¼ teaspoon freshly ground black pepper

**1. HEAT** the oil in a large pot over medium heat. Add the corn, onion, and thyme and cook, stirring occasionally, until softened, 10 to 12 minutes.

**2. COMBINE** the broth, milk, flour, and sugar. Pour into the pot. Cook, stirring, until slightly thickened and just starting to boil, 10 to 11 minutes.

**3. REMOVE** from the heat and cool for 5 minutes. Puree in a blender in several batches.

**4. RETURN** the soup to the pot over medium heat. Add the chicken, salt, and pepper. Cook until hot, about 2 minutes.

## MAKE IT A MEAL

Small salad made with 1½ cups baby spinach, 1 teaspoon walnuts, 1 teaspoon dried cranberries, 10 sprays salad dressing spray **60 CALORIES**

# 420
**CALORIES PER MEAL**
★ ★

**PER SERVING** (1 serving = 2 cups)

| Calories | Total Fat | Saturated Fat | Sodium | Carbohydrate | Dietary Fiber | Protein | Calcium |
|----------|-----------|---------------|--------|--------------|---------------|---------|---------|
| 360 | 8 g | 2 g | 500 mg | 45 g | 5 g | 32 g | 15% |

# Autumn Chicken Stew in the Slow Cooker

**PREP TIME:** 20 MINUTES/ **COOK TIME:** 8 HOURS UNATTENDED/ MAKES 6 SERVINGS

IF YOU PREFER, SUBSTITUTE CARROTS FOR THE PARSNIPS AND USE ANY TYPE OF WINTER SQUASH. IN PLACE OF THE ROSEMARY AND THYME, TRY THE SPICE HUNTER POULTRY MIX.

- 2 parsnips, peeled and cut into thirds
- 1 medium butternut squash, peeled, halved lengthwise, seeded, and cut into 1" slices
- 1 large red onion, cut into 8 wedges
- ½ pound red potatoes, cut into 1" chunks
- ½ pound sweet potatoes, cut into 1" chunks
- 2 cups low-sodium chicken broth
- 1 teaspoon dried rosemary
- 1 teaspoon dried thyme
- ½ teaspoon salt
- 1½ pounds boneless, skinless chicken thighs
- 6 ounces baby spinach (about 6 cups)
- 2 cups cooked couscous

**1. ARRANGE** the parsnips, squash, onion, and red and sweet potatoes in a 4- or 5-quart slow cooker. Pour the broth over the vegetables and sprinkle with ½ teaspoon of the rosemary, ½ teaspoon of the thyme, and ¼ teaspoon of the salt.

**2. LAY** the chicken over the vegetables. Sprinkle with the remaining ½ teaspoon rosemary, ½ teaspoon thyme, and ¼ teaspoon salt. Cover and cook on low for 6 to 8 hours. Stir the spinach into the hot liquid until wilted and remove from the heat.

**3. TOP** each bowl with ½ cup couscous.

## 380
**CALORIES PER MEAL**
★ ★ ★

**PER SERVING** (1 serving = 2 cups)

| Calories | Total Fat | Saturated Fat | Sodium | Carbohydrate | Dietary Fiber | Protein | Calcium |
|----------|-----------|---------------|--------|--------------|---------------|---------|---------|
| 380 | 9 g | 2.5 g | 480 mg | 49 g | 8 g | 28 g | 10% |

# Lamb Stew with Rice

**PREP TIME:** 10 MINUTES/ **COOK TIME:** 1 HOUR 7 MINUTES/ MAKES 4 SERVINGS

BASMATI RICE HAS A SUBTLE NUTTY FLAVOR, AND BROWN BASMATI RICE HAS TWICE THE FIBER OF THE MORE COMMON WHITE RICE.

## 410
### CALORIES
### PER MEAL
★ ★

- 1 cup brown basmati rice
- 2 tablespoons all-purpose flour
- ½ teaspoon salt
- ¼ teaspoon freshly ground black pepper
- 1 pound lean boneless leg of lamb, cut into 1" cubes
- 1 tablespoon extra virgin olive oil
- 2 medium onions, cut into ¼"-thick wedges
- 2 carrots, cut into 1" pieces
- 1 fennel bulb, cut into ¼"-thick wedges
- 1 teaspoon dried rosemary
- ½ teaspoon dried thyme
- ¼ cup red wine
- 2 cups fat-free reduced-sodium beef broth

1. **COOK** the rice according to the package directions.

2. **MEANWHILE,** combine the flour, ¼ teaspoon of the salt, and ⅛ teaspoon of the pepper in a medium bowl. Add the lamb and toss to coat. Heat the oil in a Dutch oven over medium-high heat. Add the lamb and cook, turning occasionally, until browned, 4 to 5 minutes. Stir in the onions, carrots, fennel, rosemary, thyme, and any remaining flour mixture. Cook for 2 minutes. Add the wine. Bring to a boil and cook for 1 minute.

3. **STIR** in the broth and bring to a boil. Reduce the heat to medium-low, cover, and simmer until the lamb and vegetables are almost tender, 45 minutes. Uncover and increase the heat to medium. Simmer until tender, 15 minutes.

4. **SERVE** the stew on top of the rice.

**PER SERVING** (1 serving = 1½ cups stew, ½ cup rice)

| Calories | Total Fat | Saturated Fat | Sodium | Carbohydrates | Dietary Fiber | Protein | Calcium |
|---|---|---|---|---|---|---|---|
| 410 | 11 g | 3 g | 660 mg | 47 g | 6 g | 30 g | 6% |

# Savory Pork Stew

**PREP TIME:** 10 MINUTES/ **COOK TIME:** 1 HOUR 35 MINUTES/ MAKES 4 SERVINGS

THIS VERSATILE STEW WORKS EQUALLY WELL WITH BONELESS, SKINLESS CHICKEN THIGHS. IF YOU PREFER A STEW WITH MORE VEGETABLES, DOUBLE THE CARROTS, ADD CELERY, AND CUT OUT THE FRUIT SALAD FOR DESSERT.

| | |
|---|---|
| 3 | tablespoons all-purpose flour |
| ½ | teaspoon salt |
| ½ | teaspoon freshly ground black pepper |
| 1 | pound lean pork tenderloin, trimmed, cut into 1" chunks |
| 2 | tablespoons olive oil |
| 1 | medium onion, chopped |
| 1 | teaspoon dried basil |
| ½ | teaspoon dried thyme |
| 6 | cloves garlic, minced |
| 1 | can (14.5 ounces) fire-roasted diced tomatoes |
| ⅓ | cup red wine |
| 1 | pound red bliss potatoes, cut into ½" cubes |
| 2 | carrots, chopped |
| 3 | tablespoons tomato paste |
| 2 | tablespoons balsamic vinegar |
| ½ | cup water |

**1. COMBINE** the flour, ¼ teaspoon of the salt, and ¼ teaspoon of the pepper in a medium bowl. Add the pork and toss well to coat. Heat 1 tablespoon of the oil in a Dutch oven over medium-high heat. Add half of the pork and cook, turning occasionally, until browned, about 4 to 5 minutes. Transfer to a plate and repeat with the remaining pork.

**2. HEAT** the remaining 1 tablespoon of oil. Add the onion, basil, and thyme. Cook, stirring occasionally, until the onion starts to brown, 4 to 5 minutes. Add the garlic and cook for 1 minute. Stir in the tomatoes and wine. Cook for 2 minutes. Add the potatoes, carrots, tomato paste, vinegar, water, and remaining ¼ teaspoon salt and ¼ teaspoon pepper. Bring to a boil. Reduce the heat to medium-low and simmer, stirring occasionally, until the vegetables and pork are tender, about 1 hour 15 minutes.

## MAKE IT A MEAL

½ cup fruit salad
**50 CALORIES**

# 420
**CALORIES PER MEAL**
★ ★ ★

**PER SERVING** (1 serving = 1½ cups)

| Calories | Total Fat | Saturated Fat | Sodium | Carbohydrate | Dietary Fiber | Protein | Calcium |
|---|---|---|---|---|---|---|---|
| 370 | 10 g | 2 g | 710 mg | 39 g | 5 g | 29 g | 8% |

# Ham and Vegetable Stew

**PREP TIME:** 15 MINUTES/ **COOK TIME:** 40 MINUTES/ MAKES 4 SERVINGS

SHOP CAREFULLY WHEN BUYING HAM TO MAKE SURE THAT YOU PURCHASE AN EXTRALEAN CUT. BECAUSE THE HAM IS HIGH IN SODIUM, THE OTHER INGREDIENTS IN THIS RECIPE ARE UNSALTED.

## MAKE IT A MEAL

Chopped salad with 2 cups romaine lettuce, ¼ cup chopped cucumber, ¼ cup chopped tomato, 2 table-spoons sliced scallion, 1 teaspoon olive oil + ½ tea-spoon red wine vinegar, 1 teaspoon The Spice Hunter Spring Salad Mix, 2 tablespoons croutons
**105 CALORIES**

## 395
**CALORIES PER MEAL**
★ ★ ★ ★

| | |
|---|---|
| 1 | tablespoon olive oil |
| 8 | ounces extra-lean smoked ham steak, cut into ½" pieces |
| 1 | medium onion, coarsely chopped |
| 2 | ribs celery, cut into 1" pieces |
| 2 | carrots, cut into 1" pieces |
| 2 | cloves garlic, minced |
| ½ | teaspoon dried thyme |
| 12 | ounces russet potatoes, cut into ½" cubes |
| 1 | can (14.5 ounces) no-salt-added diced tomatoes |
| 1 | cup fat-free reduced-sodium chicken broth |
| 1 | cup frozen corn kernels |
| 1 | cup frozen peas |
| ½ | cup water |

**1. HEAT** the oil in a Dutch oven over medium-high heat. Add the ham, onion, celery, carrots, garlic, and thyme. Cook, stirring occasionally, until starting to soften, 4 to 5 minutes.

**2. STIR** in the potatoes, tomatoes, broth, corn, peas, and water. Bring to a boil. Reduce the heat to medium-low and cover. Simmer, stirring occasionally, until the vegetables are tender, 33 to 35 minutes.

**PER SERVING** (1 serving = 2 cups)

| Calories | Total Fat | Saturated Fat | Sodium | Carbohydrate | Dietary Fiber | Protein | Calcium |
|---|---|---|---|---|---|---|---|
| 290 | 7 g | 2 g | 860 mg | 40 g | 6 g | 19 g | 6% |

# New England Clam Chowder

**PREP TIME:** 15 MINUTES/ **COOK TIME:** 35 MINUTES/ MAKES 4 SERVINGS

THE HALF-AND-HALF IN THIS RECIPE IS ENOUGH TO ADD CREAMINESS WITHOUT BREAKING THE CALORIE BANK, AND IT HOLDS UP WELL DURING COOKING. TYPICAL LOWER-FAT SUBSTITUTES SUCH AS EVAPORATED MILK CAN CURDLE DURING COOKING.

| | |
|---|---|
| 2 | slices bacon, chopped |
| 1 | onion, chopped |
| 2 | ribs celery, chopped |
| ¼ | teaspoon dried thyme |
| 12 | ounces red bliss potatoes, cut into ½" cubes |
| 1 | bottle (8 ounces) clam juice |
| 2 | cans (6½ ounces each) minced clams, drained, juice reserved |
| 3 | tablespoons all-purpose flour |
| 2 | cups low-fat milk |
| ¾ | cup half-and-half |
| ⅛ | teaspoon freshly ground black pepper |
| 1 | cup low-sodium oyster crackers |

**COOK** the bacon in a Dutch oven over medium heat, stirring occasionally, until starting to brown, about 5 to 6 minutes. Stir in the onion, celery, and thyme. Cook until softened, about 6 to 7 minutes. Add the potatoes and cook for 3 minutes. Increase the heat to medium-high. Add both the bottled and the reserved clam juice and bring to a boil. Reduce the heat to medium-low and cover. Simmer until the potatoes are tender, about 15 minutes. While the broth simmers, put the flour in a small bowl. Whisk in the milk, half-and-half, and black pepper. Stir the milk mixture and the clams into the broth. Increase the heat to medium and cook, stirring with a wooden spoon, until slightly thickened, about 10 to 12 minutes. Divide among 4 bowls and serve with oyster crackers.

## MAKE IT A MEAL

Salad with 1 cup chopped Bibb lettuce, ¼ cup cherry tomatoes, ¼ cup finely chopped Hass or California avocado, 1 teaspoon olive oil, 2 teaspoons lemon juice
**110 CALORIES**

# 420
**CALORIES PER MEAL**
★ ★

**PER SERVING** (1 serving = 1½ cups)

| Calories | Total Fat | Saturated Fat | Sodium | Carbohydrate | Dietary Fiber | Protein | Calcium |
|---|---|---|---|---|---|---|---|
| 310 | 9 g | 5 g | 970 mg | 39 g | 3 g | 17 g | 25% |

# Shrimp Gazpacho

**PREP TIME:** 15 MINUTES + 2 HOURS CHILLING TIME / MAKES 4 SERVINGS

YOU CAN INCREASE OR DECREASE THE HEAT WITHOUT AFFECTING CALORIES BY CHANGING THE AMOUNT OF JALAPEÑO CHILE PEPPER. OR, FOR SMOKY OVERTONES, USE A CANNED CHIPOTLE CHILE PEPPER INSTEAD.

- 5 plum tomatoes (about 1¼ pounds total), seeded
- 1 Hass avocado, peeled, pitted, and chopped
- 2 tablespoons chopped basil leaves
- 2 teaspoons + 2 tablespoons lime juice
- ⅝ teaspoon salt
- 1 medium cucumber, peeled and chopped
- ½ medium Vidalia or other sweet onion, chopped
- 1 red bell pepper, chopped
- 1 clove garlic
- 2 cups low-sodium tomato juice
- ½ jalapeño chile pepper, wear plastic gloves when handling
- ¼ cup fresh basil leaves
- 1 pound (16–20) steamed peeled and deveined jumbo shrimp

**1. CHOP** 1 of the tomatoes and transfer to a bowl. Add the avocado, chopped basil, 2 teaspoons lime juice, ⅛ teaspoon of the salt, ¼ cup of the cucumber, and 2 tablespoons of the onion. Cover and refrigerate until ready to use.

**2. COMBINE** the bell pepper, garlic, tomato juice, chile pepper, basil leaves, and remaining tomatoes, 2 tablespoons lime juice, ½ teaspoon salt, cucumber, and onion in a blender or food processor. Process until smooth. Transfer to a bowl and chill, 1 to 2 hours.

**3. DIVIDE** the gazpacho among 4 bowls. Gently spoon one-quarter of the avocado mixture over each serving. Hang 4 or 5 shrimp off the edge of each bowl.

**PER SERVING** (1 serving = 2 cups)

| Calories | Total Fat | Saturated Fat | Sodium | Carbohydrate | Dietary Fiber | Protein | Calcium |
|----------|-----------|---------------|--------|--------------|---------------|---------|---------|
| 220 | 7 g | 1 g | 640 mg | 19 g | 6 g | 22 g | 8% |

# Salade Niçoise

**PREP TIME:** 10 MINUTES/ MAKES 4 SERVINGS

THIS CLASSIC SALAD HAS ITS ORIGINS IN NICE, A SUNNY AND VIBRANT CITY AT THE MEDITERRANEAN SEA-SIDE. TO INCREASE GOOD FATS, SWITCH FROM TUNA TO CANNED OR LEFTOVER GRILLED SALMON.

## SALAD

- 4 cups chopped romaine lettuce
- 1 can (12 ounces) tuna, rinsed and drained
- 20 black olives
- 8 new potatoes (8 ounces), boiled, drained, and chilled
- 1 cup green beans, steamed, drained, and chilled
- 2 hard-cooked eggs, sliced
- 1 cup cherry tomatoes

## DRESSING

- 1 tablespoon Penzeys Spices Sunny Paris Seasoning or other salt-free seasoning blend
- 2 tablespoons olive oil
- 2 tablespoons lemon juice
- ½ teaspoon Dijon mustard
- ½ teaspoon salt
- ½ teaspoon freshly ground black pepper

**1. TO** make the salad: Place the lettuce in a bowl or on a platter. Arrange the tuna, olives, potatoes, green beans, eggs, and tomatoes on top of the lettuce.

**2. TO** make the dressing: Whisk together the seasoning blend, oil, lemon juice, mustard, salt, and pepper. Drizzle over the salad.

## MAKE IT A MEAL

1 medium whole wheat roll
100 CALORIES

# 390
**CALORIES PER MEAL**
★ ★ ★ ★

**PER SERVING** (1 serving = 2 cups)

| Calories | Total Fat | Saturated Fat | Sodium | Carbohydrate | Dietary Fiber | Protein | Calcium |
|----------|-----------|---------------|--------|--------------|---------------|---------|---------|
| 290 | 13 g | 3 g | 830 mg | 18 g | 5 g | 28 g | 10% |

# Harvest Salad

**PREP TIME:** 10 MINUTES/ MAKES 4 SERVINGS

THE DRIED FRUIT ADDS TEXTURE TO THE DRESSING AND FLAVOR TO THE SALAD. DRIED APRICOTS INSTEAD OF THE CHERRIES IN THE DRESSING AND SALAD WOULD ADD A BOOST OF BETA-CAROTENE.

## MAKE IT A MEAL

1 slice whole grain bread
**70 CALORIES**

# 400
**CALORIES
PER MEAL**
★ ★ ★ ★

### DRESSING

- ¼ cup orange juice
- 2 tablespoons tart dried cherries or dried cranberries
- 1 tablespoon olive oil
- 1 tablespoon balsamic vinegar

### SALAD

- 8 cups mesclun or other baby lettuce
- 2 medium apples, chopped
- 8 ounces smoked or regular cooked turkey breast, cut into ½" pieces, or 6 ounces canned salmon, drained
- ½ cup walnut halves or pieces
- ¼ cup finely chopped red onion
- ¼ cup crumbled blue cheese
- ¼ cup tart dried cherries or dried cranberries

**1. TO** make the dressing: Place the orange juice and dried cherries or cranberries in a microwaveable bowl. Heat until warm, about 30 seconds. Add the oil and vinegar. Blend or process until smooth but slightly chunky. Refrigerate.

**2. TO** make the salad: Toss the mesclun or lettuce, apples, turkey or salmon, walnuts, onion, blue cheese, and dried cherries or cranberries in a large bowl. Add the dressing.

**PER SERVING** (1 serving = 3 cups)

| Calories | Total Fat | Saturated Fat | Sodium | Carbohydrate | Dietary Fiber | Protein | Calcium |
|----------|-----------|---------------|--------|--------------|---------------|---------|---------|
| 330 | 15 g | 3 g | 170 mg | 29 g | 7 g | 23 g | 10% |

# Warmed Greens Salad

**PREP TIME:** 15 MINUTES/ **COOK TIME:** 10 MINUTES/ MAKES 4 SERVINGS

TO MAINTAIN A BIT OF CRISPNESS AND VOLUME IN THE GREENS, QUICKLY SAUTÉ AND IMMEDIATELY REMOVE THE GREENS FROM THE SKILLET. SPINACH WOULD ADD EVEN MORE NUTRIENTS TO THIS SALAD.

| | |
|---|---|
| 8 | cups mixed baby greens, baby lettuces, or mixed Mediterranean greens |
| ¼ | cup chopped walnuts |
| 1 | tablespoon olive oil |
| 1 | teaspoon walnut oil |
| 2 | teaspoons balsamic vinegar |
| ¼ | teaspoon sea salt |
| ¾ | pound salmon fillet |
| | Ken's Lite Accents Honey Mustard salad spray |

1. **WASH** and spin the greens until very dry.

2. **HEAT** a large skillet over medium heat. Add the walnuts and toast for 1 minute. Remove the walnuts from the skillet and set aside.

3. **HEAT** ½ tablespoon of the olive oil in the skillet over medium heat. Add half of the greens and cook gently for up to 1 minute. Place the greens in a medium salad bowl. Repeat with the remaining olive oil and greens. Toss the warmed greens with the walnut oil, balsamic vinegar, and salt.

4. **PLACE** an oven rack approximately 8" from the broiler element. Preheat the broiler on high. Place the salmon skin side down in an ovenproof dish. Coat the fish's surface with 8 sprays salad spray. Broil until the fish is just cooked, 8 to 10 minutes, depending on thickness.

5. **CUT** the fish into 4 servings and place on top of the greens.

## MAKE IT A MEAL

Arnold Select Multigrain Sandwich Thins
100 CALORIES

# 370
**CALORIES PER MEAL**
★ ★ ★ ★

**PER SERVING** (1 serving = 1 cup)

| Calories | Total Fat | Saturated Fat | Sodium | Carbohydrate | Dietary Fiber | Protein | Calcium |
|---|---|---|---|---|---|---|---|
| 270 | 19 g | 3 g | 390 mg | 5 g | 2 g | 20 g | 6% |

# Mediterranean Chopped Salad

**PREP TIME:** 15 MINUTES/ MAKES 4 SERVINGS

YOU CAN MODIFY THIS REFRESHING SALAD BY ADDING MORE OR LESS OF SOME VEGETABLES, CHANGING THE PARSLEY TO MINT OR CILANTRO, OR INCORPORATING ADDITIONAL VEGGIES SUCH AS RED OR GREEN BELL PEPPER. ZA'ATAR, A COMBINATION OF THYME, SESAME SEEDS, GROUND SUMAC, SALT, AND OTHER SEASONINGS, IS AVAILABLE AT MIDDLE EASTERN MARKETS.

| | |
|---|---|
| 4 | cups chopped romaine lettuce |
| 1 | medium tomato, chopped |
| 1 | small cucumber, chopped |
| 4 | radishes, chopped |
| 4 | scallions, chopped |
| ¼ | cup parsley, finely chopped |
| 2 | tablespoons olive oil |
| | Juice of 1 lemon |
| ¼ | teaspoon salt |
| ¼ | teaspoon freshly ground black pepper |
| ½ | teaspoon za'atar (optional) |

**COMBINE** the lettuce, tomato, cucumber, radishes, scallions, parsley, oil, lemon, salt, black pepper, and za'atar (if desired) in a large bowl. Toss well.

## MAKE IT A MEAL

½ cup hummus
210 CALORIES

½ whole wheat pita
90 CALORIES

# 390
**CALORIES PER MEAL**
★ ★ ★

**PER SERVING** (1 serving = 3 cups)

| Calories | Total Fat | Saturated Fat | Sodium | Carbohydrate | Dietary Fiber | Protein | Calcium |
|---|---|---|---|---|---|---|---|
| 90 | 7 g | 1 g | 160 mg | 7 g | 3 g | 2 g | 4% |

# Couscous and Vegetable Salad

**PREP TIME:** 15 MINUTES + 30 MINUTES CHILL TIME/ **COOK TIME:** 5 MINUTES/ MAKES 6 SERVINGS

YOU MAY NOT KNOW THAT COUSCOUS IS A VERY FINELY CUT PASTA, NOT A TYPE OF GRAIN. THIS COLORFUL, VEGETABLE-PACKED SALAD WOULD BE A FILLING AND COLORFUL ADDITION TO A LUNCH BUFFET.

1½  cups water

¼  teaspoon salt

1  teaspoon + 1 tablespoon olive oil

1  cup whole wheat couscous

1  can (15 ounces) chickpeas, rinsed and drained (3 tablespoons of liquid reserved)

½  cup frozen peas, thawed

1  medium carrot, coarsely shredded

1  small tomato, chopped

1  small red or yellow bell pepper, chopped

2½  tablespoons currants

2½  tablespoons finely chopped fresh chives

1½  tablespoons pistachios or pine nuts

1½  tablespoons lemon juice

¼  teaspoon dried thyme

¼  teaspoon dried oregano

Angostura bitters (optional)

**1. BRING** the water, salt, and 1 teaspoon of the oil to a boil in a medium saucepan over high heat. Stir in the couscous. Remove from the heat and cover. Let stand for 5 minutes, or until the liquid is absorbed. Fluff with a fork.

**2. TRANSFER** the couscous to a large bowl. Add the chickpeas (setting aside the liquid), peas, carrot, tomato, pepper, currants, chives, and nuts. Toss gently until mixed.

**3. WHISK** together the lemon juice, thyme, oregano, bitters (if desired), reserved chickpea liquid, and remaining tablespoon of oil in a small bowl. Mix and pour over the salad. Toss to mix well.

**4. COVER** and refrigerate for 30 minutes to blend the flavors.

## MAKE IT A MEAL

3 ounces tuna mixed with 1 tablespoon light mayo
**140 CALORIES**

# 400
**CALORIES PER MEAL**
★ ★ ★ ★

**PER SERVING** (1 serving = 1½ cups)

| Calories | Total Fat | Saturated Fat | Sodium | Carbohydrate | Dietary Fiber | Protein | Calcium |
|----------|-----------|---------------|--------|--------------|---------------|---------|---------|
| 260 | 6 g | 0.5 g | 180 mg | 44 g | 13 g | 9 g | 30% |

# Italian Salad

**PREP TIME:** 10 MINUTES/ MAKES 4 SERVINGS

HERB AND SPICE BLENDS HELP TAKE THE GUESSWORK OUT OF ADDING INTERNATIONAL FLAIR TO YOUR MEALS. ITALIAN SEASONING BLENDS CONTAIN DIFFERENT COMBINATIONS; YOU MAY WANT TO TRY A FEW TO FIND THE ONE YOU LIKE BEST. TO BE SODIUM SMART, PICK BRANDS WITHOUT ADDED SALT. (SEE THE CHART ON PAGE 41 FOR SOME BRANDS WE LIKE.)

**400**
**CALORIES**
**PER MEAL**
★ ★ ★

- 6 cups shredded romaine lettuce
- 2 tomatoes, chopped
- 1 roasted bell pepper, sliced
- 10 black olives, sliced
- 1 can (14–19 ounces) chickpeas, rinsed and drained
- 1 cup shredded part-skim mozzarella cheese
- 2 cups cooked whole grain macaroni
- 2 tablespoons olive oil
- 2 tablespoons balsamic vinegar
- 1 tablespoon Italian seasoning

**TOSS** the lettuce, tomatoes, pepper, olives, chickpeas, cheese, macaroni, oil, vinegar, and seasoning in a large bowl.

**PER SERVING** (1 serving = 3 cups)

| Calories | Total Fat | Saturated Fat | Sodium | Carbohydrate | Dietary Fiber | Protein | Calcium |
|---|---|---|---|---|---|---|---|
| 400 | 17 g | 5 g | 420 mg | 49 g | 10 g | 18 g | 30% |

# Mexican Flag Salad with Crispy Tortilla Topping

**PREP TIME:** 15 MINUTES/ **COOK TIME:** 15 MINUTES/ MAKES 4 SERVINGS

THIS LIGHT SALAD, PACKED WITH VEGETABLES AND GOOD FATS FROM THE AVOCADO, IS PARTICULARLY REFRESHING ON A HOT SUMMER DAY. AN ICE CREAM BAR IS A PERFECT DESSERT TO FOLLOW WITH.

| | |
|---|---|
| 6 | corn tortillas |
| ½ | cup cilantro |
| 2 | tablespoons olive oil |
| 2 | tablespoons lime juice |
| 2 | cloves garlic |
| ½ | teaspoon salt |
| ¼ | teaspoon freshly ground black pepper |
| 4 | cups romaine lettuce |
| 2 | scallions |
| 2 | medium tomatoes, each cut into 6 slices |
| 1 | Hass or California avocado, cut into 12 slices |
| 6 | ounces light *queso blanco*, cut into 12 slices |

**1. PREHEAT** the oven to 350°F. Coat a baking sheet with cooking spray.

**2. TO** make the tortilla topping: Coat each tortilla with cooking spray. Stack the tortillas and cut into ¼"-wide strips. Place the strips on the baking sheet and bake until crisp, about 15 minutes.

**3. TO** make the dressing: Put the cilantro, oil, lime juice, garlic, salt, and pepper in a small food processor and process until smooth. Refrigerate.

**4. TO** assemble the salad: Place the lettuce and scallions in a large bowl. Arrange the tomatoes, avocado, and cheese in rows or in a spiral, 1 slice of tomato partially topped by 1 slice of avocado and 1 slice of cheese. Repeat 11 times.

**5. DRIZZLE** the dressing over the salad. Top with the crisp tortilla strips.

MAKE IT
A MEAL

The Skinny Cow
Fudge Bar
100 CALORIES

400
CALORIES
PER MEAL
★ ★ ★

**PER SERVING** (1 serving = 1½ cups)

| Calories | Total Fat | Saturated Fat | Sodium | Carbohydrate | Dietary Fiber | Protein | Calcium |
|---|---|---|---|---|---|---|---|
| 300 | 17 g | 4 g | 640 mg | 28 g | 7 g | 13 g | 8% |

# Curried Tofu with Asian Slaw

**PREP TIME:** 30 MINUTES + 4 HOURS MARINATING/ **COOK TIME:** 12 MINUTES/ MAKES 4 SERVINGS

EVEN PEOPLE WHO ARE RELUCTANT TO TRY TOFU WILL LOVE THIS DISH THAT HAS IT ALL—A MEDLEY OF FLAVORS AND TEXTURES, LOTS OF NUTRIENTS, AND A REASONABLE CALORIE COUNT. STIR IN LEFTOVER BROWN RICE TO ROUND OUT THE SALAD WITH A WHOLE GRAIN.

## MAKE IT A MEAL

½ cup cooked
brown rice
**110 CALORIES**

# 420
**CALORIES
PER MEAL**
★ ★ ★ ★

### MARINADE

- ¼ cup canned light coconut milk
- 2 tablespoons curry powder
- 1 tablespoon minced garlic
- 1 tablespoon reduced-sodium soy sauce
- 1 container (14 ounces) extra-firm tofu, drained, patted dry, and cut into ½"-thick, 1" × 2" strips

### DRESSING

- ⅓ cup rice wine vinegar
- ¼ cup peanut butter
- 2 tablespoons reduced-sodium soy sauce
- 1 tablespoon lime juice
- 1 tablespoon honey
- 2 teaspoons minced garlic
- ½ teaspoon red curry paste (sold in the ethnic food section of most supermarkets)

### SALAD

- 1 small head napa or savoy cabbage, thinly sliced (about 4 cups)
- 2 medium red bell peppers, julienned (about 2 cups)
- 4 medium carrots, julienned (about 2 cups)
- 1 cup thinly sliced scallions
- ⅓ cup chopped fresh cilantro

**1. TO** make the marinade: Combine the coconut milk, curry powder, garlic, and soy sauce in a small bowl. Place the tofu in a wide bowl. Add the marinade and turn each piece of tofu to coat. Marinate at least ½ hour and up to 4 hours. (Cover and chill in the refrigerator if more than 2 hours.)

**2. PREHEAT** the broiler. Arrange the tofu slices in a single layer on a foil-lined baking sheet. Broil for 6 minutes. Gently turn the tofu and broil 6 minutes longer, or until golden brown. Remove from the broiler and cool slightly.

**3. TO** make the dressing: Whisk together the vinegar, peanut butter, soy sauce, lime juice, honey, garlic, and curry paste in a medium bowl.

**4. TO** make the salad: Combine the tofu, cabbage, peppers, carrots, scallions, and half of the cilantro in a large bowl. Add the dressing and toss well to coat. Divide among 4 bowls and top with the remaining cilantro.

Adapted from a recipe by Lia Huber

**PER SERVING** (1 serving = 2½ cups)

| Calories | Total Fat | Saturated Fat | Sodium | Carbohydrate | Dietary Fiber | Protein | Calcium |
|----------|-----------|---------------|--------|--------------|---------------|---------|---------|
| 310 | 15 g | 4 g | 560 mg | 26 g | 8 g | 20 g | 20% |

# Multi-Bean Salad

**PREP TIME:** 15 MINUTES + 2 HOURS CHILL TIME/ MAKES 12 SERVINGS

PREPARE THIS FIBER-PACKED SALAD WHEN YOU'RE COOKING FOR A CROWD. CILANTRO ADDS A FRESH AND BRIGHT FLAVOR.

## MAKE IT A MEAL

Dr. Praeger's California Veggie Burger with whole wheat hamburger bun, 2 tomato slices, 2 lettuce leaves, 1 tablespoon ketchup
**255 CALORIES**

# 395
**CALORIES PER MEAL**
★ ★

### SALAD

- ½ pound green beans, trimmed or halved
- 1 can (14–19 ounces) kidney beans, rinsed and drained
- 1 can (14–19 ounces) white kidney beans, rinsed and drained
- 1 can (14–19 ounces) black beans, rinsed and drained
- ½ cup chopped red bell pepper
- ¼ cup finely chopped red onion

### DRESSING

- ⅓ cup canola, safflower, or cottonseed oil
- ⅓ cup red wine vinegar
- ¼ cup white sugar
- ½ teaspoon sea salt
- ½ cup chopped fresh cilantro

1. **BRING** ½" water to a boil in a medium saucepan. Add the green beans and cover. Boil for 2 minutes. Remove from the heat. Drain and place the green beans in large bowl of ice water.

2. **TO** make the dressing: Combine the oil, vinegar, sugar, and salt in a small saucepan. Bring to a simmer over medium heat until the sugar dissolves, about 5 minutes. Remove from the heat.

3. **DRAIN** the green beans and place them in a large bowl or a 1-gallon resealable plastic bag. Add the kidney beans, white kidney beans, black beans, bell pepper, and onion. Pour on the dressing and mix gently. Refrigerate for at least 2 hours.

4. **STIR** in the cilantro just before serving.

**PER SERVING** (1 serving = ½ cup)

| Calories | Total Fat | Saturated Fat | Sodium | Carbohydrate | Dietary Fiber | Protein | Calcium |
|----------|-----------|---------------|--------|--------------|---------------|---------|---------|
| 140 | 7 g | 0.5 g | 220 mg | 18 g | 5 g | 5 g | 4% |

# Smoked Turkey, Black Bean, and Edamame Salad

**PREP TIME:** 15 MINUTES/ MAKES 4 SERVINGS

YOU CAN FIND SMOKED TURKEY AS EITHER TURKEY BREAST IN THE DELI SECTION OR SMOKED PARTS IN THE MEAT SECTION. EDAMAME (SOYBEANS) ARE A GOOD FREEZER STAPLE FOR A QUICK SNACK OR ADDITION TO A SALAD.

- 2 **cups cubed smoked turkey meat**
- 1 **can (14–19 ounces) black beans, rinsed and drained**
- 1 **can (14–19 ounces) no-salt-added corn kernels**
- 1 **cup shelled edamame, cooked according to package directions and cooled**
- 1 **medium red bell pepper, chopped**
- ½ **cup finely chopped red onion**
- ¼ **cup finely chopped fresh cilantro (optional)**
- 1 **tablespoon minced garlic**
- 1 **teaspoon McCormick Salt Free Original Perfect Pinch**
- 2 **tablespoons olive oil**
- 2 **tablespoons cider vinegar**
- 1 **teaspoon Dijon mustard**
- 4 **cups field greens**

1. **COMBINE** the turkey, beans, corn, edamame, bell pepper, onion, cilantro (if desired), garlic, and Perfect Pinch. Whisk together the oil, vinegar, and mustard and pour over the turkey and vegetables. Toss to combine. Season with salt and pepper.

2. **PLACE** the lettuce on each of 4 plates. Top with the turkey and vegetable mixture.

**390 CALORIES PER MEAL**
★ ★ ★ ★

**PER SERVING** (1 serving = 2 cups)

| Calories | Total Fat | Saturated Fat | Sodium | Carbohydrate | Dietary Fiber | Protein | Calcium |
|----------|-----------|---------------|--------|--------------|---------------|---------|---------|
| 390 | 14 g | 3 g | 280 mg | 39 g | 10 g | 31 g | 10% |

# Chinese Chicken Salad

**PREP TIME:** 15 MINUTES/ **COOK TIME:** 5 MINUTES/ MAKES 4 SERVINGS

WE CUT DOWN THE CALORIES IN THIS LUNCH CLASSIC BY BAKING THE WONTON WRAPPERS RATHER THAN BUYING THEM FRIED AND BY USING MUCH LESS OIL IN THE DRESSING. FORTUNE COOKIES ARE SOLD IN THE ASIAN FOOD SECTION OF THE SUPERMARKET AND AT ASIAN GROCERY STORES.

## MAKE IT A MEAL

½ cup canned
pineapple chunks
**50 CALORIES**

1 fortune cookie
**30 CALORIES**

# 390
**CALORIES
PER MEAL**
★ ★ ★

| | |
|---|---|
| 12 | square wonton wrappers |
| 4 | cups mesclun or torn romaine lettuce |
| 2 | cups chopped cooked chicken |
| ½ | package (about 3½ ounces) enoki mushrooms |
| 1 | can sliced water chestnuts, drained |
| 3 | scallions, sliced into thin rounds |
| 1 | rib celery, finely chopped |
| 2 | tablespoons rice vinegar |
| 1 | tablespoon peanut oil |
| 1 | tablespoon sesame seeds |
| 1 | tablespoon hoisin sauce |
| 1 | teaspoon sesame oil |
| 1 | teaspoon mustard powder |
| ½ | teaspoon sriracha sauce (optional) |

**1. PREHEAT** the oven to 350°F. Cut the wonton wrappers into ½" strips. Place the strips on a nonstick baking sheet. Coat with cooking spray and bake until crisp and lightly browned, about 5 minutes.

**2. COMBINE** the lettuce, chicken, mushrooms, water chestnuts, scallions, and celery in a large salad bowl. In another bowl, whisk together the vinegar, peanut oil, sesame seeds, hoisin sauce, sesame oil, mustard powder, and sriracha sauce (if desired). Pour the sauce over the chicken and vegetables. Toss to blend. Top with the crisp wonton skins.

**PER SERVING** (1 serving = 1½ cups)

| Calories | Total Fat | Saturated Fat | Sodium | Carbohydrate | Dietary Fiber | Protein | Calcium |
|---|---|---|---|---|---|---|---|
| 310 | 12 g | 3 g | 290 mg | 28 g | 6 g | 23 g | 8% |

# Tabbouleh with Grilled Chicken

**PREP TIME:** 20 MINUTES/ **COOK TIME:** 8 MINUTES/ MAKES 4 SERVINGS

TABBOULEH IS MADE FROM BULGUR WHEAT, WHOLE WHEAT KERNELS THAT ARE BOILED, DRIED, AND CUT INTO SMALL PIECES RANGING FROM FINE TO COARSE. ZA'ATAR, A COMBINATION OF THYME, SESAME SEEDS, GROUND SUMAC, SALT, AND OTHER SEASONINGS, IS AVAILABLE AT MIDDLE EASTERN MARKETS.

| | |
|---|---|
| 1 | cup No. 2 medium or No. 3 coarse bulgur |
| 2 | cups boiling water |
| 1½ | cups finely chopped parsley |
| 1 | cup finely chopped mint leaves |
| 2 | cups chopped tomato |
| 4 | scallions, thinly sliced |
| 2 | tablespoons olive oil |
| 3 | tablespoons lemon juice |
| ¼ | teaspoon salt |
| ⅛ | teaspoon freshly ground black pepper |
| 1 | pound boneless, skinless chicken breasts |
| 2 | teaspoons za'atar or 1 teaspoon dried thyme, ¾ teaspoon sesame seeds, and ¼ teaspoon salt |
| ½ | teaspoon garlic powder |
| ½ | teaspoon ground cumin |

**1. PLACE** the bulgur wheat in a medium bowl. Cover with the boiling water and let sit until most of the water is absorbed, about 20 minutes.

**2. MEANWHILE,** toss together the parsley, mint, tomato, and scallions in a large bowl. Drain the bulgur and combine with the vegetables. Add the oil and mix to coat. Add the lemon juice, salt, and pepper. Refrigerate.

**3. IF** the chicken breasts are thick, pound to ½" thickness. Combine the za'atar, garlic powder, and cumin in a small bowl. Rub half of the spice mixture onto each side of the chicken breast. Cut into ½"-wide strips and place in a broiling pan. Broil for 4 minutes. Turn the pieces over and broil for 4 more minutes.

**4. ARRANGE** the chicken on top of the tabbouleh.

MAKE IT
A MEAL

1 cup cubed
watermelon
**50 CALORIES**

# 390
**CALORIES
PER MEAL**
★ ★ ★ ★

**PER SERVING** (1 serving = 1½ cups tabbouleh, ½ cup chicken)

| Calories | Total Fat | Saturated Fat | Sodium | Carbohydrate | Dietary Fiber | Protein | Calcium |
|---|---|---|---|---|---|---|---|
| 340 | 11 g | 2 g | 370 mg | 35 g | 10 g | 29 g | 10% |

# Grilled Chopped Steakhouse Salad

**PREP TIME:** 25 MINUTES + 10 MINUTES STAND TIME/ **COOK TIME:** 20 MINUTES/ MAKES 4 SERVINGS

THIS SALAD IS JUST LIKE ONE YOU MIGHT ORDER AT YOUR FAVORITE STEAKHOUSE, BUT MUCH HEALTHIER AND LOWER IN CALORIES. OLIVE OIL, BALSAMIC VINEGAR, DIJON MUSTARD, AND SHALLOTS MAKE A TASTY AND LIGHT DRESSING.

4 ounces French bread, cut into ¾" cubes

¾ pound flank steak, trimmed

½ teaspoon salt

¼ teaspoon freshly ground black pepper

1 small head iceberg lettuce, chopped (4 cups)

1 large cucumber, peeled, seeded, and chopped

1 pint grape tomatoes, halved

2 carrots, chopped

1 large red bell pepper, chopped

1 Gala apple, peeled, cored, and chopped

½ small red onion, chopped

3 tablespoons finely chopped shallots

2 tablespoons balsamic vinegar

1 teaspoon Dijon mustard

1 tablespoon extra virgin olive oil

**1. PREHEAT** the oven to 425°F. Coat a baking sheet with cooking spray.

**2. ARRANGE** the bread cubes on the baking sheet in a single layer. Bake until lightly golden and crisp, 7 to 8 minutes. Cool on the pan.

**3. HEAT** a large nonstick grill pan coated with cooking spray over medium-high heat. Sprinkle the steak with ¼ teaspoon of the salt and ⅛ teaspoon of the pepper. Set the steak on the grill pan. Cook for 5 to 6 minutes per side for medium-rare to medium. Transfer to a cutting board and let stand for 10 minutes.

**4. COMBINE** the bread cubes, lettuce, cucumber, tomatoes, carrots, bell pepper, apple, and onion in a large bowl. Combine the shallots, vinegar, mustard, and remaining ¼ teaspoon salt and ⅛ teaspoon pepper in a separate bowl. Whisk in the oil until well combined. Pour over the salad and toss well. Divide among 4 serving plates. Thinly slice the steak across the grain and top each salad with one-quarter of the steak.

## MAKE IT A MEAL

1 cup sweet iced tea
**60 CALORIES**

# 400
**CALORIES PER MEAL**
★ ★

**PER SERVING** (1 serving = 3 cups)

| Calories | Total Fat | Saturated Fat | Sodium | Carbohydrate | Dietary Fiber | Protein | Calcium |
|----------|-----------|---------------|--------|--------------|---------------|---------|---------|
| 340 | 11 g | 4 g | 590 mg | 36 g | 5 g | 24 g | 8% |

# Healthy Souvlaki Sandwich

**PREP TIME:** 20 MINUTES + 20 MINUTES STAND TIME/ **COOK TIME:** 10 MINUTES/ MAKES 4 SERVINGS

SOUVLAKI OFTEN IS MADE WITH LAMB, WHICH IS MUCH HIGHER IN FAT THAN CHICKEN BREAST. AVOID OVERCOOKING THE CHICKEN SO IT STAYS MOIST.

**390 CALORIES PER MEAL**
★ ★

- 1 pound boneless, skinless chicken breast, cut into 20 cubes
- 1 teaspoon dried oregano
- 2 tablespoons red wine vinegar
- 5 teaspoons extra virgin olive oil
- 3 cloves garlic, minced
- 2 cups shredded romaine lettuce
- 2 plum tomatoes, chopped
- ½ medium cucumber, peeled, seeded, and thinly sliced
- ½ small white onion, finely chopped
- ½ teaspoon salt
- ¼ teaspoon freshly ground black pepper
- 1 container (6 ounces) Greek-style plain fat-free yogurt
- 4 whole grain pitas (6½" diameter), top ¼ sliced off

1. **COMBINE** the chicken, oregano, vinegar, 2 teaspoons of the oil, and 2 of the garlic cloves in a medium bowl. Let stand 20 minutes, tossing occasionally.

2. **MEANWHILE,** combine the lettuce, tomatoes, cucumber, onion, ¼ teaspoon of the salt, ⅛ teaspoon of the pepper, and the remaining 1 tablespoon vinegar and 3 teaspoons oil in a separate medium bowl. Combine the yogurt and remaining garlic in a bowl.

3. **PREHEAT** the broiler. Coat a broiler pan with cooking spray.

4. **THREAD** 5 chicken cubes onto each of 4 skewers. Sprinkle with the remaining ¼ teaspoon salt and ⅛ teaspoon pepper. Set on the broiler pan and cook 4" to 5" from the heat source for 8 to 10 minutes, turning often. Let cool slightly. Remove the chicken from the skewers and combine with the yogurt in a bowl.

5. **FILL** each pita with a quarter of the lettuce mixture (about ½ cup) and a quarter of the chicken and yogurt mixture.

**PER SERVING (1 serving = 1 pita sandwich)**

| Calories | Total Fat | Saturated Fat | Sodium | Carbohydrate | Dietary Fiber | Protein | Calcium |
|----------|-----------|---------------|--------|--------------|---------------|---------|---------|
| 390 | 10 g | 2 g | 710 mg | 42 g | 6 g | 34 g | 8% |

# Double A Butter Panini

**PREP TIME:** 5 MINUTES/ **COOK TIME:** 9 MINUTES/ MAKES 4 SERVINGS

THIS RECIPE IS EVEN EASIER IF YOU HAVE A PANINI MAKER. THE ALMOND BUTTER HAS A MORE SOPHISTI-CATED FLAVOR THAN PEANUT BUTTER, BUT EITHER WORKS WELL AND PROVIDES PLENTY OF GOOD FATS.

½  of 1-pound loaf whole wheat Italian bread

5  tablespoons almond butter

3  tablespoons apple butter

1  medium apple, sliced very thin

**1. SLICE** the bread in half lengthwise. Spread one half with the almond butter and the other half with the apple butter. Top one half with the apple slices and cover with the other half.

**2. HEAT** a large nonstick skillet over medium-low heat. Place the sandwich in the skillet. Top with a heavy lid or press down with a spatula to flatten as it cooks. Cook for 5 minutes, or until lightly browned on cooked surface. Turn sandwich over, press down, and cook for 4 minutes, or until lightly browned.

**3. CUT** into 4 pieces and serve.

## MAKE IT A MEAL

1 cup low-fat milk
**100 CALORIES**

# 410
**CALORIES
PER MEAL**
★ ★

**PER SERVING** (1 serving = 1 piece)

| Calories | Total Fat | Saturated Fat | Sodium | Carbohydrate | Dietary Fiber | Protein | Calcium |
|---|---|---|---|---|---|---|---|
| 310 | 14 g | 2 g | 360 mg | 39 g | 6 g | 10 g | 10% |

# Mashed Edamame White Bean Pita Party Sandwiches

**PREP TIME:** 20 MINUTES/ **COOK TIME:** 30 MINUTES/ MAKES 6 SERVINGS

WE LIGHTENED UP THIS FILLING BY ADDING WHITE BEANS TO EDAMAME (SOYBEANS) RATHER THAN USING EDAMAME ALONE. THE MINI PITAS ARE WORTH A TRIP TO TRADER JOE'S; PICK UP AN EXTRA PACKAGE TO KEEP IN THE FREEZER FOR YOUR NEXT PARTY.

## MAKE IT A MEAL

10 baby carrots
**40 CALORIES**

1 tablespoon guacamole
**30 CALORIES**

5 ounces red wine
**120 CALORIES**

# 420
**CALORIES PER MEAL**
★ ★ ★

- 1 cup water
- 1½ cups frozen shelled edamame
- 1 clove garlic, minced
- 1 cup canned white or cannellini beans, rinsed and drained
- 3 ounces reduced-fat feta cheese, crumbled
- 1 tablespoon chopped fresh parsley
- 1 teaspoon McCormick Mediterranean Super Spice or 1 teaspoon dried oregano
- 2 tablespoons balsamic vinegar
- 1 tablespoon olive oil
- 4 cups shredded romaine lettuce
- 1 tomato, finely chopped
- ½ small red onion, finely chopped
- 1 package (6 ounces) Trader Joe's whole wheat mini pitas, or 6 (1 ounce each) whole wheat pitas

1. **BRING** the water to a boil in a medium saucepan. Add the edamame and garlic. Reduce the heat to medium and cover. Cook for 25 to 30 minutes, or until the edamame are very soft.

2. **PUREE** the edamame mixture with the white beans in a food processor or blender. Pour the mixture into a medium bowl. Stir in the cheese, parsley, and seasoning.

3. **WHISK** together the vinegar and oil in a large bowl. Add the lettuce, tomato, and onion. Toss to coat.

4. **OPEN** each pita about halfway around. Carefully spread the bean mixture inside each pita. Add the salad.

**PER SERVING** (1 serving = 4 mini pita sandwiches)

| Calories | Total Fat | Saturated Fat | Sodium | Carbohydrate | Dietary Fiber | Protein | Calcium |
|----------|-----------|---------------|--------|--------------|---------------|---------|---------|
| 230 | 7 g | 2 g | 420 mg | 30 g | 7 g | 12 g | 10% |

# Turkey Club

**PREP TIME:** 10 MINUTES/ **COOK TIME:** 5 MINUTES/ MAKES 4 SERVINGS

YOU CAN FIND NITRITE-FREE BACON AT A HEALTH FOOD STORE, AS WELL AS AT MANY SUPERMARKETS. TRY THIS SANDWICH WITH MASHED RIPE AVOCADO INSTEAD OF GUACAMOLE WHEN AVOCADOS ARE AVAILABLE AND REASONABLY PRICED.

- 4 ounces nitrite-free turkey bacon (we used Applegate Farms)
- 2 whole wheat Portuguese *padinha* rolls (about 4 ounces each) or other Portuguese rolls
- 4 tablespoons guacamole or mashed Hass or California avocado
- 3 tablespoons light mayonnaise
- 1 tablespoon minced shallots
- 4 thin slices red onion
- 8 ounces deli turkey breast, in 1-ounce slices
- 1 medium tomato, cut into 8 slices
- 4 leaves romaine lettuce

**1. COOK** the turkey bacon according to package directions. Drain on paper towels.

**2. SLICE** each roll into thirds crosswise. Stir together the guacamole or avocado, mayonnaise, and shallots.

**3. SPREAD** 2 tablespoons of the guacamole on the bottommost slice of each roll. Top each with 1 onion slice, 2 slices turkey, 2 slices tomato, 1 slice bacon, and 1 leaf lettuce. Top with the middle slice of each roll. Repeat in the same order. Top with the topmost slice of roll.

**4. SECURE** each roll with tall wooden picks. Slice in half diagonally.

## MAKE IT A MEAL

¼ cup deli potato salad
80 CALORIES

# 400
**CALORIES PER MEAL**
★ ★ ★

**PER SERVING** (1 serving = ½ roll)

| Calories | Total Fat | Saturated Fat | Sodium | Carbohydrate | Dietary Fiber | Protein | Calcium |
|----------|-----------|---------------|--------|--------------|---------------|---------|---------|
| 320 | 11 g | 2 g | 450 mg | 36 g | 6 g | 23 g | 6% |

# Sliders with Sautéed Mushrooms and Onions

**PREP TIME:** 15 MINUTES/ **COOK TIME:** 26 MINUTES/ MAKES 4 SERVINGS

THE KETCHUP-MAYO SPREAD AND THE SAUTÉED MUSHROOMS AND ONION IMPART MOISTURE THAT HELPS BALANCE THE EXTRA-LEAN GROUND BEEF.

## 370
**CALORIES
PER MEAL**
★ ★

- 3 slices bacon
- 1 package (8 ounces) sliced fresh mushrooms
- 1 large onion, sliced (about 1½ cups)
- ¼ teaspoon dried thyme
- 2 cloves garlic, minced
- ¼ teaspoon salt
- ¼ teaspoon freshly ground black pepper
- 1 pound extra-lean ground round
- ¼ cup ketchup
- 2 tablespoons reduced-fat mayonnaise
- 8 whole wheat slider rolls (1.3 ounces each)

1. **COOK** the bacon in a medium nonstick skillet over medium-high heat until crisp, about 4 minutes per side. Transfer to a plate covered with a paper towel, drain, and chop. Return the skillet to the heat. Add the mushrooms, onion, and thyme. Cook, stirring occasionally, until browned, about 9 to 10 minutes. Stir in the garlic, salt, and pepper. Cook for 2 minutes longer. Remove from the heat and stir in the bacon. Keep warm.

2. **MEANWHILE,** form the beef into 8 patties. Heat a ridged grill pan coated with cooking spray over medium-high heat. Add the patties and cook until nicely marked and cooked through, about 3 minutes per side for medium.

3. **WHILE** the patties cook, combine the ketchup and mayonnaise in a bowl. Arrange the roll bottoms on 4 plates, 2 per plate. Spread each with the ketchup mixture. Top with the patties, mushroom mixture, and roll tops. Serve hot.

**PER SERVING** (1 serving = 2 sliders)

| Calories | Total Fat | Saturated Fat | Sodium | Carbohydrates | Dietary Fiber | Protein | Calcium |
|---|---|---|---|---|---|---|---|
| 370 | 10 g | 3 g | 830 mg | 41 g | 9 g | 38 g | 10% |

# Pizza-Style Turkey Sliders

**PREP TIME:** 15 MINUTES/ **COOK TIME:** 9 MINUTES/ MAKES 4 SERVINGS

THE PESTO SAUCE, A BLEND OF BASIL, OLIVE OIL, CHEESE, AND PINE NUTS, ADDS MOISTURE AND FLAVOR TO THE GROUND TURKEY BREAST. TURKEY BREAST IS SO LEAN THAT IT TENDS TO BE DRY ON ITS OWN.

## 400
**CALORIES
PER MEAL**
★ ★

- 12 ounces ground turkey breast
- ¼ cup prepared pesto sauce
- 1 large egg white
- ¼ cup finely chopped Vidalia or other sweet onion
- 3 tablespoons Italian-style bread crumbs
- ⅛ teaspoon salt
- ¼ teaspoon freshly ground black pepper
- ½ cup shredded part-skim mozzarella cheese
- 8 whole wheat slider rolls (1.3 ounces each)
- 1 large plum tomato, cut into 8 slices

1. **PREHEAT** the broiler. Coat the broiler rack with cooking spray and line the broiler pan with foil.

2. **COMBINE** the turkey, pesto, egg white, onion, bread crumbs, salt, and pepper in a medium bowl. Mix gently without overworking. Form into 8 patties and set on the prepared broiler rack.

3. **BROIL** the patties for 4 minutes per side. Top each with 1 tablespoon of the cheese and broil for 10 to 15 seconds longer, or until the cheese melts.

4. **SET** 2 roll bottoms on each of 4 plates. Top each with a burger and a tomato slice. Top with the remaining halves of the rolls.

**PER SERVING** (1 serving = 2 sliders)

| Calories | Total Fat | Saturated Fat | Sodium | Carbohydrate | Dietary Fiber | Protein | Calcium |
|----------|-----------|---------------|--------|--------------|---------------|---------|---------|
| 400 | 13 g | 4 g | 680 mg | 37 g | 9 g | 41 g | 30% |

# Ham and Cheese Panini

**PREP TIME:** 10 MINUTES/ **COOK TIME:** 20 MINUTES/ MAKES 4 SERVINGS

ENJOY THIS RECIPE AS WRITTEN OR CUSTOMIZE IT TO YOUR TASTE BY SWITCHING TO DELI TURKEY, PICKING A DIFFERENT TYPE OF REDUCED-FAT CHEESE, AND EVEN SWAPPING THE TOMATO FOR THINLY SLICED APPLE OR ONION.

- 4 teaspoons Dijon mustard
- 1 tablespoon reduced-fat mayonnaise
- 8 slices whole grain bread
- 1 medium tomato, cut into 8 slices
- 6 ounces deli-thin sliced ham (8 slices)
- 4 1-ounce slices reduced-fat sharp Cheddar cheese

**1. COMBINE** the mustard and mayonnaise in a small bowl. Spread the mixture over 1 side of 4 slices of bread. Top each with 2 slices tomato, 2 slices ham, 1 slice cheese, and the remaining bread slices.

**2. HEAT** a large ridged grill pan over medium heat.

**3. COAT** the outside of each sandwich lightly with cooking spray. Place the sandwiches on the grill pan, in 2 batches if necessary. Set a large, heavy skillet on top and press down slightly. Cook until the center is warm and the bread is marked and toasted, about 4 to 5 minutes per side. Cut each in half and serve hot.

## MAKE IT A MEAL

Large salad with 2 cups lettuce, 1 tomato, 10 salad dressing sprays
**60 CALORIES**

1 cup cantaloupe
**50 CALORIES**

# 410
**CALORIES PER MEAL**
★ ★ ★

**PER SERVING** (1 serving = 1 sandwich)

| Calories | Total Fat | Saturated Fat | Sodium | Carbohydrate | Dietary Fiber | Protein | Calcium |
|----------|-----------|---------------|--------|--------------|---------------|---------|---------|
| 300 | 10 g | 5 g | 970 mg | 28 g | 4 g | 22 g | 25% |

# Oven-Baked Chicken Fingers

**PREP TIME:** 15 MINUTES/ **COOK TIME:** 20 MINUTES/ MAKES 4 SERVINGS

IN ADDITION TO SUPPLYING GOOD FATS, PEANUTS ARE THE PERFECT PARTNER FOR CHILI POWDER IN THIS CROWD-PLEASING DISH. DIP THESE CHICKEN FINGERS IN NATURAL APPLESAUCE INSTEAD OF KETCHUP AND ENJOY WITH A BAKED SWEET POTATO, A VEGETABLE SO RICH IN VITAMINS THAT IT DESERVES A SPOT ON YOUR PLATE—AND NOT JUST ON THANKSGIVING.

### MAKE IT A MEAL

½ cup unsweetened applesauce
**50 CALORIES**

Medium baked sweet potato
**100 CALORIES**

# 410
**CALORIES PER MEAL**
★ ★ ★

¼ cup lightly salted dry-roasted peanuts
½ cup panko
½ tablespoon chili powder
1 egg
1 teaspoon Dijon mustard
1 pound boneless, skinless chicken breasts, cut into 1"-thick strips

1. **PREHEAT** the oven to 400°F. Coat a baking sheet with cooking spray.

2. **CHOP** the peanuts in a food processor until fine. Place the peanuts, panko, and chili powder in a large resealable plastic bag or container. Shake to mix.

3. **WHISK** together the egg and mustard in a large bowl. Add the chicken and combine until all strips are covered. Place the strips in the plastic bag or container. Seal and shake until well coated. Place the strips on the baking sheet. Bake until the coating is crisp and the chicken is cooked through, 15 to 20 minutes.

### STAR SYSTEM

★ PROTEIN
★ FIBER
★ GOOD FATS
★ FRUITS/VEGGIES

**PER SERVING** (1 serving = 2 or 3 chicken fingers)

| Calories | Total Fat | Saturated Fat | Sodium | Carbohydrate | Dietary Fiber | Protein | Calcium |
|---|---|---|---|---|---|---|---|
| 260 | 10 g | 2 g | 160 mg | 8 g | 1 g | 33 g | 4% |

# Barbecue Chicken

**PREP TIME:** 10 MINUTES/ **COOK TIME:** 1 HOUR 20 MINUTES/ MAKES 4 SERVINGS

SURE, YOU CAN BUY A BOTTLE OF BARBECUE SAUCE FROM THE MARKET, BUT IT'S A LOT MORE FUN TO MAKE YOUR OWN. YOU DON'T HAVE A LOT OF CALORIE WIGGLE ROOM FOR PLAYING WITH THE MAIN INGREDIENTS, BUT YOU CAN SPICE UP THIS RECIPE BY ALTERING THE SEASONINGS.

- 2 teaspoons olive oil
- ½ cup chopped onion
- 1 cup tomato puree
- 2 tablespoons honey
- 2 tablespoons molasses or brown sugar
- 2⅓ tablespoons cider vinegar
- 1 tablespoon + ½ teaspoon Worcestershire sauce
- 2½ teaspoons mustard powder
- ¾ teaspoon sea salt
- ½ teaspoon freshly ground black pepper
- ½ teaspoon liquid smoke
- 4 split bone-in chicken breasts (7–8 ounces each), skin removed

**1. HEAT** the oil in a small saucepan over medium heat. Add the onion and cook until soft, about 3 minutes. Add the tomato puree, honey, molasses or brown sugar, vinegar, Worcestershire sauce, mustard powder, salt, pepper, liquid smoke, and chicken. Stir and cover. Simmer on low heat for 20 minutes. Uncover and simmer for an additional 10 minutes, or until thick. Refrigerate until ready to use.

**2. PREHEAT** the oven to 350°F. Place the chicken in a baking pan and brush generously with barbecue sauce. Bake for approximately 45 minutes, or until the juices run clear.

**3. SERVE** with the remaining barbecue sauce.

## MAKE IT A MEAL

Medium ear corn on the cob
**80 CALORIES**

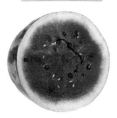

½ cup watermelon
**20 CALORIES**

# 380
**CALORIES PER MEAL**
★ ★

**PER SERVING** (1 serving = 1 chicken breast)

| Calories | Total Fat | Saturated Fat | Sodium | Carbohydrate | Dietary Fiber | Protein | Calcium |
|---|---|---|---|---|---|---|---|
| 280 | 6 g | 2 g | 740 mg | 25 g | 2 g | 31 g | 6% |

# Quick Chicken Parm Bites over a Bed of Pasta

**PREP TIME:** 10 MINUTES/ **COOK TIME:** 15 MINUTES/ MAKES 4 SERVINGS

WE PICKED WHOLE WHEAT SPAGHETTI FOR ITS EXTRA FIBER AND MINERALS. TO TURN THIS INTO A PARTY DISH, ELIMINATE THE PASTA AND BRING OUT THE WOODEN PICKS.

## MAKE IT A MEAL

Small green salad with 10 salad dressing sprays
**30 CALORIES**

# 410
**CALORIES PER MEAL**
★ ★

- 1 pound thick chicken breasts, cut into 1" pieces
- 1 large egg
- ½ teaspoon Dijon mustard
- ¾ cup panko
- ¼ cup grated Parmesan cheese
- 1 tablespoon salt-free Italian seasoning
- 1 teaspoon garlic powder
- 2 cups jarred pasta sauce
- 2 cups cooked whole wheat spaghetti, kept warm
- 8 tablespoons grated part-skim mozzarella cheese

1. **PREHEAT** the oven to 350°F. Coat a baking sheet with cooking spray.

2. **PLACE** the chicken in a large bowl. Whisk together the egg and mustard in a small bowl. Pour the egg mixture over the chicken and stir to coat all pieces. Remove the chicken and shake off the extra egg. Place the chicken on a rack to allow excess egg to drain off.

3. **MEANWHILE,** combine the panko, Parmesan cheese, seasoning, and garlic powder in a large resealable plastic bag or container. Add the chicken and shake to cover all pieces. Remove the chicken, place on the baking sheet, and bake for 30 minutes, or until lightly browned and sizzling.

4. **HEAT** the pasta sauce while the chicken is cooking.

5. **SERVE** ½ cup spaghetti with one-quarter of the chicken, 2 tablespoons mozzarella cheese, and ½ cup pasta sauce.

**PER SERVING** (1 serving = ½ cup spaghetti, 8 pieces chicken, 2 tablespoons cheese, ½ cup sauce)

| Calories | Total Fat | Saturated Fat | Sodium | Carbohydrate | Dietary Fiber | Protein | Calcium |
|---|---|---|---|---|---|---|---|
| 380 | 9 g | 4 g | 650 mg | 39 g | 4 g | 37 g | 25% |

# Slow-Cooker Chicken Cacciatore

**PREP TIME:** 20 MINUTES/ **COOK TIME:** 4–8 HOURS/ MAKES 8 SERVINGS

BONELESS, SKINLESS CHICKEN THIGHS BECOME MOIST AND TENDER IN THE SLOW COOKER, AND THEY ELIMINATE THE NEED TO FISH OUT STRAY BONES THAT CAN SEPARATE FROM CHICKEN PARTS DURING COOKING.

- 2 pounds boneless, skinless chicken thighs, each cut into quarters
- 1 medium yellow onion, coarsely chopped
- 1 large red bell pepper, coarsely chopped
- 1 cup white mushrooms, halved
- 1 can (28 ounces) crushed tomatoes
- 1 can (6 ounces) tomato paste
- 1 cup reduced-sodium chicken broth
- ½ cup red wine
- 3 cloves garlic, minced
- 1 bay leaf
- 2 tablespoons fresh or 2 teaspoons dried parsley
- 2 teaspoons salt-free Italian seasoning (we used McCormick Perfect Pinch Italian Seasoning)
- ½ teaspoon salt
- ½ teaspoon freshly ground black pepper
- 12 ounces rotini or linguine pasta

**1. COMBINE** the chicken, onion, bell pepper, mushrooms, crushed tomatoes, tomato paste, broth, wine, garlic, bay leaf, parsley, seasoning, salt, and black pepper in a large slow cooker. Cover and cook on high for 3 hours. Remove the lid and cook for 1 hour longer to thicken the sauce. Alternatively, cook on low for 8 hours, remove the lid, and cook for 2 hours longer.

**2. PREPARE** the pasta according to package directions approximately 30 minutes before serving.

**3. REMOVE** the bay leaf from the chicken mixture and serve the chicken and sauce over the pasta.

## 380
### CALORIES
### PER MEAL
★ ★

**PER SERVING** (1 serving = 4 pieces chicken, 1 cup sauce, ⅔ cup pasta)

| Calories | Total Fat | Saturated Fat | Sodium | Carbohydrate | Dietary Fiber | Protein | Calcium |
|----------|-----------|---------------|--------|--------------|---------------|---------|---------|
| 380 | 6 g | 2 g | 420 mg | 47 g | 5 g | 32 g | 8% |

# Chicken, Broccoli, and Candied Cashew Stir-Fry

**PREP TIME:** 15 MINUTES/ **COOK TIME:** 20 MINUTES/ MAKES 4 SERVINGS

THIS METHOD OF CANDYING CASHEWS ALSO WORKS WELL FOR WALNUTS AND PECANS. MICROWAVING THE VEGETABLES HELPS CUT DOWN ON COOKING TIME AND ALSO PRESERVES MORE OF THEIR VITAMINS.

**420**
**CALORIES PER MEAL**
★ ★ ★

- ½ cup roasted unsalted cashews, broken into pieces
- 1 tablespoon sugar
- ⅛ teaspoon salt
- 3 cups small broccoli florets
- 2 large carrots, julienned
- 1 cup fresh snow peas
- ½ cup reduced-sodium chicken broth
- 2 tablespoons reduced-sodium soy sauce
- 1 tablespoon hoisin sauce
- ½ teaspoon sesame oil
- ½ teaspoon chili oil or additional ½ teaspoon sesame oil
- 1 teaspoon peanut oil
- 1 tablespoon finely chopped fresh ginger
- 3 cloves garlic, minced
- ¾ pound boneless, skinless chicken thighs, cut into 1" pieces, combined with 1 tablespoon cornstarch
- 3 medium scallions, thinly sliced, including ⅔ of green parts
- 2 cups cooked brown rice

1. **SOAK** the cashews in water for 2 minutes. Drain well and place in a microwaveable bowl. Mix together with the sugar and salt. Microwave in 30-second intervals for 1½ to 2 minutes, checking on the cashews after each 30 seconds, until the sugar appears thick and the cashews are slightly browned. Carefully place the cashews on a nonstick baking sheet or silicone mat. Spread out using a spoon. Cool.

2. **PLACE** the broccoli, carrots, and snow peas in a microwaveable bowl. Add 2 tablespoons water, cover, and microwave for 2 minutes. Meanwhile, combine the broth, soy sauce, hoisin sauce, sesame oil, and chili oil or additional sesame oil in a small bowl. Set aside.

3. **COAT** a wok well with cooking spray. Heat the peanut oil over medium heat. Cook the ginger and garlic for 1 minute. Add the microwaved vegetables and cook for 5 minutes over medium-high heat, stirring often to prevent sticking or burning. Add the chicken and cook for 6 minutes, stirring often. Add the sauce and cover. Simmer for 3 minutes, or until the vegetables reach the desired degree of doneness.

4. **STIR** in the scallions. Top with the cashews. Serve over the rice.

**PER SERVING** (1 serving = 1½ cups stir-fry over ½ cup rice)

| Calories | Total Fat | Saturated Fat | Sodium | Carbohydrate | Dietary Fiber | Protein | Calcium |
|---|---|---|---|---|---|---|---|
| 420 | 18 g | 4 g | 530 mg | 42 g | 4 g | 23 g | 6% |

# Island Chicken with Piña Colada Salsa

**PREP TIME:** 10 MINUTES + 24 HOURS MARINATING/ **COOK TIME:** 14 MINUTES/ MAKES 4 SERVINGS

TRY SERVING THIS DISH COLD FOR A REFRESHING SUMMER LUNCH. COMBINING PINEAPPLE AND COCONUT WITH CILANTRO AND LIME EVOKES A COMBINATION OF HAWAII AND THE CARIBBEAN.

- 1 pound boneless, skinless chicken breasts, cut into 8 pieces
- ¼ cup orange juice
- 1½ tablespoons curry powder (hot or sweet)
- 1 tablespoon reduced-sodium soy sauce
- 1 tablespoon honey
- 2 cloves garlic, finely chopped
- 1 tablespoon + ¼ cup finely chopped fresh mint
- 1 can (20 ounces) unsweetened crushed pineapple (with juice)
- ½ cup chopped red onion
- ¼ cup chopped scallions or chives
- 2 tablespoons finely chopped fresh cilantro
- 2 tablespoons lime juice
- 2 tablespoons shredded coconut, preferably unsweetened
- ¼ teaspoon red-pepper flakes
  Pinch of salt
- 1 cup uncooked brown rice, prepared according to package directions

**1. PLACE** the chicken on a flat pan or in a resealable plastic bag. Whisk together the orange juice, curry powder, soy sauce, honey, garlic, and 1 tablespoon of the mint. Pour over the chicken. Turn the chicken to coat. Refrigerate for at least 4 hours and up to 24 hours, moving the pieces around occasionally.

**2. TO** make the salsa: Strain the pineapple. Combine the pineapple, onion, scallions, cilantro, lime juice, coconut, red-pepper flakes, salt, and the remaining ¼ cup mint in a medium bowl. Refrigerate.

**3. REMOVE** the chicken from the marinade. Grill or broil for 5 to 7 minutes on each side, or until no longer pink in the center. Check by inserting the tip of a sharp knife into 1 breast.

**4. PLACE** one-quarter of the rice on each of 4 plates. Top with 2 pieces of chicken and ¼ cup salsa. Serve the remaining salsa at the table.

## 400
**CALORIES
PER MEAL**
★ ★

**PER SERVING** (1 serving = ⅔ cup cooked rice, 2 pieces chicken, ¼ cup salsa)

| Calories | Total Fat | Saturated Fat | Sodium | Carbohydrate | Dietary Fiber | Protein | Calcium |
|----------|-----------|---------------|--------|--------------|---------------|---------|---------|
| 400 | 5 g | 2 g | 280 mg | 59 g | 5 g | 32 g | 6% |

# Chicken Tacos with Charred Tomato Salsa

**PREP TIME:** 20 MINUTES + 4 HOURS MARINATING/ **COOK TIME:** 20 MINUTES/ MAKES 4 SERVINGS

THE BROILER MAKES QUICK WORK OF CHARRING VEGETABLES FOR THIS SMOKY SALSA. FOR LESS HEAT, REMOVE SEEDS FROM THE JALAPEÑO CHILE PEPPER.

## MAKE IT A MEAL

Edy's Lime Fruit Bar
**60 CALORIES**

# 400
**CALORIES PER MEAL**
★ ★ ★

- 1 pound boneless, skinless chicken breasts
- Grated peel of 2 limes
- Juice of 3 limes
- ¼ cup orange juice
- ¼ cup + 2 tablespoons chopped fresh cilantro
- 1 tablespoon + 1 teaspoon minced garlic
- ½ teaspoon ground cumin
- 8 plum tomatoes
- 1–2 jalapeño chile peppers (wear plastic gloves when handling)
- ⅓ cup chopped scallions
- ⅛ teaspoon salt
- 1 large red onion, thinly sliced
- 4 whole wheat (7½" diameter) tortillas (2 ounces each)
- 2 cups finely shredded leaf lettuce

**1. PLACE** the chicken on a baking sheet or in a resealable plastic bag. Whisk together the lime peel and juice of 2 limes, orange juice, ¼ cup of the cilantro, 1 tablespoon of the garlic, and cumin. Pour the lime mixture over the chicken. Turn the chicken pieces to coat. Refrigerate for at least 1 hour and up to 4 hours. Turn at least once while marinating.

**2. MEANWHILE,** cut the tomatoes in half lengthwise and place them cut side down on a baking sheet. Place the peppers on the baking sheet. Broil until the tomato and pepper skins are charred, turning so that all sides char. Remove from the heat and lightly cover with foil. Let stand until the vegetables are cool enough to handle.

**3. REMOVE** and discard the skins and seeds from the peppers. Finely chop and transfer them to a medium bowl. Gently squeeze the tomatoes to remove the seeds. Coarsely chop and add them to the bowl. Stir in the scallions, juice of 1 lime, salt, the remaining 2 tablespoons of cilantro, and remaining 1 teaspoon of garlic.

**4. COAT** a skillet with cooking spray. Cook the onion slices over medium heat until they begin to soften, about 3 minutes. Remove the chicken from the marinade and cut into 1" strips. Add them to the skillet and cook for about 6 minutes, or until no longer pink in the center when tested with a knife.

**5. SERVE** the chicken with the warm tortillas, salsa, and shredded lettuce.

**PER SERVING** (1 serving = 1 taco)

| Calories | Total Fat | Saturated Fat | Sodium | Carbohydrate | Dietary Fiber | Protein | Calcium |
|---|---|---|---|---|---|---|---|
| 340 | 3 g | 0.5 g | 450 mg | 53 g | 8 g | 33 g | 8% |

# Slow-Cooker Stuffed Peppers

**PREP TIME:** 20 MINUTES/ **COOK TIME:** 4 HOURS/ MAKES 4 SERVINGS

WE WENT OVER OUR CALORIE LIMIT FOR THIS DISH BECAUSE IT NEEDS A SLICE OF BREAD FOR MOPPING UP THE TASTY SAUCE. THE POTENT COMBO OF TOMATO PUREE, CHILE AND BELL PEPPERS, AND ONION OVERFLOWS WITH VITAMINS A AND C, LYCOPENE, AND OTHER PHYTOCHEMICALS. QUINOA, A PROTEIN-PACKED GRAIN FROM SOUTH AMERICA, LENDS ITS UNIQUE NUTTY FLAVOR TO THIS MEAL.

## MAKE IT A MEAL

1 small slice
(1 ounce) Italian
bread
**80 CALORIES**

## 430
**CALORIES
PER MEAL**
★ ★ ★

- ¾ pound lean ground turkey
- ½ cup uncooked quinoa
- ¼ cup chopped cilantro
- 3 scallions, chopped
- 1 small yellow onion, finely chopped
- 1 small jalapeño chile pepper, finely chopped
- 1 clove garlic, minced
- ¼ teaspoon salt
- ¼ teaspoon freshly ground black pepper
- 4 large green bell or Cubanelle peppers
- 2 cups reduced-sodium chicken broth
- 1 can (28 ounces) tomato puree (choose one that has less than 50 mg sodium per ½ cup)
- ¾ teaspoon dried oregano
- 2 tablespoons chopped fresh parsley

  Salt

  Freshly ground black pepper

**1. COMBINE** the turkey, quinoa, ¼ cup cilantro, scallions, onion, jalapeño pepper, garlic, salt, and black pepper in a large bowl.

**2. CUT** the tops off the bell or Cubanelle peppers and scoop out the seeds. Stuff each pepper with one-quarter of the turkey mixture. Replace the pepper tops and place in the slow cooker.

**3. COMBINE** the broth, tomato puree, and oregano in a medium bowl. Pour over the peppers in the slow cooker. Position the peppers carefully so that they are covered by the liquid. Cook on high heat for 4 hours.

**4. SPRINKLE** each pepper with the parsley before serving. Season with salt and black pepper.

**PER SERVING** (1 serving = 1 stuffed pepper)

| Calories | Total Fat | Saturated Fat | Sodium | Carbohydrate | Dietary Fiber | Protein | Calcium |
|---|---|---|---|---|---|---|---|
| 350 | 10 g | 3 g | 330 mg | 44 g | 9 g | 26 g | 10% |

# Spinach-Stuffed Chicken Roulades

**PREP TIME:** 20 MINUTES/ **COOK TIME:** 45 MINUTES/ MAKES 4 SERVINGS

THIS DISH IS SIMPLE BUT ELEGANT. THE CHICKEN CUTLETS MUST BE SLICED THIN SO THAT THEY'RE EASY TO ROLL AROUND THE FILLING.

| | |
|---|---|
| 1 | teaspoon olive oil |
| ¼ | cup finely chopped onion |
| 1 | clove garlic, minced |
| ¼ | teaspoon red-pepper flakes |
| ¼ | cup grated Parmesan cheese |
| 2 | The Laughing Cow Light French Onion Wedges |
| 1 | package (10 ounces) frozen chopped spinach, thawed, drained, and squeezed dry |
| 4 | chicken breast cutlets, sliced thin (about 1 pound) |
| 2 | tablespoons finely chopped dry-packed sun-dried tomatoes |
| ½ | cup reduced-sodium chicken broth |
| 4 | tablespoons pine nuts, toasted |

**1. PREHEAT** the oven to 350°F. Coat a small-to-medium ovenproof pan with cooking spray.

**2. HEAT** the oil in a medium nonstick skillet over medium heat. Add the onion, garlic, and red-pepper flakes and cook for about 3 minutes, until softened. Remove from the heat. Combine the onion mixture, Parmesan cheese, French onion cheese, and spinach in a small bowl.

**3. PUT** the chicken on a work surface, smooth side down. Sprinkle the tomatoes evenly over the chicken. Divide the spinach mixture evenly among the cutlets. Pat the mixture to the edges of 3 sides of each cutlet, leaving about 1" at the narrow tip free of spinach. Loosely roll up the cutlet, ending with the narrow tip.

**4. PLACE** the roulades in the baking pan, seam side down. Add the broth. Cover and bake for 40 minutes, or until the chicken is entirely white in color. Remove from the heat. Allow the roulades to rest for 5 minutes.

**5. CUT** the roulades into diagonal slices and arrange on individual plates. Drizzle with the pan juices. Sprinkle each serving with 1 tablespoon pine nuts.

## MAKE IT A MEAL

½ cup brown rice
**110 CALORIES**

1 cup broccoli steamed with garlic
**20 CALORIES**

# 390
**CALORIES PER MEAL**
★ ★ ★

**PER SERVING** (1 serving = 1 roulade)

| Calories | Total Fat | Saturated Fat | Sodium | Carbohydrate | Dietary Fiber | Protein | Calcium |
|---|---|---|---|---|---|---|---|
| 260 | 13 g | 3 g | 370 mg | 7 g | 3 g | 31 g | 20% |

# Greek Chicken with Vegetables and Potatoes

**PREP TIME:** 20 MINUTES/ **COOK TIME:** 45 MINUTES/ MAKES 4 SERVINGS

WE PARTIALLY PRECOOKED THE POTATO IN THE MICROWAVE SO THAT ALL COMPONENTS OF THIS DISH WOULD BE FULLY COOKED AT THE SAME TIME.

**MAKE IT A MEAL**

1 slice angel food cake
70 CALORIES

**420**
CALORIES PER MEAL
★ ★ ★ ★

- 4 skinless, bone-in split chicken breasts (about 1½ pounds)
- 1 medium red bell pepper, seeded and cut into 8 wedges
- 1 medium orange bell pepper, seeded and cut into 8 wedges
- ¾ pound Yukon gold potatoes, cut into 12 wedges and microwaved for 2 minutes
- 1 medium red onion, cut into 8 wedges
- 2 medium zucchini, cut into ½" slices
- 20 pitted kalamata olives
- 1 tablespoon extra virgin olive oil
  Juice and grated peel of 1 lemon
- 2 cloves garlic, minced
- 2 teaspoons dried oregano or 1 tablespoon chopped fresh oregano
- ¾ teaspoon freshly ground black pepper
- ¾ teaspoon paprika

**1. PREHEAT** the oven to 400°F. Coat a roasting pan with cooking spray, or prepare a 17" × 12" rimmed baking pan: Tear off 2 sheets of nonstick aluminum foil, each 24" long. Put the dull (nonstick) sides together and fold over the edge on one side twice, to make a seam. Open up the seam, and line and cover the edges of the baking pan. (The dull side of the foil should face up.)

**2. PLACE** the chicken on one side of the pan. Place the bell peppers, potatoes, onion, and zucchini on the other.

**3. PUREE** the olives, olive oil, lemon peel and juice, garlic, oregano, black pepper, and paprika in a small food processor. Spread the puree over the chicken and the vegetables. Toss the vegetables to coat.

**4. ROAST,** turning the chicken and stirring the vegetables halfway through cooking, for 40 to 45 minutes, or until a meat thermometer registers 160°F when inserted into the thickest part of the chicken (not touching bone). If the chicken is done before the vegetables are tender, remove the chicken and cover with foil. Increase the temperature to 450°F and cook the vegetables for an additional 5 to 10 minutes. Arrange 1 chicken breast and one-quarter of the vegetables on each of 4 plates.

**PER SERVING** (1 serving = 1 chicken breast, ¼ cup vegetables)

| Calories | Total Fat | Saturated Fat | Sodium | Carbohydrate | Dietary Fiber | Protein | Calcium |
|---|---|---|---|---|---|---|---|
| 350 | 12 g | 2 g | 390 mg | 29 g | 5 g | 32 g | 8% |

# Beer Can Chicken

**PREP TIME:** 15 MINUTES/ **COOK TIME:** 1 HOUR 15 MINUTES/ MAKES 8 SERVINGS

THE LIQUID IN THE BEER CAN—IT DOESN'T HAVE TO BE BEER; ANY LIQUID WILL DO—STEAMS THE CHICKEN FROM THE INSIDE WHILE THE GRILL COOKS THE OUTSIDE, YIELDING TENDER, JUICY MEAT.

½ cup chopped onion

4 cloves garlic

1 tablespoon olive oil

2 tablespoons chili powder

¾ teaspoon salt

½ teaspoon freshly ground black pepper

1 large roasting chicken, (approximately 4½ pounds)

1 can (12 ounces) beer, any type, or other liquid

**1. PREPARE** an outdoor grill. If using a charcoal kettle, spread the lit coals around the perimeter of the coal grate. If using a gas grill, leave the middle burners off and set the side burners to medium.

**2. COMBINE** the onion, garlic, oil, chili powder, salt, and pepper in a small food processor or blender. Blend until smooth.

**3. LOOSEN** the skin of the chicken. Spread the onion mixture between the skin and flesh. Spread extra on the skin.

**4. OPEN** the can of beer and pour off half of the beer so that it doesn't bubble over during cooking. Holding the can upright, place the chicken on top of the can, inserting the can as far as it will go into the cavity of the chicken. Position the beer can and chicken in the center of the grill. Position the chicken legs in front of the chicken to help steady the chicken.

**5. COVER** the grill and cook for about 1 hour 15 minutes, or until the skin is browned and the thigh temperature reaches 170°F. Carefully remove the chicken from the grill and remove the beer can. Cover the chicken with a foil tent. Allow to rest for 10 minutes.

**6. CUT** the chicken into serving pieces: 2 legs, 2 thighs, 2 wings, and 4 chicken breast quarters. Remove the skin before eating.

**PER SERVING** (1 serving = 1 piece of chicken)

| Calories | Total Fat | Saturated Fat | Sodium | Carbohydrate | Dietary Fiber | Protein | Calcium |
|---|---|---|---|---|---|---|---|
| 170 | 6 g | 1 g | 340 mg | 3 g | 1 g | 27 g | 2% |

## MAKE IT A MEAL

⅔ cup Uncle Ben's Whole Grain Brown Ready Rice
**145 CALORIES**

1½ cups Dole Very Veggie Salad
**20 CALORIES**

2 tablespoons Newman's Own Lighten Up or other light Italian dressing
**60 CALORIES**

# 395
**CALORIES PER MEAL**
★ ★

# Chicken and Seven Vegetables Couscous

**PREP TIME:** 20 MINUTES/ **COOK TIME:** 30 MINUTES/ MAKES 4 SERVINGS

*COUSCOUS AUX SEPT LEGUME,* FRENCH FOR "COUSCOUS WITH SEVEN VEGETABLES," IS A CLASSIC, WITH VEGETABLES VARYING FROM SEASON TO SEASON.

## 400
**CALORIES PER MEAL**
★ ★ ★

- 1 teaspoon olive oil
- 1 medium onion, finely chopped
- 1 pound boneless, skinless chicken thighs, cut into bite-size pieces
- 1 pound winter squash or pumpkin, cut into 1" cubes
- 3 medium carrots, cut into 1" pieces
- 2 small zucchini, sliced into rounds (about 2 cups)
- 1 medium turnip, cut into 1" cubes
- 1 medium green bell pepper, cut into 1" pieces
- 2 cups reduced-sodium chicken broth
- 2 teaspoons ground cinnamon
- 1 teaspoon dried ginger
- ½ teaspoon ground allspice
- ¼ teaspoon salt
- 2 cups baby spinach
- ½ cup chopped fresh cilantro
- ½ cup chopped fresh parsley
- 2 cups cooked whole wheat couscous
  Harissa or hot sauce (optional)

**1. HEAT** the oil in a large pot or Dutch oven over medium heat. Add the onion and cook until soft, about 1 minute. Add the chicken, squash or pumpkin, carrots, zucchini, turnip, bell pepper, broth, cinnamon, ginger, allspice, and salt. Bring to a boil. Reduce to a simmer, cover, and cook until the vegetables reach the desired doneness, about 30 minutes.

**2. STIR** in the spinach, cilantro, and parsley. Spoon the chicken and vegetables over ½-cup servings of couscous. Serve with the hot sauce.

**PER SERVING** (1 serving = 2 cups chicken and vegetables, ½ cup couscous)

| Calories | Total Fat | Saturated Fat | Sodium | Carbohydrate | Dietary Fiber | Protein | Calcium |
|----------|-----------|---------------|--------|--------------|---------------|---------|---------|
| 400 | 11 g | 3 g | 370 mg | 48 g | 10 g | 34 g | 15% |

# Sweet and Tangy Mustard-Molasses Chicken

**PREP TIME:** 10 MINUTES/ **COOK TIME:** 25 MINUTES/ MAKES 4 SERVINGS

IT'S EASY TO FEEL GUILTY BECAUSE THIS RECIPE IS SO EASY, BUT IF YOU DON'T SAY ANYTHING, NOBODY WILL KNOW. OVEN-BAKED FRIES ARE A PERFECT LOWER-CALORIE SUBSTITUTE FOR FRENCH FRIES.

2 pounds bone-in skinless chicken breasts

1 medium onion, sliced thin

¼ cup deli mustard

¼ cup molasses

**1. PREHEAT** the oven to 400°F. Remove the skin from the chicken and place it in the pan. If the chicken breasts are large (1 pound each), cut in half. Top with the onion slices.

**2. COMBINE** the mustard and molasses and brush on the chicken breasts.

**3. BAKE** for 25 minutes, or until cooked through, turning the chicken halfway through.

## MAKE IT A MEAL

½ medium potato, cut into wedges, tossed with ½ teaspoon olive oil and salt-free seasoning, and baked until crisp
**100 CALORIES**

½ cup cooked carrots
**30 CALORIES**

# 410
**CALORIES PER MEAL**
★ ★

**PER SERVING** (1 serving = ¼ pound chicken breast)

| Calories | Total Fat | Saturated Fat | Sodium | Carbohydrate | Dietary Fiber | Protein | Calcium |
|---|---|---|---|---|---|---|---|
| 280 | 3 g | 0.5 g | 320 mg | 18 g | 0 g | 42 g | 6% |

**PER SERVING** (1 serving = 3 oz rotisserie chicken and ½ cup plum-walnut relish, ½ cup mango salsa, ⅓ cup pineapple sauce)

| Calories | Total Fat | Saturated Fat | Sodium | Carbohydrate | Dietary Fiber | Protein | Calcium |
|----------|-----------|---------------|--------|--------------|---------------|---------|---------|
| 330 | 11 g | 2 g | 730 mg | 37 g | 4 g | 25 g | 6% |

# Rotisserie Chicken Three Ways

**PREP TIME:** 30 MINUTES/ **COOK TIME:** 6 MINUTES/ MAKES 4 SERVINGS

ROTISSERIE CHICKEN FROM THE MARKET IS A GREAT TIME SAVER, AND THESE THREE FRUIT SAUCES CAN BE MADE QUICKLY RIGHT BEFORE THE MEAL. DEPENDING ON WHICH FRUITS ARE IN SEASON, YOU CAN SUBSTITUTE PEACHES, APRICOTS, AND EVEN MELON FOR THE PLUMS OR MANGO. FOR THE MEAL, SERVE 3-OUNCE PORTIONS OF THE ROTISSERIE CHICKEN ALONG WITH ONE-QUARTER OF EACH SAUCE PER PERSON. ENJOY ANY REMAINING CHICKEN THE NEXT DAY.

### PLUM-WALNUT RELISH

- 2 medium black plums, pitted and chopped
- ¼ cup orange juice
- 2 tablespoons chopped onion
- 1 tablespoon honey
- ¼ cup finely chopped walnuts
- ½ teaspoon curry powder
- ¼ teaspoon salt
- ¼ teaspoon red-pepper flakes

### MANGO SALSA

- 1 medium mango, diced
- 1 cup bottled salsa
- ¼ cup chopped fresh cilantro
- 2 tablespoons finely chopped red onion

### PINEAPPLE SAUCE

- 1 can (8 ounces) crushed pineapple in juice
- 1 tablespoon finely chopped yellow onion
- 1 tablespoon reduced-sodium soy sauce
- 1 tablespoon rice vinegar
- 1 teaspoon finely chopped ginger
- 1 clove garlic, minced
- ½ tablespoon cornstarch mixed with 1 tablespoon cold water
- 2 scallions, sliced into thin rounds

**1. TO** make the Plum-Walnut Relish: Combine the plums, orange juice, onion, honey, walnuts, curry powder, salt, and red-pepper flakes in a medium bowl.

**2. TO** make the Mango Salsa: Combine the mango, salsa, cilantro, and red onion in a medium bowl.

**3. TO** make the Pineapple Sauce: Combine the pineapple, onion, soy sauce, vinegar, ginger, and garlic in a small saucepan. Simmer for 5 minutes. Add the cornstarch mixture and simmer for 1 minute, or until the pineapple mixture thickens. Remove from the heat and stir in the scallions.

## MAKE IT
## A MEAL

Small dinner roll
**80 CALORIES**

# 410
**CALORIES
PER MEAL**
★ ★

# Warm Sesame-Peanut Noodles with Chicken

**PREP TIME:** 10 MINUTES/ **COOK TIME:** 15 MINUTES/ MAKES 4 SERVINGS

THIS RECIPE IS EQUALLY DELICIOUS, AND EVEN HIGHER IN GOOD FATS, WHEN MADE WITH COOKED OR CANNED SALMON. WAREHOUSE STORES SELL STIR-FRY COMBOS WITH UP TO 10 DIFFERENT VEGETABLES THAT WILL GIVE GREAT COLOR AND FLAVOR TO THIS DISH.

## 380 CALORIES PER MEAL
★ ★ ★ ★

- 4 ounces whole wheat spaghetti
- 1 teaspoon peanut oil
- 1 tablespoon peeled, finely chopped ginger
- 1 tablespoon minced garlic
- 1 cup thinly sliced scallions
- 6 cups frozen stir-fry vegetables
- ¼ cup peanut butter
- 2 tablespoons reduced-sodium soy sauce
- 2 tablespoons lime juice
- 1 tablespoon honey
- 1 teaspoon toasted sesame oil
- 1 teaspoon grated lemon peel
- 1½ cups cubed cooked chicken
- Cayenne (optional)
- Salt (optional)

**1. PREPARE** the spaghetti according to the package directions. Drain, reserving ¼ cup of the cooking water.

**2. WHILE** the pasta is cooking, heat the peanut oil in a large skillet over medium heat. Add the ginger, garlic, and ½ cup of the scallions and cook until soft, about 2 minutes. Add the stir-fry vegetables and cover. Reduce the heat to medium-low and cook until the veggies are crisp-tender, about 5 minutes.

**3. WHISK** together the peanut butter, soy sauce, lime juice, honey, sesame oil, lemon peel, and reserved pasta water in a large serving bowl. Add the spaghetti, chicken, and vegetables. Toss to mix well. Add the cayenne pepper and salt, if using. Garnish with the remaining ½ cup scallions.

**PER SERVING** (1 serving = 2 cups)

| Calories | Total Fat | Saturated Fat | Sodium | Carbohydrate | Dietary Fiber | Protein | Calcium |
|----------|-----------|---------------|--------|--------------|---------------|---------|---------|
| 380 | 14 g | 3 g | 440 mg | 42 g | 8 g | 27 g | 8% |

# North African Turkey Meatballs with Caramelized Onions

**PREP TIME:** 15 MINUTES/ **COOK TIME:** 35 MINUTES/ MAKES 4 SERVINGS

GROUND TURKEY IS LEANER THAN GROUND BEEF AND STAYS MOIST WHEN COOKED IN THIS TOMATO SAUCE. TRY THE ONIONS WITH THE CINNAMON FOR AN UNUSUAL AND FLAVORFUL COMBINATION.

| | |
|---|---|
| 1 | pound lean ground turkey or ground turkey breast |
| ¼ | cup chopped fresh cilantro |
| 1 | tablespoon ground cumin |
| ½ | teaspoon freshly ground black pepper |
| 2 | tablespoons minced garlic |
| ½ | teaspoon ground cinnamon |
| 1 | can (28 ounces) crushed tomatoes |
| 1 | tablespoon olive oil |
| ¾ | pound yellow onions, chopped |
| 1 | teaspoon honey |
| | Salt |

**1. COMBINE** the turkey, cilantro, cumin, pepper, 1 tablespoon of the garlic, and ¼ teaspoon of the cinnamon in a large bowl. Form the turkey mixture into 24 small meatballs and chill in the refrigerator for 15 minutes.

**2. IN** a medium pot, combine the tomatoes and remaining 1 tablespoon garlic. Simmer for about 15 minutes. Add the meatballs and simmer for another 15 to 20 minutes, until the meatballs are cooked through.

**3. WHILE** the meatballs are cooking, heat the oil in a large skillet over medium heat. Add the onions, honey, salt, and remaining ¼ teaspoon cinnamon. Cover and cook for 5 minutes to soften the onions. Uncover and cook until soft and light brown in color, up to 20 minutes.

**4. SERVE** the meatballs topped with the caramelized onions.

## MAKE IT A MEAL

½ cup cooked brown rice
110 CALORIES

420
**CALORIES PER MEAL**
★ ★ ★

**PER SERVING** (1 serving = 6 meatballs)

| Calories | Total Fat | Saturated Fat | Sodium | Carbohydrate | Dietary Fiber | Protein | Calcium |
|---|---|---|---|---|---|---|---|
| 310 | 14 g | 3 g | 520 mg | 27 g | 6 g | 25 g | 15% |

# Thai-Inspired Chicken Lettuce Wraps

**PREP TIME:** 20 MINUTES/ **COOK TIME:** 20 MINUTES/ MAKES 4 SERVINGS

THIS RECIPE HAS BECOME SO POPULAR IN RESTAURANTS THAT WE DECIDED TO TRY IT OURSELVES WITH LEFTOVER CHICKEN. THE VEGETABLES CAN BE VARIED TO SUIT YOUR TASTES.

### MAKE IT A MEAL

½ cup brown rice
**110 CALORIES**

# 390

**CALORIES PER MEAL**

★ ★ ★

- 1 tablespoon peanut oil
- 3 cloves garlic, minced
- 1 1" piece ginger, finely chopped
- 2 cups bean sprouts
- 4 or 5 mushrooms, sliced
- 2 medium carrots, julienned or grated
- 2 scallions, sliced into thin rings
- ½ cup thinly sliced green cabbage
- 2 cups cooked chicken, cut into 1" cubes
- 1 tablespoon lime juice
- 1 tablespoon mirin (rice wine)
- 1 tablespoon sugar
- 1 teaspoon toasted sesame oil
- 2 teaspoons reduced-sodium soy sauce
- ½ teaspoon anchovy paste or 2 tablespoons fish sauce
- 8 inner iceberg lettuce leaves
- 1 cup basil leaves, cut into thin slices
- ¼ cup unsalted peanuts, chopped

**1. HEAT** the peanut oil in a wok or large skillet over medium heat. Add the garlic and ginger and cook for 1 minute. Add the bean sprouts, mushrooms, carrots, scallions, and cabbage. Stir briefly and cover. Cook over medium-low heat for 10 to 15 minutes, or until the vegetables are almost soft.

**2. WHILE** the vegetables are cooking, combine the chicken with the lime juice, mirin, sugar, sesame oil, soy sauce, and anchovy paste or fish sauce in a medium bowl.

**3. ADD** the chicken and the lime juice mixture to the vegetables and cook for 5 minutes, or until the chicken is warm.

**4. SERVE** in the lettuce leaf cups, topped with the basil and peanuts.

**PER SERVING** (1 serving = 2 wraps)

| Calories | Total Fat | Saturated Fat | Sodium | Carbohydrate | Dietary Fiber | Protein | Calcium |
|---|---|---|---|---|---|---|---|
| 280 | 14 g | 3 g | 270 mg | 17 g | 4 g | 24 g | 8% |

# Turkey and Bean Burritos

**PREP TIME:** 10 MINUTES/ **COOK TIME:** 20 MINUTES/ MAKES 8 SERVINGS

THIS RECIPE CALLS FOR A BIGGER TORTILLA SO THERE'S ROOM TO STUFF IN THE LETTUCE AND TOMATO.

**390**
**CALORIES PER MEAL**
★

- 1 teaspoon olive oil
- 1 medium onion, chopped
- 1 clove garlic, minced
- 1 pound ground turkey
- 1 can (14–19 ounces) pinto beans, rinsed and drained
- 1 can (8 ounces) no-salt-added tomato sauce
- ⅓ cup salsa
- 1 tablespoon chili powder
- 1 teaspoon ground cumin
- 8 flour tortillas (10" diameter)
- 8 tablespoons guacamole
- 2 cups shredded romaine lettuce
- 16 tablespoons chopped tomato

1. **HEAT** the oil in a large skillet over medium heat. Add the onion and garlic and cook for 1 minute. Add the turkey and cook for 8 to 10 minutes, breaking up the turkey as it cooks, until no trace of pink remains.

2. **STIR** in the beans, tomato sauce, salsa, chili powder, and cumin. Cover and cook over low heat, stirring occasionally, for 10 minutes.

3. **TO** make the burritos, spread each tortilla with 1 tablespoon guacamole and top with a rounded ½ cup of turkey and beans, ¼ cup of the lettuce, and 2 tablespoons of the tomato. Fold into a burrito shape.

**PER SERVING** (1 serving = 1 burrito)

| Calories | Total Fat | Saturated Fat | Sodium | Carbohydrate | Dietary Fiber | Protein | Calcium |
|----------|-----------|---------------|--------|--------------|---------------|---------|---------|
| 390 | 12 g | 3 g | 710 mg | 50 g | 6 g | 19 g | 15% |

# Turkey Sausage, Peppers, and Onions

**PREP TIME:** 10 MINUTES/ **COOK TIME:** 20 MINUTES/ MAKES 4 SERVINGS

A SWITCH TO YELLOW AND ORANGE BELL PEPPERS OR TO A RED ONION ADDS COLOR TO THIS RECIPE. YOU MAY WANT TO SERVE THIS WITH A CUP OF COOKED PASTA INSTEAD OF THE ROLL.

- 2 tablespoons reduced-sodium chicken broth
- 2 cloves garlic, minced
- 1 large onion, thinly sliced
- 1 pound Cubanelle or bell peppers, sliced
- 12 ounces turkey sausage, chopped
- 1 teaspoon McCormick Garlic & Herb Seasoning
- ¼ teaspoon red-pepper flakes (optional)
- 4 (4-ounce) Italian rolls

**1. PLACE** the broth and garlic in a large skillet over medium-low heat. Cover and simmer for 1 minute. Add the onion and the Cubanelle or bell peppers and cover. Simmer until the onion and peppers are soft, about 8 minutes. Add the sausage, seasoning, and red-pepper flakes, if desired. Cover and cook for 10 minutes.

**2. MEANWHILE,** cut each roll in half and remove as much of the inside as possible. Each roll should weigh about 2½ ounces after the insides are removed.

**3. SPOON** the sausage mixture into the bottom half of each roll. Top with the top half of the roll.

## 380
**CALORIES
PER MEAL**
★ ★

**PER SERVING** (1 serving = 1 roll)

| Calories | Total Fat | Saturated Fat | Sodium | Carbohydrate | Dietary Fiber | Protein | Calcium |
|---|---|---|---|---|---|---|---|
| 380 | 10 g | 2 g | 900 mg | 47 g | 4 g | 25 g | 10% |

# Slow-Cooker Italian-Style Turkey Meat Loaf

**PREP TIME:** 5 MINUTES/ **COOK TIME:** 4 HOURS/ MAKES 4 SERVINGS

YOU MIGHT NOT THINK OF MAKING MEAT LOAF IN THE SLOW COOKER, BUT IT COMES OUT INCREDIBLY MOIST AND FLAVORFUL. THE RECIPE WORKS WITH ANY TYPE OF PASTA SAUCE.

**400**
**CALORIES
PER MEAL**
★

- 1 pound lean ground turkey
- 1 medium onion, finely chopped
- ½ cup fresh, soft whole wheat bread crumbs (from 1 slice)
- ½ cup sliced mushrooms
- 1 egg
- 1 tablespoon Dijon mustard
- 1 tablespoon Penzeys Spices Pizza Seasoning
- 2 cups marinara sauce
- ½ cup reduced-sodium chicken broth
- 2 cups cooked brown rice

1. **COMBINE** the turkey, onion, bread crumbs, mushrooms, egg, mustard, and seasoning in a large bowl. Form into a round loaf.

2. **COMBINE** the marinara sauce and broth in the bottom of a slow cooker. Place the meat loaf on top, spoon sauce over the meat loaf, and cook on high for 4 hours, turning and spooning sauce on the top after 2 hours.

3. **SERVE** over the brown rice.

**PER SERVING** (1 serving = ¼ meat loaf, ½ cup sauce, ½ cup brown rice)

| Calories | Total Fat | Saturated Fat | Sodium | Carbohydrates | Dietary Fiber | Protein | Calcium |
|---|---|---|---|---|---|---|---|
| 400 | 14 g | 4 g | 790 mg | 39 g | 5 g | 28 g | 8% |

# Stuffed Cornish Hens

**PREP TIME:** 15 MINUTES/ **COOK TIME:** 1 HOUR 25 MINUTES/ MAKES 4 SERVINGS

THIS ELEGANT MAIN DISH IS PERFECT FOR SERVING TO GUESTS. WE PICKED DRIED CRANBERRIES FOR THEIR COLOR AND FLAVOR AND PECANS FOR THEIR GOOD FAT AND RICH TASTE.

- 1 box (6 ounces) long-grain and wild rice pilaf
- ¼ cup dried cranberries
- ¼ cup pecan halves, broken into pieces
- 2 Cornish hens (1¼ pounds each)

  Seasoning blend

**1. PREHEAT** the oven to 400°F. Place a wire rack in the bottom of a pan large enough for the hens.

**2. PREPARE** the pilaf according to package directions, omitting the oil or butter, using only 1 tablespoon of the enclosed seasoning mix, and adding the dried cranberries. When the pilaf is done, stir in the pecans.

**3. STUFF** the hens loosely with the pilaf and reserve the leftover pilaf. Place the stuffed hens on the rack. Sprinkle with your choice of seasoning blend.

**4. BAKE** for approximately 1 hour, or until the juices run clear. Let rest for 5 minutes and cut each hen in half. Serve with the remaining pilaf.

## MAKE IT A MEAL

½ cup cooked broccoli
**30 CALORIES**

**400**
**CALORIES**
**PER MEAL**
★ ★

**PER SERVING** (1 serving = ½ Cornish hen, additional pilaf)

| Calories | Total Fat | Saturated Fat | Sodium | Carbohydrate | Dietary Fiber | Protein | Calcium |
|----------|-----------|---------------|--------|--------------|---------------|---------|---------|
| 370 | 9 g | 2 g | 360 mg | 39 g | 2 g | 32 g | 4% |

# Slow-Cooker Chili con Carne

**PREP TIME:** 15 MINUTES/ **COOK TIME:** 3 HOURS 45 MINUTES/ MAKES 4 SERVINGS

SLOW COOKING IS SO GENTLE THAT IT PRESERVES THE SHAPES AND TEXTURES OF THE BEANS AND VEGE-TABLES. TO COOK THIS OVERNIGHT OR WHILE YOU ARE AT WORK, SET THE HEAT TO LOW AND DOUBLE THE COOKING TIME.

## 410 CALORIES PER MEAL
★ ★ ★

- 2 teaspoons olive oil
- 1 pound extra-lean ground round
- 1 medium onion, chopped
- 1 medium green bell pepper, chopped
- 1 jalapeño chile pepper, finely chopped (wear plastic gloves when handling)
- 4 cloves garlic, minced
- 1 can (14–19 ounces) no-salt-added red kidney beans, rinsed and drained
- 1 can (14.5 ounces) fire-roasted diced tomatoes
- 1 tablespoon chili powder
- 2 teaspoons packed brown sugar
- 1½ teaspoons ground cumin
- 1½ teaspoons dried oregano
- ½ teaspoon salt
- 4 ounces whole grain spaghetti
- 4 tablespoons low-fat sour cream

**1. HEAT** the oil in a large nonstick skillet over medium-high heat. Add the beef and cook, stirring occasionally, until no longer pink, about 4 minutes. Add the onion, bell pepper, chile pepper, and garlic. Cook until the beef is browned, about 7 to 8 minutes. Transfer to a 4- or 5-quart slow cooker and add the beans, tomatoes, chili powder, sugar, cumin, oregano, and salt. Cover and cook on high for 3 to 3½ hours, or until the beef is tender.

**2. DURING** the last half hour that the chili cooks, bring a large pot of lightly salted water to a boil. Add the spaghetti. Cook according to package directions and drain. Divide the spaghetti among 4 bowls. Top with the chili and sour cream.

**PER SERVING** (1 serving = 2 cups)

| Calories | Total Fat | Saturated Fat | Sodium | Carbohydrate | Dietary Fiber | Protein | Calcium |
|---|---|---|---|---|---|---|---|
| 410 | 9 g | 3 g | 600 mg | 50 g | 12 g | 35 g | 13% |

# White Style Chili with Pork and Beans

**PREP TIME:** 20 MINUTES/ **COOK TIME:** 30 MINUTES/ MAKES 4 SERVINGS

TO ALLOW THE FLAVORS TO DEVELOP, COOK THIS CHILI THE DAY BEFORE AND REFRIGERATE. MAKE THE
PASTA THE DAY THAT YOU PLAN TO SERVE THIS DISH.

- 4 ounces elbow macaroni
- 2 teaspoons canola oil
- 1 pound lean pork tenderloin, trimmed and cut into 1" cubes
- 1 medium onion, chopped
- 1 medium green bell pepper, chopped
- 1 medium red bell pepper, chopped
- 1 cup fresh or frozen and thawed corn kernels
- 3 cloves garlic, minced
- 2 teaspoons chili powder
- 1 cup fat-free, reduced-sodium chicken broth
- 1 cup rinsed and drained canned white kidney beans
- 2 tablespoons chopped fresh cilantro
- ¼ teaspoon freshly ground black pepper
- ¾ cup (3 ounces) shredded 50% less fat sharp Cheddar cheese

1. **BRING** a large pot of lightly salted water to a boil. Add the macaroni and cook according to the package directions.

2. **HEAT** 1 teaspoon of the oil in a nonstick Dutch oven over medium-high heat. Add the pork and cook, turning occasionally, until browned, 4 to 5 minutes. Transfer the pork to a plate. Heat the remaining 1 teaspoon oil. Add the onion and bell peppers and cook, stirring occasionally, until crisp-tender, 5 to 6 minutes. Stir in the corn and garlic. Cook for 2 minutes. Add the chili powder and cook for 15 seconds. Add the broth, beans, and pork. Bring to a boil and cover. Reduce the heat to medium-low and simmer until the pork is tender, 15 to 20 minutes. Remove from the heat. Stir in the cilantro and black pepper. Serve over the elbow macaroni and top with the cheese.

## 420
**CALORIES
PER MEAL**
★ ★

**PER SERVING** (1 serving = 2 cups)

| Calories | Total Fat | Saturated Fat | Sodium | Carbohydrate | Dietary Fiber | Protein | Calcium |
|---|---|---|---|---|---|---|---|
| 420 | 10 g | 4 g | 360 mg | 45 g | 6 g | 39 g | 20% |

# Classic Pot Roast with Pearl Onions and Carrots

**PREP TIME:** 15 MINUTES + 10 MINUTES STAND TIME/ **COOK TIME:** 2 HOURS 10 MINUTES/ MAKES 6 SERVINGS

EYE OF ROUND IS AMONG THE LEANEST CUTS OF BEEF, BUT IT HAS ENOUGH SURFACE FAT TO BE BROWNED ON THE STOVE TOP IN ONLY A SMALL AMOUNT OF OIL.

| | |
|---|---|
| 3 | tablespoons all-purpose flour |
| 1 | teaspoon dried basil |
| ½ | teaspoon salt |
| ¼ | teaspoon freshly ground black pepper |
| 2 | pounds lean eye of round roast, trimmed |
| 2 | teaspoons olive oil |
| ⅓ | cup red wine |
| ¾ | cup fat-free, reduced-sodium beef broth |
| 2 | teaspoons Dijon mustard |
| 1 | teaspoon Worcestershire sauce |
| 12 | ounces baby carrots |
| 2½ | cups frozen small white onions, thawed |
| 3 | ribs celery, cut into 1½" pieces |
| 8 | cloves garlic |
| 3 | cups cooked egg noodles |

1. **COMBINE** the flour, basil, ¼ teaspoon of the salt, and ⅛ teaspoon of the black pepper in a large bowl. Add the roast and turn to coat.

2. **HEAT** the oil in a nonstick Dutch oven over medium-high heat. Add the roast and cook until browned, turning occasionally, about 8 minutes. Pour in the wine and cook for 2 minutes, scraping up any browned bits.

3. **MEANWHILE,** combine any remaining flour mixture with the broth, mustard, and Worcestershire sauce. Add to the Dutch oven with the carrots, onions, celery, and garlic.

4. **BRING** the mixture to a boil. Cover and reduce the heat to medium-low. Simmer until tender, turning the beef occasionally, about 2 hours. Remove from the heat. Stir in the remaining ¼ teaspoon salt and ⅛ teaspoon black pepper. Cool for 10 minutes before slicing.

5. **SERVE** each portion with ½ cup egg noodles.

## 420
**CALORIES PER MEAL**
★ ★

**PER SERVING** (1 serving = 4 oz beef, ½ cup egg noodles, 1½ cups vegetables)

| Calories | Total Fat | Saturated Fat | Sodium | Carbohydrate | Dietary Fiber | Protein | Calcium |
|---|---|---|---|---|---|---|---|
| 420 | 9 g | 3 g | 420 mg | 43 g | 3 g | 39 g | 8% |

# Almond Beef Kebabs

**PREP TIME:** 20 MINUTES + 30 MINUTES MARINATING/ **COOK TIME:** 20 MINUTES/ MAKES 4 SERVINGS

THE ALMONDS ADD HEALTHY MONOUNSATURATED FATTY ACIDS AND GIVE THE COATING A MORE COMPLEX FLAVOR. THESE CAN BE COOKED ON THE GRILL OVER INDIRECT HEAT.

## MAKE IT A MEAL

½ cup brown rice
**110 CALORIES**

½ cup strawberries
**30 CALORIES**

# 420
**CALORIES PER MEAL**
★ ★

- 1 large egg white, lightly beaten
- 1 tablespoon grated fresh ginger
- ¼ teaspoon salt
- ¼ teaspoon freshly ground black pepper
- 2 tablespoons hoisin sauce
- 1 pound beef tenderloin, trimmed, cut into 16 equal cubes
- 2 tablespoons reduced-sodium soy sauce
- 1 tablespoon seasoned rice vinegar
- 1 tablespoon honey
- 1 tablespoon lemon juice
- ⅛ teaspoon red-pepper flakes
- ¼ cup unsalted roasted almonds
- 3 tablespoons panko
- 4 scallions, trimmed and each cut into 4 pieces
- 4 cherry tomatoes

**1. COMBINE** the egg white, ginger, salt, black pepper, and 1 tablespoon of the hoisin sauce in a bowl. Add the beef cubes and toss well. Marinate for 30 minutes. Meanwhile, combine the soy sauce, vinegar, honey, lemon juice, red-pepper flakes, and remaining 1 tablespoon hoisin sauce. Set aside.

**2. PREHEAT** the oven to 425°F. Coat a baking sheet and wire rack with cooking spray.

**3. GRIND** the almonds in a food processor until finely ground. Transfer to a large plate and add the panko. Alternately thread 4 beef cubes and 4 scallion pieces onto each of 4 skewers. Working with one at a time, roll each skewer in the almond mixture, coating lightly. Spoon the mixture over each to coat. Set the skewers on the rack on the baking sheet and top the end of each skewer with 1 tomato.

**4. BAKE** for 18 to 20 minutes, until lightly browned and the beef is cooked to the desired doneness (medium-rare or medium). Drizzle with the reserved hoisin mixture and serve.

**PER SERVING** (1 serving = 1 skewer)

| Calories | Total Fat | Saturated Fat | Sodium | Carbohydrate | Dietary Fiber | Protein | Calcium |
|---|---|---|---|---|---|---|---|
| 280 | 12 g | 3 g | 730 mg | 15 g | 2 g | 29 g | 6% |

# Shepherd's Pie with Vegetables

**PREP TIME:** 15 MINUTES + 10 MINUTES STAND TIME/ **COOK TIME:** 1 HOUR 15 MINUTES/ MAKES 4 SERVINGS

LAMB IS AMONG THE HIGHER-FAT MEATS, SO WE PAIRED IT WITH EXTRA-LEAN GROUND BEEF FOR FLAVOR
WITHOUT ADDING TOO MUCH FAT OR TOO MANY CALORIES.

## 380

### CALORIES
### PER MEAL
★ ★

- 1½ pounds baking potatoes, peeled and cubed
- ½ cup low-fat milk
- ¼ cup grated Parmesan cheese
- 4 ounces ground lamb
- 4 ounces extra-lean ground round
- 1 teaspoon dried oregano
- 2 cloves garlic, minced
- 1 package (10 ounces) frozen peas and carrots
- 1 cup frozen small white onions
- 1 cup frozen cauliflower florets
- 2 tablespoons tomato paste
- 1 teaspoon Worcestershire sauce
- 1 cup reduced-sodium beef broth
- 1½ tablespoons cornstarch
- ¼ teaspoon salt

1. **PREHEAT** the oven to 350°F. Coat a 10-cup baking dish with cooking spray.

2. **COMBINE** the potatoes in a large saucepan with enough water to cover by 2". Bring to a boil over high heat. Reduce the heat to medium-high and cook until very tender, 15 to 20 minutes. Drain and place in a bowl. Add the milk and cheese to the bowl and mash the potatoes.

3. **HEAT** a large nonstick skillet over medium-high heat. Add the lamb, beef, and oregano. Cook, stirring occasionally, until no longer pink, about 4 to 5 minutes. Add the garlic and cook for 1 minute. Stir in the peas and carrots, onions, and cauliflower. Cook until the lamb and beef are browned, 5 to 6 minutes. Stir in the tomato paste and Worcestershire sauce. Cook, stirring, for 1 minute. Combine the beef broth, corn-starch, and salt. Pour into the skillet and cook until thickened, about 1 minute. Transfer to the prepared baking dish. Top with the mashed potatoes, smoothing with a spatula. Bake for 38 to 40 minutes, or until the top is lightly browned. Let stand for 10 minutes before serving.

**PER SERVING** (1 serving = 2 cups)

| Calories | Total Fat | Saturated Fat | Sodium | Carbohydrate | Dietary Fiber | Protein | Calcium |
|---|---|---|---|---|---|---|---|
| 380 | 10 g | 5 g | 540 mg | 54 g | 6 g | 22 g | 15% |

# Pepper Steak

**PREP TIME:** 10 MINUTES/ **COOK TIME:** 10 MINUTES/ MAKES 4 SERVINGS

WE PAIRED THIS DISH WITH MINI EGG ROLLS, WHICH CAN BE FOUND IN THE FROZEN-FOODS SECTION. ALTERNATIVELY, YOU CAN MAKE UP THE EXTRA CALORIES WITH CRUDITÉS AND A LIGHT DIP OR WITH A LIGHT DESSERT.

- 12 ounces top round steak, cut into ¼" strips
- 2 tablespoons reduced-sodium soy sauce
- 1 tablespoon cornstarch
- ½ cup reduced-sodium beef broth
- 3 tablespoons oyster-flavored sauce
- 1 tablespoon honey
- ½ teaspoon chili-garlic sauce
- 3 teaspoons toasted sesame oil
- 1 medium onion, sliced
- 1 tablespoon grated fresh ginger
- 1 medium red bell pepper, sliced
- 1 medium green bell pepper, sliced
- 2 cups hot cooked brown rice

1. **COMBINE** the beef, 1 tablespoon of the soy sauce, and 1 teaspoon of the cornstarch in a large bowl. Combine 2 teaspoons of the cornstarch, the broth, oyster-flavored sauce, honey, chili-garlic sauce, and the remaining 1 table-spoon soy sauce in a small bowl.

2. **HEAT** 1 teaspoon of the sesame oil in a large nonstick skillet over medium-high heat. Add the beef and cook, stirring occasionally, until no longer pink, about 2 minutes. Transfer to a plate. Heat the remaining 2 teaspoons oil. Add the onion and ginger. Cook, stirring often, until starting to soften, 1 to 2 minutes. Add the bell peppers and cook, stirring occasionally, until crisp-tender, 2 to 3 minutes. Stir in the broth mixture. Bring to a boil and cook, stirring occasion-ally, until thickened, about 1 minute. Serve over the rice.

## MAKE IT A MEAL

2 mini egg rolls with 1 tablespoon duck sauce
**90 CALORIES**

**420**

**CALORIES PER MEAL**
★ ★

**PER SERVING** (1 serving = ½ cup steak, ½ cup rice)

| Calories | Total Fat | Saturated Fat | Sodium | Carbohydrate | Dietary Fiber | Protein | Calcium |
|----------|-----------|---------------|--------|--------------|---------------|---------|---------|
| 330 | 8 g | 2 g | 1,100 mg | 40 g | 3 g | 24 g | 2% |

# Grilled Korean Marinated Flank Steak

**PREP TIME:** 5 MINUTES + 2 HOURS MARINATING/ **COOK TIME:** 12 MINUTES/ MAKES 4 SERVINGS

GRILL THE VEGETABLES FIRST, AS THEY TAKE MUCH LONGER TO COOK THAN THE MEAT DOES. SERVE THIS WITH WHITE OR BROWN RICE.

## MAKE IT A MEAL

¼ medium red pepper, ¼ medium green pepper, ¼ medium zucchini, ¼ portobello mushroom, brushed with ½ teaspoon peanut oil and grilled
**50 CALORIES**

½ cup rice
**100 CALORIES**

# 420
**CALORIES PER MEAL**
★ ★

- 4 cloves garlic, minced
- 1 tablespoon grated fresh ginger
- 3 tablespoons honey
- 2 tablespoons reduced-sodium soy sauce
- 2 tablespoons hoisin sauce
- 2 tablespoons seasoned rice vinegar
- 2 teaspoons chili-garlic paste
- 1 pound flank steak, trimmed

1. **COMBINE** the garlic, ginger, honey, soy sauce, hoisin sauce, vinegar, and chili-garlic paste in a glass baking dish. Add the flank steak and turn to coat. Marinate for at least 4 hours and up to 12 hours.

2. **COAT** a grill rack with cooking spray. Prepare the grill for medium-hot grilling.

3. **REMOVE** the steak from the marinade. Place the steak on the grill rack and cook until well marked and cooked through, about 5 to 6 minutes per side for medium. Transfer to a cutting board and let stand 5 minutes before thinly slicing against the grain.

**PER SERVING** (1 serving = ¼ pound steak)

| Calories | Total Fat | Saturated Fat | Sodium | Carbohydrate | Dietary Fiber | Protein | Calcium |
|----------|-----------|---------------|--------|--------------|---------------|---------|---------|
| 270 | 10 g | 4 g | 660 mg | 21 g | 1 g | 25 g | 4% |

# Stir-Fried Beef and Broccoli

**PREP TIME:** 10 MINUTES/ **COOK TIME:** 10 MINUTES/ MAKES 4 SERVINGS

MANY DISHES IN CHINESE RESTAURANTS HAVE SODIUM COUNTS WELL OVER 1,000 OR EVEN 2,000 MILLI-GRAMS, SO MAKING YOUR OWN MAKES GOOD NUTRITIONAL SENSE. EVEN BETTER, YOU CAN DECIDE EX-ACTLY WHICH VEGETABLES YOU WANT.

1 pound top round steak, cut into ¼" strips

1 tablespoon reduced-sodium soy sauce

8 tablespoons orange juice

3 tablespoons sherry

2 teaspoons cornstarch

⅓ cup hoisin sauce

⅛ teaspoon red-pepper flakes

1 tablespoon toasted sesame oil

1 tablespoon grated fresh ginger

5 cups broccoli florets

2 carrots, sliced

3 tablespoons water

6 scallions, chopped

2 cups hot cooked brown rice

1. **COMBINE** the beef, soy sauce, 2 tablespoons of the orange juice, 1 tablespoon of the sherry, and 1 teaspoon of the cornstarch. Combine the hoisin sauce, red-pepper flakes, and remaining 6 tablespoons orange juice, 2 tablespoons sherry, and 1 teaspoon cornstarch in a separate bowl.

2. **HEAT** 1 teaspoon of the oil in a large nonstick skillet over medium-high heat. Add the beef, in batches if necessary so as not to overcrowd the skillet, and cook, stirring often, until lightly browned, about 2 minutes. Transfer to a plate and set aside.

3. **RETURN** the skillet to medium-high heat and stir in the remaining 2 teaspoons oil. Add the ginger and cook for 30 seconds, or until fragrant. Stir in the broccoli and cook for 1 minute. Add the carrots and water.

4. **COVER** and simmer for 2 to 3 minutes, or until crisp-tender. Uncover and stir in the beef and orange juice mixture. Cook, stirring, until thick and bubbly, 1 to 2 minutes. Remove from the heat and stir in the scallions. Serve over the rice.

## 410
### CALORIES
### PER MEAL
★ ★

**PER SERVING** (1 serving = 1½ cups stir-fry, ½ cup rice)

| Calories | Total Fat | Saturated Fat | Sodium | Carbohydrate | Dietary Fiber | Protein | Calcium |
|----------|-----------|---------------|--------|--------------|---------------|---------|---------|
| 410 | 9 g | 2 g | 750 mg | 52 g | 5 g | 30 g | 8% |

# Sweet and Sour Pork

**PREP TIME:** 10 MINUTES/ **COOK TIME:** 11 MINUTES/ MAKES 4 SERVINGS

THIS SLIMMED-DOWN VERSION OF A CHINESE RESTAURANT FAVORITE ELIMINATES THE BREADING AND FRYING OF THE PORK. INSTEAD WE COMBINE IT WITH CORNSTARCH TO CREATE A VERY LIGHT COATING.

**390**
CALORIES
PER MEAL
★ ★

- 1  pound lean pork tenderloin, trimmed and cut into ½" pieces
- 2  tablespoons cornstarch
- 2  tablespoons reduced-sodium soy sauce
- ¼  cup ketchup
- 3  tablespoons cider vinegar
- 3  tablespoons sugar
- 1  can (8 ounces) pineapple chunks in juice, drained and juice reserved
- 5  teaspoons safflower oil
- 4  teaspoons grated fresh ginger
- 1  clove garlic, minced
- 1  small red bell pepper, chopped
- 1  small green bell pepper, chopped
- 1  medium onion, chopped
- 2  cups hot cooked brown rice

1. **COMBINE** the pork, 1 tablespoon of the cornstarch, and 1 tablespoon of the soy sauce in a large bowl. Toss well. Combine the ketchup, vinegar, sugar, reserved pineapple juice, the remaining 1 tablespoon cornstarch, and the remaining 1 tablespoon soy sauce in a small bowl.

2. **HEAT** the oil in a large nonstick skillet over medium-high heat. Add the pork and cook, stirring often, until the pink is almost gone, about 3 to 4 minutes. Add the ginger and garlic. Cook until fragrant, about 30 seconds. Stir in the bell peppers, onion, and pineapple. Cook until crisp-tender, 4 to 5 minutes. Stir in the ketchup mixture. Bring to a boil and cook until thickened, about 1 minute. Serve over the rice.

**PER SERVING** (1 serving = 1 cup pork over ½ cup rice)

| Calories | Total Fat | Saturated Fat | Sodium | Carbohydrate | Dietary Fiber | Protein | Calcium |
|----------|-----------|---------------|--------|--------------|---------------|---------|---------|
| 390 | 9 g | 2 g | 570 mg | 50 g | 3 g | 28 g | 2% |

# Pulled Pork

**PREP TIME:** 10 MINUTES/ **COOK TIME:** 1 HOUR/ MAKES 4 SERVINGS

TO CUT DOWN ON THE SODIUM IN THIS DISH, SWITCH TO REDUCED-SODIUM KETCHUP, WHICH CAN BE FOUND IN HEALTH FOOD STORES AS WELL AS SUPERMARKETS.

- 1 pound lean pork loin, trimmed and cut into 2" pieces
- ⅓ cup ketchup
- 2 tablespoons cider vinegar
- 2 tablespoons packed brown sugar
- 2 teaspoons smoked paprika
- 1½ teaspoons chili powder
- 1 teaspoon ground cumin
- ½ teaspoon garlic powder
- ¼ teaspoon salt

COMBINE the pork, ketchup, vinegar, sugar, paprika, chili powder, cumin, garlic powder, and salt in a medium saucepan over medium-high heat. Bring to a simmer. Reduce the heat to medium-low and cover. Gently simmer, stirring occasionally, until very tender, about 1 hour. Transfer the pork and sauce to a bowl. Shred with 2 forks.

## MAKE IT A MEAL

Whole wheat hamburger bun
**110 CALORIES**

2 tablespoons bread-and-butter pickles
**20 CALORIES**

Salad with ½ cup sliced tomato topped with ½ tablespoon balsamic vinegar, 1 teaspoon olive oil, ⅛ teaspoon salt
**65 CALORIES**

**415 CALORIES PER MEAL**
★

**PER SERVING** (1 serving = 2 cups)

| Calories | Total Fat | Saturated Fat | Sodium | Carbohydrate | Dietary Fiber | Protein | Calcium |
|----------|-----------|---------------|--------|--------------|---------------|---------|---------|
| 220 | 8 g | 3 g | 420 mg | 13 g | 1 g | 23 g | 4% |

# Guava Pork Tenderloin

**PREP TIME:** 10 MINUTES + 40 MINUTES STAND TIME/ **COOK TIME:** 28 MINUTES/ MAKES 4 SERVINGS

TO GRILL THE MANGO AND PINEAPPLE THAT ACCOMPANY THIS RECIPE, PLACE THEM ON A GRILL RACK OVER DIRECT HEAT UNTIL SEAR MARKS FORM, TURN AND CREATE SEAR MARKS ON THE OTHER SIDE, AND THEN MOVE THE FRUIT ONTO INDIRECT HEAT UNTIL IT SOFTENS, UP TO 10 MINUTES.

## MAKE IT A MEAL

¼ mango, grilled
**30 CALORIES**

1 pineapple ring, grilled
**30 CALORIES**

½ cup brown rice
**110 CALORIES**

## 400
**CALORIES PER MEAL**
★ ★

- 1 tablespoon packed brown sugar
- 1 teaspoon garlic powder
- 1 teaspoon paprika
- ¼ teaspoon ground coriander
- ½ teaspoon salt
- ¼ teaspoon freshly ground black pepper
- 1 pound lean pork tenderloin, trimmed
- 2 teaspoons olive oil
- ⅓ cup guava jelly
- 2 teaspoons reduced-sodium soy sauce
- 2 teaspoons grated fresh ginger
- 1 teaspoon cider vinegar

**1. COAT** a grill rack with cooking spray. Prepare the grill for indirect heat grilling.

**2. COMBINE** the sugar, garlic powder, paprika, coriander, salt, and black pepper in a small bowl. Brush the pork with the oil. Rub the pork with the sugar mixture to coat. Let stand for 30 minutes.

**3. MEANWHILE,** combine the jelly, soy sauce, ginger, and vinegar in a small saucepan. Cook over medium heat, stirring, until dissolved. Remove from the heat and cool.

**4. SET** the pork on the grill rack away from the heat source. Close the cover and cook, turning occasionally, for 20 minutes. Brush the pork with one-third of the jelly mixture. Cover the grill and cook for 2 minutes. Turn the pork and brush with one-third of the jelly mixture. Cover the grill and cook for 2 minutes longer. Turn the pork and brush with the remaining jelly mixture. Cover the grill and cook for about 2 to 4 minutes, until a thermometer inserted into the thickest part of the pork registers 150°F. Let stand for 5 to 10 minutes before slicing.

**PER SERVING** (1 serving = 3–4 slices)

| Calories | Total Fat | Saturated Fat | Sodium | Carbohydrate | Dietary Fiber | Protein | Calcium |
|---|---|---|---|---|---|---|---|
| 230 | 5 g | 1 g | 450 mg | 22 g | 0 g | 24 g | 2% |

# BBQ Spice-Rubbed Pork Loin Roast

**PREP TIME:** 5 MINUTES/ **COOK TIME:** 55 MINUTES/ MAKES 8 SERVINGS

PORK LOIN IS EXTREMELY LEAN, SO PULL IT OUT OF THE OVEN AS SOON AS IT REACHES 150°F TO AVOID DRYING IT OUT.

## MAKE IT A MEAL

Medium sweet potato mashed with ½ teaspoon butter, 1 teaspoon maple syrup, and salt to taste
**140 CALORIES**

2 cups collard greens cooked with 1 clove garlic, 1 teaspoon olive oil, and salt until wilted
**70 CALORIES**

# 420
## CALORIES PER MEAL
★ ★

| | |
|---|---|
| 2 | tablespoons packed brown sugar |
| 1 | tablespoon chili powder |
| 2 | teaspoons smoked paprika |
| 1½ | teaspoons ground cumin |
| 1 | teaspoon garlic powder |
| ¾ | teaspoon onion powder |
| ½ | teaspoon ground thyme |
| 1 | teaspoon salt |
| ½ | teaspoon freshly ground black pepper |
| 2 | pounds boneless center-cut pork loin roast, trimmed |
| ½ | cup prepared barbecue sauce |

1. **PREHEAT** the oven to 425°F. Coat a wire rack and a shallow roasting pan with cooking spray.

2. **COMBINE** the sugar, chili powder, paprika, cumin, garlic powder, onion powder, thyme, salt, and pepper in a medium bowl. Rub the spice mixture over the pork to coat. Set the pork on the rack in the roasting pan and roast for 45 to 55 minutes, until a thermometer inserted into the thickest part registers 150°F. Remove from the oven. Let stand for 10 minutes before slicing. Serve with the barbecue sauce.

**PER SERVING** (1 serving = 3–4 slices)

| Calories | Total Fat | Saturated Fat | Sodium | Carbohydrate | Dietary Fiber | Protein | Calcium |
|---|---|---|---|---|---|---|---|
| 210 | 8 g | 3 g | 520 mg | 12 g | 0 g | 23 g | 4% |

# Hot Italian Sausage–Topped Salad Pizza

**PREP TIME:** 15 MINUTES + 30 MINUTES STAND TIME/ **COOK TIME:** 22 MINUTES/ MAKES 4 SERVINGS

THE SAUSAGE IN THIS SALAD PIZZA MAKES IT A HEARTIER AND MORE FILLING MEAL. WHOLE WHEAT PIZZA DOUGH WILL GIVE THE CRUST A COMPLETELY DIFFERENT FLAVOR.

- 1 fresh or frozen and thawed pizza dough (15 ounces)
- ¼ cup grated Parmesan cheese
- 6 ounces hot Italian sausage, removed from casing
- 3 cloves garlic, sliced
- 1 bunch arugula, trimmed (about 4 cups)
- 1 cup halved grape tomatoes
- ½ medium Vidalia or other sweet onion, thinly sliced
- 1 can (14 ounces) artichoke hearts, 5–6 pieces, quartered
- 1 jarred roasted red bell pepper, rinsed, patted dry, and cut into strips
- 2 tablespoons balsamic vinegar
- 1 tablespoon extra virgin olive oil
- ⅛ teaspoon salt

1. **COAT** a 16" pizza pan with cooking spray. On a lightly floured surface, roll or stretch the dough into a large circle to fit the pan. Cover the pan loosely with plastic wrap. Allow the dough to rise in a warm place (85°F) for 30 minutes.

2. **PREHEAT** the oven to 425°F.

3. **SPRINKLE** the dough with the cheese. Bake until golden, 12 to 15 minutes.

4. **MEANWHILE,** heat a medium nonstick skillet over medium-high heat. Add the sausage and cook, breaking into smaller pieces with a wooden spoon, until starting to brown, 4 to 5 minutes. Add the garlic and cook until starting to brown, 2 minutes. Remove the skillet from the heat.

5. **TOSS** the arugula, tomatoes, onion, artichoke hearts, roasted pepper, vinegar, oil, and salt in a large bowl. Spread over the pizza crust. Sprinkle evenly with the sausage mixture. Cut into 8 slices.

## 400
**CALORIES PER MEAL**
★

**PER SERVING** (1 serving = 2 slices)

| Calories | Total Fat | Saturated Fat | Sodium | Carbohydrate | Dietary Fiber | Protein | Calcium |
|----------|-----------|---------------|--------|--------------|---------------|---------|---------|
| 400 | 13 g | 3 g | 990 mg | 58 g | 3 g | 19 g | 15% |

# Veal Marsala

**PREP TIME:** 15 MINUTES/ **COOK TIME:** 18 MINUTES/ MAKES 4 SERVINGS

THE COMBINATION OF DRIED AND FRESH MUSHROOMS ADDS TO THE ELEGANCE OF THIS DISH.

## MAKE IT A MEAL

²⁄₃ cup cooked whole wheat linguine
120 CALORIES

## 410
CALORIES PER MEAL
★

- ½ ounce dried porcini mushrooms
- ½ cup boiling water
- ¼ cup all-purpose flour
- ¼ teaspoon salt
- ¼ teaspoon freshly ground black pepper
- 1 pound veal scallops, pounded to ⅛" thickness
- 3 teaspoons olive oil
- 1 package (10 ounces) sliced mushrooms
- 1 shallot, finely chopped
- 1 clove garlic, minced
- ½ cup dry marsala
- ¾ cup reduced-sodium beef broth
- 1 tablespoon unsalted butter
- 4 teaspoons chopped fresh parsley

**1. PLACE** the dried porcini mushrooms in a small bowl and pour in the boiling water. Let stand for 10 minutes, until softened. Drain and chop.

**2. MEANWHILE,** combine the flour, salt, and pepper on a large plate. Dredge the veal in the flour mixture to coat. Shake off any excess flour. Heat 2 teaspoons of the oil in a large nonstick skillet over medium-high heat. Add the veal and cook until browned, about 1 to 2 minutes per side. Transfer to a platter. Heat the remaining 1 teaspoon oil and add the sliced mushrooms and shallot. Cook, stirring occasionally, until the mushrooms start to brown, 5 to 6 minutes. Add any leftover flour, the porcini mushrooms, and the garlic. Cook for 2 minutes, until the garlic starts to brown. Pour in the marsala and broth. Bring to a boil and cook until slightly thickened, 2 to 3 minutes. Return the veal to the skillet and cook, turning once, until hot, 1 to 2 minutes. Remove the skillet from the heat. Swirl in the butter until melted. Divide among 4 plates and sprinkle with the parsley.

**PER SERVING** (1 serving = ¼ skillet contents)

| Calories | Total Fat | Saturated Fat | Sodium | Carbohydrate | Dietary Fiber | Protein | Calcium |
|---|---|---|---|---|---|---|---|
| 290 | 9 g | 3 g | 310 mg | 15 g | 2 g | 29 g | 2% |

# Greek Country-Style Meat Loaf

**PREP TIME:** 15 MINUTES + 20 MINUTES STAND TIME/ **COOK TIME:** 50 MINUTES/ MAKES 6 SERVINGS

GROUND LAMB IS RELATIVELY HIGH IN FAT, SO THIS RECIPE COMPENSATES BY COMBINING IT WITH VERY LEAN BEEF AND ALSO CALLING FOR FAT-FREE FETA CHEESE.

⅓ cup golden raisins

½ cup boiling water

2 tablespoons red wine vinegar

1 pound extra-lean ground round

8 ounces ground lamb

2 large egg whites

½ medium green bell pepper, chopped

½ medium onion, chopped

½ cup Italian-style bread crumbs

¼ cup chopped fresh parsley

3 ounces crumbled fat-free feta cheese

1 teaspoon dried mint

½ teaspoon salt

¼ teaspoon freshly ground black pepper

¾ cup no-salt-added tomato sauce

1. **PREHEAT** the oven to 375°F. Coat a baking sheet with cooking spray.

2. **COMBINE** the raisins, boiling water, and vinegar in a small bowl. Let stand for 10 minutes. Drain.

3. **COMBINE** the raisins, beef, lamb, egg whites, bell pepper, onion, bread crumbs, parsley, feta cheese, mint, salt, black pepper, and ¼ cup tomato sauce in a large bowl. Mix gently. Transfer to the prepared baking sheet and form into a 9" × 4" × 2" loaf. Spread the remaining ½ cup tomato sauce over the top of the meat loaf. Bake for about 45 to 50 minutes, until a thermometer inserted into the thickest part of the meat loaf registers 165°F. Let stand for 10 minutes before slicing.

## MAKE IT A MEAL

Large salad with 2 cups romaine lettuce, ¼ cup chopped tomato, 3 kalamata olives, 1 teaspoon olive oil, 2 teaspoons lemon juice
**105 CALORIES**

# 405
**CALORIES PER MEAL**
★ ★ ★

**PER SERVING** (1 serving = ⅙ meat loaf)

| Calories | Total Fat | Saturated Fat | Sodium | Carbohydrate | Dietary Fiber | Protein | Calcium |
|---|---|---|---|---|---|---|---|
| 300 | 12 g | 5 g | 570 mg | 18 g | 1 g | 28 g | 4% |

# Pasta with Garlic, Sausage, White Beans, and Broccoli

**PREP TIME:** 10 MINUTES/ **COOK TIME:** 20 MINUTES/ MAKES 4 SERVINGS

KEEP BROCCOLI IN YOUR FRIDGE AT ALL TIMES—IT HOLDS UP WELL AND IS AN EXCELLENT SOURCE OF VITAMINS A AND C.

8 ounces rotini

4 cups broccoli florets

4 ounces sweet Italian sausage, removed from the casing

1 tablespoon extra virgin olive oil

6 cloves garlic, sliced

1 can (14–19 ounces) cannellini beans, rinsed and drained

¾ cup reduced-sodium chicken broth

⅛ teaspoon salt

¼ teaspoon freshly ground black pepper

¼ cup grated Romano cheese

**1. BRING** a large pot of lightly salted water to a boil. Add the pasta and cook according to the package directions. Add the broccoli to the pot during the final 2 minutes of cooking. Drain the pasta and broccoli.

**2. HEAT** a large nonstick skillet over medium-high heat. Add the sausage and cook, breaking it into smaller pieces with a wooden spoon, until the sausage starts to brown, 4 to 5 minutes. Add the oil and garlic and cook until the garlic starts to brown, 1 to 2 minutes. Stir in the beans and cook for 1 minute. Add the broth and bring to a boil. Stir in the pasta-broccoli mixture, salt, and black pepper. Cook until hot, about 1 minute. Remove from the heat and stir in the cheese. Serve immediately.

## 400 CALORIES PER MEAL
★ ★ ★

**PER SERVING** (1 serving = 2 cups)

| Calories | Total Fat | Saturated Fat | Sodium | Carbohydrate | Dietary Fiber | Protein | Calcium |
|----------|-----------|---------------|--------|--------------|---------------|---------|---------|
| 400 | 9 g | 3 g | 550 mg | 60 g | 7 g | 20 g | 15% |

# 13.

# SEAFOOD & VEGETARIAN RECIPES

# Speedy Fish Tacos

**PREP TIME:** 10 MINUTES/ **COOK TIME:** 13 MINUTES/ MAKES 4 SERVINGS

ALMOST ANY TYPE OF FISH WILL WORK IN THIS QUICK AND EASY RECIPE. IF YOU PREFER, SPRINKLE THE FISH WITH SEASONINGS AND COOK IT ON AN OUTDOOR GRILL.

## 370
**CALORIES PER MEAL**
★ ★ ★

- 1 small white onion, thinly sliced
- ½ jalapeño chile pepper, finely chopped, wear plastic gloves when handling
- 1 tablespoon lime juice
- 1 tablespoon chopped fresh cilantro
- ½ teaspoon salt
- 1 tablespoon canola oil
- 1 pound halibut fillet
- 1 teaspoon chili powder
- 1 teaspoon ground cumin
- 8 corn tortillas
- 2 cups shredded romaine lettuce
- 1 medium tomato, chopped
- 1 avocado, sliced

1. **COMBINE** the onion, chile pepper, lime juice, cilantro, and ¼ teaspoon of the salt in a medium bowl.

2. **HEAT** the oil in a large nonstick skillet over medium-high heat. Sprinkle the halibut with the chili powder, cumin, and remaining ¼ teaspoon salt. Add to the skillet and cook until the fish flakes easily with a fork, about 5 to 6 minutes per side. Remove from the skillet.

3. **HEAT** the tortillas according to package directions. Fill the tortillas with the halibut, lettuce, tomato, and avocado. Top with the onion mixture.

## STAR SYSTEM
- ★ PROTEIN
- ★ FIBER
- ★ GOOD FATS
- ★ FRUITS/VEGGIES

**PER SERVING** (1 serving = 2 tacos)

| Calories | Total Fat | Saturated Fat | Sodium | Carbohydrate | Dietary Fiber | Protein | Calcium |
|----------|-----------|---------------|--------|--------------|---------------|---------|---------|
| 370 | 14 g | 2 g | 430 mg | 35 g | 6 g | 27 g | 8% |

# Dill Salmon Burgers

**PREP TIME:** 10 MINUTES/ **COOK TIME:** 22 MINUTES/ MAKES 4 SERVINGS

SALMON CANNED WITH ITS BONES SUPPLIES EXTRA CALCIUM; THE BONES DISINTEGRATE DURING MIXING. THIS RECIPE ALSO WORKS WITH CANNED CRAB OR TUNA.

- 2 cans (6 ounces each) or 1 can (14.75 ounces) salmon, drained
- 1 small onion, finely chopped
- 1 egg
- ⅓ cup bread crumbs
- ¼ cup light mayonnaise
- 1 tablespoon fresh dill, finely chopped (or 1 teaspoon dried dill)
- 2 tablespoons Greek-style fat-free yogurt
- 1 teaspoon country-style Dijon mustard
- 4 whole wheat rolls (1½–2 ounces each)

  Lettuce

  Tomato slices

**1. PREHEAT** the oven to 350°F. Coat a small baking sheet with cooking spray, or use a nonstick baking sheet.

**2. MIX** together the salmon, onion, egg, bread crumbs, mayonnaise, and dill. Make 4 patties (½ cup of salmon mixture each) approximately 4" in diameter.

**3. PLACE** the patties on the baking sheet and bake for approximately 20 to 22 minutes, until lightly browned.

**4. COMBINE** the yogurt and mustard in a small bowl. Stir to mix thoroughly. Divide the yogurt mixture evenly and spread it on the rolls. Serve the burgers on the rolls and top with the lettuce and tomato.

**PER SERVING** (1 serving = 1 burger)

| Calories | Total Fat | Saturated Fat | Sodium | Carbohydrate | Dietary Fiber | Protein | Calcium |
|----------|-----------|---------------|--------|--------------|---------------|---------|---------|
| 320 | 12 g | 2 g | 720 mg | 29 g | 4 g | 25 g | 30% |

# Pan-Seared Salmon with Garlic, Tomatoes, and Basil

**PREP TIME:** 10 MINUTES/ **COOK TIME:** 10 MINUTES/ MAKES 4 SERVINGS

IF TOMATOES AND FRESH BASIL ARE EITHER NOT AVAILABLE OR NOT IN SEASON, SWITCH TO CANNED DICED TOMATOES WITH BASIL OR ITALIAN SEASONING. YOU MIGHT NEED TO COOK THE TOMATOES LONGER TO REDUCE THE LIQUID. COMPARE BRANDS TO FIND THOSE LOWEST IN SODIUM.

## MAKE IT A MEAL

1 cup raspberries
**60 CALORIES**

**410**
**CALORIES PER MEAL**
★ ★ ★ ★

4   salmon fillets (¼ pound each)

½   teaspoon salt

¼   teaspoon freshly ground black pepper

1   medium onion, chopped

2   cloves garlic, minced

3   cups halved grape tomatoes

3   tablespoons chopped fresh basil

1   cup dry whole wheat couscous

**1. COAT** a nonstick skillet with cooking spray and heat over medium-high heat. Sprinkle the salmon with ¼ teaspoon of the salt and ⅛ teaspoon of the pepper. Add the fillets to the skillet and cook, turning once, until the fish is browned and flakes easily with a fork, 9 to 10 minutes. Transfer to a plate and keep warm. Add the onion and garlic to the skillet. Cook, stirring occasionally, until slightly softened, 4 to 5 minutes. Stir in the tomatoes and cook until wilted, about 3 to 4 minutes. Remove from the heat. Stir in the basil and the remaining ¼ teaspoon salt and ⅛ teaspoon pepper.

**2. MEANWHILE,** prepare the couscous according to the package directions. Serve the salmon and vegetables over the couscous.

**PER SERVING** (1 serving = 1 fillet, ½ cup couscous, ½ cup vegetables)

| Calories | Total Fat | Saturated Fat | Sodium | Carbohydrate | Dietary Fiber | Protein | Calcium |
|---|---|---|---|---|---|---|---|
| 350 | 13 g | 3 g | 360 mg | 30 g | 5 g | 28 g | 4% |

# Tuna Spaghetti Casserole

**PREP TIME:** 10 MINUTES/ **COOK TIME:** 40 MINUTES/ MAKES 6 SERVINGS

THE FAT-FREE MILK AND FLOUR COMBO IN THIS RECIPE CREATES A CREAMY, FAT-FREE SAUCE THAT ADDS AN EXTRA BOOST OF PROTEIN AND CALCIUM.

- 8  ounces spaghetti
- 1  tablespoon olive oil
- 1  medium onion, chopped
- 1  package (8 ounces) sliced mushrooms
- ½  teaspoon dried thyme
- ¼  teaspoon salt
- ¼  teaspoon freshly ground black pepper
- 1  cup frozen peas
- 3  cloves garlic, minced
- 2  cups fat-free milk
- 2  tablespoons all-purpose flour
- 2  cans (6 ounces each) solid white tuna packed in water, drained
- ¼  cup chopped fresh parsley
- 1  cup french fried onions, such as French's

**1. PREHEAT** the oven to 375°F. Coat an 8" × 8" baking dish with cooking spray.

**2. BRING** a large pot of lightly salted water to a boil. Add the spaghetti and cook according to package directions. Drain.

**3. HEAT** the oil in a large nonstick skillet over medium-high heat. Add the onion, mushrooms, thyme, salt, and pepper. Cook, stirring occasionally, until browned, about 10 to 12 minutes. Add the peas and garlic. Cook for 2 minutes, or until the garlic starts to brown. Reduce the heat to medium. Stir together the milk and flour and stir into the skillet. Cook, stirring, until slightly thickened, about 4 to 5 minutes.

**4. TRANSFER** to a bowl and add the spaghetti, tuna, and parsley. Toss well. Transfer to the prepared baking dish. Sprinkle the top with the fried onions and cover with aluminum foil.

**5. BAKE** for 15 minutes. Uncover and bake for 5 minutes longer, or until the top is browned and the filling is bubbly. Cool for 10 minutes before serving.

## MAKE IT A MEAL

10 cherry tomatoes
**30 CALORIES**

**400**
**CALORIES**
**PER MEAL**
★ ★

**PER SERVING** (1 serving = 2 cups)

| Calories | Total Fat | Saturated Fat | Sodium | Carbohydrate | Dietary Fiber | Protein | Calcium |
|---|---|---|---|---|---|---|---|
| 370 | 10 g | 3 g | 460 mg | 45 g | 3 g | 24 g | 15% |

# Fish en Papillote

**PREP TIME:** 15 MINUTES/ **COOK TIME:** 45 MINUTES/ MAKES 4 SERVINGS

WHITE-FLESHED FISH ARE VERY LOW IN FAT AND CALORIES, LEAVING YOU PLENTY OF ROOM FOR EXTRAS IN THIS MEAL. BROCCOLI SLAW, RICH IN ANTIOXIDANT VITAMINS, ADDS WONDERFUL FLAVOR AND TEXTURE TO THIS DISH.

## MAKE IT A MEAL

½ cup light vanilla ice cream
110 CALORIES

½ cup frozen berries
30 CALORIES

# 390
CALORIES PER MEAL
★ ★ ★

- 1  pound new potatoes, quartered
- ¼  teaspoon salt
- ¼  teaspoon paprika
- 2  tablespoons olive oil
- 1  package (12 ounces) broccoli slaw
- ½  teaspoon McCormick Perfect Pinch or other salt-free seasoning blend or herbs
- ½  teaspoon shallot salt or onion salt
- 4  cod fillets (¼ pound each) or other firm white fish such as scrod, tilapia, monkfish, or halibut
- 8  lemon slices
-    Parchment paper or foil

**1. PREHEAT** the oven to 425°F. Toss the potatoes with the salt, paprika, and 1 tablespoon of the oil. Place on a nonstick baking sheet or pan and cook for 15 minutes.

**2. COMBINE** the broccoli slaw with the remaining 1 tablespoon olive oil, seasoning blend or herbs, and salt in a microwave-proof bowl. Cover and microwave for 2 minutes, or until the slaw has softened.

**3. PLACE** 1 cup of the slaw in the middle of each of four 12" × 24" pieces of parchment paper or foil. Top the slaw with a fish fillet and 2 lemon slices. Fold over the parchment or foil and crimp the edges, sealing in the fish and vegetables.

**4. PLACE** each fish packet upside down on a large baking sheet. Reduce the oven heat to 400°F, leaving the potatoes in the oven. Place the fish in the oven and bake for 15 to 30 minutes, depending on the thickness of the fillets. To check for doneness, pierce the packet and fish with a skewer. The skewer should come out smoothly. Remove the potatoes from the oven.

**5. PLACE** each packet on a dinner plate and cut open. Serve with the potatoes.

**PER SERVING** (1 serving = 1 packet, ½ cup potatoes)

| Calories | Total Fat | Saturated Fat | Sodium | Carbohydrate | Dietary Fiber | Protein | Calcium |
|---|---|---|---|---|---|---|---|
| 250 | 8 g | 1 g | 320 mg | 24 g | 5 g | 23 g | 6% |

# Crunchy Dijon Snapper

**PREP TIME:** 10 MINUTES/ **COOK TIME:** 15 MINUTES/ MAKES 4 SERVINGS

ALTHOUGH MANY STORES SELL THESE FISH FROZEN, FRESH FILLETS ARE LESS WATERY AND YIELD A CRISPIER CRUST.

- 4 red snapper or sole, flounder, or other thin fish fillets (¼ pound each)
- 1 tablespoon Dijon mustard
- 1 tablespoon Miracle Whip Light or low-fat mayonnaise
- ¼ cup panko

1. **PREHEAT** the oven to 350°F. Place the fish fillets on a baking sheet.

2. **STIR** together the mustard and Miracle Whip in a small bowl. Brush the mustard mixture on the top surface of the fillets. Sprinkle with the panko.

3. **BAKE** for about 10 minutes, or until the fillets are firm to the touch. Turn on the broiler and broil the fish about 8" from the heat source until the panko is browned, about 3 minutes.

## MAKE IT A MEAL

1 cup broccoli, sautéed with garlic and ½ teaspoon olive oil
**40 CALORIES**

2-ounce piece garlic bread
**210 CALORIES**

# 380
**CALORIES PER MEAL**
★ ★

**PER SERVING** (1 serving = 1 fillet)

| Calories | Total Fat | Saturated Fat | Sodium | Carbohydrate | Dietary Fiber | Protein | Calcium |
|----------|-----------|---------------|--------|--------------|---------------|---------|---------|
| 130 | 3 g | 0 g | 180 mg | 4 g | 0 g | 22 g | 4% |

# Tandoori Spiced Snapper with Minted Yogurt

**PREP TIME:** 15 MINUTES + 4 HOURS MARINATING/ **COOK TIME:** 12 MINUTES/ MAKES 4 SERVINGS

GREEK YOGURT IS THICKER THAN REGULAR YOGURT AND STICKS WELL TO FOODS WHEN USED AS A MARINADE. TILAPIA, SOLE, AND OTHER FLAT FISH ARE WELL SUITED FOR THIS RECIPE.

## MAKE IT A MEAL

2 cups spinach, sautéed with 1 garlic clove and 1 teaspoon peanut oil
**60 CALORIES**

½ cup brown basmati rice
**110 CALORIES**

# 400
**CALORIES PER MEAL**
★ ★

| | |
|---|---|
| 2 | tablespoons lemon juice |
| 1 | tablespoon paprika |
| 1 | tablespoon grated fresh ginger |
| 3 | cloves garlic, minced |
| 2 | teaspoons curry powder |
| 1½ | cups fat-free Greek yogurt |
| 4 | skinless snapper fillets (6 ounces each, 1"–1½" thick) |
| ½ | medium cucumber, grated and excess liquid squeezed out |
| 1 | tablespoon chopped fresh mint |
| ¾ | teaspoon salt |
| ¼ | teaspoon freshly ground black pepper |

**1. COMBINE** the lemon juice, paprika, ginger, garlic, curry powder, and 1 cup yogurt in a large bowl. Add the snapper fillets and turn to coat. Refrigerate for 1½ hours or up to 4 hours.

**2. COMBINE** the cucumber, mint, ¼ teaspoon salt, ⅛ teaspoon of the black pepper, and the remaining ½ cup yogurt in a small bowl. Refrigerate until ready to use.

**3. PREHEAT** the broiler. Coat a broiler-pan rack with cooking spray.

**4. REMOVE** the snapper fillets from the bowl and discard the marinade. Place the fish on the broiler-pan rack and sprinkle with the remaining salt and pepper. Broil, turning once, until the fish is firm and opaque throughout, 10 to 12 minutes. Serve topped with the yogurt sauce.

**PER SERVING** (1 serving = 1 fillet, ¼ of the sauce)

| Calories | Total Fat | Saturated Fat | Sodium | Carbohydrate | Dietary Fiber | Protein | Calcium |
|---|---|---|---|---|---|---|---|
| 230 | 3 g | 0.5 g | 580 mg | 7 g | 1 g | 43 g | 15% |

# Blackened Catfish
# with Shallot Remoulade

**PREP TIME:** 10 MINUTES/ **COOK TIME:** 10 MINUTES/ MAKES 4 SERVINGS

THE NATURALLY SWEET FLAVOR OF THE CATFISH PAIRS WELL WITH THE REDUCED-FAT MAYONNAISE, WHICH ADDS MOISTURE. HOMEMADE COLESLAW HAS LESS MAYO AND IS MUCH LOWER IN CALORIES THAN STORE-BOUGHT. IT CAN BE SEASONED TO YOUR TASTES.

- ½ cup reduced-fat mayonnaise
- 1 shallot, finely chopped
- 2 teaspoons Dijon mustard
- 2 teaspoons drained capers, chopped
- 1 tablespoon paprika
- 1½ teaspoons dried oregano
- ¾ teaspoon dried thyme
- 1 teaspoon garlic powder
- ½ teaspoon salt
- ¼ teaspoon ground red pepper
- ¼ teaspoon freshly ground black pepper
- 4 catfish fillets (¼ pound each)

**1. COMBINE** the mayonnaise, shallot, mustard, and capers in a small bowl.

**2. COMBINE** the paprika, oregano, thyme, garlic powder, salt, ground red pepper, and black pepper in a small bowl. Sprinkle the paprika mixture over both sides of the catfish.

**3. HEAT** a nonstick skillet coated with cooking spray over medium-high heat until very hot. Add the catfish, flesh side down, and cook, turning once, until the fish flakes easily with a fork, 8 to 10 minutes. Transfer the catfish to serving plates and dollop with the mayonnaise mixture.

## MAKE IT
## A MEAL

½ cup brown rice
**110 CALORIES**

1 cup coleslaw mix
with 1 tablespoon
light mayonnaise
**70 CALORIES**

# 400
**CALORIES
PER MEAL**
★ ★

**PER SERVING** (1 serving = 1 fillet)

| Calories | Total Fat | Saturated Fat | Sodium | Carbohydrate | Dietary Fiber | Protein | Calcium |
|---|---|---|---|---|---|---|---|
| 220 | 13 g | 3 g | 720 mg | 8 g | 1 g | 18 g | 2% |

# Lemon-Oregano Grilled Tilapia with Parsley Rice

**PREP TIME:** 10 MINUTES + 10 MINUTES STAND TIME/ **COOK TIME:** 8 MINUTES/ MAKES 4 SERVINGS

THE FISH PORTION IS LARGER THAN THE STANDARD 4–OUNCE SERVING BECAUSE TILAPIA AND OTHER WHITE-FLESHED FISH ARE RELATIVELY LOW IN CALORIES.

## MAKE IT A MEAL

Salad with ½ cup sliced cucumber, 1 teaspoon red vinegar, ½ teaspoon sugar, ½ teaspoon dried or 2 teaspoons fresh dill
**20 CALORIES**

## 420
**CALORIES PER MEAL**
★

| | |
|---|---|
| 4 | tilapia fillets (6 ounces each) |
| 1 | tablespoon extra virgin olive oil |
| 2 | tablespoons lemon juice |
| 2 | teaspoons grated lemon peel |
| 1 | teaspoon dried oregano |
| ¼ | teaspoon salt |
| ⅛ | teaspoon freshly ground black pepper |
| 2 | packages (8.8 ounces each) Uncle Ben's Ready Rice Whole Grain Brown |
| ¼ | cup chopped fresh parsley |

**1. COMBINE** the tilapia, oil, lemon juice, lemon peel, oregano, salt, and pepper in a large bowl. Turn the tilapia to coat and let stand for 10 minutes.

**2. HEAT** a ridged grill pan coated with cooking spray over medium-high heat. Remove the tilapia from the marinade and sprinkle with additional salt and pepper. Place the tilapia on the grill pan and cook until the fish flakes easily with a fork, 4 minutes per side. (Cook the fish in 2 batches if necessary.) Transfer to a serving plate.

**3. MEANWHILE,** prepare the rice according to package directions. Transfer the rice to a bowl and stir in the parsley. Divide the rice among 4 plates and serve with 1 fillet apiece.

**PER SERVING** (1 serving = 1 fillet, ½ package rice)

| Calories | Total Fat | Saturated Fat | Sodium | Carbohydrate | Dietary Fiber | Protein | Calcium |
|---|---|---|---|---|---|---|---|
| 400 | 10 g | 2 g | 240 mg | 38 g | 1 g | 39 g | 2% |

# Rosemary-Dijon Swordfish Skewers

**PREP TIME:** 20 MINUTES/ **COOK TIME:** 10 MINUTES/ MAKES 4 SERVINGS

SWORDFISH IS AMONG THE HIGHER FAT FISH AND, LIKE ITS RELATIVES, IT PROVIDES PLENTY OF HEART-HEALTHY, FLAT-BELLY-FRIENDLY MONOUNSATURATED FATTY ACIDS.

## MAKE IT A MEAL

½ cup blueberries
**40 CALORIES**

## 390
**CALORIES PER MEAL**
★★

| | |
|---|---|
| 3 | tablespoons Dijon mustard |
| 4 | teaspoons chopped fresh rosemary |
| 3 | cloves garlic, minced |
| 1 | tablespoon grated fresh orange peel |
| 1 | tablespoon lemon juice |
| 1 | tablespoon extra virgin olive oil |
| 1 | pound swordfish steak, cut into 16 cubes |
| 1 | small green bell pepper, cut into 12 squares |
| 1 | medium red onion, cut into 12 wedges |
| 12 | cherry tomatoes |
| ¼ | teaspoon salt |
| ⅛ | teaspoon black pepper |
| 2⅔ | cups cooked brown rice |

1. **COMBINE** the mustard, rosemary, garlic, orange peel, lemon juice, and oil in a bowl. Add the swordfish and mix well. Cover and refrigerate for 30 minutes.

2. **PREHEAT** the broiler. Coat a broiler pan with cooking spray.

3. **ALTERNATELY** thread 4 swordfish cubes, 3 bell pepper squares, 3 onion wedges, and 3 cherry tomatoes on each of 4 skewers. Sprinkle with the salt and pepper and place on the prepared broiler pan. Broil 5" from the heat source, turning ¼ turn every 2 minutes until the fish is cooked through, about 8 minutes.

4. **SERVE** with the rice.

**PER SERVING** (1 serving = 1 skewer with ⅔ cup rice)

| Calories | Total Fat | Saturated Fat | Sodium | Carbohydrate | Dietary Fiber | Protein | Calcium |
|---|---|---|---|---|---|---|---|
| 350 | 9 g | 2 g | 520 mg | 39 g | 4 g | 25 g | 4% |

# Grilled Shrimp with Mango-Habanero Relish

**PREP TIME:** 15 MINUTES/ **COOK TIME:** 30 MINUTES/ MAKES 4 SERVINGS

THE MANGO RELISH IN THIS RECIPE IS MUCH LOWER IN SUGAR AND SALT THAN COMMERCIAL RELISHES AND SALSAS. YOU MAY WANT TO SUBSTITUTE SCALLOPS OR FIRM-FLESHED WHITE FISH FOR THE SHRIMP.

| | |
|---|---|
| 2 | mangoes, peeled, pitted, and cut into ½" cubes |
| 1 | shallot, finely chopped (about 3 tablespoons) |
| ¼ | cup golden raisins |
| ¼–½ | small habanero chile pepper, seeded and finely chopped (wear plastic gloves when handling) |
| 1 | tablespoon chopped fresh mint |
| 2 | teaspoons cider vinegar |
| ¼ | teaspoon ground allspice |
| ¼ | teaspoon ground coriander |
| ¾ | teaspoon salt |
| 1 | tablespoon olive oil |
| 1½ | pounds jumbo shrimp, peeled and deveined, 16–20 per pound |
| ½ | cup brown basmati rice |
| ⅓ | cup sweetened coconut flakes |

**1. PREPARE** the grill for direct heat grilling. Coat a grill rack with cooking spray.

**2. COMBINE** the mangoes, shallot, raisins, chile pepper, mint, vinegar, allspice, coriander, and ¼ teaspoon of the salt in a large bowl. Combine the oil, shrimp, and remaining ½ teaspoon salt in a separate large bowl.

**3. PREPARE** the rice according to package directions. Meanwhile, heat a small skillet over medium heat. Add the coconut flakes and cook until lightly browned, stirring consistently, about 3 to 4 minutes. When the rice is cooked, stir in the coconut.

**4. SET** the shrimp on the grill rack. Grill for 2 to 3 minutes per side, until opaque and cooked through. Serve with the mango relish and toasted coconut rice.

## MAKE IT A MEAL

1 cup strawberries
50 CALORIES

410
CALORIES
PER MEAL
★ ★ ★

**PER SERVING** (1 serving = about 7 shrimp)

| Calories | Total Fat | Saturated Fat | Sodium | Carbohydrate | Dietary Fiber | Protein | Calcium |
|---|---|---|---|---|---|---|---|
| 360 | 8 g | 3 g | 750 mg | 46 g | 4 g | 30 g | 8% |

# Spicy Seared Shrimp Cocktail with Peach Salsa

**PREP TIME:** 15 MINUTES/ **COOK TIME:** 12 MINUTES/ MAKES 4 SERVINGS

APRICOTS, NECTARINES, MANGOES, OR EVEN CANTALOUPE CAN BE USED IN PLACE OF THE PEACHES IN THIS RECIPE. FOR A VIBRANT NONALCOHOLIC DRINK, MIX A POMEGRANATE-BERRY DRINK—WE USED POMEGRANATE-CRANBERRY—WITH SELTZER.

- 4 medium peaches, pitted and cut into ¼" cubes
- ½ small red onion, finely chopped
- 2 tablespoons lemon juice
- 1 tablespoon agave nectar
- 1 tablespoon chopped fresh mint
- ¾ teaspoon salt
- 1½ teaspoons paprika
- 1 teaspoon ground coriander
- ¾ teaspoon curry powder
- ¼ teaspoon garlic powder
- ¼ teaspoon ground ginger
- ⅛ teaspoon ground red pepper
- 24 extra-large shrimp (about 1½ pounds), peeled and deveined
- 4 teaspoons olive oil
- 3 ounces baked tortilla chips

1. **COMBINE** the peaches, onion, lemon juice, agave, mint, and ¼ teaspoon of the salt in a large bowl.

2. **COMBINE** the paprika, coriander, curry powder, garlic powder, ginger, ground red pepper, and remaining ½ teaspoon salt in a bowl. Dredge both sides of each shrimp in the spice mixture and transfer to a plate.

3. **HEAT** 2 teaspoons of the oil in a large nonstick skillet over medium-high heat. Add half of the shrimp to the skillet and cook until opaque, about 3 minutes per side. Transfer to a plate and repeat with the remaining oil and shrimp.

4. **TO** serve, spoon the peach salsa into 4 large martini glasses. Hang 6 shrimp on the rim of each glass. Serve with the tortilla chips.

## MAKE IT A MEAL

½ cup pomegranate-cranberry juice drink with ½ cup seltzer
**50 CALORIES**

# 390
**CALORIES PER MEAL**
★ ★

**PER SERVING** (1 serving = 6 shrimp, 1 cup salsa)

| Calories | Total Fat | Saturated Fat | Sodium | Carbohydrate | Dietary Fiber | Protein | Calcium |
|----------|-----------|---------------|--------|--------------|---------------|---------|---------|
| 340 | 9 g | 2 g | 840 mg | 37 g | 4 g | 30 g | 8% |

# Shrimp, Avocado, and Cilantro Seviche

**PREP TIME:** 15 MINUTES + 4 HOURS CHILL TIME/ **COOK TIME:** 10 MINUTES/ MAKES 4 SERVINGS

IN TRADITIONAL SEVICHE, CITRUS JUICE "COOKS" THE FISH OR SEAFOOD BY CAUSING ITS FLESH TO BECOME FIRM. BUT BECAUSE CITRUS DOESN'T HEAT FOOD, IT DOESN'T KILL BACTERIA. HERE, WE BRIEFLY BOIL THE SHRIMP AND THEN COMBINE IT WITH CITRUS.

## 390
### CALORIES
### PER MEAL
★ ★ ★ ★

- 1½ pounds medium shrimp (41–50 per pound), peeled and deveined
- 1 Hass avocado, finely diced
- 1 large mango, peeled, pitted, and finely chopped
- ½ medium red bell pepper, finely chopped
- ½ small white onion, finely chopped (¼ cup)
- ½ jalapeño chile pepper, finely chopped, wear plastic gloves when handling
- ¼ cup orange juice
- 3 tablespoons lime juice
- 2 tablespoons chopped fresh cilantro
- ¼ teaspoon salt
- 8 corn tortillas

1. **BRING** a large pot of lightly salted water to a boil. Add the shrimp and cook until pink and opaque, about 2 to 3 minutes. Drain, rinse under cold water, and drain well. Pat the shrimp dry with a paper towel.

2. **COMBINE** the shrimp, avocado, mango, bell pepper, onion, chile pepper, orange juice, lime juice, cilantro, and salt in a large bowl. Toss well and cover with plastic wrap. Refrigerate for at least 1 hour and up to 4 hours.

3. **HEAT** the tortillas directly over gas burners, turning frequently, until they are hot and just beginning to char, 1 to 2 minutes. Alternatively, heat according to package directions. Serve with the seviche.

**PER SERVING** (1 serving = 1½ cups seviche, 2 tortillas)

| Calories | Total Fat | Saturated Fat | Sodium | Carbohydrate | Dietary Fiber | Protein | Calcium |
|---|---|---|---|---|---|---|---|
| 390 | 10 g | 2 g | 450 mg | 45 g | 8 g | 33 g | 6% |

# Shrimp and Scallop Paella

**PREP TIME:** 15 MINUTES/ **COOK TIME:** 41 MINUTES/ MAKES 4 SERVINGS

CLAM JUICE, LIQUID FROM FRESHLY SHUCKED OR COOKED CLAMS, HAS A BRINY FLAVOR THAT COMPLEMENTS CLASSIC PAELLA INGREDIENTS.

| | |
|---|---|
| 1 | tablespoon olive oil |
| 1 | medium onion, chopped |
| 1 | large green bell pepper, chopped |
| 2 | ounces turkey kielbasa or sausage, chopped |
| 4 | cloves garlic, minced |
| ¼ | teaspoon saffron threads, lightly crushed |
| ¾ | cup rice |
| 1 | bottle (8 ounces) clam juice |
| ½ | cup water |
| 3 | plum tomatoes, seeded and chopped |
| ½ | cup frozen peas |
| 16 | Manzanilla olives |
| ¾ | pound large shrimp (36–40 per pound), peeled and deveined |
| ½ | pound sea scallops |

**1. HEAT** the oil in a nonstick Dutch oven over medium-high heat. Add the onion, bell pepper, and kielbasa. Cook, stirring occasionally, until slightly softened, 4 to 5 minutes. Stir in the garlic and saffron and cook, stirring often, 2 minutes. Add the rice and cook for 1 minute.

**2. POUR** in the clam juice and ¼ cup of the water. Bring to a boil and cover. Reduce the heat to medium-low and simmer for 10 minutes.

**3. STIR** in the tomatoes, peas, olives, and remaining ¼ cup water. Cover and return to a simmer. Cook for 15 minutes longer, or until the rice is nearly tender. Stir in the shrimp and scallops. Cover and cook for 6 to 8 minutes longer, or until the rice is tender and the seafood is cooked through.

## MAKE IT A MEAL

1 cup honeydew
**60 CALORIES**

**420**
**CALORIES
PER MEAL**
★ ★ ★

**PER SERVING** (1 serving = 2 cups)

| Calories | Total Fat | Saturated Fat | Sodium | Carbohydrate | Dietary Fiber | Protein | Calcium |
|---|---|---|---|---|---|---|---|
| 360 | 9 g | 1 g | 830 mg | 39 g | 3 g | 30 g | 8% |

# Stir-Fried Scallops in Black Bean Sauce

**PREP TIME:** 10 MINUTES/ **COOK TIME:** 45 MINUTES/ MAKES 4 SERVINGS

SEAFOOD DEPARTMENTS MAY CARRY TWO TYPES OF SCALLOPS: BAY SCALLOPS, WHICH ARE SMALL, AND THE MORE COMMON AND LARGER SEA SCALLOPS. BOTH ARE VIRTUALLY FAT FREE.

## MAKE IT A MEAL

Hunt's Snack Pack
Fat-Free Chocolate
Pudding
90 CALORIES

# 420
**CALORIES
PER MEAL**
★

- 1 cup brown basmati rice
- 3 teaspoons olive oil
- 1 tablespoon grated fresh ginger
- 2 cloves garlic, minced
- 1 pound sea scallops, drained
- 2 scallions, chopped
- 1 large carrot, sliced
- 1 red bell pepper, seeded and chopped
- 2 teaspoons fermented black beans
- 3 tablespoons sake
- 1 tablespoon reduced-sodium soy sauce
- 1 teaspoon honey

1. **COOK** the rice according to the package directions. Fluff the rice with a fork.

2. **MEANWHILE,** heat 2 teaspoons of the oil in a large nonstick skillet over medium-high heat. Add the ginger and garlic and cook for 30 seconds, or until fragrant.

3. **STIR** in the scallops and cook for 3 to 4 minutes, or until opaque. Transfer the scallops to a bowl and set aside.

4. **HEAT** the remaining 1 teaspoon oil and add the scallions, carrot, and pepper. Cook, stirring often, for 2 to 3 minutes, or until the vegetables are crisp-tender.

5. **ADD** the black beans, sake, soy sauce, and honey and cook for 45 seconds. Drain any liquid from the scallops, then add them to the skillet, toss, and cook for 1 minute, or until hot. Serve over the rice.

**PER SERVING** (1 serving = 1 cups, ½ cup rice)

| Calories | Total Fat | Saturated Fat | Sodium | Carbohydrate | Dietary Fiber | Protein | Calcium |
|---|---|---|---|---|---|---|---|
| 330 | 6 g | 1 g | 350 mg | 44 g | 3 g | 24 g | 6% |

# Pad Thai

**PREP TIME:** 20 MINUTES/ **COOK TIME:** 15 MINUTES/ MAKES 4 SERVINGS

FINISH ALL THE CUTTING AND CHOPPING BEFORE SOAKING THE NOODLES; THEY BECOME MUSHY DURING COOKING IF THEY'RE SOAKED TOO LONG. WE ADDED EXTRA VEGETABLES.

- 6 ounces rice-flour noodles
- 2 tablespoons fish sauce
- 2 tablespoons brown sugar
- 1 tablespoon reduced-sodium soy sauce
- 1 tablespoon rice wine vinegar
  Juice of 2 limes
- 1 teaspoon toasted sesame oil
- ½ teaspoon crushed red-pepper flakes
- 1 teaspoon peanut oil
- 1 tablespoon finely chopped shallots
- 3 cloves garlic, minced
- 2 cups bean sprouts
- 2 cups shredded green or savoy cabbage
- 2 cups julienned carrots
- 4 medium scallions (whites + ⅔ of green parts, thinly sliced)
- 7 ounces extra-firm tofu, cut into thin strips
- 1 large egg, lightly beaten
- ¼ cup chopped dry-roasted, unsalted peanuts
- ½ cup chopped fresh cilantro

**1. PLACE** the noodles in a large bowl. Cover with warm water and soak for up to 5 minutes. The texture should be soft but al dente. Drain.

**2. MEANWHILE,** whisk together the fish sauce, sugar, soy sauce, vinegar, lime juice, sesame oil, and red-pepper flakes.

**3. HEAT** a wok or deep skillet coated with cooking spray over medium-high heat. Add the peanut oil, shallots, and garlic and cook for 1 minute. Add the bean sprouts, cabbage, carrots, and scallions and cook, stirring constantly, for 2 minutes. Add the sauce and tofu and cook, stirring constantly, for 2 minutes longer. Remove the vegetable and tofu mixture to a large serving bowl.

**4. ADD** the egg to the wok and reduce the heat to medium. Stir until the egg begins to scramble, about 1 minute. Remove from the heat. Add the egg and noodles to the serving bowl with the vegetables and toss gently to combine.

**5. TOP** with the peanuts and cilantro.

## 390
### CALORIES
### PER MEAL
★ ★ ★

**PER SERVING** (1 serving = 2½ cups)

| Calories | Total Fat | Saturated Fat | Sodium | Carbohydrate | Dietary Fiber | Protein | Calcium |
|---|---|---|---|---|---|---|---|
| 390 | 11 g | 2 g | 920 mg | 61 g | 7 g | 15 g | 10% |

# Three-Bean Chili with Corn "Pie"

THREE-BEAN CHILI: **PREP TIME:** 30 MINUTES/ COOK TIME: 8 HOURS/ MAKES 10 SERVINGS

CORN "PIE": **PREP TIME:** 5 MINUTES/ COOK TIME: 1 HOUR/ MAKES 12 SERVINGS

**390**
CALORIES
PER MEAL
★ ★ ★

### CHILI

- ⅔ cup each dried kidney, black, and white beans
- 1 large green bell pepper, chopped
- 1 medium rib celery, chopped
- 1 large onion, chopped
- 2 medium carrots, chopped
- 3 cloves garlic, finely chopped
- 1 chipotle pepper in adobo sauce, finely chopped
- 1½ tablespoons chili powder
- 1 tablespoon ground cumin
- ½ teaspoon smoked black pepper
- 28 ounces crushed tomatoes
- 2½ cups water
- 1 tablespoon salt
  Ground red pepper (optional)
- 1 cup plain low-fat yogurt
- 1 cup grated reduced-fat Cheddar cheese
- ½ cup chopped scallions

### CORN "PIE"

- ¼ cup soft margarine
- ¼ cup plain low-fat yogurt
- 2 eggs, slightly beaten
- 1 can (14–16 ounces) no-salt-added whole kernel corn
- 1 can (14–16 ounces) creamed corn
- 1 package (8.5 ounces) corn muffin mix

CHILI KEEPS SO WELL IN THE FRIDGE OR FREEZER THAT YOU'LL BE GLAD THIS RECIPE MAKES EXTRA. IF YOU PREFER THICK CHILI WITH VERY SOFT BEANS, USE A 15-OUNCE CAN OF EACH OF THE BEANS, DRAINED AND RINSED BEFORE ADDING TO THE SLOW COOKER. THE CORN PIE IS INCREDIBLY MOIST AND GOES WELL WITH STEW OR SIMMERED GREENS, ALSO.

**1. TO** make the chili: Soak the beans overnight in 1 quart of cold water.

**2. IN** the morning, drain the beans and add them to the slow cooker along with the bell pepper, celery, onion, carrots, garlic, chipotle pepper, chili powder, cumin, black pepper, tomatoes, and water. Cook on high for 4 hours or on medium or low for 8 hours, until the beans are fully cooked.

**3. ADD** the salt, along with the ground red pepper if desired for a spicier chili.

**4. SERVE** topped with the yogurt, cheese, and scallions.

**5. TO** make the corn "pie": Preheat the oven to 350°F. Spray a 13" × 9" baking pan with cooking spray, or use a nonstick pan.

**6. MIX** together the margarine, yogurt, eggs, corn kernels, creamed corn, and muffin mix in a medium bowl.

**7. POUR** the batter into the prepared pan and bake for 45 minutes to 1 hour, until the top is light brown and a wooden pick inserted in the center comes out clean.

**8. CUT** into 3" squares.

**PER SERVING** (1 serving = 1½ cups chili; one 3" square corn pie)

| Calories | Total Fat | Saturated Fat | Sodium | Carbohydrate | Dietary Fiber | Protein | Calcium |
|---|---|---|---|---|---|---|---|
| 390 | 11 g | 4 g | 870 mg | 60 g | 13 g | 19 g | 32% |

# Tangy Tofu Stir-Fry

**PREP TIME:** 30 MINUTES/ **COOK TIME:** 12 MINUTES/ MAKES 4 SERVINGS

A FOOD PROCESSOR OR HANDHELD MANDOLINE WILL HELP MAKE QUICK WORK OF CUTTING ALL THE VEGETABLES. THE RICE VINEGAR BRINGS OUT THE FLAVOR OF THE VEGETABLES AND SOBA NOODLES.

**420**
CALORIES
PER MEAL
★ ★ ★ ★

- 1 box (14 ounces) extra-firm tofu
- 2 tablespoons sriracha sauce or other Asian chile sauce
- 8 ounces dry soba noodles
- 2 teaspoons peanut oil
- 3 cloves garlic, minced
- 1 1" piece fresh ginger, finely chopped
- 3 medium carrots, halved crosswise and cut into strips
- 1 medium red bell pepper, julienned
- 1 medium green bell pepper, julienned
- 1 cup sliced mushrooms
- 4 scallions, halved lengthwise and cut into 1" pieces
- 1 can sliced water chestnuts, drained
- 1 tablespoon cornstarch
- ½ cup reduced-sodium vegetable broth
- 3 tablespoons reduced-sodium soy sauce
- 2 tablespoons natural rice vinegar (not seasoned)
- 1 teaspoon toasted sesame oil

**1. SLICE** the tofu block in half crosswise. Press each half with paper towels to remove extra water. Cut the tofu into 1" cubes. Combine the tofu and the chile sauce in a medium bowl. Toss to coat. Marinate in the refrigerator while you cut the vegetables.

**2. PREPARE** the soba noodles according to package directions. Place in a large bowl or on a platter.

**3. HEAT** 1 teaspoon peanut oil in a wok or deep skillet coated with cooking spray over medium-high heat. Add the garlic and ginger and stir-fry for about 30 seconds. Add the carrots, bell peppers, mushrooms, scallions, and water chestnuts. Stir-fry for 3 to 5 minutes, stirring frequently to prevent sticking or burning. Remove the wok from the heat. Transfer the vegetables to a bowl.

**4. REMOVE** the tofu from the refrigerator. Toss with the cornstarch to coat.

**5. HEAT** the remaining 1 teaspoon peanut oil in the wok over medium-high heat. Add the tofu and stir-fry for 1 minute, stirring to prevent sticking. Add the broth, soy sauce, vinegar, and sesame oil. Return the vegetables to the wok and simmer for 5 minutes. The liquid will thicken. Serve the vegetables and tofu on top of the soba noodles.

**PER SERVING** (1 serving = 1½ cups tofu, ⅔ cup noodles)

| Calories | Total Fat | Saturated Fat | Sodium | Carbohydrate | Dietary Fiber | Protein | Calcium |
|---|---|---|---|---|---|---|---|
| 420 | 10 g | 2 g | 1,100 mg | 67 g | 7 g | 21 g | 15% |

# Black-Eyed Peas and Collards

**PREP TIME:** 10 MINUTES/ **COOK TIME:** 42 MINUTES/ MAKES 4 SERVINGS

TRADITIONALLY, COLLARDS AND OTHER GREENS ARE SLOW-SIMMERED WITH HAM HOCKS FOR FLAVOR (IT ALSO ADDS EXTRA FAT AND CALORIES). IN THIS VEGETARIAN VERSION, WE ADD LIQUID SMOKE AND A MEATLESS SMOKED SAUSAGE. THIS DISH IS DELICIOUS OVER RICE OR WITH CORNBREAD.

## MAKE IT A MEAL

½ cup rice
**100 CALORIES**

2 medium peaches
**120 CALORIES**

# 380
**CALORIES PER MEAL**
★ ★

- ¾ pound collard greens or other greens such as kale, mustard, or turnip
- 1 teaspoon olive oil
- 1 medium onion, chopped
- 4 cloves garlic, minced
- 1 can (15–16 ounces) black-eyed peas, rinsed and drained
- 2 cups reduced-sodium vegetable broth
- 1 teaspoon liquid smoke
- 1 meatless smoked sausage, finely chopped (we used Lightlife Chorizo Style)

**1. REMOVE** the tough stems from the collard greens. Place the leaves in a large bowl with water to remove any dirt and grit. Drain, rinse well, and cut into thin strips.

**2. HEAT** the oil in a large pot over medium heat. Add the onion and garlic and cook until soft, about 2 minutes. Add the black-eyed peas, broth, liquid smoke, and meatless sausage. Bring to a boil. Reduce the heat to low. Cover and simmer until the greens are soft, up to 40 minutes. If desired, remove the lid during the last 5 minutes to boil off some of the cooking liquid.

**PER SERVING** (1 serving = 1 cup)

| Calories | Total Fat | Saturated Fat | Sodium | Carbohydrate | Dietary Fiber | Protein | Calcium |
|----------|-----------|---------------|--------|--------------|---------------|---------|---------|
| 160 | 5 g | 0.5 g | 440 mg | 21 g | 6 g | 9 g | 15% |

# Grilled Pita Panini with Vegetables and Green Chile Chutney

**PREP TIME:** 15 MINUTES/ **COOK TIME:** 49 MINUTES/ MAKES 4 SERVINGS

YOU CAN FIND GREEN CHUTNEY IN THE STORE, BUT MAKING YOUR OWN IS EASY AND MUCH MORE FLAVORFUL. FOR A DIFFERENT LOOK AND FLAVOR, USE BROCCOLI, GREEN PEPPER, AND YELLOW ONION IN THE FILLING.

## CHUTNEY

- 1 cup fresh cilantro
- 1 tablespoon mint leaves
- 1 medium-size green chile pepper (Anaheim for medium heat, jalapeño for more heat)
- 1 ½" piece fresh ginger
- 2 cloves garlic
- 2 tablespoons wine vinegar
- 2 tablespoons unsweetened dried coconut
- 1 teaspoon sugar
- ¼ teaspoon salt

## PITA PANINI

- 4 cups fresh or frozen cauliflower florets
- 1 medium red bell pepper, quartered lengthwise
- 1 medium red onion, quartered
- 1 tablespoon + 4 teaspoons extra virgin olive oil
- ¼ cup canned chickpeas, rinsed and drained
- ½ cup hummus
- 4 Weight Watchers 100% Whole Wheat Pita Pocket Bread
- 1 medium tomato, chopped

1. **COMBINE** the cilantro, mint, chile pepper, ginger, garlic, vinegar, coconut, sugar, and salt in a food processor. Process until smooth. Refrigerate.

2. **PREHEAT** the oven to 400°F. Toss the cauliflower, bell pepper, and onion with 1 tablespoon olive oil, and add salt and pepper. Arrange in 1 layer on a rimmed baking sheet or a 13" × 9" pan and seal with foil. Roast until just tender, 20 to 25 minutes. Transfer the vegetables to a cutting board and cool. Coarsely chop the vegetables.

3. **WITH** a fork, mash the chickpeas into the hummus.

4. **BRUSH** both sides of each pita with 1 of the remaining 4 teaspoons oil. Spread 2 tablespoons hummus and 2 tablespoons chutney inside each pita. Place equal amounts of the vegetables inside each pita (you may have vegetables left over). Add the tomato.

5. **PLACE** 1 sandwich in a large skillet over medium-high heat and weigh it down with a smaller skillet. Cook for 3 minutes per side. Repeat with the remaining sandwiches. Cut each pita in half and serve hot with the extra vegetables on the side.

MAKE IT
A MEAL

1 medium apple
100 CALORIES

400
CALORIES
PER MEAL
★ ★

**PER SERVING** (1 serving = 1 panini)

| Calories | Total Fat | Saturated Fat | Sodium | Carbohydrate | Dietary Fiber | Protein | Calcium |
|----------|-----------|---------------|--------|--------------|---------------|---------|---------|
| 300 | 14 g | 3 g | 300 mg | 42 g | 14 g | 12 g | 10% |

# 7-Layer Mexican Dinner Dip

**PREP TIME:** 20 MINUTES/ **COOK TIME:** 6 MINUTES/ MAKES 4 SERVINGS

EVERYONE HAS A DIFFERENT VERSION OF THIS PARTY CLASSIC. THE TRICK TO KEEP CALORIES UNDER CONTROL IS TO SWITCH TO PLAIN YOGURT INSTEAD OF SOUR CREAM, LIMIT THE AMOUNT OF AVOCADO, CHANGE TO A LOWER-FAT CHEESE, AND, SADLY, CUT BACK ON CHIPS.

**400**
**CALORIES**
**PER MEAL**
★ ★

### LETTUCE LAYER
- 4 cups shredded romaine lettuce

### BEAN LAYER
- 1 teaspoon olive oil
- ¼ cup chopped yellow onion
- 1 clove garlic, minced
- 1 can (14–19 ounces) pinto beans, rinsed and drained
- ⅓ cup water
- 1 teaspoon ground cumin

### VEGGIE LAYER
- 2 medium tomatoes, chopped
- ¼ cup finely chopped fresh cilantro
- ¼ cup sliced green olives
- 2 scallions, thinly sliced

### AVOCADO LAYER
- 1 avocado, chopped

### SALSA LAYER
- 1 cup salsa

### "SOUR CREAM" LAYER
- 1 cup plain low-fat yogurt
- 1 teaspoon chili powder

### CHEESE LAYER
- ½ cup shredded reduced-fat Cheddar cheese
- 4 ounces baked tortilla chips

**1. TO** make the bean layer: Heat the oil in a skillet over medium heat. Cook the onion and garlic for 1 minute. Add the beans, water, and cumin. Simmer for 5 minutes. Cool for 5 minutes. Mash the bean mixture using a potato masher, immersion blender, or food processor.

**2. TO** make the veggie layer: Combine the tomatoes, cilantro, green olives, and scallions in a medium bowl.

**3. TO** make the "sour cream" layer: Mix together the yogurt and chili powder in a small bowl.

**4. TO** assemble: Place the lettuce on a platter or in a bowl. Top with the beans, veggies, avocado, salsa, "sour cream," and cheese. Serve with the tortilla chips.

**PER SERVING** (1 serving = 1½ cups dip, 1 cup lettuce)

| Calories | Total Fat | Saturated Fat | Sodium | Carbohydrate | Dietary Fiber | Protein | Calcium |
|---|---|---|---|---|---|---|---|
| 400 | 14 g | 4 g | 1,020 mg | 56 g | 12 g | 17 g | 45% |

# Vegetarian Paella

**PREP TIME:** 10 MINUTES/ **COOK TIME:** 30 MINUTES/ MAKES 4 SERVINGS

GET HIGH-QUALITY SAFFRON FOR THE BEST FLAVOR. ALTHOUGH SAFFRON IS EXTREMELY EXPENSIVE, MOST RECIPES CALL FOR ONLY A SMALL AMOUNT.

## MAKE IT A MEAL

So Delicious or other 80–100-calorie ice cream sandwich
**90 CALORIES**

## 380
**CALORIES PER MEAL**
★ ★

- 1 teaspoon olive oil
- 1 medium onion, chopped
- 3 cloves garlic, minced
- 1½ cups water
- ¾ cup rice
- 1 medium orange or red bell pepper, finely chopped
- ½ teaspoon salt
- ¼ teaspoon saffron threads
- 1 cup canned diced tomatoes
- 1½ cups frozen peas, thawed
- 1 cup cooked or canned chickpeas, rinsed and drained
- ¼ cup roasted red bell pepper, cut into thin strips
- ¼ teaspoon ground black pepper
- 2 teaspoons smoked paprika
- 2 tablespoons parsley

1. **HEAT** the oil in a large saucepan or pot over medium heat. Add the onion and garlic and cook for 1 minute. Add the water, rice, bell pepper, salt, and saffron. Bring to a boil. Reduce the heat to low. Cover and simmer for about 18 minutes, or until the rice is barely tender.

2. **ADD** the tomatoes, then the peas, chickpeas, and roasted bell peppers to the rice. Cover and simmer for at least 5 minutes, or until all the liquid is absorbed. Remove from the heat and let sit for 5 minutes.

3. **SPRINKLE** with the black pepper and gently toss with a fork to distribute the vegetables. Add the paprika and parsley before serving.

**PER SERVING** (1 serving = 1¾ cups)

| Calories | Total Fat | Saturated Fat | Sodium | Carbohydrate | Dietary Fiber | Protein | Calcium |
|----------|-----------|---------------|--------|--------------|---------------|---------|---------|
| 290 | 3 g | 0 g | 720 mg | 57 g | 8 g | 10 g | 6% |

# Veggie "Soufflé"

**PREP TIME:** 15 MINUTES/ **COOK TIME:** 1 HOUR/ MAKES 6 SERVINGS

THIS LAYERED VEGETABLE SIDE DISH IS PERFECT FOR A BRUNCH OR LUNCH. TO GIVE IT A LIGHTER TEXTURE, BEAT THE EGG WHITES FIRST BEFORE COMBINING WITH THE VEGETABLE MIXTURES.

- 1 pound cauliflower florets, fresh or frozen
- 4 tablespoons water
- 1 pound broccoli florets, fresh or frozen
- 2 teaspoons olive oil
- ½ cup chopped onion
- 1½ cups sliced mushrooms
- 2 large eggs
- 4 egg whites
- ⅔ cup panko
- 1 teaspoon salt
- 1 teaspoon freshly ground black pepper
- 1 clove garlic, minced

**1. PREHEAT** the oven to 350°F. Coat a loaf pan with cooking spray or use a nonstick loaf pan.

**2. PUT** the cauliflower and 2 tablespoons of the water in a medium microwaveable bowl. Microwave for 3 to 5 minutes, or until soft. Drain off any liquid and set aside.

**3. PLACE** the broccoli and the remaining 2 tablespoons water in a medium microwaveable bowl. Microwave for 3 to 5 minutes, or until soft. Drain off any liquid and set aside.

**4. HEAT** the oil in a skillet. Add the onion and mushrooms and cook until soft, about 5 minutes. Remove from the heat and set aside.

**5. COMBINE** the cauliflower, onion, mushrooms, 1 of the eggs, 2 of the egg whites, ⅓ cup of the panko, ½ teaspoon of the salt, and ½ teaspoon of the pepper in a food processor. Pulse until almost smooth. Scrape into the loaf pan.

**6. COMBINE** the broccoli, garlic, and remaining 1 egg, 2 egg whites, ⅓ cup panko, ½ teaspoon salt, and ½ teaspoon pepper in the food processor. Pulse until almost smooth. Set aside.

**7. LAYER** the mushroom mixture over the cauliflower layer in the loaf pan. Gently spread the broccoli over the top.

**8. BAKE** for 45 to 50 minutes, or until a wooden pick inserted into the center comes out clean.

## MAKE IT A MEAL

3 ounces grilled salmon
**180 CALORIES**

½ cup brown rice
**110 CALORIES**

**410**
**CALORIES PER MEAL**
★ ★

**PER SERVING** (1 serving = 1½"-thick slice)

| Calories | Total Fat | Saturated Fat | Sodium | Carbohydrate | Dietary Fiber | Protein | Calcium |
|----------|-----------|---------------|--------|--------------|---------------|---------|---------|
| 120 | 5 g | 1 g | 510 mg | 15 g | 5 g | 10 g | 6% |

# Roasted Vegetable Lasagna

**PREP TIME:** 35 MINUTES/ **COOK TIME:** 1 HOUR 20 MINUTES/ MAKES 8 SERVINGS

PACKED WITH VEGETABLES, THIS RECIPE DELICIOUSLY DISHES UP PLENTY OF VITAMIN A, VITAMIN C, AND PHYTONUTRIENTS. CUT IT INTO SERVINGS, WRAP WELL IN FOIL, LABEL, AND FREEZE FOR A QUICK PACKAGED MEAL WHEN YOU'RE SHORT ON TIME.

## MAKE IT A MEAL

1-ounce slice Italian bread spread with roasted garlic, sprinkled with a couple drops of olive oil, covered, and roasted in the microwave for 10 to 15 seconds
**80 CALORIES**

## 410
**CALORIES PER MEAL**
★ ★ ★

- 3 medium zucchini, cut lengthwise into ¼"-thick slices
- 2 large red bell peppers, cut into 1"-wide strips
- 1 teaspoon olive oil
- 8 ounces sliced mushrooms
- 4 medium carrots, coarsely shredded
- 1 package (10 ounces) frozen chopped spinach, thawed and squeezed dry
- 1 container (15 ounces) part-skim ricotta cheese
- ⅓ cup grated Parmesan cheese
- 1 large egg
- 3 cups pasta sauce
- 9 no-boil or regular lasagna noodles
- 1½ cups shredded part-skim mozzarella cheese

1. **PREHEAT** the oven to 450°F. Coat the bottoms and sides of 1 large or 2 medium baking sheets with cooking spray. Arrange the zucchini and bell peppers on the baking sheets and coat with cooking spray. Roast for 15 to 20 minutes, or until tender. Remove the baking sheets and reduce the oven temperature to 350°F.

2. **HEAT** the oil in a large nonstick skillet over medium-high heat. Add the mushrooms and cook, stirring frequently, for 4 minutes, or until lightly browned. Stir in the carrots and cook for 1 minute longer. Set aside.

3. **STIR** together the spinach, ricotta, Parmesan, and egg in a medium bowl until blended.

4. **SPREAD** ½ cup of the pasta sauce over the bottom of a 13" × 9" × 2" baking dish. Top with 3 of the no-boil or cooked noodles, overlapping if necessary. Spoon on half of the ricotta mixture, spreading to cover the noodles. Top with half of the roasted vegetables and half of the mushroom mixture. Spoon ½ cup of the sauce over the vegetables and sprinkle with ½ cup of the mozzarella. Repeat the layering. Top with the remaining 3 noodles. Spread the remaining sauce over the noodles. Cover the dish with foil. Bake for 30 minutes. Uncover and sprinkle with the remaining ½ cup mozzarella. Bake for 20 to 25 minutes longer, or until hot and bubbly. Let stand for 15 minutes before serving.

**PER SERVING** (1 serving = one 3" x 4" square)

| Calories | Total Fat | Saturated Fat | Sodium | Carbohydrate | Dietary Fiber | Protein | Calcium |
|---|---|---|---|---|---|---|---|
| 330 | 13 g | 6 g | 690 mg | 34 g | 6 g | 20 g | 40% |

# Creamy Pasta with Beans, Tomatoes, and Basil

**PREP TIME:** 15 MINUTES/ **COOK TIME:** 15 MINUTES/ MAKES 4 SERVINGS

CANNED CANNELLINI OR WHITE BEANS BECOME VERY SOFT DURING COOKING, GIVING THIS DISH A CREAMY CONSISTENCY. IF BASIL IS NOT AVAILABLE, SUBSTITUTE PARSLEY.

- 8 ounces rotini, ziti, or penne
- ½ tablespoon olive oil
- 2 cloves garlic, minced
- ½ cup chopped onion
- 2 medium tomatoes, chopped
- 1 cup chopped parsley
- 1 can (14–19 ounces) cannellini beans
- ¼ cup water (optional)
- 4 tablespoons Parmesan cheese
- 2 tablespoons chopped fresh basil and pepper to taste

  Salt

  Freshly ground black pepper

**1. COOK** the pasta according to package directions.

**2. HEAT** the oil in a large skillet over medium heat. Add the garlic and onion and cook until soft, about 2 minutes. Add the tomatoes and parsley and cook for an additional 2 minutes, until the tomatoes begin to soften.

**3. ADD** the beans with their liquid and cover. Cook over medium heat for 5 minutes. Add the water if the sauce is too thick.

**4. STIR** in the Parmesan cheese and basil. Add the pasta and toss together. Season with salt and pepper.

## MAKE IT A MEAL

1 cup steamed broccoli
50 CALORIES

# 390
**CALORIES PER MEAL**
★ ★ ★

**PER SERVING** (1 serving = 1½ cups)

| Calories | Total Fat | Saturated Fat | Sodium | Carbohydrate | Dietary Fiber | Protein | Calcium |
|----------|-----------|---------------|--------|--------------|---------------|---------|---------|
| 340 | 3 g | 1 g | 370 mg | 65 g | 8 g | 18 g | 15% |

# Mushroom Onion Pizza

**PREP TIME:** 15 MINUTES/ **COOK TIME:** 33 MINUTES/ MAKES 4 SERVINGS

MANY SUPERMARKETS SELL BOTH WHOLE WHEAT AND REGULAR PIZZA DOUGH IN THE DAIRY CASE, USUALLY NEAR THE MOZZARELLA CHEESE. THE WHOLE WHEAT FLOUR IN WHOLE WHEAT DOUGH HAS MORE FIBER, MINERALS, AND HEALTHFUL PHYTOCHEMICALS.

1 tablespoon olive oil

1 cup sliced mushrooms

1 cup sliced onions

¼ teaspoon sea salt

1 package (15–16 ounces) refrigerated whole wheat pizza dough

1 tablespoon flour

½ cup pasta sauce

1 cup grated part-skim mozzarella cheese

¼ cup grated Parmesan or Parmigiano-Reggiano cheese

**1. PREHEAT** the oven to 450°F. Remove the dough from the refrigerator.

**2. HEAT** the oil in a large skillet. Add the mushrooms and onions and stir briefly. Cover the pan and cook for 3 minutes. Remove the cover and cook for 5 minutes longer, or until almost all the liquid boils off. Add the salt and remove from the heat.

**3. FORM** the dough into a ball and roll or pat out on a large, lightly floured baking sheet until no thicker than ¼". Spread the pasta sauce on the dough and sprinkle with the cheeses. Top with the mushrooms and onions.

**4. BAKE** for 25 minutes, or until the crust is lightly browned and the cheese is bubbly. Cut into 8 slices.

## 400 CALORIES PER MEAL
★

**PER SERVING** (1 serving = 2 slices)

| Calories | Total Fat | Saturated Fat | Sodium | Carbohydrate | Dietary Fiber | Protein | Calcium |
|---|---|---|---|---|---|---|---|
| 400 | 15 g | 5 g | 940 mg | 55 g | 9 g | 19 g | 30% |

# Naan Pizza

**PREP TIME:** 10 MINUTES/ **COOK TIME:** 21 MINUTES/ MAKES 2 SERVINGS

THE VEGETABLES SHOULD BE AS DRY AS POSSIBLE TO PREVENT THE PIZZA FROM BECOMING SOGGY. POCK-ETLESS PITA CAN BE SUBSTITUTED FOR THE NAAN, AND GRATED PART-SKIM MOZZARELLA CHEESE CAN BE USED INSTEAD OF THE SMOKED MOZZARELLA.

MAKE IT
A MEAL

½ cup sorbet
80 CALORIES

**410**
CALORIES
PER MEAL
★ ★

| | |
|---|---|
| 1 | International Fabulous Flats Tandoori Naan, Whole Grain |
| ¼ | cup pasta or pizza sauce |
| 2 | teaspoons olive oil |
| 1 | cup sliced white button mushrooms |
| 1 | small onion, chopped |
| ½ | cup chopped red or green bell pepper |
| 1 | bag (6 ounces) baby spinach |
| ½ | teaspoon dried basil |
| | Salt |
| | Freshly ground black pepper |
| 2 | ounces smoked fresh mozzarella cheese, grated |

1. **PREHEAT** the oven to 350°F. Place the naan on a baking sheet.

2. **PLACE** the pasta sauce in a small strainer or colander over a small bowl. Allow the liquid to drain off, thickening the sauce.

3. **MEANWHILE,** heat the oil in a large nonstick skillet over medium heat. Add the mushrooms, onion, and bell pepper and cook, stirring often, for about 8 minutes, or until tender. Add the spinach in batches, stirring until wilted, about 5 minutes. Transfer the vegetables to a small bowl, leaving behind any liquid that accumulated during cooking. Season the vegetables with the basil, salt, and pepper.

4. **SPREAD** the naan with the sauce and top with the vegetable mixture. Sprinkle evenly with the cheese and bake for about 8 minutes, or until the cheese has warmed and is lightly browned. Cut the naan in half and serve.

**PER SERVING** (1 serving = ½ pizza)

| Calories | Total Fat | Saturated Fat | Sodium | Carbohydrate | Dietary Fiber | Protein | Calcium |
|---|---|---|---|---|---|---|---|
| 330 | 12 g | 6 g | 320 mg | 46 g | 9 g | 14 g | 25% |

# Vegetarian Egg Lover's Salad Sandwich

**PREP TIME:** 10 MINUTES + 35 MINUTES REFRIGERATION/ **COOK TIME:** 1½ MINUTES/ MAKES 4 SERVINGS

EURASIAN SEA SALT HAS AN EGGLIKE FLAVOR THAT MAKES THIS TOFU-BASED SALAD TASTE AS IF IT CONTAINS EGGS. PRESSING THE WATER OUT OF THE TOFU HELPS PREVENT THE SALAD FROM BEING TOO WATERY.

- ½  package extra-firm tofu (not silken), about 7 ounces
- ¼  cup low-fat eggless mayonnaise
- 3  tablespoons chopped yellow onion
- 2  tablespoons chopped celery
- 1  tablespoon pickle relish
- 1  tablespoon sliced green olives
- 1  clove garlic, minced
- 1  teaspoon Dijon mustard
- ⅛  teaspoon sea salt, preferably Eurasian
- 8  slices whole wheat bread, toasted
- 4  thick slices tomato
- 4  leaves romaine lettuce

**1. HEAT** the tofu in the microwave for 90 seconds. Refrigerate for 20 minutes, then gently press out as much water as possible from the tofu.

**2. COMBINE** the mayonnaise, onion, celery, relish, olives, garlic, mustard, and salt in a medium bowl. Add the tofu and mash to a chunky texture. Chill for 15 minutes.

**3. FORM** the sandwiches with the tomato, lettuce, and about ⅓ cup filling between 2 slices whole wheat toast.

## MAKE IT A MEAL

½ cup deli three-bean salad
**90 CALORIES**

½ cup fruit salad
**50 CALORIES**

# 380
**CALORIES PER MEAL**
★ ★

**PER SERVING** (1 serving = 1 sandwich)

| Calories | Total Fat | Saturated Fat | Sodium | Carbohydrate | Dietary Fiber | Protein | Calcium |
|----------|-----------|---------------|--------|--------------|---------------|---------|---------|
| 240 | 8 g | 1 g | 540 mg | 30 g | 5 g | 13 g | 10% |

# Red Beans and Rice

**PREP TIME:** 15 MINUTES/ **COOK TIME:** 21 MINUTES/ MAKES 4 SERVINGS

FOR THIS MEATLESS VERSION, WE OMITTED THE HAM AND ADDED LIQUID SMOKE TO REPLACE THE SMOKY FLAVOR HAM IMPARTS. SMOKED BLACK PEPPER WOULD ADD A SIMILAR FLAVOR. IF YOU PREFER, ADD 4 OUNCES OF SMOKED TURKEY BREAST AND YOU'LL STILL STAY WITHIN THE 400-CALORIE RANGE.

**380**
**CALORIES PER MEAL**
★ ★

1 tablespoon olive oil

1 medium onion, chopped

1 medium rib celery, chopped

1 medium green bell pepper, chopped

¼ cup chopped roasted red bell pepper, rinsed and drained before chopping

3 scallions, sliced

4 cloves garlic, minced

2 cans (14–19 ounces each) small red beans, rinsed and drained

½ cup reduced-sodium vegetable broth

1 teaspoon Worcestershire sauce

1 teaspoon liquid smoke

1 teaspoon chili powder

½ teaspoon dried thyme

½ teaspoon salt

¼ teaspoon freshly ground black pepper

¼ teaspoon ground red pepper

¼ cup chopped parsley

2 cups cooked brown rice

1. **HEAT** the oil for 30 seconds in a medium saucepan over medium heat. Add the onion, celery, bell pepper, roasted red pepper, scallions, and garlic. Cook for 5 minutes. Add the beans, broth, Worcestershire sauce, liquid smoke, chili powder, thyme, salt, black pepper, and red pepper. Cover and simmer for at least 15 minutes.

2. **STIR** in the parsley and serve over brown rice.

**PER SERVING** (1 serving = 1½ cups beans, ½ cup rice)

| Calories | Total Fat | Saturated Fat | Sodium | Carbohydrate | Dietary Fiber | Protein | Calcium |
|---|---|---|---|---|---|---|---|
| 380 | 5 g | 0.5 g | 380 mg | 67 g | 19 g | 16 g | 6% |

# Lentils with Zesty Tomatoes

**PREP TIME:** 5 MINUTES + 10 MINUTES DURING COOKING TIME/ **COOK TIME:** 28 MINUTES/ MAKES 4 SERVINGS

EXPOSING TOMATOES TO HEAT HELPS RELEASE THEIR LYCOPENE, A PHYTOCHEMICAL THAT IS FOUND MAINLY IN TOMATOES. IF YOU PREFER A LESS SPICY DISH, USE CANNED DICED TOMATOES WITH ITALIAN SEASONING IN PLACE OF THE TOMATOES AND CHILE PEPPERS.

- 1 cup brown lentils, picked over and rinsed
- 3 cups water
- ¼ teaspoon paprika
- ½ teaspoon freshly ground black pepper
- 2 teaspoons extra virgin olive oil
- 2 cloves garlic, minced
- 1 cup canned fire-roasted tomatoes with green chile peppers
- 2 medium tomatoes, cut into ½" chunks
- 2 tablespoons chopped fresh cilantro
- ¼ teaspoon salt
- 1 cup low-fat or fat-free plain yogurt
- 2 tablespoons snipped fresh chives or scallion greens

**1. COMBINE** the lentils, water, paprika, and ¼ teaspoon of the black pepper in a large saucepan. Bring to a boil over high heat. Reduce the heat to low and cover. Simmer for 25 minutes, or until the lentils are tender but still hold their shape. Remove from the heat and drain.

**2. WHILE** the lentils are cooking, heat the oil in a large skillet over medium-high heat. Add the garlic and cook, stirring, for 30 seconds, or until fragrant. Add the canned and fresh tomatoes and the remaining ¼ teaspoon black pepper. Cook, stirring occasionally, for about 5 minutes. Remove from the heat and stir in the cilantro.

**3. TRANSFER** the lentil mixture to a shallow serving dish and sprinkle with salt. Spoon the tomato mixture over the lentils. Top with the yogurt and sprinkle with the chives or scallion greens.

### MAKE IT A MEAL

6" whole wheat pita
**170 CALORIES**

# 420
**CALORIES PER MEAL**
★ ★ ★ ★

**PER SERVING** (1 serving = 1½ cups)

| Calories | Total Fat | Saturated Fat | Sodium | Carbohydrate | Dietary Fiber | Protein | Calcium |
|----------|-----------|---------------|--------|--------------|---------------|---------|---------|
| 250 | 4 g | 1 g | 340 mg | 38 g | 12 g | 17 g | 15% |

# 14.
## SNACKS & DESSERTS

# Warm Artichoke Dip with Vegetables

**PREP TIME:** 10 MINUTES/ **COOK TIME:** 40 MINUTES/ MAKES 4 SERVINGS

THIS RECIPE WILL MAKE VEGETABLE LOVERS OUT OF YOUR FAMILY AND FRIENDS; FEEL FREE TO SWITCH TO ANY COMBO OF RAW VEGETABLES. IF YOU PREFER, SKIP THE BEER AND ADD ANOTHER PITA TO THE RECIPE.

## MAKE IT A MEAL

12 ounces light beer
**100 CALORIES**

## 410
**CALORIES PER MEAL**
★

### STAR SYSTEM

- ★ PROTEIN
- ★ FIBER
- ★ GOOD FATS
- ★ FRUITS/VEGGIES

| | |
|---|---|
| 2 | slices bacon |
| 1 | medium onion, chopped |
| 2 | cloves garlic, minced |
| 4 | ounces fat-free cream cheese, at room temperature |
| 2 | ounces Neufchâtel cheese, at room temperature |
| ¼ | cup reduced-fat mayonnaise |
| ¼ | cup reduced-fat sour cream |
| ¼ | cup grated Parmesan cheese |
| 1 | teaspoon lemon juice |
| 1 | package (9 ounces) frozen artichoke hearts, thawed and chopped |
| ¼ | teaspoon salt |
| ¼ | teaspoon freshly ground black pepper |
| 4 | cups precut vegetables, such as carrots, cucumbers, jicama, and celery |
| 2 | pitas (6" diameter), each cut into 8 wedges |

**1. PREHEAT** the oven to 375°F. Coat a 6-cup baking dish with cooking spray.

**2. COOK** the bacon in a medium skillet over medium-high heat until crisp, turning once, 5 to 6 minutes. Transfer to a plate covered with a paper towel. Drain and chop. Return the skillet to medium-high heat. Add the onion and garlic and cook until beginning to brown, 4 to 5 minutes. Remove from the heat and cool for 5 minutes.

**3. BEAT** together the cream cheese, Neufchâtel cheese, mayonnaise, sour cream, Parmesan, and lemon juice in a large bowl. Stir in the onion mixture, bacon, artichoke hearts, salt, and pepper. Transfer to the prepared baking dish and smooth with a spatula.

**4. BAKE** until the dip is bubbly and the top begins to brown slightly, about 28 to 30 minutes. Serve with the cut vegetables and pita wedges.

**PER SERVING** (1 serving = ¾ cup dip, 1 cup vegetables)

| Calories | Total Fat | Saturated Fat | Sodium | Carbohydrate | Dietary Fiber | Protein | Calcium |
|---|---|---|---|---|---|---|---|
| 310 | 11 g | 5 g | 940 mg | 38 g | 6 g | 15 g | 35% |

# Black Bean–Chipotle Dip with Tortilla Chips

**PREP TIME:** 10 MINUTES/ MAKES 6 SERVINGS

INSTEAD OF LIGHT BEER, YOU CAN PAIR THIS MEAL WITH A VERY SMALL (4-OUNCE) BLENDED MARGARITA (110 CALORIES) OR A 100-CALORIE FROZEN DESSERT.

## MAKE IT A MEAL

12 ounces light Mexican beer
**100 CALORIES**

## 370
**CALORIES PER MEAL**
★

- ½ can (16 ounces) refried black beans
- ½ cup jarred chipotle salsa
- 1½ Hass avocados, peeled and pitted
- 1 tablespoon lime juice
- 1 tablespoon chopped fresh cilantro
- ¼ teaspoon salt
- ⅔ cup low-fat sour cream
- ½ cup shredded reduced-fat Mexican four-cheese blend
- 2 scallions, chopped
- 6 ounces baked tortilla chips

**MIX** together the beans and salsa in a medium bowl. Spoon the bean mixture into a 3-cup straight-sided ceramic or glass dish. Combine the avocados, lime juice, cilantro, and salt into another bowl. Mash together with a fork until fairly smooth. Spread over the bean mixture. Top with the sour cream and sprinkle with the cheese and scallions. Serve with the tortilla chips.

**PER SERVING** (1 serving = ⅔ cup)

| Calories | Total Fat | Saturated Fat | Sodium | Carbohydrate | Dietary Fiber | Protein | Calcium |
|----------|-----------|---------------|--------|--------------|---------------|---------|---------|
| 270 | 11 g | 4 g | 520 mg | 37 g | 6 g | 9 g | 20% |

# Classic Hors D'Oeuvres

HAM SALAD TEA SANDWICHES: **PREP TIME:** 15 MINUTES/ MAKES 4 SERVINGS
DEVILED EGGS: **PREP TIME:** 15 MINUTES/ **COOK TIME:** 12 MINUTES/ MAKES 4 SERVINGS

WE LIGHTENED UP TWO 1950S CLASSICS THAT CONTINUE TO BE CROWD-PLEASERS TODAY. IF YOU PREFER,
SERVE CALORIE-FREE BEVERAGES AND ADD A PLATTER OF CRUDITÉS TO THE MENU.

## SANDWICHES

- 4 ounces deli-sliced Virginia ham, finely chopped
- 3 tablespoons finely chopped celery
- 3 tablespoons light mayonnaise
- 2 tablespoons finely chopped onion
- 5 teaspoons sweet pickle relish
- 1 teaspoon prepared yellow mustard
- 10 thin slices whole wheat bread

## DEVILED EGGS

- 5 eggs
- 2 tablespoons light sour cream
- 1 tablespoon light mayonnaise
- 1 tablespoon sweet pickle relish
- ½ teaspoon Dijon mustard
- ¼ teaspoon grated fresh lemon peel
- ⅛ teaspoon salt
- ⅛ teaspoon freshly ground black pepper
- 2 teaspoons chopped fresh chives (optional)

**1. TO** make the sandwiches: Combine the ham, celery, mayonnaise, onion, relish, and mustard in a bowl. Arrange 5 slices of bread on a work surface. Spread each evenly with ham mixture and top with the remaining bread. Trim the crusts and cut each sandwich into 4 squares or triangles.

**2. TO** make the eggs: Place the eggs in a medium saucepan and cover with cold water. Bring to a boil over high heat. Cover the pan, remove it from the heat, and let it stand for 12 minutes. Cool the eggs under cold running water. Tap the eggs against the side of the pan and gently remove the shells.

**3. CUT** the eggs in half lengthwise. Place 3 whole yolks and 1 white in a bowl and mash with a fork until fairly smooth; discard the remaining 2 yolks. Add the sour cream, mayonnaise, relish, mustard, lemon peel, salt, and pepper and mix well. Spoon the filling into the hollows of the eggg whites, mounding to fill. Place the egg halves on a platter, cover with plastic, and chill for at least 1 hour before serving. Sprinkle with the chives, if desired, just before serving.

## MAKE IT A MEAL

1 cup half lemonade/ half unsweetened iced tea
**50 CALORIES**

# 400
CALORIES
PER MEAL

**PER SERVING** (1 serving = 5 sandwich squares, 2 deviled eggs halves)

| Calories | Total Fat | Saturated Fat | Sodium | Carbohydrate | Dietary Fiber | Protein | Calcium |
|----------|-----------|---------------|--------|--------------|---------------|---------|---------|
| 350 | 13 g | 2.5 g | 930 mg | 35 g | 5 g | 19 g | 10% |

# Caramelized Pineapple with Vanilla Frozen Yogurt

**PREP TIME:** 5 MINUTES/ **COOK TIME:** 15 MINUTES/ MAKES 4 SERVINGS

JUST A TEASPOON OF BUTTER IS ENOUGH TO GIVE THE PINEAPPLE A SUBTLE CARAMEL FLAVOR. BE PATIENT AND ALLOW THE JUICE TO THICKEN TO A SYRUPLIKE CONSISTENCY. SERVE WARM OR REFRIGERATE FIRST TO COOL.

## MAKE IT A MEAL

3 ounces grilled chicken breast
**140 CALORIES**

2 cups spinach sautéed with 1 clove garlic and 1 teaspoon peanut oil
**60 CALORIES**

# 410
**CALORIES PER MEAL**
★ ★

---

1 teaspoon unsalted butter

1 tablespoon packed brown sugar

1 can (20 ounces) crushed pineapple or pineapple chunks in juice

2 cups Edy's or Breyer's vanilla frozen yogurt (100–120 calories per ½ cup)

**1. MELT** the butter in a medium skillet over medium-low heat. Add the brown sugar and swirl to combine. Add the pineapple with juice and simmer over medium-low heat, uncovered, for 15 minutes, or until the juice thickens.

**2. SERVE** over the frozen yogurt.

---

**PER SERVING** (1 serving = 5 oz pineapple, ½ cup frozen yogurt)

| Calories | Total Fat | Saturated Fat | Sodium | Carbohydrate | Dietary Fiber | Protein | Calcium |
|----------|-----------|---------------|--------|--------------|---------------|---------|---------|
| 210 | 3 g | 2 g | 60 mg | 44 g | 1 g | 5 g | 20% |

# Baked Filled Wontons

**PREP TIME:** 20 MINUTES/ **COOK TIME:** 20 MINUTES/ MAKES 4 SERVINGS

THE AUTHENTIC FLAVOR OF THESE WONTONS COMES FROM THEIR TRADITIONAL VEGETABLE COMBO, ALONG WITH THE SEASONING FROM THE GINGER, GARLIC, HOISIN SAUCE, AND SOY SAUCE. IN A SHOW OF ASIAN FUSION, WE PAIR THIS CHINESE DISH WITH JAPANESE WASABI SOYBEANS TO SNACK ON.

- 2 teaspoons toasted sesame oil
- 6 ounces mushrooms, chopped
- 2 teaspoons grated fresh ginger
- 1 clove garlic, minced
- 3 cups shredded napa cabbage
- 1 carrot, grated
- 2 scallions, chopped
- 1 tablespoon hoisin sauce
- 1 tablespoon reduced-sodium soy sauce
- ⅛ teaspoon freshly ground black pepper
- 2 ounces Neufchâtel cheese
- 2 tablespoons chopped fresh cilantro
- 24 wonton wrappers
- 2 tablespoons Chinese mustard
- ¼ cup duck sauce

**1. PREHEAT** the oven to 425°F. Coat a large baking sheet with cooking spray.

**2. HEAT** the oil in a large nonstick skillet over medium-high heat. Add the mushrooms and cook until starting to brown, 5 to 6 minutes. Add the ginger and garlic and cook for 1 minute. Stir in the cabbage and carrot. Cook, stirring occasionally, until wilted, about 4 to 5 minutes. Add the scallions and cook for 1 minute. Stir in the hoisin sauce, soy sauce, and pepper. Cook for 30 seconds. Transfer to a bowl and cool for 5 minutes. Stir in the Neufchâtel and cilantro.

**3. ARRANGE** the wonton wrappers on a clean work surface. Place a rounded teaspoon of the mushroom filling in the center of each wonton. Dampen the edges and fold over to form a triangle. Press the edges with your fingers to seal. Place the wontons on the prepared baking sheet and lightly coat with cooking spray. Bake until lightly browned and crisp, about 10 to 12 minutes. Serve with the mustard and duck sauce.

## MAKE IT A MEAL

¼ cup wasabi soybeans
**140 CALORIES**

**410**
**CALORIES**
**PER MEAL**
★ ★

**PER SERVING** (1 serving = 6 wontons)

| Calories | Total Fat | Saturated Fat | Sodium | Carbohydrate | Dietary Fiber | Protein | Calcium |
|----------|-----------|---------------|--------|--------------|---------------|---------|---------|
| 270 | 6 g | 3 g | 790 mg | 42 g | 3 g | 9 g | 10% |

# Tart Cherry and Camembert Phyllo Tartlets

**PREP TIME:** 20 MINUTES/ **COOK TIME:** 10 MINUTES/ MAKES 6 SERVINGS

THE PHYLLO TART SHELLS MAKE QUICK WORK OF THIS ELEGANT HORS D'OEUVRE. BLENDING THE CAMEMBERT WITH NEUFCHÂTEL BRINGS DOWN THE CALORIES WHILE MAINTAINING THE CHARACTERISTIC CREAMINESS AND FLAVOR OF THE CAMEMBERT.

| | |
|---|---|
| 90 | dried tart cherries (about ¾ cup) |
| ½ | cup boiling water |
| 30 | mini phyllo tart shells (from 2 boxes, 1.9 ounces each) |
| 4 | ounces Neufchâtel cheese |
| 4 | ounces Camembert cheese, rind removed, cut into 30 small slices |
| 2½ | tablespoons cherry preserves |
| 4 | basil leaves, very thinly sliced |

**1. PREHEAT** the oven to 350°F.

**2. SET** aside 30 cherries. Combine the remaining cherries and the water in a small bowl and let stand for 2 minutes. Drain.

**3. ARRANGE** the tart shells in a single layer on a large baking sheet. Place 2 drained cherries in the bottom of each tart shell. Top with the Neufchâtel and Camembert. Bake until the cheese is hot, about 7 minutes. Remove from the oven and, working quickly, top each shell with ¼ teaspoon of the cherry preserves and 1 reserved cherry. Sprinkle with the sliced basil. Serve warm or at room temperature.

## MAKE IT A MEAL

5 ounces crisp white wine
120 CALORIES

# 400
CALORIES PER MEAL

**PER SERVING** (1 serving = 5 tartlets)

| Calories | Total Fat | Saturated Fat | Sodium | Carbohydrate | Dietary Fiber | Protein | Calcium |
|---|---|---|---|---|---|---|---|
| 280 | 14 g | 6 g | 280 mg | 28 g | 4 g | 9 g | 10% |

# Chocolate Chip Pecan Cookies

**PREP TIME:** 10 MINUTES/ **COOK TIME:** 14 MINUTES/ MAKES 18 SERVINGS

MINI CHOCOLATE CHIPS ARE A FAVORITE BECAUSE A LITTLE BIT GOES A LONG WAY TO ADD A BURST OF CHOCOLATE. THE EGG WHITES ADD LIGHTNESS TO THESE COOKIES.

- 1¼ cups all-purpose flour
- ½ teaspoon baking soda
- ½ teaspoon salt
- 1 large egg
- ¼ cup soft margarine (trans-free but not reduced fat)
- 1 egg white
- ¾ cup sugar
- 1 tablespoon corn syrup
- 1 teaspoon vanilla extract
- ½ cup mini chocolate chips
- ¼ cup chopped pecans

**1. PREHEAT** the oven to 350°F. Coat 2 large baking sheets with cooking spray.

**2. COMBINE** the flour, baking soda, and salt in a large bowl. Separate the egg and set aside the egg white. Mix together the margarine and egg yolk in a small bowl.

**3. WHIP** the egg whites (one from the egg you separated and one by itself) in a medium bowl until foamy. Slowly add the sugar while continuing to whip. The egg whites should thicken and appear meringuelike. Slowly add the corn syrup and continue to whip until the egg whites form soft peaks. Gently fold in the egg yolk mixture.

**4. ADD** the vanilla extract to the egg mixture. Fold into the flour mixture until well blended. Fold in the chocolate chips and pecans.

**5. DROP** the batter by rounded teaspoonfuls onto the baking sheet, leaving about 1" between cookies. Bake for about 12 to 14 minutes, or until the cookies are lightly browned. Cool for 5 minutes. Remove to a rack and cool completely. Store in an airtight container.

**PER SERVING** (1 serving = 2 cookies)

| Calories | Total Fat | Saturated Fat | Sodium | Carbohydrate | Dietary Fiber | Protein | Calcium |
|---|---|---|---|---|---|---|---|
| 130 | 5 g | 2 g | 130 mg | 19 g | 1 g | 2 g | 0% |

# Double-Ginger Ginger Snaps

**PREP TIME:** 10 MINUTES/ **COOK TIME:** 15 MINUTES/ MAKES 30 COOKIES

THE CANDIED GINGER GIVES THESE COOKIES A BRIGHTER GINGER FLAVOR THAT PARTNERS BEAUTIFULLY WITH VANILLA ICE CREAM AND CANNED PEARS. CHOOSE A BRAND OF ICE CREAM WITH ABOUT 140 CALORIES PER $\frac{1}{2}$ CUP TO STAY WITHIN THE 400-CALORIE WINDOW.

## MAKE IT A MEAL

$\frac{1}{2}$ cup vanilla ice cream
**140 CALORIES**

$\frac{1}{2}$ pear canned in juice
**40 CALORIES**

# 390
**CALORIES PER MEAL**

- 1 cup all-purpose flour
- 1 cup whole wheat flour
- $\frac{3}{4}$ teaspoon baking soda
- 1 teaspoon ground ginger
- $\frac{1}{2}$ teaspoon ground cinnamon
- $\frac{1}{4}$ teaspoon ground allspice
- $\frac{1}{4}$ cup finely chopped candied ginger
- $\frac{1}{2}$ cup packed brown sugar
- $\frac{1}{2}$ cup molasses
- $\frac{1}{3}$ cup butter, tub margarine (trans free but not reduced-fat), or combination
- 1 egg

**1. PREHEAT** the oven to 375°F. Coat a large baking sheet with cooking spray or cover with a silicone sheet or parchment paper.

**2. COMBINE** the all-purpose flour, whole wheat flour, baking soda, ground ginger, cinnamon, allspice, and candied ginger in a large bowl.

**3. MIX** together the sugar, molasses, butter or margarine, and egg in a medium bowl until fully combined.

**4. ADD** the sugar mixture to the flour mixture and mix until fully combined. The dough will be quite stiff, so you may have to use your hands or a powerful mixer.

**5. ROLL** the dough into tablespoon-size balls. Place the cookies about 1" apart on the baking sheet. Use the bottom of a drinking glass or the palm of your hand to flatten the balls into $\frac{1}{4}$"-thick disks.

**6. BAKE** for about 15 minutes, or until browned and crisp.

**PER SERVING** (1 serving = 3 cookies)

| Calories | Total Fat | Saturated Fat | Sodium | Carbohydrate | Dietary Fiber | Protein | Calcium |
|----------|-----------|---------------|--------|--------------|---------------|---------|---------|
| 210 | 8 g | 3 g | 135 mg | 39 g | 3 g | 3 g | 6% |

# Strawberry Shortcake

**PREP TIME:** 15 MINUTES/ MAKES 4 SERVINGS

FOR A MORE ELEGANT PRESENTATION, CUT THE CAKE ROUNDS TO FIT INTO A BRANDY SNIFTER OR RED WINE GLASS. CANNED WHIPPED CREAM WORKS FINE, BUT WE PREFER THE FLAVOR OF FRESHLY MADE.

- 4 slices (2½" thick) angel food cake
- 1 pint strawberries, hulled and sliced
- ½ tablespoon balsamic vinegar
- 1 tablespoon sugar
- ¼ cup heavy cream
- ¼ teaspoon vanilla extract

**1. CUT** a round disk of cake from each slice using a drinking glass. Place each slice on a dessert plate or in a small bowl. Break the leftover scraps into small pieces.

**2. TOSS** the strawberries with the vinegar and ½ tablespoon of the sugar in a medium bowl. Set aside.

**3. COMBINE** the heavy cream, vanilla extract, and remaining ½ tablespoon sugar in a medium bowl. Whip with an electric mixer until soft peaks form.

**4. TOP** each cake disk with the strawberries and the broken cake pieces. Drizzle with the liquid from the strawberries. Top with the whipped cream.

## MAKE IT A MEAL

3 ounces grilled rib eye
**160 CALORIES**

Salad with 2 cups lettuce, 1 teaspoon olive oil, ½ teaspoon vinegar
**60 CALORIES**

# 380
**CALORIES PER MEAL**
★ ★

**PER SERVING** (1 serving = 1 disk, ½ cup berries, ¼ cup whipped cream)

| Calories | Total Fat | Saturated Fat | Sodium | Carbohydrate | Dietary Fiber | Protein | Calcium |
|---|---|---|---|---|---|---|---|
| 160 | 6 g | 4 g | 220 mg | 26 g | 2 g | 2 g | 6% |

# Molten Brownie Bites

**PREP TIME:** 5 MINUTES/ **COOK TIME:** 10 MINUTES/ MAKES 12 SERVINGS

*THE SURPRISE INGREDIENT, LOW-FAT MAYONNAISE, IMPARTS MOISTURE AND TEXTURE WHILE ADDING ONLY A LITTLE EXTRA FAT. IF YOU ACCIDENTALLY OVERBAKE THEM, YOU'LL STILL HAVE DELICIOUS SINGLE-SERVING BROWNIES.*

- 1 box (20 ounces) Ghirardelli Double or Triple Chocolate Brownie Mix
- 2 eggs
- 1 egg yolk
- ¼ cup low-fat mayonnaise
- ½ cup unsalted butter, melted

**1. PREHEAT** the oven to 400°F. Coat a 24-cup mini muffin (2") pan well with cooking spray, covering the insides of the cups and the top of the pan.

**2. PLACE** the brownie mix in a large bowl. Beat together the eggs, egg yolk, and mayonnaise in a small bowl with an electric mixer on high speed for 2 minutes. Add to the brownie mix, along with the butter.

**3. PLACE** the batter in the muffin pan, filling each cup to the top or to slightly extend above the top. Bake for 10 minutes, or until the top surface is just cooked and the inside is still soft.

**4. IMMEDIATELY** and gently remove the brownie bites from the pan using a tablespoon and serve.

## MAKE IT A MEAL

1 cup low-fat or fat-free milk
**100 CALORIES**

# 400
**CALORIES PER MEAL**

**PER SERVING** (1 serving = 2 brownie bites)

| Calories | Total Fat | Saturated Fat | Sodium | Carbohydrate | Dietary Fiber | Protein | Calcium |
|----------|-----------|---------------|--------|--------------|---------------|---------|---------|
| 300 | 15 g | 8 g | 220 mg | 38 g | 1 g | 3 g | 0% |

# Mini Mocha Pots de Crème

**PREP TIME:** 10 MINUTES + 4 HOURS REFRIGERATION/ **COOK TIME:** 1½ MINUTES/ MAKES 8 SERVINGS

WE TOOK OUR INSPIRATION FROM THE FRENCH, WHO ENJOY INDULGENT DESSERTS SERVED BEAUTIFULLY IN MODEST PORTIONS. THIS DESSERT CAN ALSO BE MADE WITH MILK, BUT IT WILL BE MUCH LESS CREAMY.

- 2 tablespoons sugar
- 2 tablespoons cocoa powder
- Pinch of salt
- 6 ounces bittersweet chocolate, chopped into small pieces (do not use unsweetened chocolate)
- ⅔ cup half-and-half
- ⅓ cup very strong espresso
- ½ teaspoon vanilla extract
- ¼ cup pasteurized egg or 1 egg, whisked
- 4 tablespoons whipped cream

**1. STIR** together the sugar, cocoa powder, and salt in a small bowl. Combine the sugar mixture, chocolate, half-and-half, espresso, and vanilla extract in a medium microwaveable bowl. Microwave for 1 minute. Whisk, microwave for 30 seconds longer, and whisk again. The chocolate should be completely melted, and the liquid should be very hot but not boiling. Pour into a blender. Blend, slowly adding the egg, for about 1 minute.

**2. POUR** about ⅓ cup into each of 8 champagne flutes, small dessert cups, or demitasse cups. Refrigerate for at least 4 hours.

**3. TOP** each serving with 1 tablespoon whipped cream.

**PER SERVING** (1 serving = ⅓ cup)

| Calories | Total Fat | Saturated Fat | Sodium | Carbohydrate | Dietary Fiber | Protein | Calcium |
|---|---|---|---|---|---|---|---|
| 180 | 15 g | 8 g | 40 mg | 16 g | 2 g | 3 g | 4% |

# Oatmeal Cranberry Chocolate Chip Cookies

**PREP TIME:** 15 MINUTES/ **COOK TIME:** 15 MINUTES/ MAKES 21 SERVINGS

THE COMBINATION OF OIL AND HONEY GIVES THESE COOKIES A MOIST AND CHEWY TEXTURE. MINI CHOCOLATE CHIPS SPREAD WELL THROUGHOUT THE DOUGH, SO EACH COOKIE HAS BURSTS OF CHOCOLATE.

| | |
|---|---|
| 1½ | cups old-fashioned oats |
| ½ | cup all-purpose flour |
| ½ | cup whole wheat flour |
| ½ | teaspoon baking soda |
| ½ | teaspoon salt |
| ½ | teaspoon ground nutmeg |
| ½ | cup packed brown sugar |
| ¼ | cup vegetable or canola oil |
| 2 | tablespoons honey |
| 1 | large egg |
| 1 | teaspoon vanilla extract |
| ¼ | cup dried cranberries |
| ¼ | cup mini chocolate chips |

**1. PREHEAT** the oven to 350°F. Coat a baking sheet with cooking spray.

**2. COMBINE** the oats, all-purpose flour, whole wheat flour, baking soda, salt, and nutmeg in a large bowl. Combine the sugar, oil, honey, egg, and vanilla extract in a medium bowl. Add to the oat mixture and combine until well blended. The dough will be firm and sticky. Fold in the dried cranberries and chocolate chips.

**3. DROP** teaspoonfuls of the dough onto the prepared baking sheet. Press down slightly with damp fingers. Bake for 15 minutes, or until lightly browned.

## MAKE IT A MEAL

Salad with 2 cups romaine lettuce, 1 medium tomato, 1 tablespoon pine nuts, 2 tablespoons grated Parmesan cheese, 1 small pear, 1 teaspoon olive oil, 1 tablespoon balsamic vinegar
**280 CALORIES**

# 390
**CALORIES
PER MEAL**
★ ★ ★

**PER SERVING** (1 serving = 2 cookies)

| Calories | Total Fat | Saturated Fat | Sodium | Carbohydrate | Dietary Fiber | Protein | Calcium |
|---|---|---|---|---|---|---|---|
| 110 | 4 g | 0.5 g | 90 mg | 18 g | 1 g | 2 g | 2% |

# Vanilla, Chocolate, and Lemon Cupcake Medley

**PREP TIME:** 15 MINUTES + 30 MINUTES COOLING TIME/ **COOK TIME:** 20 MINUTES/ MAKES 12 SERVINGS

COMBINE THE INGREDIENTS WITHOUT OVERMIXING, BECAUSE LOWER-FAT BATTERS PRODUCE SPONGY CAKES IF THEY'RE STIRRED TOO MUCH. WE TRIED A FEW DIFFERENT LOWER-CALORIE FROSTINGS WITHOUT SUCCESS. HERE, WHIPPING THE FROSTING MAKES IT SO EASY TO SPREAD THAT YOU USE LESS THAN A TABLESPOON PER CUPCAKE.

## MAKE IT A MEAL

Open-faced burger with ½ whole wheat hamburger bun, one 3-ounce (cooked weight) extra-lean burger patty, 2 tomato slices
**200 CALORIES**

# 420
**CALORIES PER MEAL**
★

| | |
|---|---|
| 1½ | cups all-purpose flour |
| ⅔ | cup sugar |
| 1 | teaspoon baking soda |
| ½ | teaspoon baking powder |
| 1 | cup low-fat vanilla yogurt |
| ¼ | cup low-fat milk |
| ¼ | cup butter, melted |
| 2 | large eggs |
| 1 | teaspoon vanilla extract |
| 1 | tablespoon grated lemon peel |
| 1 | teaspoon lemon extract |
| 4 | drops yellow food coloring |
| 2 | tablespoons hot cocoa mix (not diet) |
| ½ | cup canned frosting, any flavor |

1. **PREHEAT** the oven to 350°F. Place muffin liners in a 12-muffin pan.

2. **COMBINE** the flour, sugar, baking soda, and baking powder in a large bowl and mix well.

3. **WHISK** together the yogurt, milk, butter, eggs, and vanilla extract in a medium bowl. Add to the flour mixture and stir until just mixed. Avoid overmixing. Remove 1 cup batter, place it in a small bowl, and stir in the lemon peel, lemon extract, and food coloring. Remove another cup batter, place it in a small bowl, and stir in the cocoa mix. Place the batter in the muffin cups. Each batter flavor should fill 4 muffin cups.

4. **BAKE** for 20 minutes, or until a wooden pick inserted in the center of a cupcake comes out clean. Cool completely.

5. **PLACE** the frosting in a small bowl. Whip with an electric mixer until soft and fluffy. Frost the cupcakes.

**PER SERVING** (1 serving = 1 cupcake)

| Calories | Total Fat | Saturated Fat | Sodium | Carbohydrate | Dietary Fiber | Protein | Calcium |
|---|---|---|---|---|---|---|---|
| 220 | 7 g | 4 g | 180 mg | 36 g | 1 g | 4 g | 8% |

# Apple-Whatever Cobbler

**PREP TIME:** 10 MINUTES/ **COOK TIME:** 45 MINUTES/ MAKES 8 SERVINGS

THIS DESSERT GOT ITS NAME BECAUSE YOU CAN ADD WHATEVER FRUIT YOU LIKE TO PARTNER WITH THE APPLES, DEPENDING ON WHAT YOU HAVE ON HAND AND WHICH FRUITS ARE IN SEASON. VANILLA FROZEN YOGURT IS A PERFECT TOPPING.

## FILLING

- 2 pounds Golden Delicious, Mutsu, or other pie apples, cored and thinly sliced
- ½ cup dried cranberries or 1 cup fresh or frozen raspberries, cranberries, blueberries, or peach slices
- ½ cup water
- ¼ cup maple syrup
- 1 teaspoon cinnamon

## TOPPING

- 2 tablespoons all-purpose flour
- 2 tablespoons packed brown sugar
- 2 tablespoons butter
- 1 teaspoon cinnamon
- ¾ cup old-fashioned oats

2⅔ cups 100-calorie vanilla frozen yogurt

**1. PREHEAT** the oven to 350°F. Lightly coat a 13" x 9" baking dish with cooking spray.

**2. TO** make the filling: Place the apples and whatever fruit in the pan. Combine the water and syrup in a small bowl and pour over the apples. Sprinkle with the cinnamon.

**3. TO** make the topping: Combine the flour, brown sugar, butter, and cinnamon in a food processor or blender. Process or blend until crumbly. Add the oats and process or blend for just a few seconds longer. Pour evenly over the apples.

**4. COVER** the baking dish with foil and bake for 20 minutes. Remove the foil and bake for an additional 25 minutes, or until the apples are bubbly and the topping is browned.

**5. SERVE** topped with ⅓ cup frozen yogurt per serving.

## MAKE IT A MEAL

Large salad with 2 cups lettuce, 1 tomato, 2 ounces grilled chicken breast, 10 sprays salad dressing spray
**150 CALORIES**

# 400
**CALORIES PER MEAL**
★ ★ ★

**PER SERVING** (1 serving = 1 cup cobbler, ⅓ cup frozen yogurt)

| Calories | Total Fat | Saturated Fat | Sodium | Carbohydrate | Dietary Fiber | Protein | Calcium |
|----------|-----------|---------------|--------|--------------|---------------|---------|---------|
| 250 | 5.5 g | 3 g | 24 mg | 50 g | 4 g | 3 g | 9% |

# Granita di Caffe with Hazelnut-Ricotta Cream

**PREP TIME:** 10 MINUTES + 4 HOURS FREEZING TIME/ MAKES 4 SERVINGS

WE AVOIDED FAT-FREE RICOTTA CHEESE BECAUSE ITS TEXTURE IS TOO GRAINY FOR THIS DESSERT. IF YOUR BLENDER ISN'T STRONG ENOUGH TO CRUSH THE ESPRESSO CUBES, PUT THE ESPRESSO IN A SMALL METAL PAN AND PLACE IT IN THE FREEZER. BREAK UP THE ICE CRYSTALS WITH A FORK EVERY 30 MINUTES OR SO UNTIL THE MIXTURE RESEMBLES SHAVED ICE.

### MAKE IT A MEAL

2 biscotti
180 CALORIES

## 390
CALORIES
PER MEAL

- 1½ cups strong hot brewed espresso
- ¼ cup sugar
- ⅓ cup heavy cream
- ⅓ cup reduced-fat ricotta cheese
- 3 tablespoons Nutella

**1. TO** make the granita: Stir together the espresso and sugar until the sugar dissolves. Pour into ice cube trays and freeze until almost solid. Place the espresso cubes in a food processor or blender. Process or blend until slushy. Return to the freezer until ready to serve.

**2. TO** make the hazelnut-ricotta cream: Whip the heavy cream with an electric mixer until firm peaks form. Beat in the ricotta cheese and Nutella.

**3. TO** serve, layer the granita with the hazelnut cream in 4 dessert or tall parfait glasses.

**PER SERVING** (1 serving = 1 parfait)

| Calories | Total Fat | Saturated Fat | Sodium | Carbohydrate | Dietary Fiber | Protein | Calcium |
|----------|-----------|---------------|--------|--------------|---------------|---------|---------|
| 210 | 12 g | 9 g | 50 mg | 22 g | 1 g | 3 g | 8% |

# Cardamom Rice Pudding

**PREP TIME:** 5 MINUTES/ **COOK TIME:** 1 HOUR/ MAKES 4 SERVINGS

THIS INDIAN RICE PUDDING COMBINES LEFTOVER RICE WITH MILK, EGG, AND SEVERAL DIFFERENT FLAVORINGS. BECAUSE IT IS A HEARTY DESSERT, WE PAIRED IT WITH A LIGHT MEAL OF PAN-SEARED TILAPIA AND A SPINACH SALAD.

1⅓ cups cooked rice

2⅔ cups low-fat milk

1 egg, beaten

¼ cup sugar

3 tablespoons coarsely ground almonds

1 teaspoon vanilla extract

½ teaspoon ground cinnamon

½ teaspoon ground cardamom

**1. PREHEAT** the oven to 350°F. Coat a medium round ceramic dish with cooking spray.

**2. COMBINE** the rice, milk, egg, sugar, almonds, vanilla extract, cinnamon, and cardamom in a large bowl. Spread evenly in the prepared pan.

**3. BAKE** for 15 minutes. Stir to recombine. Repeat twice for a total cooking time of 45 minutes. Bake for an additional 10 to 15 minutes, or until the pudding reaches the desired consistency. Refrigerate.

## MAKE IT A MEAL

3 ounces pan-seared tilapia seasoned with any McCormick Perfect Pinch
**110 CALORIES**

Salad made with 1½ cups baby spinach, 10 sprays salad dressing spray
**30 CALORIES**

# 380
**CALORIES PER MEAL**
★ ★

**PER SERVING** (1 serving = ⅔ cup)

| Calories | Total Fat | Saturated Fat | Sodium | Carbohydrate | Dietary Fiber | Protein | Calcium |
|----------|-----------|---------------|--------|--------------|---------------|---------|---------|
| 240 | 5 g | 2 g | 90 mg | 37 g | 1 g | 10 g | 20% |

# Indulgent Tiramisu

**PREP TIME:** 20 MINUTES + 4 HOURS REFRIGERATION/ **COOK TIME:** 13 MINUTES/ MAKES 12 SERVINGS

THIS DESSERT TASTES SO GOOD THAT IT'S HARD TO BELIEVE THERE'S ROOM FOR A LIGHT MEAL WITHOUT TOPPING 400 CALORIES. DON'T BE PUT OFF BY THE BEATING OF THE EGG WHITES. THE RESULTING CREAMINESS ALLOWED US TO CUT WAY BACK ON HIGH-FAT INGREDIENTS.

- 3 large egg whites, at room temperature
- ⅔ cup sugar
- 3 tablespoons cold water
- ¼ teaspoon cream of tartar
- ½ cup mascarpone cheese
- ½ cup 2% Greek yogurt
- 4 ounces Neufchâtel cheese, at room temperature
- ½ teaspoon vanilla extract
- ¾ cup strong espresso
- 22 ladyfingers
- 1 teaspoon Hershey's Special Dark cocoa powder

**1. BRING** about 2" of water to a simmer in a medium pot or double boiler. Combine the egg whites, sugar, cold water, and cream of tartar in a medium heatproof bowl that will fit over the pot or in the top of the double boiler. Place the bowl over the pot or double boiler. Beat for 4 minutes using an electric mixer on low speed. Increase the speed to high and beat for 4 minutes longer, or until very thick. Remove the bowl from the pot or double boiler. Beat for another 4 minutes, or until the mixture is very light and fluffy.

**2. PLACE** the mascarpone, yogurt, Neufchâtel, and vanilla extract in a large bowl. Using the same beaters, beat until creamy. Add 1 cup of the egg-white mixture and beat until smooth. Gradually fold in the remaining egg-white mixture.

**3. POUR** the espresso into a shallow bowl. Dip 7 ladyfingers in the espresso and arrange at the bottom of a 2½-quart square baking dish. Top with one-third of the mascarpone mixture. Repeat twice, ending with a layer of mascarpone. Break the extra ladyfinger into pieces to fill in any holes in the top ladyfinger layer. Dust with the cocoa powder. Cover and refrigerate for at least 4 hours and up to 3 days before serving.

**PER SERVING** (1 serving = one 2½" x 4" square)

| Calories | Total Fat | Saturated Fat | Sodium | Carbohydrate | Dietary Fiber | Protein | Calcium |
|---|---|---|---|---|---|---|---|
| 230 | 12 g | 6 g | 100 mg | 25 g | 0 g | 8 g | 0% |

# Caramelized Pear Clafouti

**PREP TIME:** 10 MINUTES/ **COOK TIME:** 53 MINUTES/ MAKES 6 SERVINGS

THIS DESSERT SHOULD HAVE THE CONSISTENCY OF A SOFT, MOIST PANCAKE. CLAFOUTI, SOMETIMES SPELLED *CLAFOUTIS*, TRADITIONALLY IS MADE WITH CHERRIES.

## MAKE IT A MEAL

Sandwich with whole wheat English muffin, 2 ounces sliced turkey breast, 1 teaspoon honey mustard, 2 lettuce leaves, 2 tomato slices
**220 CALORIES**

# 420
**CALORIES PER MEAL**
★ ★

- 2 teaspoons unsalted butter
- 3 tablespoons packed brown sugar
- 1 can (15 ounces) pears canned with juice, drained and thinly sliced, or 2 cups pears, thinly sliced
- ¾ cup all-purpose flour
- 3 large eggs
- 1 cup low-fat milk
- 1 carton (6 ounces) low-fat vanilla yogurt (not light)
- 1 teaspoon almond extract

**1. PREHEAT** the oven to 350°F. Coat a large ovenproof skillet with cooking spray.

**2. HEAT** the skillet over medium heat. Add the butter and sugar and cook for 3 minutes, stirring constantly. Remove from the heat. Spread the butter-sugar mixture to distribute evenly on the bottom of the pan. Arrange the pear slices on top of the butter-sugar mixture.

**3. WHISK** together the flour, eggs, milk, yogurt, and almond extract until smooth. Pour over the pears.

**4. BAKE** for 45 to 50 minutes, or until light brown and puffy. A knife inserted in the center should come out clean.

**PER SERVING** (1 serving = 1 cup)

| Calories | Total Fat | Saturated Fat | Sodium | Carbohydrate | Dietary Fiber | Protein | Calcium |
|----------|-----------|---------------|--------|--------------|---------------|---------|---------|
| 200 | 5 g | 2 g | 75 mg | 32 g | 2 g | 8 g | 10% |

# Stuffed Baked Apples

**PREP TIME:** 10 MINUTES/ **COOK TIME:** 30 MINUTES/ MAKES 4 SERVINGS

THE COOKING LIQUID SWEETENS AND FLAVORS THE PLAIN YOGURT THAT WE CHOSE AS AN ACCOMPANIMENT. YOU MIGHT PREFER ICE CREAM OR FROZEN YOGURT INSTEAD.

- 4 medium Golden Delicious apples, about 6 ounces each
- ½ cup apple butter
- 2 tablespoons dried cranberries
- ¼ cup chopped walnuts
- ¼ cup chopped crystallized ginger
- 1 teaspoon ground cinnamon
- 1 can (11½ ounces) pear nectar

**1. PREHEAT** the oven to 350°F. Spray the inside of a 2- to 3-quart baking dish with cooking spray.

**2. CORE** the apples. Combine the apple butter, cranberries, walnuts, ginger, and cinnamon in a medium bowl. Pack into the cored center of each apple. Place the apples in the baking dish and add any remaining filling to the dish. Pour in the pear nectar. Cover and bake for 30 minutes, or until the apples reach the desired degree of doneness.

## MAKE IT A MEAL

6 ounces 2% fat plain Greek yogurt
130 CALORIES

# 410
CALORIES
PER MEAL
★ ★

**PER SERVING** (1 serving = 1 apple)

| Calories | Total Fat | Saturated Fat | Sodium | Carbohydrate | Dietary Fiber | Protein | Calcium |
|----------|-----------|---------------|--------|--------------|---------------|---------|---------|
| 280 | 5 g | 0.5 g | 10 mg | 61 g | 5 g | 2 g | 6% |

# Wine-Poached Ginger Pears

**PREP TIME:** 10 MINUTES + 8 HOURS CHILL TIME/ **COOK TIME:** 40 MINUTES/ MAKES 4 SERVINGS

THIS SURPRISINGLY SIMPLE DESSERT ALWAYS IMPRESSES FAMILY AND FRIENDS. IF YOU PREFER NOT TO USE WINE, SWITCH TO APPLE JUICE, PEAR NECTAR, OR, FOR BRIGHT RED COLOR, CRANBERRY OR POMEGRANATE JUICE.

- 4 ripe, firm medium-size pears
- 4 pieces (1" each) crystallized ginger
- 1 cup red wine
- 1 cup water
- 2 tablespoons honey
- 3 thin strips lemon peel
- ½ teaspoon ground cinnamon

**1. PEEL** the pears, leaving the stems intact. Use a corer or sharp knife to remove the bottom "flower" and about 1½" of the core. Place one piece of the ginger into each hollow.

**2. PLACE** the pears upright in a medium pot. Combine the wine, water, honey, lemon peel, and cinnamon in a medium bowl and pour over the pears. Cover the pot and place over medium-low heat. Simmer the pears for 20 minutes. Uncover the pot and gently lay the pears on their sides. Cover and simmer for 10 minutes. Uncover and gently turn each pear over to its other side. Simmer uncovered for 10 minutes.

**3. STAND** the pears upright in a medium glass bowl. Pour the wine syrup over the pears. Cover and refrigerate for several hours or overnight.

## MAKE IT A MEAL

4 ounces (raw weight) grilled tilapia
**110 CALORIES**

Small (4-ounce) baked potato with salt-free seasoning
**110 CALORIES**

# 420
**CALORIES PER MEAL**
★ ★ ★

**PER SERVING** (1 serving = 1 pear)

| Calories | Total Fat | Saturated Fat | Sodium | Carbohydrate | Dietary Fiber | Protein | Calcium |
|----------|-----------|---------------|--------|--------------|---------------|---------|---------|
| 200 | 0 g | 0 g | 5 mg | 41 g | 6 g | 1 g | 2% |

# Maple-Pecan Praline Pumpkin Pie

**PREP TIME:** 25 MINUTES + 3 HOURS CHILL TIME/ **COOK TIME:** 7 MINUTES FOR PRALINES + 55 MINUTES FOR PIE/ MAKES 12 SERVINGS

## MAPLE-PECAN PRALINES
- ½ cup packed brown sugar
- ¼ cup maple syrup
- 2 tablespoons evaporated milk
- 1 cup pecan pieces
- 1 teaspoon vanilla extract
- 1 tablespoon chilled unsalted butter, cut into pieces

## CRUST
- 1¼ cups all-purpose flour
- ½ teaspoon salt
- ⅓ cup very cold unsalted butter, cut into small pieces
- 1 teaspoon lemon juice
- ¼ cup ice water
- ¼ cup Maple-Pecan Pralines
- 1 pound dried kidney beans

## FILLING
- 3 eggs, at room temperature
- 1¾ cups canned pumpkin
- 1 cup low-fat evaporated milk
- 1 cup packed brown sugar
- 1 teaspoon ground cinnamon
- ½ teaspoon ground nutmeg
- ½ teaspoon ground ginger
- ¼ teaspoon ground allspice
- 1 cup Maple-Pecan Pralines

**1. TO** make the pralines: Combine the sugar, syrup, and milk in a small saucepan over medium heat. Bring to a boil and cook, stirring constantly, until the mixture reaches 242°F, about 5 to 7 minutes, at which stage it will almost form a hard ball. Remove from the heat and stir in the pecans, vanilla extract, and butter. Spread on a silicone sheet or parchment paper. When cool (about 10 minutes), crumble and place in an airtight resealable plastic container. This will make 2 cups of pralines. You'll use 1¼ cups for the pie.

**2. TO** make the crust: Place the flour and salt in the bowl of a food processor and pulse for 5 seconds. Add the butter and lemon juice and pulse 10 to 15 times, until the mixture resembles coarse sand. With the processor running, add the ice water 1 tablespoon at a time until the dough just begins to form. If needed, add more water 1 teaspoon at a time until dough forms. Place the dough in a medium bowl and shape gently into a ball. Flatten into a round disk. Cover with plastic wrap and refrigerate for 1 hour.

PUMPKIN PIE IS AMONG THE LOWEST-CALORIE PIES—IT HAS LESS SUGAR THAN MANY FRUIT PIES AND IS MADE WITHOUT A TOP CRUST. WE ADDED GOOD FATS WITH THE PRALINE TOPPING. THERE WILL BE LEFT-OVER PRALINES, WHICH YOU CAN ADD TO SALAD, YOGURT, OR CEREAL (ABOUT 50 CALORIES PER TABLE-SPOON). TO SAVE TIME AND HASSLE, YOU CAN MAKE THIS PIE WITH A PREPARED PIE CRUST.

**3. REMOVE** the dough from the refrigerator. On a lightly floured cutting board, carefully roll out the dough to a 12" circle. Gently transfer to a 9" pie pan and press to fit the pan, fluting the edges. Avoid overhandling the dough. Press the pralines into the bottom of the crust. Freeze the crust for at least 20 minutes.

**4. PREHEAT** the oven to 375°F. Cover the entire crust, including the edges, with a piece of foil. Place the beans on top of the foil. While you make the pie filling (see below), bake the crust for 7 to 10 minutes, remove from the oven, and carefully lift off the foil and beans. Discard the beans.

**5. TO MAKE** the filling: Mix together the eggs, pumpkin, milk, sugar, cinnamon, nutmeg, ginger, and allspice by hand or using a mixer until completely combined. Pour into the hot crust and bake for 40 to 45 minutes, or until the top is lightly browned and a knife inserted in the center comes out clean. Remove from the oven and top with the pralines while the pie is still hot. Let cool and refrigerate for 1 to 2 hours before serving.

## MAKE IT A MEAL

2 ounces roast turkey breast with 2 tablespoons turkey gravy
**95 CALORIES**

# 395
**CALORIES PER MEAL**
★

**PER SERVING** (1 serving = 1/12 pie)

| Calories | Total Fat | Saturated Fat | Sodium | Carbohydrate | Dietary Fiber | Protein | Calcium |
|----------|-----------|---------------|--------|--------------|---------------|---------|---------|
| 300 | 12 g | 5 g | 150 mg | 43 g | 2 g | 6 g | 10% |

# Chocolate Chocolate Cake

**PREP TIME:** 5 MINUTES/ **COOK TIME:** 25 MINUTES/ MAKES 16 SERVINGS

DARK COCOA POWDER ADDS EXTRA CHOCOLATE FLAVOR TO THIS MOIST CAKE. AVOID OVERMIXING THE BATTER—LOWER-FAT CAKES GET SPONGY IF THEY'RE STIRRED TOO MUCH.

- 1¼ cups all-purpose flour
- ¾ cup sugar
- ¼ cup unsweetened dark cocoa powder
- 1 teaspoon baking powder
- 1 teaspoon baking soda
- 1 cup buttermilk
- ¼ cup melted butter
- 2 large eggs
- 1 teaspoon vanilla extract
- ½ cup mini chocolate chips
- 1 tablespoon confectioners' sugar (optional)

**1. PREHEAT** the oven to 350°F. Coat a 9" x 9" baking pan with cooking spray.

**2. COMBINE** the flour, sugar, cocoa, baking powder, and baking soda in a large bowl. Whisk together the buttermilk, butter, eggs, and vanilla extract in a medium bowl. Add to the flour mixture and stir to combine thoroughly without overmixing. Fold in the chocolate chips. Pour into the prepared pan.

**3. BAKE** for 25 minutes, or until a wooden pick inserted in the center comes out clean. Cool in the pan on a rack. When cool, dust the top with the confectioners' sugar, if using.

**PER SERVING** (1 serving = one 2¼" x 2¼" square)

| Calories | Total Fat | Saturated Fat | Sodium | Carbohydrate | Dietary Fiber | Protein | Calcium |
|----------|-----------|---------------|--------|--------------|---------------|---------|---------|
| 140 | 6 g | 3 g | 135 mg | 22 g | 1 g | 3 g | 4% |

# Frozen Yogurt Pie

**PREP TIME:** 5 MINUTES + AT LEAST 3 HOURS FREEZING TIME/ **COOK TIME:** 10 MINUTES/ MAKES 8 SERVINGS

THIS PIE BRINGS BACK MEMORIES OF THE '70S, WHEN FROZEN YOGURT FIRST BECAME POPULAR. WE TRIED TO MAKE THIS RECIPE USING WHIPPING CREAM INSTEAD OF THE COOL WHIP THAT THE ORIGINAL RECIPES CALL FOR, BUT THE PIE TURNED OUT TOO ICY.

| | |
|---|---|
| 20 | graham cracker squares, ground into crumbs (1 cup) |
| 3 | tablespoons unsalted butter, melted |
| 2 | cartons (6 ounces each) blended raspberry yogurt or any other flavor of blended or smooth yogurt |
| 2 | cups Cool Whip Lite whipped topping |
| 2 | cups frozen raspberries, thawed |

**1. PREHEAT** the oven to 350°F.

**2. RESERVE** 1 tablespoon of the graham cracker crumbs for the top of the pie. In an 8" pie pan, combine the butter and remaining crumbs. Pat firmly into the pan. Bake for 10 minutes. Cool completely.

**3. GENTLY** fold the yogurt into the whipped topping. Spoon into the pie pan. Cover and freeze until firm, at least 3 hours.

**4. REMOVE** the pie from the freezer 30 minutes before serving. Top with the raspberries before cutting.

## MAKE IT A MEAL

Boca burger on ½ whole wheat bun, 2 leaves lettuce, 2 slices tomato, 1 tablespoon ketchup
**195 CALORIES**

# 405

**CALORIES PER MEAL**

★ ★

**PER SERVING** (1 serving = ⅛ pie)

| Calories | Total Fat | Saturated Fat | Sodium | Carbohydrate | Dietary Fiber | Protein | Calcium |
|---|---|---|---|---|---|---|---|
| 210 | 9 g | 5 g | 125 mg | 32 g | 2 g | 3 g | 6% |

# Conclusion
# LIVE THE 400-CALORIE LIFE

ALTHOUGH EXPERTS CONTINUE TO DEBATE the causes of our tremendous collective weight gain over the past 30 years, the role of food—too much of it—is pretty clear. Sure, activity (and lack thereof) plays its part, but the perfect storm of big and bigger portions, family-size packages, oversize plates and bowls, and size-as-value in fast-food fare has created an environment in which it is plain hard work to stay lean.

Here's the good news: The 400 Calorie Fix was created to show you that weight gain does not have to be your destiny. The latest scientific studies say that controlling calories is in fact the smartest way to achieve a healthy weight and a healthy body. And the 400 Calorie Fix teaches you how to control calories by regulating the amount you eat in a way that is sensible, satisfying, and delicious. Better yet, we count the calories for you!

The 400 Calorie Fix gives you an important gift—the tools and fixes to help you see your meals through a 400 Calorie Lens—for life.

## THE TOOLS

In order to fix something, you need a tool kit. Of course, depending on the job, you might choose to use all the tools in the kit, or just one or two favorites. The same holds true for fixing your weight. That's why the 400 Calorie Fix provides you with a well-stocked tool kit; you decide which tools are best for you. Each on its own puts you on the path to healthier eating the 400-calorie way. All together, they're a powerful resource for taking charge of your eating, your weight, and your health. As you go out into the world armed with your new knowledge, I want to encourage you to use the tools that best fit your goals and your personality. Here's a recap:

❖ **Four hundred 400-calorie meals**—a carefully chosen selection of 250 prepared foods, takeout, casual dining, and quick-fix meals, plus 150 recipe meals, each with approximately 400 calories.

❖ **400 Calorie Lens**—visual tricks and shortcuts for selecting foods that add up to 400 calories, wherever you eat.

❖ **2 Week Quick Slim**—a 14-day jump-start with three 400-calorie meals each day.

❖ **400 Calorie Menus**—2-day meal plans for seven different lifestyles, eating challenges, and health concerns: From-the-Freezer, On-the-Run, Dining-Out, Family-Friendly, Vegetarian, Diabetes-Friendly, and Heart-Healthy.

❖ **4 Star Nutrition System**—your guide to nutritional balance, with meals starred based on their protein, fiber, good fats, and fruits and vegetables content.

# THE FIXES

### THE BIG FIX EAT 400-CALORIE MEALS.

Remember that 400 calories per meal is our chosen number. It's big enough for plenty of food and variety. It's small enough to help you lose weight. And 400-calorie meals are filling, especially when packed with hunger-quelling foods like fruits and vegetables, protein-rich options, choices that are high in fiber, and nuts and other healthy fats.

### MINI FIX #1 EAT THE RIGHT NUMBER OF MEALS.

You've had the opportunity to try out your chosen number of daily meals, based on your gender, level of physical activity, and weight-loss goals. Now is a good time to determine whether you're at the correct level. If you are losing up to 2 pounds each week and are not yet at your goal weight—or if you're holding steady at your goal weight—stick with your current meal pattern. If your weight loss is continuing at a faster clip, especially after the first couple of weeks, when weight loss tends to be fastest, consider adding one more daily meal. And if you're gaining weight, you may need to cut out one meal. Whatever you choose, don't go below three meals, or 1,200 calories, a day; eating too few calories can cause your metabolism to slow, plus it's virtually impossible to meet your body's nutrition needs at that level. Also, before you cut out a

meal, be sure to double-check your portion sizes just in case you're dishing up more food than you think.

### MINI FIX #2 SPACE MEALS EVENLY THROUGHOUT THE DAY.

Do what you can to eat every 4 to 5 hours. You'll find that you're hungry by mealtime but not so hungry that it's hard to control your eating and food decisions.

### MINI FIX #3 REMAIN VIGILANT ABOUT PORTION SIZES.

It's important to keep up your portion training in order to stay sharp and on top of your game. So use at least one of the 400-calorie tools every week or so to double-check whether your eyes are still seeing foods through the 400 Calorie Lens. You might be surprised. Several of our test panelists, seasoned dieters all, initially resisted going back to measuring portions during the 2 Week Quick Slim. Imagine their shock upon learning that over time, their eyes had up-sized portions and that they were eating way more than they thought.

### MINI FIX #4 SEEK NUTRITION.

Your body needs both the right number of calories and the right nutrition, and the 4 Star Nutrition System is an easy-to-use guide for making sure that your daily diet provides important nutrients—vitamins and minerals from fruits and vegetables, plus fiber, protein, and good fats. We recommend four different stars—one from each category—as the minimum; more stars mean more nutrition in your day. Remember to check calcium information to find meals that are highest in this important mineral and strive for a total of at least 100 percent as often as possible.

## MINI FIX #5 WEIGH YOURSELF.

Weighing yourself at a regular interval—whether it's daily, a few days a week, or once a week—helps you see how well you're doing. Getting on that scale really does work. Participants in the National Weight Control Registry, a database of more than 5,000 individuals who lost 30 pounds or more and kept it off for at least a year, say that they weigh themselves frequently.[1] This enables them to spot any weight gain right when it begins and make necessary adjustments to their diets before things get out of control. Keep track of your weight in a journal (like our 400 Calorie Fix Tracker), or use *Prevention*'s online Health Tracker at www.prevention.com/healthtracker, so you can follow your progress.

## MINI FIX #6 KEEP A FOOD JOURNAL.

Write down what you eat at least once per week, either in your journal or online. We're not asking you to count calories, unless of course you want to. But the process of writing down your food intake keeps you accountable and might help stop you in your tracks before you veer too far off course. People who monitor themselves by keeping a food journal, along with other measures like weighing themselves regularly, have an easier time managing their weight.[2-4] In a study conducted at the University of Pennsylvania, 49 participants who kept a daily food log and attended group meetings in addition to taking a weight-loss medication lost 27 pounds over the course of a year, while 45 participants on medication alone lost just 11 pounds.[5]

## MINI FIX #7 GET MOVING.

The 400 Calorie Fix is about food. But we recognize just how important it is (for our health, our energy, and our sleep) to get plenty of physical activity. Plus, I know that when I exercise, I feel healthier and more confident and I'm more motivated to eat the 400-calorie way.

The 400 Calorie Fix has changed my relationship with food. My number-one goal is to eat healthy, balanced 400-calorie meals every day. At the same time, I now know that nothing is off-limits, as long as I use my 400-calorie tools to guide me to the right portion sizes. You too can take charge of your eating, one 400-calorie meal at a time, and feel confident in your ability to choose foods and meals that will control your weight and improve your health.

# A

# 400 Calorie
# MENUS

WE ALL HAVE DIFFERENT LIFESTYLES AND NEEDS. Maybe you leave the house too early in the morning for breakfast, or your job requires a lot of travel. Maybe you don't have time to cook and your closest friends never met a takeout menu that they didn't love. Or maybe you prefer to avoid eating meat. That's why we created the 400 Calorie Menus. It's impossible for one eating plan to meet everyone's needs.

As I travel around the country visiting with readers, I ask them what they want from a diet or eating plan. Time and time again, they request meal ideas and menus that will fit their busy lifestyles—meals to eat on the go, restaurant picks, fast-food choices, and packaged foods from the supermarket. We could have done a whole book with just the sample menus you requested, but then we wouldn't have the space to give you 400 different meals to choose from! Instead, we limited ourselves to seven different types of menus—From-the-Freezer, On-the-Run, Dining-Out, Family-Friendly, Vegetarian, Diabetes-Friendly, and Heart-Healthy—based on the meals in the rest of this book.

❖ From-the-Freezer shows you how to put together meals from make-ahead and freezer-friendly fare. We suggest setting aside a little bit of time on the weekend or in the evening—when you're not running to meetings, social events, and activities—to cook a few meals, pack them in portions into resealable containers or bags, label them, and put them in the freezer. It's like having your own line of frozen meals.

❖ On-the-Run combines convenience foods with foods and dishes that are really easy to prepare. This menu is, of course, ideal if you don't have time to cook, but also is perfect for long days and late nights at the office, where often the only piece of cooking equipment is a microwave.

❖ Dining-Out pulls together a selection of meals from takeout and sit-down restaurants. We included foods from a couple of national chains, as well as dishes that are pretty easy to order in a deli or coffee shop. This is great for frequent travelers, as well as social butterflies, people who need to entertain for business, and folks who hate to cook.

❖ Family-Friendly does more than just keep the kids happy: It also includes dishes that are easy to double or even triple if you're feeding a crowd. They don't take long to make or contain a lot of expensive ingredients, and they come together quickly should hungry surprise guests show up for dinner. Mindy also made sure to design them with plenty of calcium to meet the needs of both growing kids and healthy moms and dads.

✤ **Vegetarian** showcases just a few of the many tasty lacto-ovo-vegetarian meals that we developed or discovered in putting together this book.

✤ **Diabetes-Friendly** includes meals that have a lot of fiber and also are not excessively high in carbohydrates, a combination that helps keep blood sugar levels steady. Not just for people with diabetes, these menus deliver about twice the recommended amount of fiber for a 1,600-calorie meal plan. Because people with diabetes can eat sugar as long as they count it toward their total carbs for the meal or day, we didn't select sugar-free foods for our meals. Instead, we pulled together a few of our lower-sugar selections.

✤ **Heart-Healthy** addresses one of today's major nutrition hot buttons—the excess amounts of sodium in the average American's diet and the higher blood pressure that often results. The sample menus also include oats, beans, and good fats, all of which are part of heart-healthy eating for everyone, not just people at risk for heart disease.

You'll also see that all of our menus follow the 4 Star Nutrition System that we described in Chapter 3. We've mixed and matched so that each menu includes each of the four stars at least once. In Chapters 6 through 14, you can find full nutritional information on each meal.

As we mentioned, you don't need to follow any of these menus to reap the benefits of the 400 Calorie Fix. For each of our seven plans, we've created a 2-day sample just to give you an idea of how all the different 400-calorie tools work together. After you feel comfortable, feel free to create your own menus to fit your lifestyle. Maybe a hybrid of these plans works best for you (it does for me), so experiment away and be inspired to create your own themes!

**STAR SYSTEM**
★ PROTEIN
★ FIBER
★ GOOD FATS

# From-the-Freezer Menu

## DAY 1

### BANANA WALNUT BREAD
(page 209)                          calories

★ ★

| | |
|---|---|
| Banana Walnut Bread, one ¾"-thick slice | 230 |
| Light cream cheese, 1 Tbsp | 40 |
| Fruit salad, ½ cup | 50 |
| Latte made with ¾ cup low-fat milk | 80 |
| **Total = 400** | |

### CREAMY VEGETABLE SOUP
(page 232)                          calories

★ ★ ★

| | |
|---|---|
| Creamy Vegetable Soup, 2 cups | 170 |
| Toasted whole wheat English muffin, 1 | 130 |
| So Delicious or other 80–100-calorie ice cream sandwich | 90 |
| **Total = 390** | |

### NORTH AFRICAN TURKEY MEATBALLS WITH CARAMELIZED ONIONS
(page 305)                          calories

★ ★ ★

| | |
|---|---|
| North African Turkey Meatballs with Caramelized Onions, 6 meatballs | 310 |
| Brown rice, ½ cup cooked | 110 |
| **Total = 420** | |

### MANY WAYS GRANOLA
(page 206)                          calories

★ ★ ★

| | |
|---|---|
| Many Ways Granola, ½ cup | 200 |
| 1% cottage cheese, ½ cup | 80 |
| Walnut halves, 2 Tbsp | 80 |
| Chopped apple, ½ medium | 50 |
| **Total = 410** | |

## DAY 2

### PEANUT BUTTER BREAKFAST SHAKE
(page 229)                          calories

★

| | |
|---|---|
| Peanut Butter Breakfast Shake, 1 | 290 |
| Pepperidge Farm Brown Sugar Cinnamon Mini Bagel, 1 | 120 |
| **Total = 410** | |

### CHICKEN AND SAUSAGE GUMBO
(page 244)                          calories

★ ★

| | |
|---|---|
| Chicken and Sausage Gumbo, 2 cups | 380 |
| **Total = 380** | |

### OLD-FASHIONED BEEF STEW
(page 248)                          calories

★ ★

| | |
|---|---|
| Old-Fashioned Beef Stew, 2 cups | 410 |
| **Total = 410** | |

### CASCADIAN FARM FRUIT & NUT GRANOLA
(page 81)                          calories

★ ★ ★

| | |
|---|---|
| Cascadian Farm Fruit & Nut Granola, ½ cup | 140 |
| Stonyfield Farm Fat Free Plain Yogurt, 6 oz | 80 |
| Blueberries, 1 cup | 80 |
| Walnut halves, 2 Tbsp | 80 |
| **Total = 380** | |

# On-the-Run Menu

## DAY 1

### BREAKFAST TRAIL MIX
(page 164)                    calories

★ ★

| | |
|---|---:|
| Barbara's Bakery Puffins, Cinnamon, ⅔ cup | 100 |
| Peanuts, 1 Tbsp | 50 |
| Slivered almonds, 1 Tbsp | 40 |
| Dried cranberries, 2 Tbsp | 50 |
| Raisins, 2 Tbsp | 50 |
| Steamed low-fat milk with sugar-free vanilla syrup, 1 cup | 100 |
| **Total = 390** | |

### SPINACH SALAD
(page 176)                    calories

★ ★

| | |
|---|---:|
| Spinach, 2 cups | 15 |
| Light tuna, ¼ cup | 50 |
| Hard-cooked egg, 1 | 80 |
| Crumbled blue cheese, 2 Tbsp | 60 |
| Salad dressing spray, 10 sprays | 10 |
| Whole wheat English muffin, 1 | 130 |
| Sweet iced tea, 1 cup | 60 |
| **Total = 405** | |

### 90% LEAN BURGER
(page 185)                    calories

★

| | |
|---|---:|
| 90% lean cooked hamburger, one 3-oz patty | 180 |
| Hamburger bun, 1 | 120 |
| Lettuce, 1 leaf | 5 |
| Tomato, 1 medium slice | 5 |
| Ketchup, 1 Tbsp | 20 |
| Pickle slices, 2 | 0 |
| Potato salad, ¼ cup | 80 |
| **Total = 410** | |

### PUDDING PARFAIT
(page 197)                    calories

★ ★ ★

| | |
|---|---:|
| Instant vanilla sugar-free pudding made with ½ cup low-fat milk | 80 |
| Frozen berries, 1 cup | 60 |
| Low-fat granola, ⅓ cup | 130 |
| Chopped walnuts, 2 Tbsp | 100 |
| Cool Whip Lite, 2 Tbsp | 20 |
| **Total = 390** | |

## DAY 2

### WHOLE GRAIN TOAST
(page 167)                    calories

★ ★ ★

| | |
|---|---:|
| Pepperidge Farm Whole Grain Double Fiber Bread, 2 slices | 200 |
| The Laughing Cow Mini Babybel Light, 2 rounds | 100 |
| Fruit salad, 1 cup | 100 |
| **Total = 400** | |

### GRILLED CHICKEN AND PESTO SANDWICH
(page 180)                    calories

★ ★ ★

| | |
|---|---:|
| Whole grain bread, 2 slices | 140 |
| Grilled chicken breast, 3 oz | 140 |
| Pesto, 1 Tbsp | 80 |
| Tomato slices, 2 | 10 |
| Broccoli florets, 1 cup | 20 |
| Fat-free ranch dressing, 1 Tbsp | 20 |
| **Total = 410** | |

### GORTON'S CLASSIC GRILLED SALMON
(page 102)                    calories

★ ★ ★

| | |
|---|---:|
| Gorton's Classic Grilled Salmon, 1 fillet | 100 |
| Uncle Ben's Ready Rice Whole Grain Brown, ½ cup | 110 |
| Green Giant Broccoli & Carrots (Family Size bag), 1 cup cooked (2½ cups frozen) | 80 |
| Nabisco Ginger Snaps, 4 cookies | 120 |
| **Total = 410** | |

### PITA CHIPS
(page 188)                    calories

★ ★

| | |
|---|---:|
| Whole wheat pita chips, 12 | 140 |
| Hummus, ¼ cup | 100 |
| Olives, 10 | 100 |
| Baby carrots, 10 | 40 |
| **Total = 380** | |

# Dining-Out Menu

## DAY 1

### STARBUCKS APPLE BRAN MUFFIN
(page 112)                               calories

★

| | |
|---|---|
| Starbucks Apple Bran Muffin, 1 | 310 |
| Starbucks Skinny Caramel Latte, tall (12 oz) | 90 |
| **Total = 400** | |

### APPLEBEE'S GARLIC HERB CHICKEN FAJITA
(page 143)                               calories

★ ★

| | |
|---|---|
| Grilled chicken breast, 3 oz | 110 |
| Grilled peppers and onions, ½ cup | 90 |
| Salsa, 2 Tbsp | 10 |
| Guacamole, 2 Tbsp | 40 |
| Flour tortilla, one 7½" | 140 |
| **Total = 390** | |

### CHILI'S GUILTLESS CEDAR PLANK TILAPIA
(page 140)                               calories

★

| | |
|---|---|
| Chili's Guiltless Cedar Plank Tilapia, 1 | 200 |
| Chili's rice, 1 cup | 190 |
| **Total = 390** | |

### JAMBA JUICE MEGA MANGO
(page 127)                               calories

★ ★

| | |
|---|---|
| Jamba Juice Mega Mango, 16 oz | 230 |
| Jamba Juice Omega-3 Chocolate Brownie Cookie, 1 | 150 |
| **Total = 380** | |

## DAY 2

### DUNKIN' DONUTS EGG WHITE TURKEY SAUSAGE FLATBREAD SANDWICH
(page 112)                               calories

★ ★

| | |
|---|---|
| Dunkin' Donuts Egg White Turkey Sausage Flatbread Sandwich, 1 | 280 |
| Orange juice, 1 cup | 110 |
| **Total = 390** | |

### WENDY'S CHILI
(page 115)                               calories

★ ★

| | |
|---|---|
| Wendy's Chili, large, 1 | 280 |
| Wendy's Saltine Crackers, 1 package | 30 |
| Wendy's Shredded Cheddar Cheese, 2 Tbsp | 70 |
| **Total = 380** | |

### RED ROBIN GRILLED SALMON BURGER
(page 144)                               calories

★ ★

| | |
|---|---|
| Red Robin Grilled Salmon patty with lettuce, balsamic and marinated tomato, onion, fajita veggies, avocado, 1 | 400 |
| **Total = 400** | |

### HEALTHY CHOICE ICE CREAM SANDWICH
(page 106)                               calories

★ ★ ★

| | |
|---|---|
| Healthy Choice Ice Cream Sandwich, 1 | 130 |
| Fruit salad, 1 cup | 100 |
| Cascadian Farm Fruit and Nut Granola, ½ cup | 140 |
| Chopped pistachios, 1 Tbsp | 40 |
| **Total = 410** | |

# Family-Friendly Menu

## DAY 1

### CHEERIOS
(page 82)                                    calories

★ ★

| | |
|---|---|
| Cheerios, 1½ cups | 150 |
| Sliced almonds, 4 Tbsp | 130 |
| Low-fat or fat-free milk, 1 cup | 100 |
| **Total = 380** | |

### DOUBLE A BUTTER PANINI
(page 273)                                   calories

★ ★

| | |
|---|---|
| Double A Butter Panini, 1 | 310 |
| Low-fat milk, 1 cup | 100 |
| **Total = 410** | |

### TACO SALAD
(page 145)                                   calories

★ ★ ★

| | |
|---|---|
| Shredded lettuce, 2 cups | 10 |
| Chopped tomato, ¼ cup | 10 |
| Ground beef, ¼ cup cooked | 60 |
| Refried beans, ¼ cup | 50 |
| Guacamole, 2 Tbsp | 60 |
| Grated cheese, 2 Tbsp | 60 |
| Salsa, 2 Tbsp | 10 |
| Tortilla chips, 10 chips (1 oz) | 140 |
| **Total = 400** | |

### POUND CAKE
(page 197)                                   calories

★ ★

| | |
|---|---|
| Pound cake, one 2-oz slice | 220 |
| Raspberries, 1 cup | 60 |
| Fresh whipped cream, ¼ cup | 100 |
| **Total = 380** | |

## DAY 2

### APPLE PUDDING PANCAKE
(page 218)                                   calories

★

| | |
|---|---|
| Apple Pudding Pancake, ¼ of one 10–12"-diameter pancake | 300 |
| Honey, 1 teaspoon | 20 |
| Chobani 1% Plain Greek Yogurt, ½ of 6-ounce container | 70 |
| **Total = 390** | |

### HEALTHY CHOICE MINESTRONE SOUP
(page 91)                                    calories

★ ★

| | |
|---|---|
| Healthy Choice Minestrone Soup, 1 cup | 200 |
| Arnold Select Multi-Grain Sandwich Thins, 1 roll | 100 |
| The Laughing Cow Mini Babybel Light, 1 round | 50 |
| Seedless grapes, ½ cup | 60 |
| **Total = 410** | |

### GREEK CHICKEN WITH VEGETABLES AND POTATOES
(page 298)                                   calories

★ ★ ★ ★

| | |
|---|---|
| Greek Chicken with ¼ of the Vegetables and Potatoes, 1 chicken breast | 350 |
| Angel food cake, 1 slice | 70 |
| **Total = 420** | |

### VANILLA WAFERS
(page 194)                                   calories

★

| | |
|---|---|
| Vanilla wafers, 8 | 130 |
| Nutella, 1 Tbsp | 100 |
| Banana, ½ medium | 50 |
| Low-fat or fat-free milk, 1 cup | 100 |
| **Total = 380** | |

# Vegetarian Menu

## DAY 1

### AMY'S ORGANIC TOFU SCRAMBLE
(page 85)                    calories

★ ★

| | |
|---|---|
| Amy's Organic Tofu Scramble, 1 | 320 |
| Grapefruit juice, 1 cup | 90 |
| **Total = 410** | |

### BURGER KING BK VEGGIE BURGER
(page 115)                    calories

★ ★

| | |
|---|---|
| Burger King BK Veggie Burger (no mayo), 1 | 340 |
| American cheese, 1 slice | 45 |
| **Total = 385** | |

### ASIAN-STYLE SOUP
(page 172)                    calories

★ ★ ★

| | |
|---|---|
| Low-sodium chicken or vegetable broth, or miso soup, 1 cup | 40 |
| Baby spinach, 1 cup | 10 |
| Silken tofu, 3 oz (about ¼ box) | 50 |
| Soba noodles, 2 oz | 190 |
| Low-fat frozen yogurt, ½ cup | 110 |
| **Total = 400** | |

### CASCADIAN FARM FRUIT & NUT GRANOLA
(page 81)                    calories

★ ★ ★

| | |
|---|---|
| Cascadian Farm Fruit & Nut Granola, ½ cup | 140 |
| Stonyfield Farm Fat Free Plain Yogurt, 6 oz | 80 |
| Blueberries, 1 cup | 80 |
| Walnut halves, 2 Tbsp | 80 |
| **Total = 380** | |

## DAY 2

### TOASTED BARLEY-ALMOND CEREAL WITH ROASTED FRUIT
(page 207)                    calories

★ ★

| | |
|---|---|
| Toasted Barley-Almond Cereal with Roasted Fruit, 1 cup | 300 |
| Low-fat or fat-free milk, 1 cup | 100 |
| **Total = 400** | |

### TOFU RICE BOWL
(page 186)                    calories

★

| | |
|---|---|
| Leftover brown rice, ⅔ cup | 150 |
| Extra-firm tofu, 4 oz | 100 |
| Thai-style frozen vegetables, ¾ cup | 30 |
| Mrs. Dash Spicy Teriyaki 10-Minute Marinade, 1 Tbsp | 25 |
| Fat-free chocolate pudding snack, 1 pudding cup | 90 |
| **Total = 395** | |

### VEGETARIAN PAELLA
(page 364)                    calories

★ ★

| | |
|---|---|
| Vegetarian Paella, 1¾ cups | 290 |
| So Delicous or other 80–100-calorie ice cream sandwich | 90 |
| **Total = 380** | |

### ENGLISH MUFFIN WITH NUT BUTTER
(page 168)                    calories

★ ★ ★

| | |
|---|---|
| Toasted whole wheat English muffin, 1 | 130 |
| Peanut or almond butter, 4 tsp | 130 |
| Sliced banana, ½ medium | 50 |
| Low-fat or fat-free milk, 1 cup | 100 |
| **Total = 410** | |

# Diabetes-Friendly Menu

## DAY 1

### KASHI GOLEAN CEREAL

(page 81)                                    calories

★ ★ ★

| | |
|---|---|
| Kashi GOLEAN cereal, 1 cup | 140 |
| Blueberries, 1 cup | 80 |
| Low-fat or fat-free milk, 1 cup | 100 |
| Hard-boiled egg, 1 | 70 |
| **Total = 390** | |

### RUBY TUESDAY WHITE BEAN CHICKEN CHILI

(page 139)                                   calories

★ ★ ★

| | |
|---|---|
| Ruby Tuesday White Bean Chicken Chili, 1 | 320 |
| Ruby Tuesday Fresh Steamed Broccoli, 1 | 90 |
| **Total = 410** | |

### SMOKED TURKEY, BLACK BEAN, AND EDAMAME SALAD

(page 267)                                   calories

★ ★ ★ ★

| | |
|---|---|
| Smoked Turkey, Black Bean, and Edamame Salad, 2 cups | 390 |
| **Total = 390** | |

### SNYDER'S OF HANOVER HONEY WHEAT STICKS

(page 109)                                   calories

★ ★

| | |
|---|---|
| Snyder's of Hanover Honey Wheat Sticks, 1 oz | 120 |
| Kraft String-Ums String Cheese, 2 sticks | 160 |
| Baby carrots, 10 | 40 |
| Apple, 1 medium | 100 |
| **Total = 420** | |

## DAY 2

### CHEERIOS

(page 82)                                    calories

★ ★

| | |
|---|---|
| Cheerios, 1½ cups | 150 |
| Sliced almonds, 4 Tbsp | 130 |
| Low-fat or fat-free milk, 1 cup | 100 |
| **Total = 380** | |

### ASIAN CHICKEN SALAD

(page 176)                                   calories

★ ★ ★ ★

| | |
|---|---|
| Field greens, 2 cups | 20 |
| Cooked chicken breast strips, ½ cup | 120 |
| Sunflower seeds, 2 Tbsp | 90 |
| Shelled edamame, ¼ cup | 50 |
| Sliced water chestnuts, ¼ cup | 30 |
| Newman's Own Asian Sesame Natural Salad Mist, 10 sprays | 10 |
| Rice crackers, 6 | 110 |
| **Total = 430** | |

### HEALTHY CHOICE FRESH MIXERS ZITI & MEAT SAUCE

(page 98)                                    calories

★ ★

| | |
|---|---|
| Healthy Choice Fresh Mixers Ziti & Meat Sauce, 1 | 340 |
| Large salad with 2 cups lettuce, 1 tomato, salad dressing spray | 60 |
| **Total = 400** | |

### PANDA EXPRESS CHICKEN POT STICKERS

(page 127)                                   calories

★

| | |
|---|---|
| Panda Express Chicken Potstickers, 3 pieces | 220 |
| Panda Express Veggie Spring Rolls, 2 | 160 |
| Panda Express fortune cookie, 1 | 30 |
| **Total = 410** | |

# Heart-Healthy Menu

## DAY 1

### STARBUCKS PERFECT OATMEAL
(page 112)                    calories

★

| | |
|---|---|
| Starbucks Perfect Oatmeal, 1 bowl | 140 |
| Starbucks Nut Medley, 1 packet | 100 |
| Starbucks Brown Sugar, 1 packet | 50 |
| Starbucks Skinny Latte, tall (12 oz) | 100 |
| **Total = 390** | |

### AMY'S MEXICAN CASSEROLE
(page 95)                    calories

★ ★

| | |
|---|---|
| Amy's Mexican Casserole (light in sodium), 1 | 370 |
| Low-sodium V8 juice, 1 cup | 50 |
| **Total = 420** | |

### THAI-INSPIRED CHICKEN LETTUCE WRAPS
(page 306)                    calories

★ ★ ★

| | |
|---|---|
| Thai-Inspired Chicken Lettuce Wraps, 2 | 280 |
| Brown rice, ½ cup | 110 |
| **Total = 390** | |

### RAISIN BRAN MUFFIN
(page 170)                    calories

★ ★

| | |
|---|---|
| Raisin bran muffin, 2 oz | 150 |
| All-fruit strawberry jam, 2 tsp | 20 |
| Plain low-fat yogurt, ¾ cup | 120 |
| Wheat germ, 1 Tbsp | 30 |
| Mixed berries, 1 cup | 100 |
| **Total = 420** | |

## DAY 2

### ALL-IN-ONE SMOOTHIE
(page 171)                    calories

★ ★ ★

| | |
|---|---|
| Low-fat or fat-free milk, 1 cup | 100 |
| Banana (peel, slice, and freeze the night before), small | 90 |
| Frozen berries, ½ cup | 30 |
| Old-fashioned oats, ¼ cup | 80 |
| Peanut butter, 1 Tbsp | 90 |
| **Total = 390** | |

### PASTA WITH GARLIC, SAUSAGE, WHITE BEANS, AND BROCCOLI
(page 331)                    calories

★ ★ ★

| | |
|---|---|
| Pasta with Garlic, Sausage, White Beans, and Broccoli, 2 cups | 400 |
| **Total = 400** | |

### GRILLED SALMON
(page 186)                    calories

★ ★ ★

| | |
|---|---|
| Salmon fillet, 4 oz raw, brushed with 1 tsp Mrs. Dash Spicy Teriyaki 10-Minute Marinade | 250 |
| Spinach, 2 cups, sautéed with 1 minced clove garlic, 1 tsp peanut oil | 60 |
| Brown rice, ½ cup cooked | 110 |
| **Total = 420** | |

### QUAKER OATMEAL SQUARES
(page 81)                    calories

★ ★ ★

| | |
|---|---|
| Quaker Oatmeal Squares, ⅔ cup | 150 |
| Low-fat or fat-free milk, ¾ cup | 80 |
| Peaches canned in juice, drained, 1 cup chopped | 110 |
| Chopped pecans, 1 Tbsp | 50 |
| **Total = 390** | |

APPENDIX

# B

# 400-Calorie
# FRESH
# FOODS

THROUGHOUT MOST OF THIS BOOK, we focus on assessing single-portion sizes of the foods you find everywhere, from your own pantry to your neighborhood bar. But sometimes it's easier to think in blocks of calories, like when you're building your own 400-calorie meals, for example. In cases like that, it might be easier to group portions of vegetables, fruits, and proteins into blocks of 100 or 200 calories.

Remember that diagram on page 34 that explains how your plate should be divided into six sections, with one section full of protein, two sections full of grains, and three of vegetables? Think of these lists just like that, only instead of dividing a plate, you're dividing a 400-calorie meal!

The following portion guides make last-minute meal planning a cinch by showing you how many cups of celery or eggplant or raspberries you could eat to consume 100 calories of fruits or vegetables and how many ounces of filet mignon or tablespoons of peanut butter will give you 200 calories of protein. With so many foods listed side by side, you'll be amazed at how such different portion sizes can supply the same number of calories. For example, you can get 100 calories from 20 cups of lettuce ... or just ¾ cup of corn!

### VEGETABLES
I'm sure it's no surprise to you that vegetables give you the most nutrition bang for your calorie buck. In fact, as you know, many green vegetables are so low in calories that we even list them in our Freebies box on page 38—it's virtually impossible to overindulge on cucumbers and celery! But not all vegetables are alike in their caloric density, so choose carefully.

### FRUITS
Fruits and vegetables often are grouped together, even though their calorie counts and characteristic vitamins and minerals are different. The natural sugar in fruits pushes up their calories. A budget of 100 calories, more than you're likely to use in a meal, buys you 2 cups of strawberries and most melons, a cup of cherries, or ¾ cup (1 medium) sliced banana. Many fruits supply an abundance of vitamin C and each fruit color—green, red, orange, white—means a different group of health-promoting phytochemicals.

### PROTEINS
Protein foods, both meat and meatless, vary a lot in calories. You can blame fat; for the same 200 calories that we use as a reference, a portion of a higher-fat meat like a lamb chop is a little more than half the size of a portion of lean pork tenderloin. Most fish varieties are very low in fat, so the theoretical 200-calorie portion is larger. Meatless proteins are very different from each other in nutrients and calories.

# 100-Calorie PORTION GUIDE

# VEGETABLE

THOUGH ALL VEGGIES ARE GOOD for you and are low in calories compared to other kinds of foods, they still vary in calories quite a bit. Here are the amounts of raw veggies that you can eat for 100 calories.

**ICEBERG LETTUCE, SHREDDED**
100 calories
**20 CUPS**

**SPINACH, CHOPPED**
100 calories
**14 CUPS**

**CUCUMBER, SLICED**
100 calories
**7 CUPS**

**CELERY**
100 calories
**6½ CUPS**

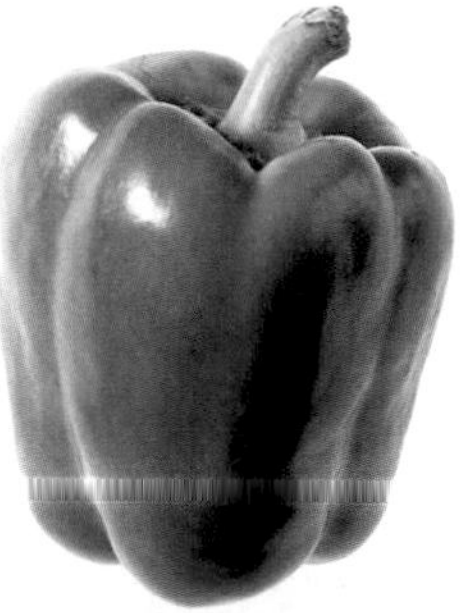

**GREEN BELL PEPPERS, SLICED**
100 calories
**5½ CUPS**

**ZUCCHINI, SLICED**
Amount for
100 calories
**5½ CUPS**

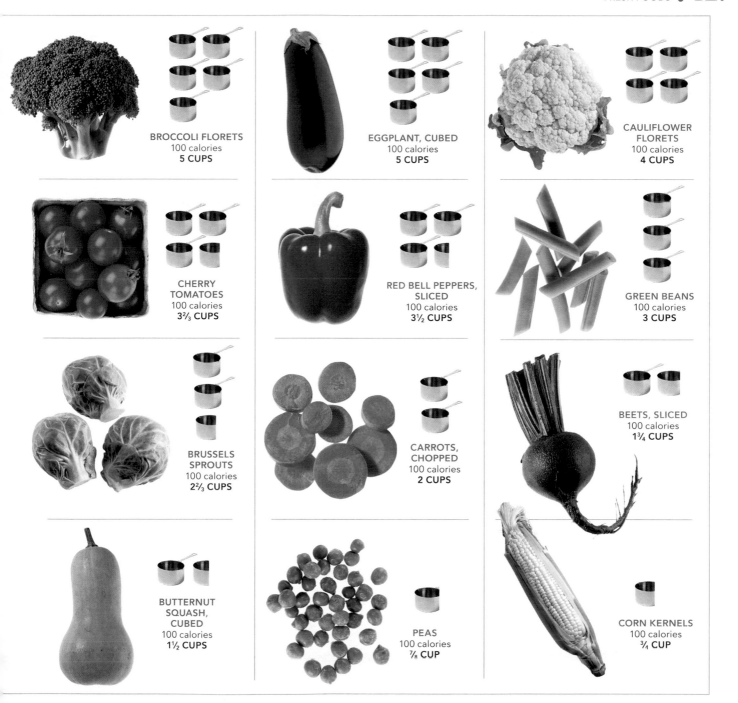

**BROCCOLI FLORETS**
100 calories
**5 CUPS**

**EGGPLANT, CUBED**
100 calories
**5 CUPS**

**CAULIFLOWER FLORETS**
100 calories
**4 CUPS**

**CHERRY TOMATOES**
100 calories
**3⅔ CUPS**

**RED BELL PEPPERS, SLICED**
100 calories
**3½ CUPS**

**GREEN BEANS**
100 calories
**3 CUPS**

**BRUSSELS SPROUTS**
100 calories
**2⅔ CUPS**

**CARROTS, CHOPPED**
100 calories
**2 CUPS**

**BEETS, SLICED**
100 calories
**1¾ CUPS**

**BUTTERNUT SQUASH, CUBED**
100 calories
**1½ CUPS**

**PEAS**
100 calories
**⅞ CUP**

**CORN KERNELS**
100 calories
**¾ CUP**

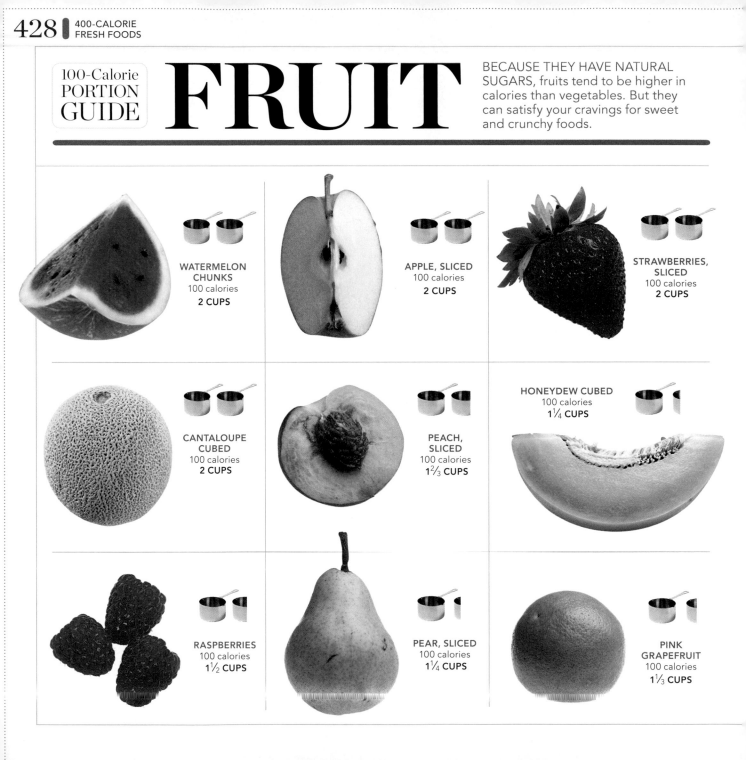

## 100-Calorie PORTION GUIDE

# FRUIT

BECAUSE THEY HAVE NATURAL SUGARS, fruits tend to be higher in calories than vegetables. But they can satisfy your cravings for sweet and crunchy foods.

**WATERMELON CHUNKS**
100 calories
**2 CUPS**

**APPLE, SLICED**
100 calories
**2 CUPS**

**STRAWBERRIES, SLICED**
100 calories
**2 CUPS**

**CANTALOUPE CUBED**
100 calories
**2 CUPS**

**PEACH, SLICED**
100 calories
**1⅔ CUPS**

**HONEYDEW CUBED**
100 calories
**1¼ CUPS**

**RASPBERRIES**
100 calories
**1½ CUPS**

**PEAR, SLICED**
100 calories
**1¼ CUPS**

**PINK GRAPEFRUIT**
100 calories
**1⅓ CUPS**

**PLUM, SLICED**
100 calories
**1⅓ CUPS**

**PINEAPPLE
CHUNKS**
100 calories
**1¼ CUPS**

**ORANGE, SLICED**
100 calories
**1⅕ CUPS**

**BLUEBERRIES**
100 calories
**1⅕ CUPS**

**SEEDLESS GRAPES**
100 calories
**1 CUP**

**MANGO, SLICED**
100 calories
**1 CUP**

**KIWI, SLICED**
100 calories
**1 CUP**

**CHERRIES**
100 calories
**1 CUP**

**BANANA**
100 calories
**¾ CUP**

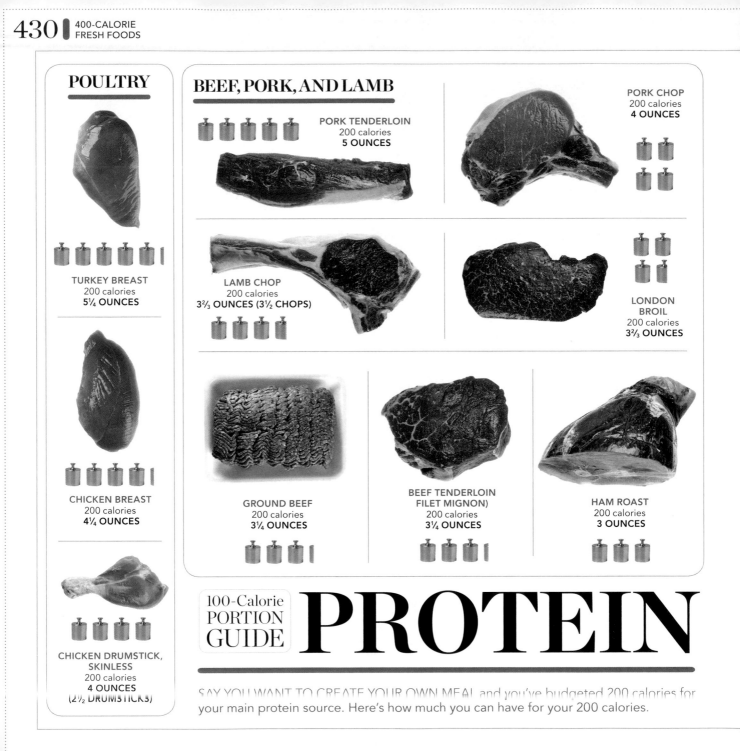

## POULTRY

**TURKEY BREAST**
200 calories
**5¼ OUNCES**

**CHICKEN BREAST**
200 calories
**4¼ OUNCES**

**CHICKEN DRUMSTICK, SKINLESS**
200 calories
**4 OUNCES**
**(2½ DRUMSTICKS)**

## BEEF, PORK, AND LAMB

**PORK TENDERLOIN**
200 calories
**5 OUNCES**

**PORK CHOP**
200 calories
**4 OUNCES**

**LAMB CHOP**
200 calories
**3⅔ OUNCES (3½ CHOPS)**

**LONDON BROIL**
200 calories
**3⅔ OUNCES**

**GROUND BEEF**
200 calories
**3¼ OUNCES**

**BEEF TENDERLOIN FILET MIGNON)**
200 calories
**3¼ OUNCES**

**HAM ROAST**
200 calories
**3 OUNCES**

## 100-Calorie PORTION GUIDE PROTEIN

SAY YOU WANT TO CREATE YOUR OWN MEAL, and you've budgeted 200 calories for your main protein source. Here's how much you can have for your 200 calories.

# FISH AND SEAFOOD

**MUSSELS, MEDIUM**
200 calories
**8⅛ OUNCES (14 MUSSELS)**

**LOBSTER, STEAMED**
200 calories
**7¼ OUNCES**

**SHRIMP, STEAMED**
200 calories
**7 OUNCES**

**COD, BAKED**
200 calories
**6¾ OUNCES**

**YELLOWFIN SASHIMI/
SUSHI TUNA**
200 calories
**6½ OUNCES**

**LIGHT TUNA, WATER-
PACKED, DRAINED**
200 calories
**6 OUNCES**

**TILAPIA, BAKED**
200 calories
**5½ OUNCES**

**SALMON, BROILED**
200 calories
**3⅓ OUNCES**

# MEATLESS

**CANNED
BEANS**
200 calories
**8 OUNCES
(ABOUT 1 CUP)**

**EDAMAME**
200 calories
**5¼ OUNCES (1 CUP)**

**TOFU, EXTRA FIRM**
200 calories
**4¾ OUNCES (⅝ CUP)**

**EGGS**
200 calories
**4⅔ OUNCES
(3 MEDIUM)**

**ORIGINAL
BOCA BURGER**
200 calories
**2¼ OUNCES
(2 PATTIES)**

**ALMONDS**
200 calories
**1¼ OUNCES
(29 ALMONDS)**

**CASHEWS**
200 calories
**1⅕ OUNCES
(22 CASHEWS)**

**PEANUT
BUTTER**
200 calories
**1⅛ OUNCES
(2 TABLE-
SPOONS)**

# Conversion Chart

## THESE EQUIVALENTS HAVE BEEN SLIGHTLY ROUNDED TO MAKE MEASURING EASIER.

### Volume Measurements

| US | Imperial | Metric |
|---|---|---|
| ¼ tsp | – | 1 ml |
| ½ tsp | – | 2 ml |
| 1 tsp | – | 5 ml |
| 1 Tbsp | – | 15 ml |
| 2 Tbsp (1 oz) | 1 fl oz | 30 ml |
| ¼ cup (2 oz) | 2 fl oz | 60 ml |
| ⅓ cup (3 oz) | 3 fl oz | 80 ml |
| ½ cup (4 oz) | 4 fl oz | 120 ml |
| ⅔ cup (5 oz) | 5 fl oz | 160 ml |
| ¾ cup (6 oz) | 6 fl oz | 180 ml |
| 1 cup (8 oz) | 8 fl oz | 240 ml |

### Weight Measurements

| US | Metric |
|---|---|
| 1 oz | 30 g |
| 2 oz | 60 g |
| 4 oz (¼ lb) | 115 g |
| 5 oz (⅓ lb) | 145 g |
| 6 oz | 170 g |
| 7 oz | 200 g |
| 8 oz (½ lb) | 230 g |
| 10 oz | 285 g |
| 12 oz (¾ lb) | 340 g |
| 14 oz | 400 g |
| 16 oz (1 lb) | 455 g |
| 2.2 lb | 1 kg |

### Length Measurements

| US | Metric |
|---|---|
| ¼″ | 0.6 cm |
| ½″ | 1.25 cm |
| 1″ | 2.5 cm |
| 2″ | 5 cm |
| 4″ | 11 cm |
| 6″ | 15 cm |
| 8″ | 20 cm |
| 10″ | 25 cm |
| 12″ (1′) | 30 cm |

### Pan Sizes

| US | Metric |
|---|---|
| 8″ cake pan | 20 × 4 cm sandwich or cake tin |
| 9″ cake pan | 23 × 3.5 cm sandwich or cake tin |
| 11″ × 7″ baking pan | 28 × 18 cm baking tin |
| 13″ × 9″ baking pan | 32.5 × 23 cm baking tin |
| 15″ × 10″ baking pan | 38 × 25.5 cm baking tin (Swiss roll tin) |
| 1½ qt baking dish | 1.5 liter baking dish |
| 2 qt baking dish | 2 liter baking dish |
| 2 qt rectangular baking dish | 30 × 19 cm baking dish |
| 9″ pie plate | 22 × 4 or 23 × 4 cm pie plate |
| 7″ or 8″ springform pan | 18 or 20 cm springform or loose-bottom cake tin |
| 9″ × 5″ loaf pan | 23 × 13 cm or 2 lb narrow loaf tin or pâté tin |

### Temperatures

| Fahrenheit | Centigrade | Gas |
|---|---|---|
| 140° | 60° | – |
| 160° | 70° | – |
| 180° | 80° | – |
| 225° | 105° | ¼ |
| 250° | 120° | ½ |
| 275° | 135° | 1 |
| 300° | 150° | 2 |
| 325° | 160° | 3 |
| 350° | 180° | 4 |
| 375° | 190° | 5 |
| 400° | 200° | 6 |
| 425° | 220° | 7 |
| 450° | 230° | 8 |
| 475° | 245° | 9 |
| 500° | 260° | – |

# ENDNOTES

## CHAPTER 1

1 Wells HF, Buzby JC. *Dietary assessment of major trends in US food consumption, 1970–2005.* Economic Information Bulletin Number 33, March 2008; and USDA Economic Research Service. Average daily per capita calories from the U.S. food availability, adjusted for spoilage and other waste. February 27, 2009.

2 Wansink B, van Ittersum K. Portion size me: downsizing our consumption norms. *J Am Diet Assoc* 2007;107:1103–6.

3 Mintel Portion Control—U.S., April 2009.

4 Wansink B, van Ittersum K, Painter JE. Ice cream illusions: bowls, spoons, and self-served portion sizes. *Am J Prev Med* 2006;31:240–3.

5 Wansink B, Payne CR. *The Joy of Cooking* too much: 70 years of calorie increases in classic recipes. *Ann Intern Med* 2009;150:291–2.

6 International Food Information Council. 2009 Food & Health Survey: consumer attitudes toward food, nutrition and health. www.ific.org.

7 Bassett MT et al. Purchasing behavior and calorie information at fast-food chains in New York City, 2007. *Am J Publ Health* 2008;98: 1457–9.

8 Sacks FM, et al. Comparison of weight-loss diets with different compositions of fat, protein, and carbohydrates. *N Engl J Med* 2009;360:859–73.

9 Brinkworth GD, et al. Long-term effects of a very-low-carbohydrate weight loss diet compared with an isocaloric low-fat diet after 12 mo. *Am J Clin Nutr* 2009; 90:23–32.

10 Redman LM, Ravussin E. Endocrine alterations in response to calorie restriction in humans. *Mol Cell Endocrinol* 2009 Feb 5;299:129–36.

11 International Food Information Council. 2008 Food & Health Survey: consumer attitudes toward food, nutrition and health. www.ific.org.

12 California Center for Public Health Advocacy. March 20–31, 2007 statewide poll. http://www. publichealthadvocacy.org/menulabelingpoll. html.

13 Godwin S, et al. Accuracy of reporting dietary intake using various portion-size aids in-person and via telephone. *J Am Diet Assoc* 2004;104:585–94.

14 Burton S, et al. Attacking the obesity epidemic: the potential health benefits of providing nutrition information in restaurants. *Am J Public Health* 2006;96:1669–75.

## CHAPTER 2

1 USDA Economic Research Service. Loss adjusted food availability. http://www.ers.usda.gov/Data/ FoodConsumption/FoodGuideIndex.htm. February 27, 2009.

2 Smeets AJ, Westerterp-Plantenga MS. Acute effects on metabolism and appetite profile of one meal difference in the lower range of meal frequency. *Brit J Nutr* 2008;99:1316–21.

3 Farshchi HR, Taylor MA, Macdonald IA. Beneficial metabolic effects of regular meal frequency on dietary thermogenesis, insulin sensitivity, and fasting lipid profiles in healthy obese women. *Am J Clin Nutr* 2005;81:16–24.

4 Farshchi HR, Taylor MA, Macdonald IA. Regular meal frequency creates more appropriate insulin sensitivity and lipid profiles compared with irregular meal frequency in healthy lean women. *Eur J Clin Nutr* 2004 Jul;58(7):1071–7.

5 Farshchi HR, Taylor MA, Macdonald IA. Decreased thermic effect of food after an irregular compared with a regular meal pattern in healthy lean women. *Int J Obes Relat Metab Disord* 2004 May;28(5):653–60.

6 Chapelot D, et al. Consequence of omitting or adding a meal in man on body composition, food intake, and metabolism. *Obesity* 2006;14:215–27.

7 Makris AP, Foster GD. Dietary approaches to the treatment of obesity. *Psychiatr Clin N Amer* 2005;28:117–39.

8 Leidy HJ, Bossingham MJ, Mattes RD, Campbell WW. Increased dietary protein consumed at breakfast leads to an initial and sustained feeling of fullness during energy restriction compared to other meal times. *Br J Nutri* 2009; 101:798–803.

9 Rolls BJ, et al. The specificity of satiety: the

influence of foods of different macronutrient content on the development of satiety. *Physiol Behav* 1988;43:145–53.

10 Paddon-Jones D, et al. Protein, weight management, and satiety. *Am J Clin Nutr* 2008;87:1558S–1561S.

11 He K, et al. Changes in intake of fruits and vegetables in relation to risk of obesity and weight gain among middle-aged women. *Int J Obes Relat Metab Disord* 2004;28:1569–74.

12 Liu S, et al. Relation between changes in intakes of dietary fiber and grain products and changes in weight and development of obesity among middle-aged women. *Am J Clin Nutr* 2003;78:920–7.

13 Lindstrom J, et al. High-fibre, low-fat diet predicts long-term weight loss and decreased type 2 diabetes risk: the Finnish Diabetes Prevention Study. *Diabetologia* 2006 May;49(5):912–20. Epub 2006 Mar 16. 19 Bell EA et al. Energy density of foods affects energy intake in normal-weight women. *Am J Clin Nutr* 1998;67:412–20.

14 Mattes RD, Kris-Etherton PM, Foster GD. Impact of peanuts and tree nuts on body weight and healthy weight loss in adults. *J Nutr* 2008;138:1741S–1745S.

15 Parra D, et al. A diet rich in long chain omega-3 fatty acids modulates satiety in overweight and obese volunteers during weight loss. *Appetite* 2008;51:676–80.

16 McManus K, Antinoro L, Sacks F. A randomized controlled trial of a moderate-fat, low-energy diet compared with a low fat, low-energy diet for weight loss in overweight adults. *Int J Obes Relat Metab Disord* 2001;25:1503–11.

17 Azadbakht L, et al. Better dietary adherence and weight maintenance achieved by a long-term moderate-fat diet. *Br J Nutr* 2007;97:399–404.

18 Pelkman CL, et al. Effects of moderate-fat (from monounsaturated fat) and low-fat weight-loss diets on the serum lipid profile in overweight and obese men and women. *Am J Clin Nutr* 2004;79:204–12.

19 Ramel A, et al. Moderate consumption of fatty fish reduces diastolic blood pressure in overweight and obese European young adults during energy restriction. *Nutrition* 2009 May 30. [Epub ahead of print]

20 Bell EA et al. Energy density of foods affects energy intake in normal-weight women. *Am J Clin Nutr* 1998;67:412–20

## CHAPTER 4

1 Schwatz J, Byrd-Bredbenner C. Portion distortion: typical portion sizes selected by young adults. *J Am Diet Assoc* 2006;106:1412–8.

2 Wansink B, van Ittersum K, Painter JE. Ice cream illusions: bowls, spoons, and self-served portion sizes. *Am J Prev Med* 2006;31:240–3.

## CONCLUSION

1 Wing RR, Phelan S. Long-term weight loss maintenance. *Am J Clin Nutr* 2005 Jul;82 (1 Suppl):222S–225S.

2 Baker R, Kirschenbaum D. Self-monitoring may be necessary for successful weight control. *Behav Ther* 1993;24:377–94.

3 Baker RC, Kirschenbaum DS. Weight control during the holidays: highly consistent self-monitoring as a potentially useful coping mechanism. *Health Psychol* 1998;17:367–70.

4 Boutelle KN, Kirschenbaum DS, Baker RC, Mitchell ME. How can obese weight controllers minimize weight gain during the high risk holiday season? By self-monitoring very consistently. *Health Psychol* 1999;18:364–8.

5 Wadden TA, Berkowitz RI, Womble LG, et al. Randomized trial of lifestyle modification and pharmacotherapy for obesity. *N Engl J Med* 2005;353:2111–20.

# INDEX

Underscored page references indicate sidebars and tables. **Boldface** references indicate photographs.